The Photographic History
of The Civil War

In Ten Volumes

ACKNOWLEDGMENT

All rights on selections in this volume are reserved by the holders of the copyrights. The publishers and others named in the following list are the proprietors, either in their own right or as agents for the authors, of the selections of which the authorship and titles are given, and of which the ownership is thus specifically noted and is hereby acknowledged.

The BOBBS-MERRILL COMPANY, Indianapolis.—"One Country," by FRANK LEBBY STANTON.

THE CENTURY COMPANY, New York.—"Farragut," by WILLIAM TUCKEY MEREDITH, from "The Century Magazine."

DOUBLEDAY, PAGE & COMPANY, New York.—"Lee on 'Traveller,'" from "Recollections and Letters of General Lee."

HENRY HOLT & COMPANY, New York.—"The Blue and the Gray," by FRANCIS MILES FINCH.

HOUGHTON MIFFLIN COMPANY, Boston.—"Sherman," "On the Life Mask of Abraham Lincoln," from "Poems," by RICHARD WATSON GILDER; "John Burns of Gettysburg," "A Second Review of the Grand Army," "The Aged Stranger," from "Poems," by BRET HARTE; "Brother Jonathan's Lament," by OLIVER WENDELL HOLMES; "Battle-Hymn of the Republic," from "From Sunset Ridge," and "Robert E. Lee," from "At Sunset," by JULIA WARD HOWE; "Ode Recited at the Harvard Commemoration," by JAMES RUSSELL LOWELL; "The Bivouac in the Snow," by MARGARET JUNKIN PRESTON; "Kearny at Seven Pines," by EDMUND CLARENCE STEDMAN; "To the South," from "Poems," by MAURICE THOMPSON; "A Message," from "Poetic Studies," by ELIZABETH STUART PHELPS WARD.

The B. F. JOHNSON PUBLISHING COMPANY, Richmond, Virginia.—"Charleston," and "Ode at Magnolia Cemetery," by HENRY TIMROD.

P. J. KENEDY & SONS, New York.—"The Conquered Banner," from "Poems: Patriotic, Religious, Miscellaneous," by ABRAM JOSEPH RYAN.

THE J. B. LIPPINCOTT COMPANY, Philadelphia.—"Sheridan's Ride," from "Poetical Works of Thomas Buchanan Read"; "A Georgia Volunteer," from "Poems," by MARY ASHLEY TOWNSEND.

LITTLE, BROWN & COMPANY, Boston.—"The Volunteer," from "War Poems," by ELBRIDGE JEFFERSON CUTLER.

MOFFAT, YARD & COMPANY, New York.—"After All," from "Poems," by WILLIAM WINTER.

The JOHN MURPHY COMPANY, Baltimore.—"Ashby," by JOHN REUBEN THOMPSON, from "Southern Poems of the War," collected by Emily Mason.

THE NEALE PUBLISHING COMPANY, New York.—"Little Giffen," from "The Poems of Francis Orray Ticknor."

G. P. PUTNAM'S SONS, New York.—"United," from "From Cliff and Scaur," by BENJAMIN SLEDD; "A Soldier's Grave," from "Poems," by JOHN ALBEE.

CHARLES SCRIBNER'S SONS, New York.—"Keenan's Charge," "Gettysburg: A Battle Ode," by GEORGE PARSONS LATHROP; "The Dying Words of Stonewall Jackson," and "The Tournament," by SIDNEY LANIER.

The JOHN C. WINSTON COMPANY, Philadelphia.—"The Picket Guard," from "All Quiet Along the Potomac," by ETHEL LYNN BEERS.

In addition to the above, the Editor begs to acknowledge permission from the following to use the selections named.

Henry Abbey, for "On a Great Warrior."

Charles Francis Adams, for "A New England Tribute to Lee," from "Three Phi Beta Kappa Addresses," published by Houghton Mifflin Co.

Matthew Page Andrews, Editor of "Poems of James Ryder Randall," for "My Maryland," and "Pelham."

Samuel H. M. Byers, for "Sherman's March to the Sea," from his "The Happy Isles, and other Poems."

General Frederick Dent Grant, for "Let Us Have Peace," from "Personal Memoirs of U. S. Grant."

John Howard Jewett, for "Those Rebel Flags."

William Gordon McCabe, for "Christmas Night of '62," and "Dreaming in the Trenches."

Dr. Edward Mayes, for text of Lamar's "Eulogy of Sumner."

Mrs. Eva M. O'Connor, for "The General's Death," by Joseph O'Connor.

Mrs. William C. Palmer, for "Stonewall Jackson's Way," by John Williamson Palmer.

General Horace Porter, for the "Eulogy of Ulysses S. Grant."

Wallace Rice, for "Wheeler's Brigade at Santiago."

John Jerome Rooney, for "Joined the Blues."

Clinton Scollard, for "The Daughter of the Regiment," from "Ballads of Valor and Victory," by Wallace Rice and Clinton Scollard.

Kate Brownlee Sherwood, for "Albert Sidney Johnston," and "Thomas at Chickamauga."

Henry Jerome Stockard, for "Over their Graves."

Will Henry Thompson, for "The High Tide at Gettysburg."

Horace Traubel, for "Bivouac on a Mountainside," "Cavalry Crossing a Ford," and "O Captain! My Captain," from "Leaves of Grass," by Walt Whitman.

Robert Burns Wilson, for "Such is the Death the Soldier Dies."

IN VIRGINIA—1865

WHAT THE WAR BROUGHT TO THE SOUTH—RUINS OF A MILL AT PETERSBURG JUST AFTER THE CAPTURE OF THE TOWN BY GRANT'S ARMY

To study this scene at the close of the war reveals the spirit of this volume. Within the stone walls of the woolen mill that now gape empty to Heaven, many a gray blanket and uniform had been woven for Lee's devoted army. Many a wheel had been turned by the stream that now plays but an idle part in the dreamy landscape. Yet the magnificent Army of the Potomac, as it rushed through the city in hot pursuit of the men soon to wear gray no longer, brought in its train an enduring prosperity. Half a century later, Petersburg, with thousands of other cities in Virginia and its sister Southern States once trampled by armies, hummed again with industry under the very flag once borne against them. North and South had learned the lasting meaning of Blue and Gray—symbols of principle and love of home, emblems of the heroism proclaimed by poets and orators of a nation united.

The Photographic History
of The Civil War

Poetry and Eloquence
from the Blue and the Gray

Francis Trevelyan Miller

Editor in Chief

Contributors

WILLIAM H. TAFT
President of the United States

HENRY WYSHAM LANIER
Art Editor and Publisher

EBEN SWIFT
Lieutenant-Colonel, U. S. A.

FRENCH E. CHADWICK
Rear-Admiral, U. S. N.

GEORGE HAVEN PUTNAM
Major, U. S. V.

MARCUS J. WRIGHT
Brigadier-General, C. S. A.

HENRY W. ELSON
Professor of History, Ohio University

JAMES BARNES
Author of " David G. Farragut "

CASTLE BOOKS ★ NEW YORK

CONTENTS

Contents

FOREWORD

THE spirit in which Dr. Miles has written his introduction and made his selections from the prose and poetry inspired by our Civil War, seems to me so admirable and so characteristically American as to need no praise and to suggest little comment that would not be superfluous. As is the case with the other volumes of this PHOTOGRAPHIC HISTORY OF THE CIVIL WAR, the present anthology brings out clearly two facts in our national history that give us great encouragement as a people—the fact that, even when the flames of war burned most fiercely, the fraternal feeling between Americans of all sections showed no signs of perishing completely, and the fact that, despite the mistakes made during the period of Reconstruction, the reestablishment of sympathy and confidence between the sections went forward with a speed and a thoroughness not previously experienced after civil wars. On these two facts alone one might base a justification of our experiment, if that word be applicable since 1865, in democratic government; and it is pleasant for the literary student to think that these facts are facts partly because of the beneficent influence exerted by our literature in affording our people an opportunity to express their better selves.

These better selves, Northern and Southern, are so well expressed in Dr. Miles' selections that one wonders why the material he has gathered has not been made more of a common literary heritage through the medium of that universally circulated book, the school-reader. Just after the war the sectional origin of most of the pieces, such as " The Blue and the Gray " and " Pelham," stood in the way of their use for national educational purposes, but now that we are truly one people in one great country, such considerations do not count,

Foreword

and the time seems to have come when the literature of our most heroic period should be rendered accessible to the children and grandchildren of the men and women who made that period memorable in the annals of human fortitude and patience. Surely no better year than the semi-centennial of the beginning of the great struggle can be found for the publication of Dr. Miles' essentially reconciliatory volume. May it stimulate our patriotism, our sense of brotherhood, our pride in our great past, and, what is more, that spirit of tolerant sympathy, which not even the passions of civil war could utterly destroy!

In the light of what has just been said we may infer that it is difficult for the American reader, to whom patriotic considerations are naturally paramount, to judge the poetry and prose gathered in this volume as dispassionately as he can judge the literature produced, let us say, during the English Civil War. I well remember, for example, how in my youth I committed the indiscretion of comparing, with some reserve of praise for the native product, certain verses produced by militant cavaliers of the South with other verses produced by English and Scotch cavaliers in the seventeenth century, and how roundly I was assured by some compatriots that I had no taste in poetry. My impression is that I was but voicing, unnecessarily perhaps, a preference for more or less original seventeenth century verse over somewhat derivative mid-nineteenth century verse, but I doubtless seemed to be combining treason with bad taste.

My taste has not sufficiently improved to enable me to prefer the poetical products of the later and much greater struggle, but I trust that I have learned to express my preferences with more suavity than of yore, and that the less perfervid American reader of to-day, who, notwithstanding the control he has acquired over his unsophisticated emotions, still values our native poetry above any foreign productions in verse, at least will stop short of feeling it necessary to assert that any

[12]

one who does not agree with him is a combination of a fool and a traitor. Quarreling over matters of politics is bad enough; quarreling over matters of taste is too absurd. It is all very well to be patriotic and to cherish our literature, but for the sake of that literature we ought to strive to pass disinterested and, as far as possible, strictly critical judgments upon the works that constitute it, even when, as in the present case, they deal with the gravest issue in our national life and represent that finest of all our achievements, national reconciliation. For we must do justice to ourselves and to posterity as well as to our ancestors, and we must also do justice to ourselves as individuals endowed with esthetic ideals, not merely to ourselves as patriotic citizens. A tolerant spirit makes for peace and for many other good things, but, while it is always to be preferred to contentiousness, especially in matters of taste, too often it makes for the triumph of intolerable mediocrity. In literature as in life it will not do to assume unreservedly that the fittest will survive, and then to argue that because something has survived, it has proved its fitness.

It will be gathered from the tone of these remarks that I do not think that much of the poetry Dr. Miles has included, suitable though it is for the present work, would find a place in a volume edited with an exigence equal to that manifested by the late Mr. Palgrave in his " Golden Treasury." But if Dr. Miles had proved as exigent an editor as Mr. Palgrave, he would have been left at the end of his labors, through no fault of his own, without a volume to give us. That would surely have been a pity, for the writers included are thoroughly representative of their time, and they display as a rule clarity of thought, rightness of feeling, and creditable powers of expression.

They rarely attain, however, in my judgment, to consummate felicity of cadence and phrase or to notable imaginative utterance. With a few exceptions such as Lincoln's " Gettysburg Address," Lowell's " Commemoration Ode," Timrod's

Foreword

" Ode at Magnolia Cemetery," and Randall's "My Maryland," the poetry and prose of the war period, like the rest of our
literature, is adequate or good, rather than remarkable or great.

One ought to add immediately that, like the rest of our
literature, that produced during and shortly after the Civil
War seems to have been excellently adapted to the needs of the
democratic public for which it was primarily written. It has
democratic soundness of substance in thought and feeling, even
if it rarely possesses aristocratic distinction of style. We do
right to collect it and to emphasize the great part it has played
in our history, as well as the great part it can play now, particularly in this semi-centennial year, in stimulating our sense
of civic brotherhood. We do right, also, to acknowledge its
esthetic limitations, but we ought, at the same time, to point to
the fact that the American is perhaps of all men the most determined to put up with nothing less than the best. As he
learns to demand more of his writers, they will learn to answer
more and more satisfactorily his legitimate demands.

NEW YORK, May 23, 1911.   W. P. TRENT.

INTRODUCTION

THE SPIRIT OF
NATIONALITY

THE END OF THE WAR—CANNON USELESS SAVE
TO BE MELTED FOR PLOWSHARES

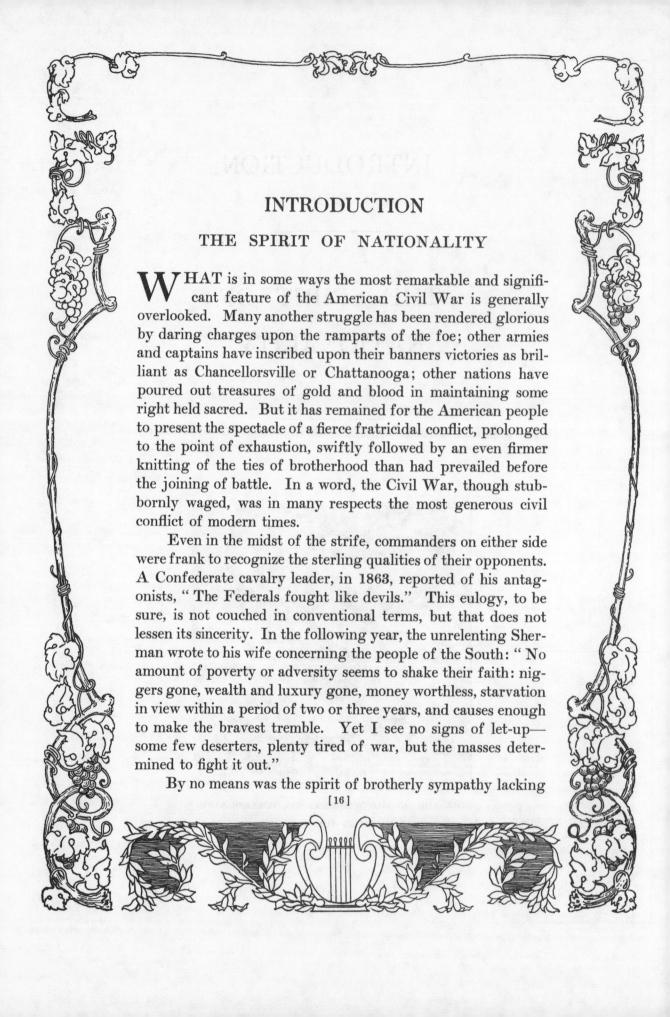

INTRODUCTION

THE SPIRIT OF NATIONALITY

WHAT is in some ways the most remarkable and significant feature of the American Civil War is generally overlooked. Many another struggle has been rendered glorious by daring charges upon the ramparts of the foe; other armies and captains have inscribed upon their banners victories as brilliant as Chancellorsville or Chattanooga; other nations have poured out treasures of gold and blood in maintaining some right held sacred. But it has remained for the American people to present the spectacle of a fierce fratricidal conflict, prolonged to the point of exhaustion, swiftly followed by an even firmer knitting of the ties of brotherhood than had prevailed before the joining of battle. In a word, the Civil War, though stubbornly waged, was in many respects the most generous civil conflict of modern times.

Even in the midst of the strife, commanders on either side were frank to recognize the sterling qualities of their opponents. A Confederate cavalry leader, in 1863, reported of his antagonists, " The Federals fought like devils." This eulogy, to be sure, is not couched in conventional terms, but that does not lessen its sincerity. In the following year, the unrelenting Sherman wrote to his wife concerning the people of the South: " No amount of poverty or adversity seems to shake their faith: niggers gone, wealth and luxury gone, money worthless, starvation in view within a period of two or three years, and causes enough to make the bravest tremble. Yet I see no signs of let-up— some few deserters, plenty tired of war, but the masses determined to fight it out."

By no means was the spirit of brotherly sympathy lacking

JULIA WARD HOWE IN 1861

The author of the magnificent "Battle-Hymn of the Republic" was born in New York in 1819, a daughter of the banker Samuel Ward. In 1843 she married the philanthropist, Dr. S. G. Howe, best known as the head of Perkins Institute for the Blind. She assisted him in editing his anti-slavery journal, the *Boston Commonwealth*. In 1861, at the time of this picture, she made her first trip to Washington, where her husband became interested in the work of the Sanitary Commission. During the visit the party was invited to a military review in the Virginia camps. On the way back she and the others in the carriage sang "John Brown's Body" to the applause of the soldiers by the roadside. Her pastor, who was in the party, suggested that she invent better words for the tune. That night the inspiration came; she wrote the best known of her poems and one of the finest products of the whole Civil War period. Her later life was devoted largely to the cause of woman suffrage. She died at Newport, October 17, 1910.

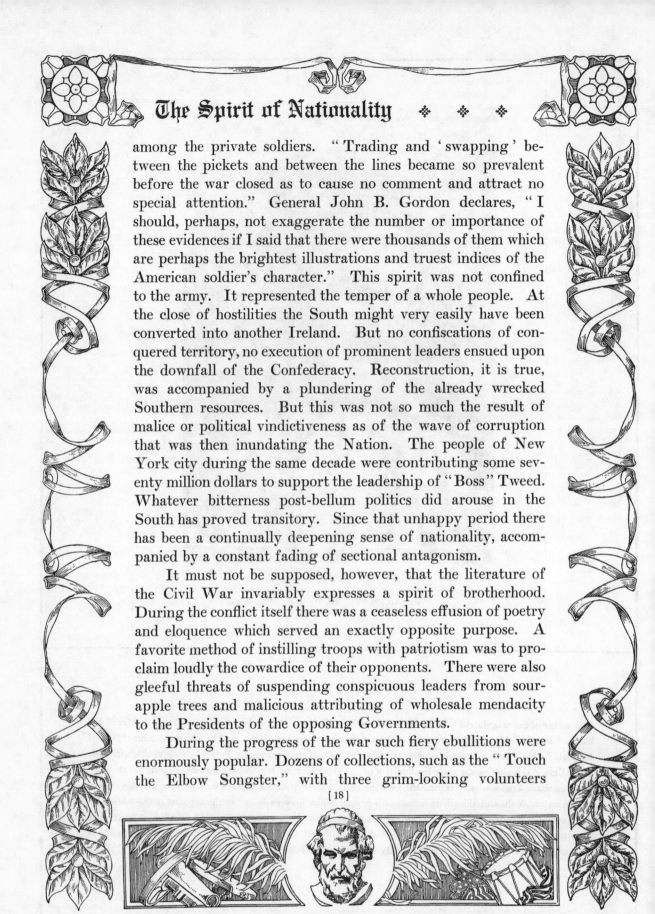

among the private soldiers. "Trading and 'swapping' between the pickets and between the lines became so prevalent before the war closed as to cause no comment and attract no special attention." General John B. Gordon declares, "I should, perhaps, not exaggerate the number or importance of these evidences if I said that there were thousands of them which are perhaps the brightest illustrations and truest indices of the American soldier's character." This spirit was not confined to the army. It represented the temper of a whole people. At the close of hostilities the South might very easily have been converted into another Ireland. But no confiscations of conquered territory, no execution of prominent leaders ensued upon the downfall of the Confederacy. Reconstruction, it is true, was accompanied by a plundering of the already wrecked Southern resources. But this was not so much the result of malice or political vindictiveness as of the wave of corruption that was then inundating the Nation. The people of New York city during the same decade were contributing some seventy million dollars to support the leadership of "Boss" Tweed. Whatever bitterness post-bellum politics did arouse in the South has proved transitory. Since that unhappy period there has been a continually deepening sense of nationality, accompanied by a constant fading of sectional antagonism.

It must not be supposed, however, that the literature of the Civil War invariably expresses a spirit of brotherhood. During the conflict itself there was a ceaseless effusion of poetry and eloquence which served an exactly opposite purpose. A favorite method of instilling troops with patriotism was to proclaim loudly the cowardice of their opponents. There were also gleeful threats of suspending conspicuous leaders from sour-apple trees and malicious attributing of wholesale mendacity to the Presidents of the opposing Governments.

During the progress of the war such fiery ebullitions were enormously popular. Dozens of collections, such as the "Touch the Elbow Songster," with three grim-looking volunteers

[18]

JAMES RYDER RANDALL

THE AUTHOR OF "MY MARYLAND," AT TWENTY–TWO

In 1861, just as he looked when he wrote his famous battle-cry, "My Maryland," James Ryder Randall, the youthful poet, faces the reader. Randall was born in Baltimore the first day of 1839. His early schooling was under Joseph H. Clark, a former teacher of Edgar Allan Poe. At Georgetown College he was the smallest boy that had ever been received as a student. After becoming known as the poet of the college, he traveled extensively in the West Indies and South America, landing in 1858 in New Orleans on his return. Then he accepted the chair of English literature at Poydras College, a flourishing Creole institution at Pointe Coupée, Louisiana. He was still teaching there when he learned through the New Orleans *Delta* of the attack on the Sixth Massachusetts in Baltimore on April 19, 1861. That night he wrote the verses that ran like wildfire through the South and were parodied numberless times in the North. The remainder of his days were chiefly spent in newspaper work, largely in Georgia. He became indifferent to his poetical work, and it was owing to the insistence of his friend, Miss Lillian McGregor Shepherd, that his verse was collected. Through her courtesy is here reproduced the intimate and appealing photograph above, a gift to her from the poet himself. He died in 1908 in Augusta, Georgia.

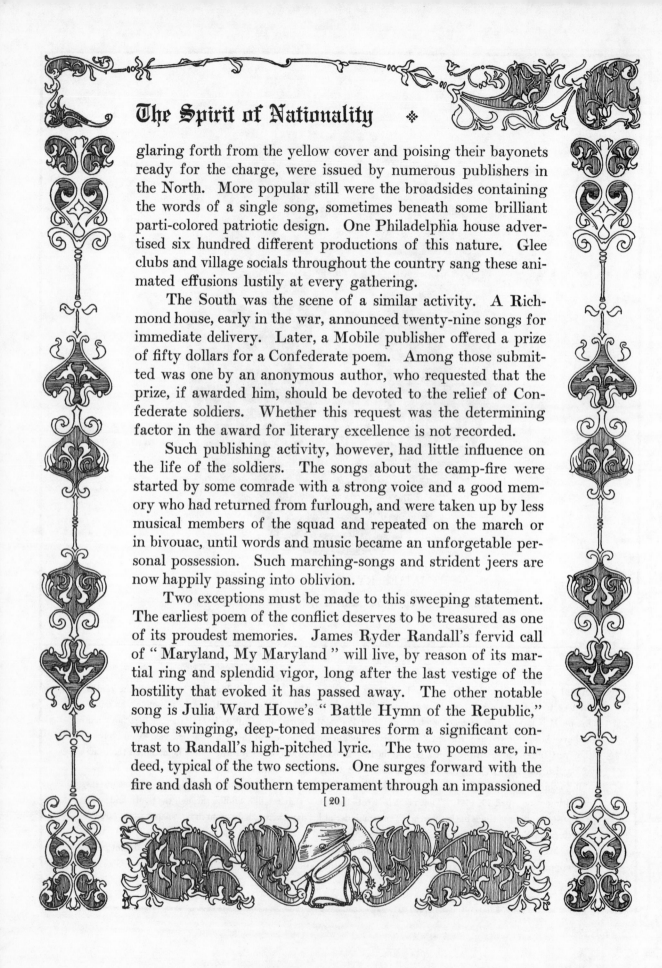

glaring forth from the yellow cover and poising their bayonets ready for the charge, were issued by numerous publishers in the North. More popular still were the broadsides containing the words of a single song, sometimes beneath some brilliant parti-colored patriotic design. One Philadelphia house advertised six hundred different productions of this nature. Glee clubs and village socials throughout the country sang these animated effusions lustily at every gathering.

The South was the scene of a similar activity. A Richmond house, early in the war, announced twenty-nine songs for immediate delivery. Later, a Mobile publisher offered a prize of fifty dollars for a Confederate poem. Among those submitted was one by an anonymous author, who requested that the prize, if awarded him, should be devoted to the relief of Confederate soldiers. Whether this request was the determining factor in the award for literary excellence is not recorded.

Such publishing activity, however, had little influence on the life of the soldiers. The songs about the camp-fire were started by some comrade with a strong voice and a good memory who had returned from furlough, and were taken up by less musical members of the squad and repeated on the march or in bivouac, until words and music became an unforgetable personal possession. Such marching-songs and strident jeers are now happily passing into oblivion.

Two exceptions must be made to this sweeping statement. The earliest poem of the conflict deserves to be treasured as one of its proudest memories. James Ryder Randall's fervid call of " Maryland, My Maryland " will live, by reason of its martial ring and splendid vigor, long after the last vestige of the hostility that evoked it has passed away. The other notable song is Julia Ward Howe's " Battle Hymn of the Republic," whose swinging, deep-toned measures form a significant contrast to Randall's high-pitched lyric. The two poems are, indeed, typical of the two sections. One surges forward with the fire and dash of Southern temperament through an impassioned

WALT WHITMAN DURING THE WAR

The most individual of American poets was born at Westhills, Long Island, in 1809, the son of a carpenter. He early learned the trade of printing; at twenty he was editor and publisher of a paper. For many years he was traveling all over the West of that day, from New Orleans to Canada. In 1855 he brought out the first edition of "Leaves of Grass," at first a thin volume of ninety-four pages, later growing until it had become several times the size of the original. At the end of the second year of the Civil War, Whitman went to Washington to care for his brother, who had been wounded in the battle of Fredericksburg. For the next three years he served as an army nurse, chiefly in the hospitals of Washington. The literary outcome of this experience was "Drum Taps," from which the poems in the present volume are taken, and which he described as "a little book containing life's darkness and blood-dripping wounds and psalms of the dead." For several years after the war he remained in Government employ in Washington, but in 1873 he moved to Camden, New Jersey, where in 1892 he died in cheerful poverty.

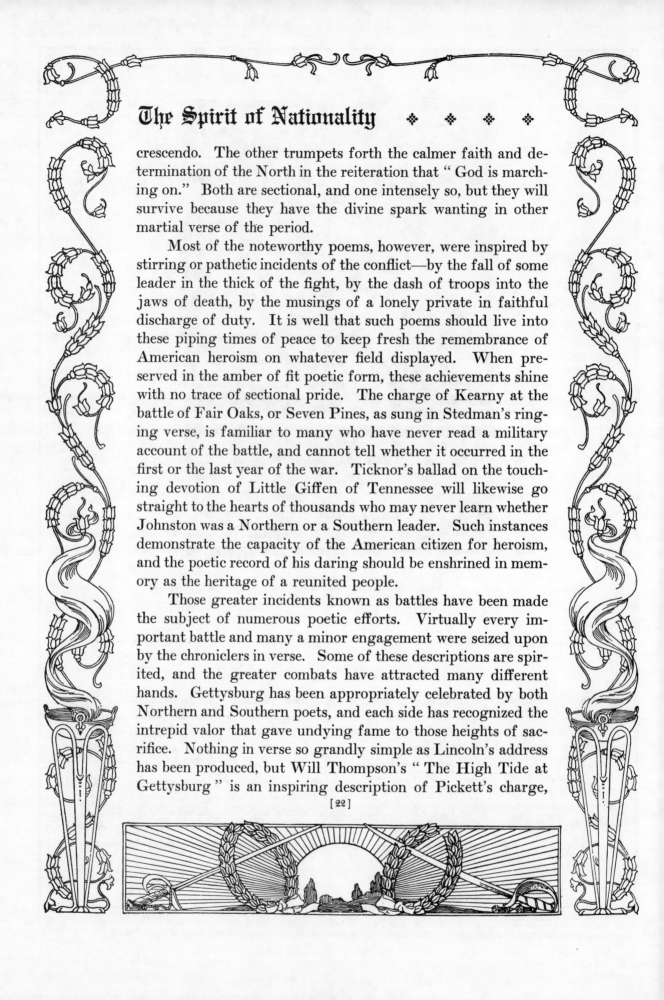

crescendo. The other trumpets forth the calmer faith and determination of the North in the reiteration that "God is marching on." Both are sectional, and one intensely so, but they will survive because they have the divine spark wanting in other martial verse of the period.

Most of the noteworthy poems, however, were inspired by stirring or pathetic incidents of the conflict—by the fall of some leader in the thick of the fight, by the dash of troops into the jaws of death, by the musings of a lonely private in faithful discharge of duty. It is well that such poems should live into these piping times of peace to keep fresh the remembrance of American heroism on whatever field displayed. When preserved in the amber of fit poetic form, these achievements shine with no trace of sectional pride. The charge of Kearny at the battle of Fair Oaks, or Seven Pines, as sung in Stedman's ringing verse, is familiar to many who have never read a military account of the battle, and cannot tell whether it occurred in the first or the last year of the war. Ticknor's ballad on the touching devotion of Little Giffen of Tennessee will likewise go straight to the hearts of thousands who may never learn whether Johnston was a Northern or a Southern leader. Such instances demonstrate the capacity of the American citizen for heroism, and the poetic record of his daring should be enshrined in memory as the heritage of a reunited people.

Those greater incidents known as battles have been made the subject of numerous poetic efforts. Virtually every important battle and many a minor engagement were seized upon by the chroniclers in verse. Some of these descriptions are spirited, and the greater combats have attracted many different hands. Gettysburg has been appropriately celebrated by both Northern and Southern poets, and each side has recognized the intrepid valor that gave undying fame to those heights of sacrifice. Nothing in verse so grandly simple as Lincoln's address has been produced, but Will Thompson's " The High Tide at Gettysburg " is an inspiring description of Pickett's charge,

JAMES RUSSELL LOWELL IN 1863

The poet who recited his ode at the Harvard Commemoration looked thus on that memorable occasion. He was born in 1819 at Cambridge, Massachusetts, of a long line of eminent New Englanders. In Harvard he was poet of his class. During the Mexican War he won immense popularity by his series of satirical poems in Yankee dialect, collected in 1848 as "The Biglow Papers." In 1855 he was appointed to succeed Longfellow in the Smith Professorship of Modern Languages. The additional distinction he had gained as editor of *The Atlantic Monthly* and later of *The North American Review* made him the logical poet at the commemoration service held by Harvard University on July 21, 1865, for its students and graduates who had perished in the war. His ode, not very enthusiastically received that day, has made him the foremost poet of American patriotism. His later life was filled with varied activities. From 1877 to 1885 he represented this country at Madrid and London. He continued to publish poetry and prose that made him at his death in 1891 the most eminent man of letters in America.

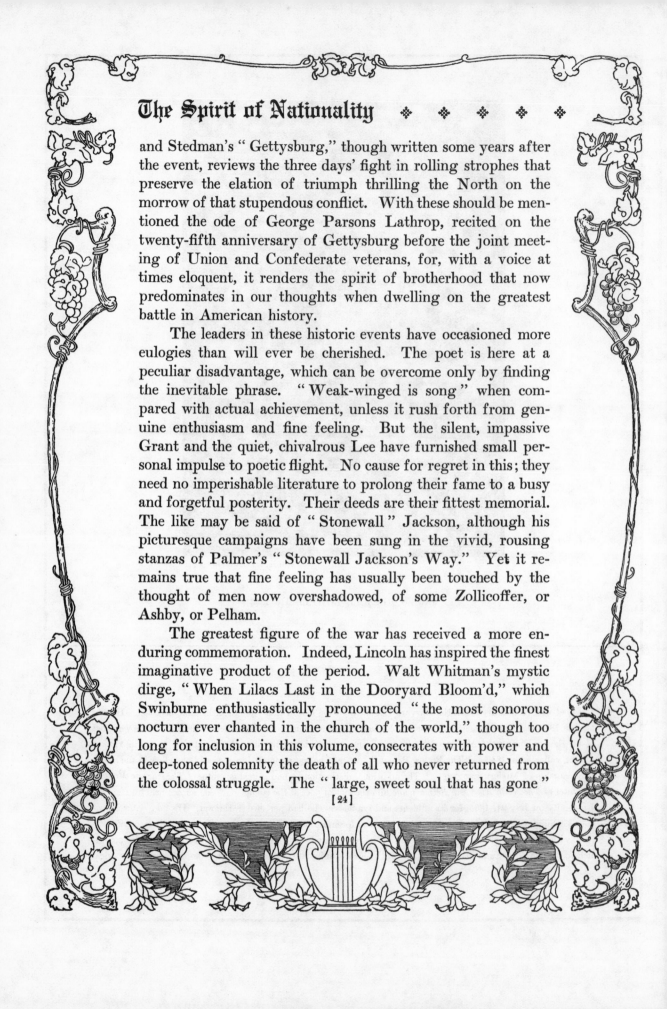

and Stedman's "Gettysburg," though written some years after
the event, reviews the three days' fight in rolling strophes that
preserve the elation of triumph thrilling the North on the
morrow of that stupendous conflict. With these should be men-
tioned the ode of George Parsons Lathrop, recited on the
twenty-fifth anniversary of Gettysburg before the joint meeting of Union and Confederate veterans, for, with a voice at
times eloquent, it renders the spirit of brotherhood that now
predominates in our thoughts when dwelling on the greatest
battle in American history.

The leaders in these historic events have occasioned more
eulogies than will ever be cherished. The poet is here at a
peculiar disadvantage, which can be overcome only by finding
the inevitable phrase. "Weak-winged is song" when compared with actual achievement, unless it rush forth from genuine enthusiasm and fine feeling. But the silent, impassive
Grant and the quiet, chivalrous Lee have furnished small personal impulse to poetic flight. No cause for regret in this; they
need no imperishable literature to prolong their fame to a busy
and forgetful posterity. Their deeds are their fittest memorial.
The like may be said of "Stonewall" Jackson, although his
picturesque campaigns have been sung in the vivid, rousing
stanzas of Palmer's "Stonewall Jackson's Way." Yet it remains true that fine feeling has usually been touched by the
thought of men now overshadowed, of some Zollicoffer, or
Ashby, or Pelham.

The greatest figure of the war has received a more enduring commemoration. Indeed, Lincoln has inspired the finest
imaginative product of the period. Walt Whitman's mystic
dirge, "When Lilacs Last in the Dooryard Bloom'd," which
Swinburne enthusiastically pronounced "the most sonorous
nocturn ever chanted in the church of the world," though too
long for inclusion in this volume, consecrates with power and
deep-toned solemnity the death of all who never returned from
the colossal struggle. The "large, sweet soul that has gone"

[24]

SIDNEY LANIER IN 1879

Sidney Lanier's war poems "The Death of Stonewall Jackson" and "The Tournament" appear in this volume. Lanier was born in Macon, Georgia, February 3, 1842. In early childhood he developed a passion for music, learning to play on many instruments without instruction. At eighteen he graduated from Oglethorpe University with the highest honors in his class. Soon after the war broke out he marched to the front with the Second Georgia Battalion of the Macon Volunteers, served through the Seven Days' Battles before Richmond, then spent two exciting years along the James in the Confederate Signal Service, and in August, 1864, was transferred to a blockade runner plying between Wilmington, North Carolina, and the Bermudas, which was captured in November of the same year. Thereafter Lanier was imprisoned for four months in Point Lookout Prison, Maryland. On securing his freedom he was emaciated to a skeleton, with the seeds of tuberculosis already developing. After the war he studied law with his father and practised for a time, but when it became apparent that he might not survive for many years, he courageously determined to devote his powers to music and literature. He settled in Baltimore in 1873 as first flute in the Peabody Symphony Concerts, eagerly studied the two arts of his love, attracted attention by his poems, and received national recognition in 1876 through the invitation to write the Centennial "Cantata." A noble feature of his writings is the absence of all sectionalism and the broadly national spirit that breathes through his verse. In 1879 he was appointed to a lectureship in literature in the recently founded Johns Hopkins University. He was winning recognition when the end came in 1881 in the mountains of North Carolina.

was there mourned in a symbolic way, but Whitman spoke in a poignant, personal way in "O Captain, My Captain," which, partly on that account and partly because of its more conventional poetic form, has become much more popular. Loftier in its flight is the ode recited by Lowell at the Harvard commemoration for her sons slain in battle. The idealism of the poet there attained its most inspired utterance, and in particular the section on Lincoln has been taken up by the whole Nation as the highest and truest characterization of the martyred President.

The features thus commemorated, however, are not peculiar to our Civil War. There have been other occasions for the display of heroism, other fields where pathetic incidents call for tears, other conflicts where leaders have arisen whom whole nations have delighted to honor. What is peculiar to the American Civil War is the generous feeling of reconciliation—the spirit of nationality which has developed since the close of hostilities.

When once the battle was joined, the forces of common tradition and of common blood asserted themselves inevitably. Numerous poems depicted scenes on the battlefield where sons of the same mother clutched each other in the death-grapple. A Southern production, popular throughout the land, was John Reuben Thompson's "Music in Camp," which in simple rimes pictured the soldiers of the recently contending hosts as hushed into silence by their recollections of home. But it is a striking fact that, in the beginning of hostilities, the poems on the Southern side were much more intense and inspired than those produced in the North. Only the fear of dissolution aroused in all its strength the latent devotion to the central Government. Only then throughout the North—

> They closed the ledger and they stilled the loom,
> The plough left rusting in the prairie farm;
> They saw but "Union" in the gathering gloom;
> The tearless women helped the men to arm.

[26]

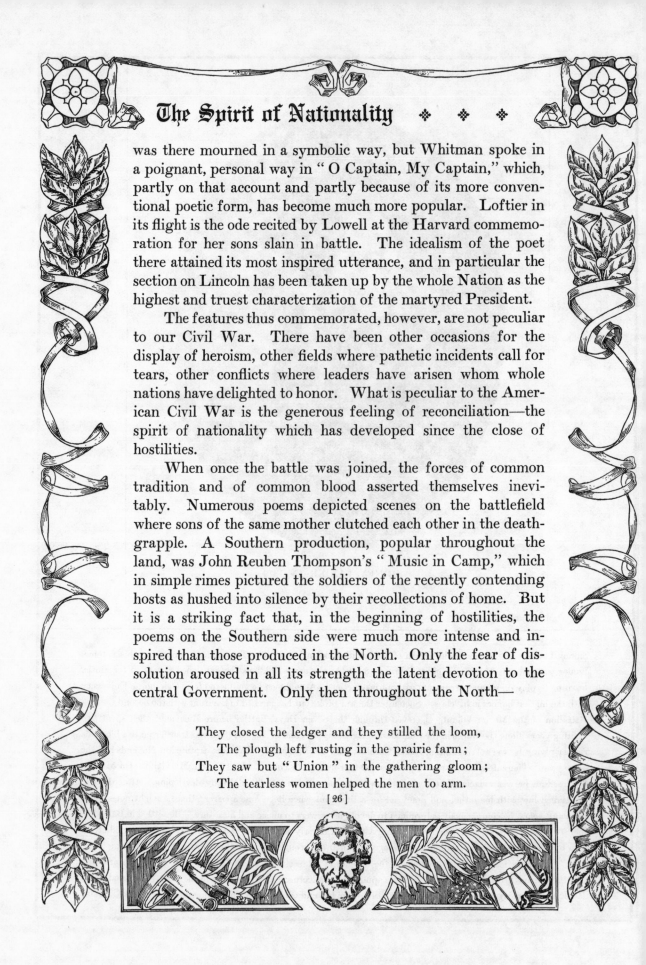

HENRY TIMROD IN 1865

Henry Timrod, born in Charleston, South Carolina, in 1829, devoted himself during all his brief life to the service of his native city and State. During his early education in the Charleston schools his love of poetry was already apparent. After leaving the University of Georgia, on account of ill-health and lack of means, he studied law for a time in Charleston. His poetic convictions led him to withdraw from the profession and accept a position as private tutor. Among the literary men of the city he soon became known as one of the choicest spirits. At the outbreak of the Civil War he entered service as a volunteer, but was ordered back by the physician as soon as he reached the front. He fired Southern hearts with several martial lyrics, proclaiming the resolution of the Confederacy to fight to the death and inspiring thousands to an intenser determination. Up to 1864 he was an army correspondent. In that year he settled in Columbia as an editor of the *South Carolinian*. In 1867 he died of tuberculosis, courageous to the end. His biographer records that "His latest occupation was correcting the proof-sheets of his own poems, and he passed away with them by his side, stained with his life-blood."

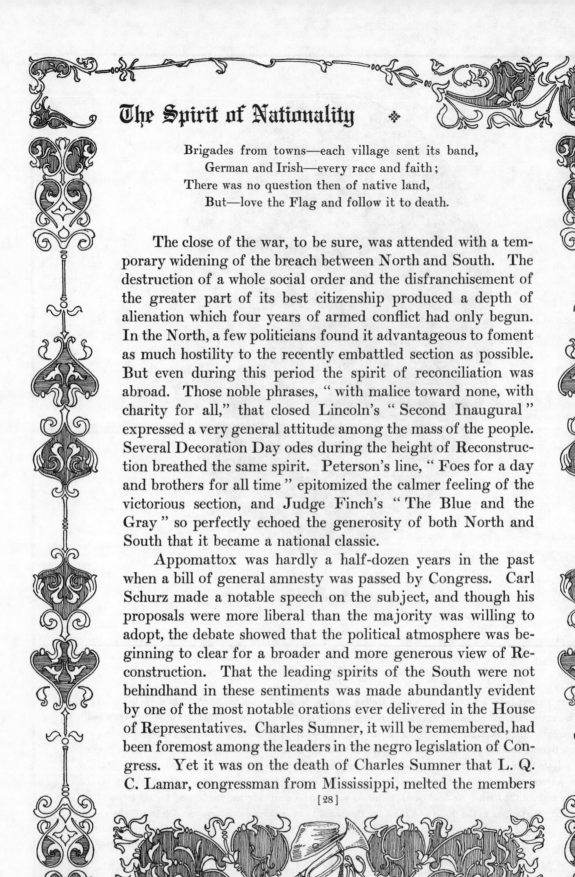

The Spirit of Nationality ❖

Brigades from towns—each village sent its band,
German and Irish—every race and faith;
There was no question then of native land,
But—love the Flag and follow it to death.

The close of the war, to be sure, was attended with a temporary widening of the breach between North and South. The destruction of a whole social order and the disfranchisement of the greater part of its best citizenship produced a depth of alienation which four years of armed conflict had only begun. In the North, a few politicians found it advantageous to foment as much hostility to the recently embattled section as possible. But even during this period the spirit of reconciliation was abroad. Those noble phrases, " with malice toward none, with charity for all," that closed Lincoln's " Second Inaugural " expressed a very general attitude among the mass of the people. Several Decoration Day odes during the height of Reconstruction breathed the same spirit. Peterson's line, " Foes for a day and brothers for all time " epitomized the calmer feeling of the victorious section, and Judge Finch's " The Blue and the Gray " so perfectly echoed the generosity of both North and South that it became a national classic.

Appomattox was hardly a half-dozen years in the past when a bill of general amnesty was passed by Congress. Carl Schurz made a notable speech on the subject, and though his proposals were more liberal than the majority was willing to adopt, the debate showed that the political atmosphere was beginning to clear for a broader and more generous view of Reconstruction. That the leading spirits of the South were not behindhand in these sentiments was made abundantly evident by one of the most notable orations ever delivered in the House of Representatives. Charles Sumner, it will be remembered, had been foremost among the leaders in the negro legislation of Congress. Yet it was on the death of Charles Sumner that L. Q. C. Lamar, congressman from Mississippi, melted the members

[28]

COPYRIGHT, 1911, REVIEW OF REVIEWS CO.

LUCIUS Q. C. LAMAR IN 1879

Taken only five years after his "Eulogy of Sumner," this photograph preserves the noble features of Lamar as he stood before the House of Representatives in 1874.   He was born in Georgia in 1825, studied at Emory College in that State, graduating at twenty; and soon began the practice of law.   In a few years he moved to Oxford, Mississippi, where he became a professor of mathematics in the State University, and continued his legal practice.   His reputation as a speaker dates from 1851, when he met Senator Foote in joint debate and   borne from the platform in triumph by the students of the University.   Six years later he went to Congress from that district.   During the war he served in the army until his health gave way, when he was sent as commissioner to Russia.   In 1872 he was elected to Congress.   Two years later, he was the best known Southerner in Washington because of his "Eulogy of Sumner."   From 1877 to 1885 he represented Mississippi in the Senate.   In 1885 he became Secretary of the Interior under Cleveland, and in 1887 he was appointed to the Supreme Court, where he served with distinction. His death in 1893 called forth tributes to his noble character and high patriotism from North and South alike.

of the House to tears and woke the applause of the Nation by a eulogy conceived in the most magnanimous temper and closing with a plea for a fuller understanding and a closer union.

How quickly the prayer was being answered appeared in 1876. The hundredth anniversary of the signing of the Declaration of Independence was celebrated by the International Industrial Exhibition at Philadelphia. The honor of writing the official cantata for this national occasion was conferred upon the Southern poet, Sidney Lanier. The cantata, composed for Dudley Buck's music, was sung " in the open air, by a chorus of many hundred voices, and with the accompaniment of a majestic orchestra." Daniel Coit Gilman thus describes the occasion: " The devotional exercises awakened no sentiment of reverence. At length came the cantata. From the overture to the closing cadence it held the attention of the vast throng of listeners, and when it was concluded loud applause rang through the air. A noble conception had been nobly rendered." The same glorification of American freedom was expressed by Lanier in the freer poetic form of the " Psalm of the West," and by including the revised ballad, " The Tournament," he voiced his own joy at the uniting of the recently antagonistic sections.

The celebration itself, followed by the immense wave of enthusiasm that ran over the country, and taken in connection with the withdrawal of Federal troops from the South in the early weeks of the Hayes administration, was significant in many ways. In the South, it marked the return to power of the responsible classes; in the North, the return of political parties to something nearer equality; and in the country as a whole, the confirmation of a conviction, arising from the panic of 1873, that problems unconnected with the war were in most pressing need of solution. The resulting consciousness of national unity, deeper and broader than had existed before, was hastened by the gathering of economic forces for an unparalleled material development. The civilization of the South was in a few

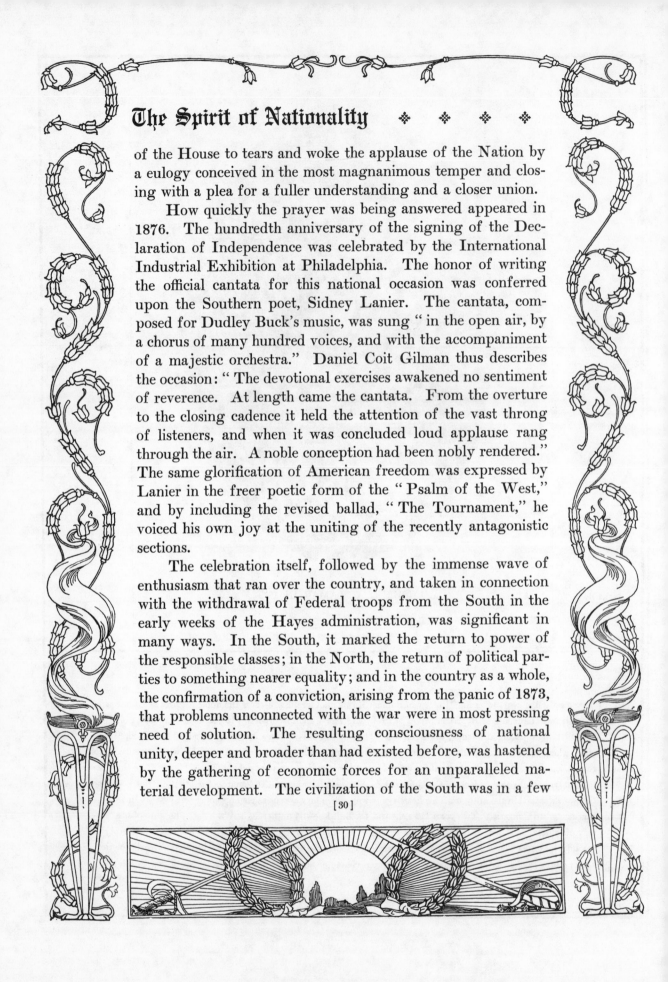

HENRY WOODFIN GRADY
THE HERALD OF THE NEW SOUTH

The Southerner who made himself famous, in 1886, by his New York address on "The New South" was born in Athens, Georgia, in 1851. After graduating at the University of Georgia, in his native town, he studied in the University of Virginia. His qualities of leadership appeared at an early age while he was editing the *Courier* of Rome, Georgia. The proprietor would not allow him to print an article denouncing a political ring, whereupon young Grady bought two other papers of the town, combined them, and carried on his campaign. After some experience on the New York *Herald* he served as reporter on the Atlanta *Constitution*. In 1880 he purchased a fourth interest in the paper and became the managing editor. He was soon recognized as a moving spirit in the progress of his city and the whole South. The reputation he gained as a speaker and editor secured him the invitation from the New England Society of New York to respond to the toast, "The South," at its banquet on December 22, 1886. The response, which was largely impromptu, was copied all over the country and brought him to a position of national importance. Some critics, however, consider his speech before the Merchants' Association of Boston in December, 1889, a superior performance. It was also his last. Hardly had he returned home when the whole Nation was grieved by the news of his death, on December 23, 1889. Every leading newspaper in the country commented upon his labors for the progress of brotherly feeling between the North and the South.

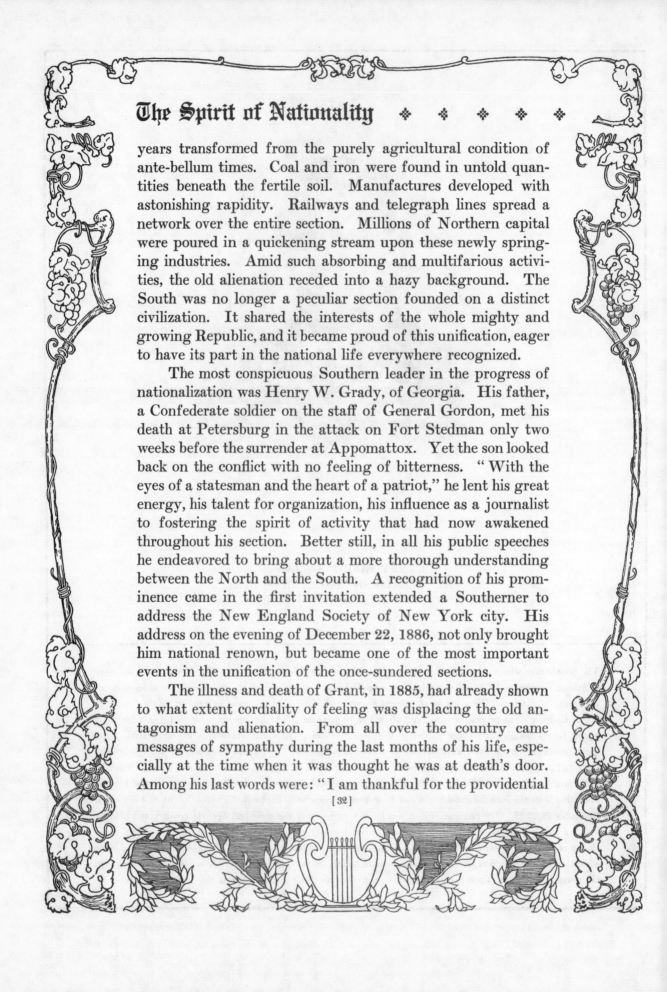

years transformed from the purely agricultural condition of ante-bellum times. Coal and iron were found in untold quantities beneath the fertile soil. Manufactures developed with astonishing rapidity. Railways and telegraph lines spread a network over the entire section. Millions of Northern capital were poured in a quickening stream upon these newly springing industries. Amid such absorbing and multifarious activities, the old alienation receded into a hazy background. The South was no longer a peculiar section founded on a distinct civilization. It shared the interests of the whole mighty and growing Republic, and it became proud of this unification, eager to have its part in the national life everywhere recognized.

The most conspicuous Southern leader in the progress of nationalization was Henry W. Grady, of Georgia. His father, a Confederate soldier on the staff of General Gordon, met his death at Petersburg in the attack on Fort Stedman only two weeks before the surrender at Appomattox. Yet the son looked back on the conflict with no feeling of bitterness. "With the eyes of a statesman and the heart of a patriot," he lent his great energy, his talent for organization, his influence as a journalist to fostering the spirit of activity that had now awakened throughout his section. Better still, in all his public speeches he endeavored to bring about a more thorough understanding between the North and the South. A recognition of his prominence came in the first invitation extended a Southerner to address the New England Society of New York city. His address on the evening of December 22, 1886, not only brought him national renown, but became one of the most important events in the unification of the once-sundered sections.

The illness and death of Grant, in 1885, had already shown to what extent cordiality of feeling was displacing the old antagonism and alienation. From all over the country came messages of sympathy during the last months of his life, especially at the time when it was thought he was at death's door. Among his last words were: "I am thankful for the providential

OLIVER WENDELL HOLMES IN WAR-TIME

Something of Holmes' gracious personality and his fastidious care for personal appearance may be traced in the portrait.   The writer of "Brother Jonathan," the first selection in this volume, was born in Cambridge, Massachusetts, in 1809.   He graduated from Harvard at the age of twenty.   At twenty-one he was famous for the stirring verses, "Old Ironsides," which preserved the old frigate *Constitution* from destruction.   In 1836, after several years spent in studying medicine both in Harvard and abroad, he began practice in Boston.   It is said that he made the announcement, "The smallest fevers thankfully received."   Certainly he is best known as a humorist. After some twenty years he was an honored professor in the Harvard Law School and a much sought after poet for social occasions.   But in 1857 his series of essays in *The Atlantic Monthly*, under the title "The Autocrat of the Breakfast Table," brought him national recognition.   Their wit and humor have made them the most popular essays written in America, and they have gained wide reception in England.   He also wrote three novels, the best known of which is "Elsie Venner."   Many of his poems, such as "The Last Leaf" and "Dorothy" will long continue to give him a warm place in the public heart.   The poem in this volume, "Brother Jonathan's Lament for Sister Caroline," is characteristic of Holmes' kindly disposition—striking as a piece of prophecy before the war had really begun.   The last thirty-four years of his life, ending in 1894, were filled with a large variety of literary work.

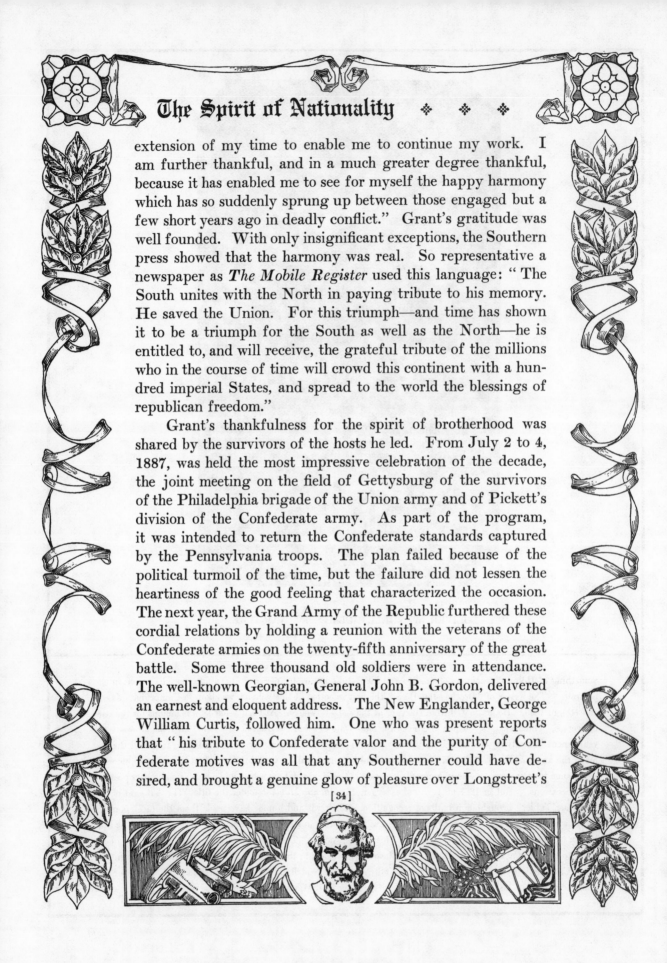

extension of my time to enable me to continue my work. I am further thankful, and in a much greater degree thankful, because it has enabled me to see for myself the happy harmony which has so suddenly sprung up between those engaged but a few short years ago in deadly conflict." Grant's gratitude was well founded. With only insignificant exceptions, the Southern press showed that the harmony was real. So representative a newspaper as *The Mobile Register* used this language: " The South unites with the North in paying tribute to his memory. He saved the Union. For this triumph—and time has shown it to be a triumph for the South as well as the North—he is entitled to, and will receive, the grateful tribute of the millions who in the course of time will crowd this continent with a hundred imperial States, and spread to the world the blessings of republican freedom."

Grant's thankfulness for the spirit of brotherhood was shared by the survivors of the hosts he led. From July 2 to 4, 1887, was held the most impressive celebration of the decade, the joint meeting on the field of Gettysburg of the survivors of the Philadelphia brigade of the Union army and of Pickett's division of the Confederate army. As part of the program, it was intended to return the Confederate standards captured by the Pennsylvania troops. The plan failed because of the political turmoil of the time, but the failure did not lessen the heartiness of the good feeling that characterized the occasion. The next year, the Grand Army of the Republic furthered these cordial relations by holding a reunion with the veterans of the Confederate armies on the twenty-fifth anniversary of the great battle. Some three thousand old soldiers were in attendance. The well-known Georgian, General John B. Gordon, delivered an earnest and eloquent address. The New Englander, George William Curtis, followed him. One who was present reports that " his tribute to Confederate valor and the purity of Confederate motives was all that any Southerner could have desired, and brought a genuine glow of pleasure over Longstreet's

BRET HARTE

One of the most American of American authors, the novelist Francis Bret Harte is represented in this volume by three poems that reveal the lighter vein of his versifying. "The Aged Stranger" is purposely humorous. "John Burns of Gettysburg" is half-humorous. "A Second Review of the Grand Army" has touches of wit in spite of its solemn subject. Harte was born in Albany, New York, in 1839. The gold-fever caught him at fifteen; he wandered to California, where he made more at school-teaching than at gold-digging. At eighteen, he entered newspaper life as a typesetter, and soon worked up to the position of editor-in-chief of the *Weekly Californian*. From 1864 to 1867, while secretary of the United States Mint in San Francisco, he wrote most of his Civil War poems and many humorous verses that made his name familiar in both East and West. During the next two years he was editor of the *Overland Monthly*, publishing in it his best-known stories—"The Luck of Roaring Camp" and "The Outcasts of Poker Flat." In 1871, he left for New York, to devote all his time to writing. Beginning with 1878, he held a succession of consular appointments. In 1885 he settled in England, where he lived till his death in 1902. A born story-teller, Harte put into his vividly realistic scenes from early California life a racy swing combined with universal sentiment that made him popular both at home and abroad.

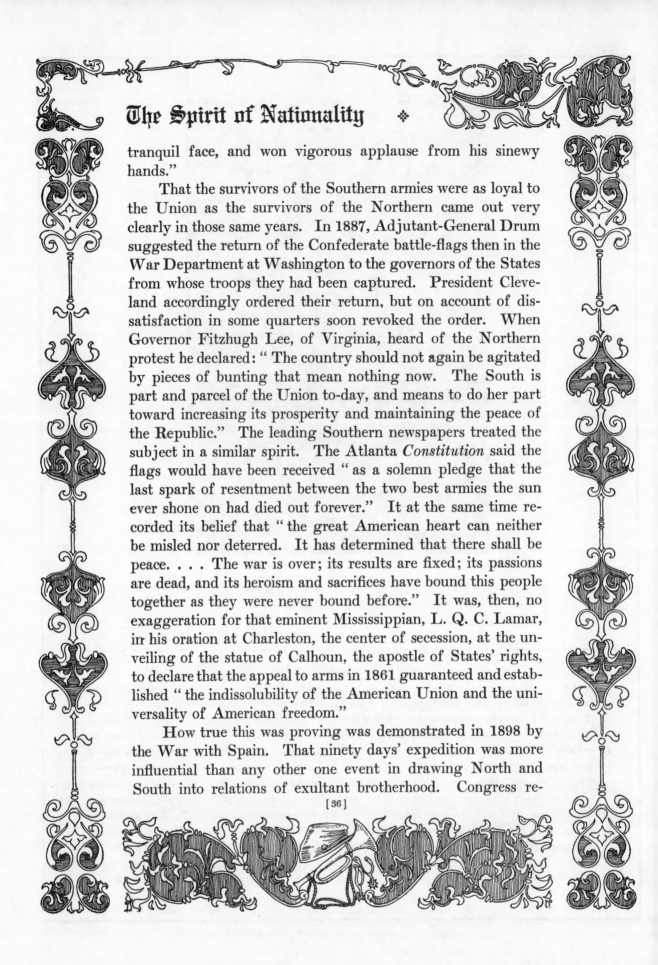

tranquil face, and won vigorous applause from his sinewy hands."

That the survivors of the Southern armies were as loyal to the Union as the survivors of the Northern came out very clearly in those same years. In 1887, Adjutant-General Drum suggested the return of the Confederate battle-flags then in the War Department at Washington to the governors of the States from whose troops they had been captured. President Cleveland accordingly ordered their return, but on account of dissatisfaction in some quarters soon revoked the order. When Governor Fitzhugh Lee, of Virginia, heard of the Northern protest he declared: "The country should not again be agitated by pieces of bunting that mean nothing now. The South is part and parcel of the Union to-day, and means to do her part toward increasing its prosperity and maintaining the peace of the Republic." The leading Southern newspapers treated the subject in a similar spirit. The Atlanta *Constitution* said the flags would have been received "as a solemn pledge that the last spark of resentment between the two best armies the sun ever shone on had died out forever." It at the same time recorded its belief that "the great American heart can neither be misled nor deterred. It has determined that there shall be peace. . . . The war is over; its results are fixed; its passions are dead, and its heroism and sacrifices have bound this people together as they were never bound before." It was, then, no exaggeration for that eminent Mississippian, L. Q. C. Lamar, in his oration at Charleston, the center of secession, at the unveiling of the statue of Calhoun, the apostle of States' rights, to declare that the appeal to arms in 1861 guaranteed and established "the indissolubility of the American Union and the universality of American freedom."

How true this was proving was demonstrated in 1898 by the War with Spain. That ninety days' expedition was more influential than any other one event in drawing North and South into relations of exultant brotherhood. Congress re-

Born in Bordentown, New Jersey, on February 8, 1844, Richard Watson Gilder was educated at Bellvue Seminary, an institution conducted by his father in Flushing, Long Island. At the age of twelve he was publishing a newspaper—a sheet a foot square, entitled *The St. Thomas Register*, for which he wrote all the articles, set all the type, and performed all the press-work. As a member of Landis's Philadelphia battery, he enlisted for the "emergency campaign" of the summer of 1863, and took part in the defense of Carlisle, Pennsylvania, when Lee made the invasion of the North ending at Gettysburg. His long editorial career began the next year, when he joined the staff of the *Newark Advertiser*, of Newark, N. J.

In 1869 he became editor of *Hours at Home*. When it was absorbed by the old *Scribner's Monthly*, Doctor J. G. Holland retained young Gilder as managing editor. Thus at twenty-six he had attained high literary influence. On the death of Doctor Holland, in 1881, Gilder became editor-in-chief of the same magazine, re-named *The Century*. His many poems, chiefly lyrical, gave him distinguished standing among American poets. But his interests exceeded the bounds of literature. All kinds of civic progress engaged his energies. He rendered valuable service in tenement-house reform in New York City and in promoting civil-service reform over the country at large. He died on November 18, 1909.

RICHARD WATSON
GILDER

AS A CADET OF
THE WAR DAYS

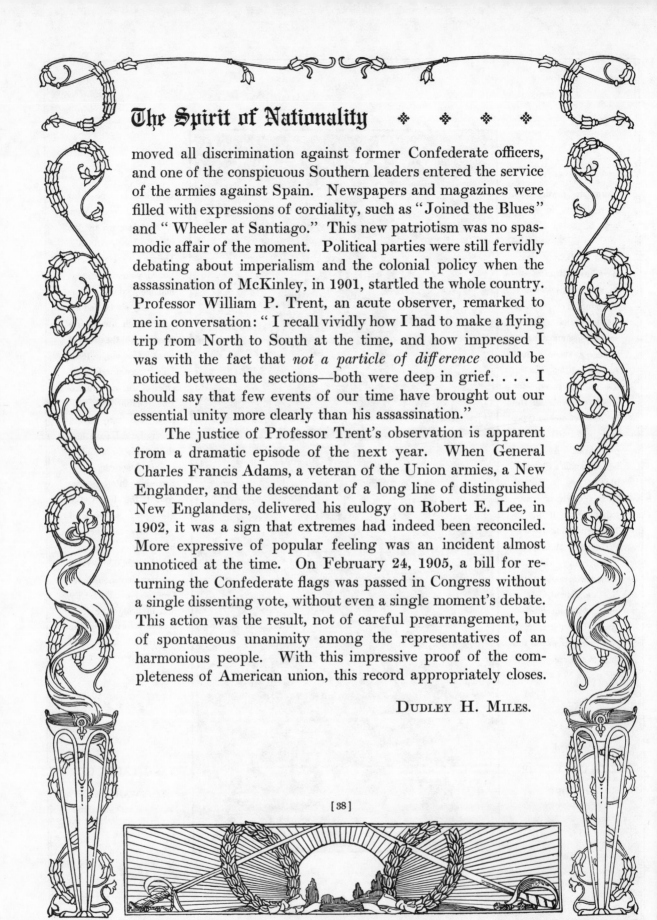

moved all discrimination against former Confederate officers, and one of the conspicuous Southern leaders entered the service of the armies against Spain. Newspapers and magazines were filled with expressions of cordiality, such as "Joined the Blues" and "Wheeler at Santiago." This new patriotism was no spasmodic affair of the moment. Political parties were still fervidly debating about imperialism and the colonial policy when the assassination of McKinley, in 1901, startled the whole country. Professor William P. Trent, an acute observer, remarked to me in conversation: "I recall vividly how I had to make a flying trip from North to South at the time, and how impressed I was with the fact that *not a particle of difference* could be noticed between the sections—both were deep in grief. . . . I should say that few events of our time have brought out our essential unity more clearly than his assassination."

The justice of Professor Trent's observation is apparent from a dramatic episode of the next year. When General Charles Francis Adams, a veteran of the Union armies, a New Englander, and the descendant of a long line of distinguished New Englanders, delivered his eulogy on Robert E. Lee, in 1902, it was a sign that extremes had indeed been reconciled. More expressive of popular feeling was an incident almost unnoticed at the time. On February 24, 1905, a bill for returning the Confederate flags was passed in Congress without a single dissenting vote, without even a single moment's debate. This action was the result, not of careful prearrangement, but of spontaneous unanimity among the representatives of an harmonious people. With this impressive proof of the completeness of American union, this record appropriately closes.

DUDLEY H. MILES.

I

SEPARATION
AND
REUNION

"IN VAIN IS
THE STRIFE"
—*Holmes*

RUINS OF CHARLESTON, 1865
FROM THE CIRCULAR CHURCH

SCENES OF '61 THAT QUICKLY FOLLOWED "BROTHER JONA- THAN" (PAGE 44)

The upper photograph shows Confederates on Monday the fifteenth of April, 1861 — one day after the momentous event which Holmes dimly prophesied in " Brother Jonathan " (page 44). The picture below, with the two following, were made on the 16th. As April wore on, North and South alike had been reluctant to strike first. When Major Robert Anderson, on December 26, 1860, removed to Fort Sumter, on an island at the entrance to Charleston

TERRE PLEIN OF THE GORGE.
Showing the Guns, "en barbette," April 15, 1861.

CONFEDERATES IN SUMTER THE DAY AFTER ANDERSON LEFT

NORTH-EASTERN ANGLE AND EASTERN FACE OF FORT SUMTER.
10 inch Columbiad in position as a Mortar pointing towards the City.

A GUN TRAINED ON CHARLESTON BY ANDERSON

Harbor, he placed himself in a position to withstand long attack. But he needed supplies. The Confederates would allow none to be landed. When at length rumors of a powerful naval force to relieve the fort reached Charleston, the Confederates demanded the surrender of the garrison. Anderson promised to evacuate by April 15th if he received no additional supplies. His terms were rejected. At half-past four on the morning of April 12th a shell from Fort Johnson "rose high in air, and curving in its course, burst almost directly over the fort." The mighty war had begun.

TWO DAYS AFTER THE BOMBARDMENT OF SUMTER, APRIL 16, 1861

Wade Hampton (the tallest figure) and other leading South Carolinians inspecting the effects of the cannonading that had forced Major Anderson to evacuate, and had precipitated the mightiest conflict of modern times—two days before.

GUNS THAT FIRED ON SUMTER

Below are some of the Confederate guns in the battery near Fort Moultrie that bore upon the fort pictured above. It was the hot shot from Fort Moultrie itself that set fire to the barracks in Fort Sumter about eight o'clock on the morning of April 13th. When the Confederate commanders saw the black smoke rise from the fort, they doubled the fire of the batteries to keep the flames from being extinguished. Sumter did not cease replying, although the intervals between shots became longer as the garrison dashed from spot to spot checking the flames.

NORTH-WEST ANGLE, SHOWING CASEMATES

THE STARS AND BARS
WAVING OVER THE CAPTURED FORT

SOUTH-WESTERN ANGLE,
Showing Sand-bag Defences and Columbiads bearing on Fort Sumter, April 16, 1861.

CONFEDERATE GUNS THAT FIRED ON SUMTER

The South Carolinians showed their admiration for their dauntless antagonists by cheering at every shot that replied to them. About half-past twelve of that day the flagstaff on Sumter was shot away. General Beauregard, who was in charge of the operations of Charleston, at once sent three of his aides to inquire if Major Anderson would accept assistance in subduing the flames and to offer terms of surrender. The terms, which allowed the gallant garrison to march out with the honors of war, were at length accepted. The first step in the war had been irrevocably taken.

The damage done by those first guns of the war, "the shots heard around the world," is shown in these faded photographs of April 16, 1861. By five A.M. of April 12th the Confederate batteries were directing a converging fire on Sumter. The garrison did not immediately reply; it had been subsisting on half rations and on this particular morning made a breakfast off pork and damaged rice. At seven it began to return the fire. During the day the duel was unremitting. The whole city poured out to witness the spectacle. The Battery, the fashionable promenade of Charleston, was thronging with

INTERIOR FACE OF GORGE.
Showing Officer's Quarters and Gate-way.

THE OFFICERS' QUARTERS
WHERE THE FIRE STARTED

WESTERN BARRACKS AND PARADE.

THE SHATTERED FLAGSTAFF (TO THE RIGHT)

ladies in holiday attire. Early on the next day the officers' quarters in Sumter caught fire from some shells or hot shot. Flames soon spread to the barracks. So fierce was the conflagration that the magazine had to be closed. The men threw themselves on the ground to avoid suffocation. Then Beauregard's terms of evacuation were accepted. On Sunday, April 14th, with colors flying and drums beating, Major Anderson and his little company marched out with a salute to the flag of fifty guns. That day the whole North was steeled to live up to the spirit of Holmes' poem.

SEPARATION AND REUNION

BROTHER JONATHAN'S LAMENT FOR SISTER CAROLINE

Both a record and a prophecy are contained in these lines by the New England poet, Oliver Wendell Holmes. A state convention meeting in Charleston had on December 20, 1860, unanimously passed an ordinance of secession, and during January and February six other states had followed. Early in February the Confederate Government had been organized at Montgomery, Alabama, with Jefferson Davis as President. Holmes dated this poem March 25, 1861. Four days later the new President of the United States, Abraham Lincoln, ordered relief to be sent to Fort Sumter in Charleston Harbor. On April 12th the attack on Sumter was made, and the war begun. How fully the sentiment of brotherhood here expressed by Holmes has been realized among the American people it has been the purpose of the Introduction to this volume and of the following selections to show.

She has gone,—she has left us in passion and pride,—
Our stormy-browed sister, so long at our side!
She has torn her own star from our firmament's glow,
And turned on her brother the face of a foe!

O Caroline, Caroline, child of the sun,
We can never forget that our hearts have been one,—
Our foreheads both sprinkled in Liberty's name,
From the fountain of blood with the finger of flame!

You were always too ready to fire at a touch;
But we said: " She is hasty,—she does not mean much."
We have scowled when you uttered some turbulent threat;
But Friendship still whispered: " Forgive and forget! "

Has our love all died out? Have its altars grown cold?
Has the curse come at last which the fathers foretold?
Then Nature must teach us the strength of the chain
That her petulant children would sever in vain.

[44]

THE RUINS OF SECESSION HALL, CHARLESTON—1865

Three months before Holmes' poem, South Carolinians had cast the die of separation in Secession Hall. It appears to the right of the Circular Church, across the narrow graveyard, its walls blasted by the fire of December, 1861. Here the vote was taken on December 20, 1860, declaring that "the union now subsisting between South Carolina and the other States under the name of the 'United States of America' is hereby dissolved." The secession convention was composed of the most experienced men in the State—men who had represented it in the national Congress, judges in the highest courts, eminent divines, and wealthy planters. On the fourth day of its session, at twelve o'clock, the ordinance quoted from above was read with flashing eyes by the venerable judge of chancery, Chancellor Inglis. At a quarter past one it was passed unanimously. The doorkeeper passed the word to the policeman without; he called to another, and so on until the sentinel at the massive iron gate proclaimed it to the impatient populace. The bells in every rocking steeple mingled their notes with the shouts of the excited throngs that filled the streets. There was no dissent in the secession sentiments here.

"THOUGH DARKENED WITH SULPHUR"

THE CHARLESTON RAILROAD DEPOT.   DESTROYED BY EXPLOSION IN 1865

These ruins form an impressive fulfilment of the prophecy in Oliver Wendell Holmes' poem. But it was not till near the end that the scene here preserved could meet the eye. It resulted from the evacuation of the city by the Confederate forces on February 17, 1865. This step had been taken with great reluctance. The movement of secession had begun at Charleston. The city was dear to every Southern heart. Yet military policy clearly dictated that the scattered troops in the Carolinas be concentrated against Sherman. Indeed, it would have been better policy to evacuate earlier. But sentiment is always powerful. Even Jefferson Davis said, "Such full preparation had been made that I had hoped for other and better results, and the disappointment to me is extremely bitter." When the Union troops from Morris Island arrived in Charleston the next morning, they found that the commissary depot had been blown up with the loss of two hundred lives, mostly of women and children. An officer reported "Public buildings, stores, warehouses, private dwellings, shipping, etc., were burning and being burned by armed Confederates." All the Negroes in the city were impressed by the Union officers to work the fire apparatus until all the fires were extinguished. But some of the fairest sections of Charleston were already in ruins.

"IN VAIN IS THE STRIFE"

THE ROMAN CATHOLIC CATHEDRAL OF ST. JOHN AND ST. FINBAR, DESTROYED BY THE FIRE OF DECEMBER, 1861—MOST OF THE ABLE BODIED
CITIZENS WERE SERVING AS SOLDIERS, AND THE FLAMES RAGED UNCHECKED.

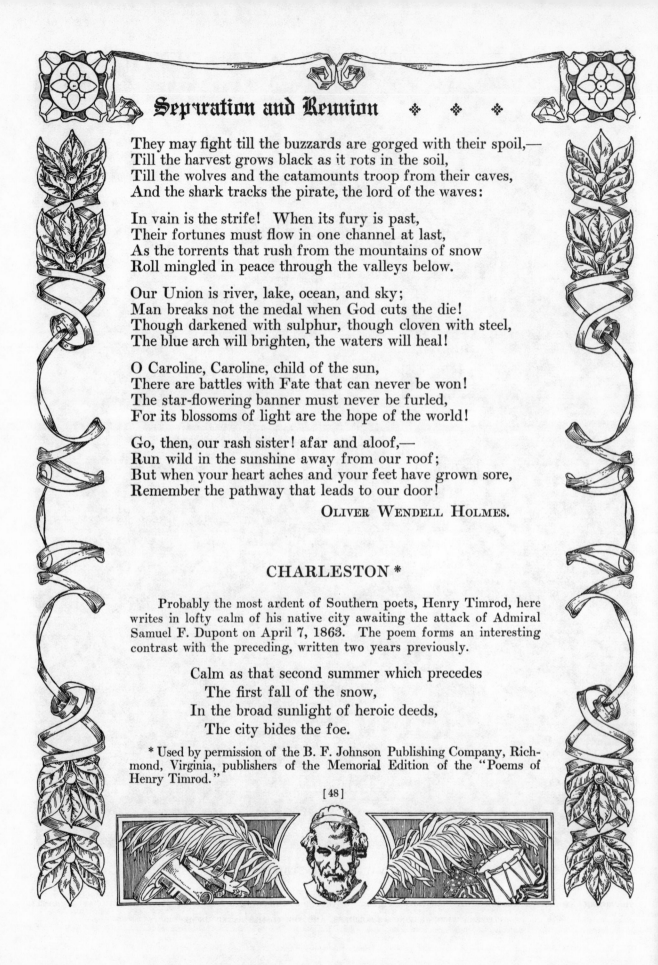

Sepiration and Reunion ❖ ❖ ❖

They may fight till the buzzards are gorged with their spoil,—
Till the harvest grows black as it rots in the soil,
Till the wolves and the catamounts troop from their caves,
And the shark tracks the pirate, the lord of the waves:

In vain is the strife! When its fury is past,
Their fortunes must flow in one channel at last,
As the torrents that rush from the mountains of snow
Roll mingled in peace through the valleys below.

Our Union is river, lake, ocean, and sky;
Man breaks not the medal when God cuts the die!
Though darkened with sulphur, though cloven with steel,
The blue arch will brighten, the waters will heal!

O Caroline, Caroline, child of the sun,
There are battles with Fate that can never be won!
The star-flowering banner must never be furled,
For its blossoms of light are the hope of the world!

Go, then, our rash sister! afar and aloof,—
Run wild in the sunshine away from our roof;
But when your heart aches and your feet have grown sore,
Remember the pathway that leads to our door!

OLIVER WENDELL HOLMES.

CHARLESTON *

Probably the most ardent of Southern poets, Henry Timrod, here
writes in lofty calm of his native city awaiting the attack of Admiral
Samuel F. Dupont on April 7, 1863. The poem forms an interesting
contrast with the preceding, written two years previously.

Calm as that second summer which precedes
    The first fall of the snow,
In the broad sunlight of heroic deeds,
    The city bides the foe.

* Used by permission of the B. F. Johnson Publishing Company, Richmond, Virginia, publishers of the Memorial Edition of the "Poems of
Henry Timrod."

[48]

"THE CITY BIDES THE FOE"

The picture of Confederate artillerymen sighting a field-piece in the outskirts of Charleston shows that there were active preparations for the expected attack. The city had, indeed, been put in a thorough state of defense by General Beauregard, who had assumed command on September 15, 1862. The forts at the entrance to the harbor were strengthened or partly rebuilt, and the waters sown with torpedoes and obstructions. The poet therefore had good reason for awaiting so calmly the naval attack of April 7, 1863. In the lower photograph, St. Michael's and the principal street of Charleston are preserved for us by the Confederate photographer Cook, just as they appeared when Timrod wrote his lines. The city was indeed a very busy one, for constant blockade-running had brought in ample munitions of war and many luxuries. It was no idle boast that Summer was brought to her courts, for silks and spices came in with every cargo. Later on, the blockading fleet, though it did not succeed in reducing Charleston, made blockade-running so dangerous that a constantly decreasing number of laden vessels arrived at the piers.

"THROUGH STREETS STILL ECHOING WITH TRADE"

CHARLESTON IN WAR TIME

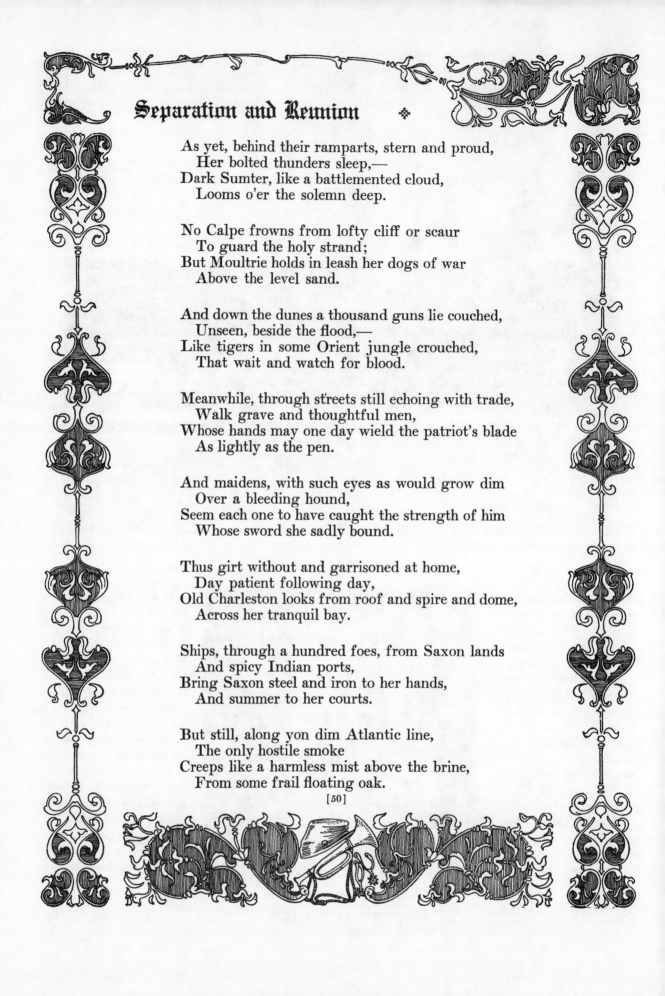

Separation and Reunion ❖

As yet, behind their ramparts, stern and proud,
    Her bolted thunders sleep,—
Dark Sumter, like a battlemented cloud,
    Looms o'er the solemn deep.

No Calpe frowns from lofty cliff or scaur
    To guard the holy strand;
But Moultrie holds in leash her dogs of war
    Above the level sand.

And down the dunes a thousand guns lie couched,
    Unseen, beside the flood,—
Like tigers in some Orient jungle crouched,
    That wait and watch for blood.

Meanwhile, through streets still echoing with trade,
    Walk grave and thoughtful men,
Whose hands may one day wield the patriot's blade
    As lightly as the pen.

And maidens, with such eyes as would grow dim
    Over a bleeding hound,
Seem each one to have caught the strength of him
    Whose sword she sadly bound.

Thus girt without and garrisoned at home,
    Day patient following day,
Old Charleston looks from roof and spire and dome,
    Across her tranquil bay.

Ships, through a hundred foes, from Saxon lands
    And spicy Indian ports,
Bring Saxon steel and iron to her hands,
    And summer to her courts.

But still, along yon dim Atlantic line,
    The only hostile smoke
Creeps like a harmless mist above the brine,
    From some frail floating oak.

"SHE WAITS THE TRIUMPH OR THE TOMB"

THE BOMBARDED GRAVEYARD OF THE CENTRAL CHURCH AT CHARLESTON

The event awaited by Timrod with faith and resignation is here directly illustrated. A sacred spot in the beautiful city of Charleston has been visited by Federal bombs. The tombs of its honored ancestors lie shattered where the ruins of fair mansions look down upon the scene. The cannonading that wrought this havoc was conducted by the Federal army under General Q. A. Gillmore after the failure of Admiral S. F. Du Pont's attack of April 7, 1863. The bombardment of the city was begun on August 21, 1863, by the famous gun, the "Swamp Angel," to enforce the evacuation of Fort Sumter. But Sumter, though reduced to a shapeless mass of ruins, did not surrender. On September 7, 1863, however, Gillmore succeeded in capturing Battery Wagner and Battery Gregg, on the northern part of Morris Island. One 30-pounder Parrott gun sent 4,523 shells toward the city, many of them landing within it destructively.

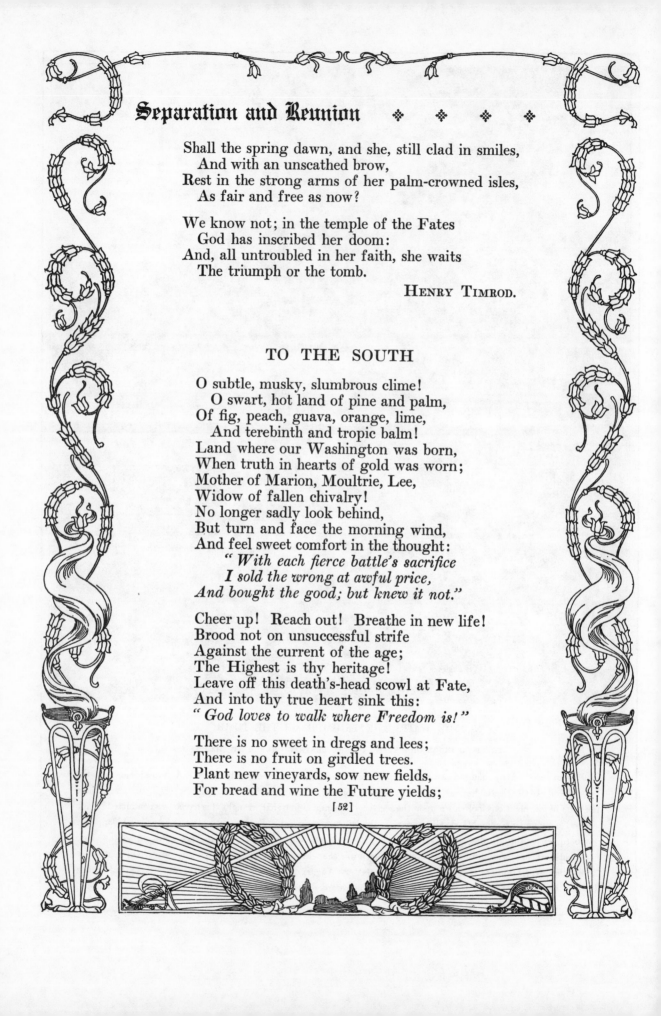

Separation and Reunion ❖ ❖ ❖ ❖

Shall the spring dawn, and she, still clad in smiles,
   And with an unscathed brow,
Rest in the strong arms of her palm-crowned isles,
   As fair and free as now?

We know not; in the temple of the Fates
   God has inscribed her doom:
And, all untroubled in her faith, she waits
   The triumph or the tomb.

HENRY TIMROD.

TO THE SOUTH

O subtle, musky, slumbrous clime!
   O swart, hot land of pine and palm,
Of fig, peach, guava, orange, lime,
   And terebinth and tropic balm!
Land where our Washington was born,
When truth in hearts of gold was worn;
Mother of Marion, Moultrie, Lee,
Widow of fallen chivalry!
No longer sadly look behind,
But turn and face the morning wind,
And feel sweet comfort in the thought:
   " With each fierce battle's sacrifice
    I sold the wrong at awful price,
And bought the good; but knew it not."

Cheer up! Reach out! Breathe in new life!
Brood not on unsuccessful strife
Against the current of the age;
The Highest is thy heritage!
Leave off this death's-head scowl at Fate,
And into thy true heart sink this:
" God loves to walk where Freedom is!"

There is no sweet in dregs and lees;
There is no fruit on girdled trees.
Plant new vineyards, sow new fields,
For bread and wine the Future yields;

"O SUBTLE, MUSKY, SLUMBEROUS CLIME"

Down the lofty nave of this forest cathedral, gleams under the open sky the tomb of some long-honored fore-father of Savannah.   The gigantic live-oaks of the stately plantation, festooned with the long Spanish moss, shadow the fragrant shrubbery growing at their feet.   The whole scene breathes the "subtle, musky, slum-berous" atmosphere sung by the poet Thompson.   Savannah, situated inland on the Savannah River, was through four years of the war unvisited by hostile armies.   But in December, 1864, it fell into the hands of Sherman's troops.   Many another lovely spot in the Southland passed through the conflict with its beauties undisturbed, as if to remind its brave people of the unbounded lavishness of nature amid the wreckage of war.   Bravely have they answered the mute appeal of such surroundings.   To-day the South can point, not only to the charms of its almost tropical clime, but to the material achievements which link it inseparably with the rapidly developing North and West.   Its people have even come to feel a thankfulness for the out-come of the war.   Typical are the whole-hearted vigorous lines of Maurice Thompson printed opposite.

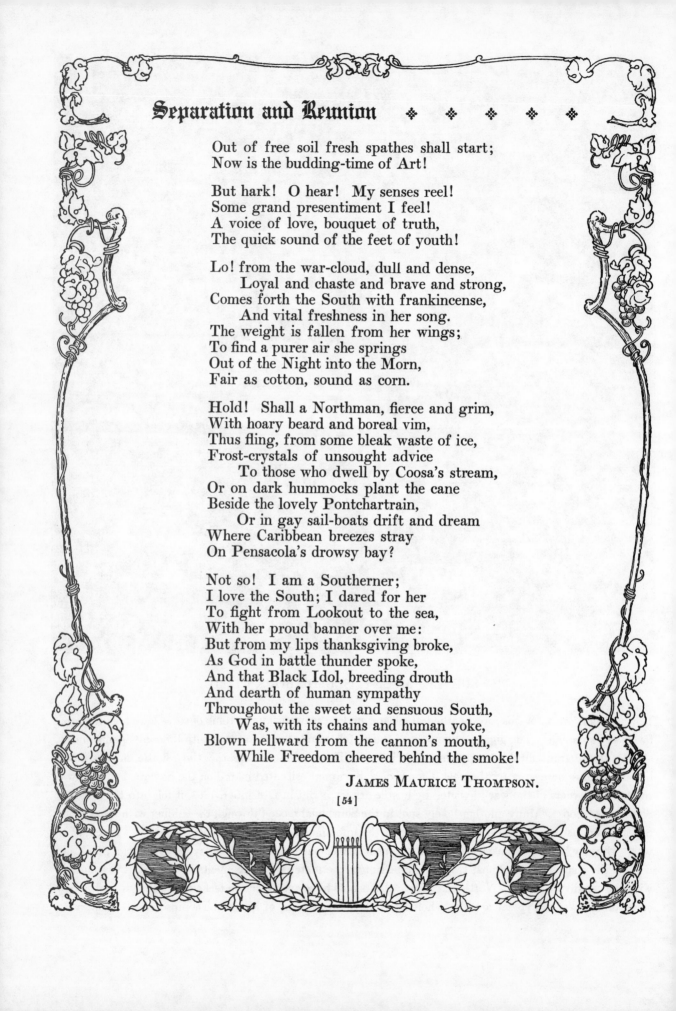

Separation and Reunion ✦ ✦ ✦ ✦ ✦

Out of free soil fresh spathes shall start;
Now is the budding-time of Art!

But hark! O hear! My senses reel!
Some grand presentiment I feel!
A voice of love, bouquet of truth,
The quick sound of the feet of youth!

Lo! from the war-cloud, dull and dense,
    Loyal and chaste and brave and strong,
Comes forth the South with frankincense,
    And vital freshness in her song.
The weight is fallen from her wings;
To find a purer air she springs
Out of the Night into the Morn,
Fair as cotton, sound as corn.

Hold! Shall a Northman, fierce and grim,
With hoary beard and boreal vim,
Thus fling, from some bleak waste of ice,
Frost-crystals of unsought advice
    To those who dwell by Coosa's stream,
Or on dark hummocks plant the cane
Beside the lovely Pontchartrain,
    Or in gay sail-boats drift and dream
Where Caribbean breezes stray
On Pensacola's drowsy bay?

Not so! I am a Southerner;
I love the South; I dared for her
To fight from Lookout to the sea,
With her proud banner over me:
But from my lips thanksgiving broke,
As God in battle thunder spoke,
And that Black Idol, breeding drouth
And dearth of human sympathy
Throughout the sweet and sensuous South,
    Was, with its chains and human yoke,
Blown hellward from the cannon's mouth,
    While Freedom cheered behind the smoke!

JAMES MAURICE THOMPSON.

[54]

II

DEEDS
OF
VALOR

"WHEN GALLANT BURNSIDE MADE DASH UPON
NEW BERNE'

FEDERAL BARRACKS AT NEW BERNE, NORTH CAROLINA, 1862

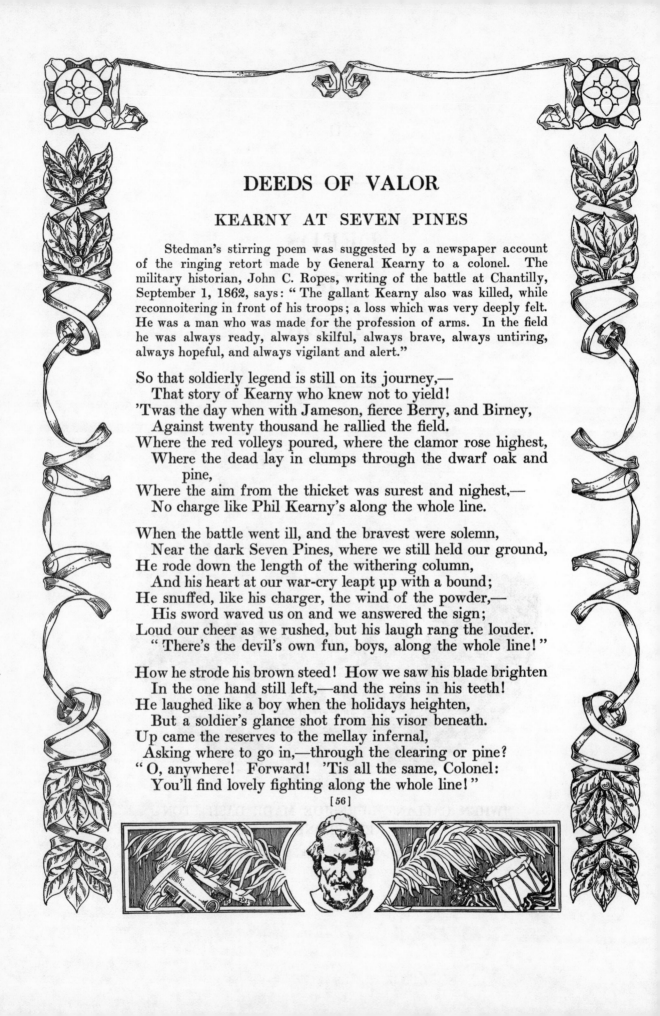

DEEDS OF VALOR

KEARNY AT SEVEN PINES

Stedman's stirring poem was suggested by a newspaper account of the ringing retort made by General Kearny to a colonel. The military historian, John C. Ropes, writing of the battle at Chantilly, September 1, 1862, says: "The gallant Kearny also was killed, while reconnoitering in front of his troops; a loss which was very deeply felt. He was a man who was made for the profession of arms. In the field he was always ready, always skilful, always brave, always untiring, always hopeful, and always vigilant and alert."

So that soldierly legend is still on its journey,—
　That story of Kearny who knew not to yield!
'Twas the day when with Jameson, fierce Berry, and Birney,
　Against twenty thousand he rallied the field.
Where the red volleys poured, where the clamor rose highest,
　Where the dead lay in clumps through the dwarf oak and
　　pine,
Where the aim from the thicket was surest and nighest,—
　No charge like Phil Kearny's along the whole line.

When the battle went ill, and the bravest were solemn,
　Near the dark Seven Pines, where we still held our ground,
He rode down the length of the withering column,
　And his heart at our war-cry leapt up with a bound;
He snuffed, like his charger, the wind of the powder,—
　His sword waved us on and we answered the sign;
Loud our cheer as we rushed, but his laugh rang the louder.
　"There's the devil's own fun, boys, along the whole line!"

How he strode his brown steed! How we saw his blade brighten
　In the one hand still left,—and the reins in his teeth!
He laughed like a boy when the holidays heighten,
　But a soldier's glance shot from his visor beneath.
Up came the reserves to the mellay infernal,
　Asking where to go in,—through the clearing or pine?
"O, anywhere! Forward! 'Tis all the same, Colonel:
　You'll find lovely fighting along the whole line!"

[56]

COPYRIGHT, 1911, REVIEW OF REVIEWS CO.

KEARNY—"HOW WE SAW HIS BLADE BRIGHTEN"

In Brigadier-General Philip Kearny, Stedman selected as the hero of his poem one of the most dashing veteran soldiers in the Civil War. He had entered the army in 1838, at the age of twenty-two, but soon went to France to study cavalry methods. After several months in the school at Saumur he entered the French service and fought with conspicuous gallantry along with veterans of Napoleon in the Arab war against Abd-el-Kader that won Algeria to France. In the American-Mexican War, at the close of the battle of Churubusco, he made a charge into Mexico City, during which he received a wound that necessitated the amputation of an arm. His love of fighting led him across the Atlantic in 1859 to take part in the Italian War against the Austrians. His bravery at Magenta and elsewhere won him the cross of the Legion of Honor. At the outbreak of the Civil War he returned—to his death.

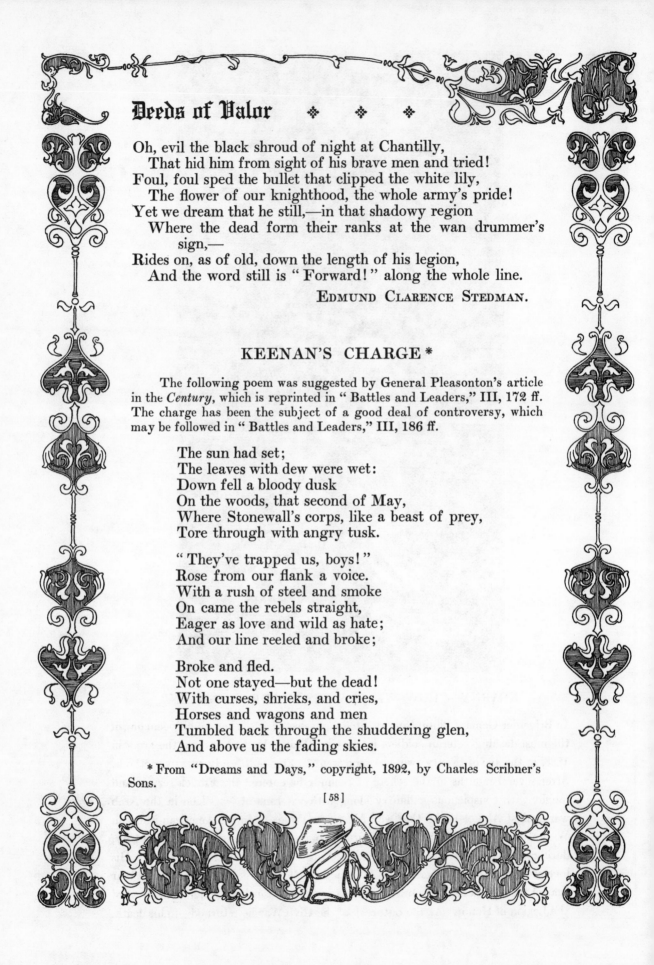

Deeds of Valor ❖ ❖ ❖

Oh, evil the black shroud of night at Chantilly,
    That hid him from sight of his brave men and tried!
Foul, foul sped the bullet that clipped the white lily,
    The flower of our knighthood, the whole army's pride!
Yet we dream that he still,—in that shadowy region
    Where the dead form their ranks at the wan drummer's
        sign,—
Rides on, as of old, down the length of his legion,
    And the word still is " Forward! " along the whole line.

               EDMUND CLARENCE STEDMAN.

KEENAN'S CHARGE *

    The following poem was suggested by General Pleasonton's article in the *Century*, which is reprinted in " Battles and Leaders," III, 172 ff. The charge has been the subject of a good deal of controversy, which may be followed in " Battles and Leaders," III, 186 ff.

    The sun had set;
    The leaves with dew were wet:
    Down fell a bloody dusk
    On the woods, that second of May,
    Where Stonewall's corps, like a beast of prey,
    Tore through with angry tusk.

    " They've trapped us, boys! "
    Rose from our flank a voice.
    With a rush of steel and smoke
    On came the rebels straight,
    Eager as love and wild as hate;
    And our line reeled and broke;

    Broke and fled.
    Not one stayed—but the dead!
    With curses, shrieks, and cries,
    Horses and wagons and men
    Tumbled back through the shuddering glen,
    And above us the fading skies.

    * From "Dreams and Days," copyright, 1892, by Charles Scribner's Sons.

KEARNY'S MEN AFTER THE BATTLE OF FAIR OAKS

This photograph directly illustrates Stedman's poem. It is June, 1862. Men of Kearny's brigade, one seated, others standing and sitting by, are gathered before the Widow Allen's house, now used as a hospital after those bloody days, May 31st and June 1st—the battle of Fair Oaks or Seven Pines. McClellan had advanced up the Peninsula to within five miles of Richmond. About noon of May 31st the Confederate attack on the Union troops about Seven Pines threatened to become heavy, but the message for reënforcements did not reach the commanding officer in the rear till three o'clock. General Kearny was sent forward. He thus reports: "On arriving at the field of battle we found certain zigzag rifle-pits sheltering crowds of men, and the enemy firing from abatis and timber in their front. General Casey remarked to me on coming up, 'If you will regain our late camp, the day will still be ours.' I had but the Third Michigan up, but they moved forward with alacrity, dashing into the felled timber, and commenced a desperate but determined contest, heedless of the shell and ball which rained upon them. . . . I directed General Berry [with the Fifth Michigan] to turn the slashings and, fighting, gain the open ground on the enemy's right flank. This was perfectly accomplished. The Thirty-seventh New York was arranged in column to support the attack. Its services in the sequel proved invaluable. In the meanwhile my remaining brigade, the One hundred and fifth and Sixty-third Pennsylvania, came up, under General Jameson. . . . Eight companies of the Sixty-third Pennsylvania, led by Lieutenant-Colonel Morgan and most spiritedly headed by General Jameson, aided by his daring chief of staff, Captain Potter, were pushed through the abatis (the portions never until now occupied by us), and nobly repelled a strong body of the enemy, who, though in a strong line and coming up rapidly and in order, just failed to reach to support this position in time, but who, nothing daunted and with a courage worthy a united cause, halted in battle array and poured in a constant heavy roll of musketry fire."

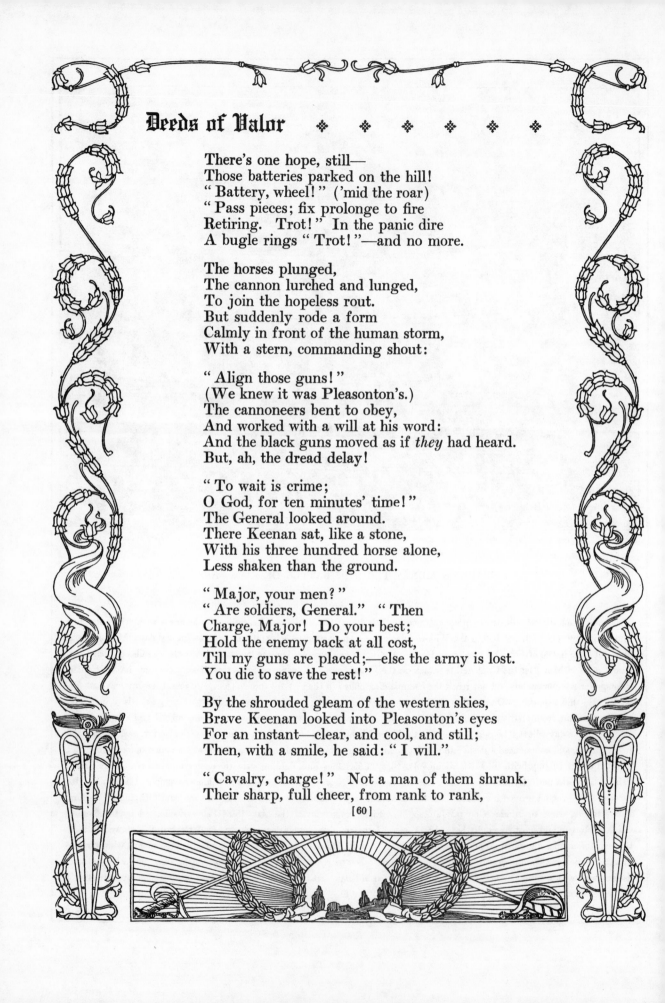

Deeds of Valor ❖ ❖ ❖ ❖ ❖ ❖

There's one hope, still—
Those batteries parked on the hill!
" Battery, wheel! " ('mid the roar)
" Pass pieces; fix prolonge to fire
Retiring.   Trot! " In the panic dire
A bugle rings " Trot! "—and no more.

The horses plunged,
The cannon lurched and lunged,
To join the hopeless rout.
But suddenly rode a form
Calmly in front of the human storm,
With a stern, commanding shout:

" Align those guns! "
(We knew it was Pleasonton's.)
The cannoneers bent to obey,
And worked with a will at his word:
And the black guns moved as if *they* had heard.
But, ah, the dread delay!

" To wait is crime;
O God, for ten minutes' time! "
The General looked around.
There Keenan sat, like a stone,
With his three hundred horse alone,
Less shaken than the ground.

" Major, your men? "
" Are soldiers, General. "   " Then
Charge, Major! Do your best;
Hold the enemy back at all cost,
Till my guns are placed;—else the army is lost.
You die to save the rest! "

By the shrouded gleam of the western skies,
Brave Keenan looked into Pleasonton's eyes
For an instant—clear, and cool, and still;
Then, with a smile, he said: " I will. "

" Cavalry, charge! " Not a man of them shrank.
Their sharp, full cheer, from rank to rank,

The pictures of the battery at "action front" and of the Germanna Plank Road as seen from the hill near the Lacy house, recall vividly the two notable events of Chancellorsville that form the theme of Lathrop's poem. On May 2, 1863, "Stonewall" Jackson had marched around the right flank of the Union army and late in the afternoon had fallen with terrific force upon Howard's (Eleventh) Corps, driving it along in confusion. Pleasonton had started out at four o'clock to pursue the Confederate wagon-train, since Jackson was supposed to be in retreat for Gordonsville, but about six he discovered that his force was needed to repel an attack. His official report runs: "I immediately ordered the Eighth Pennsylvania Cavalry to proceed at a gallop, attack the rebels, and check the attack at any cost until we could get ready for them. This service was splendidly performed, but with heavy loss, and I gained some fifteen minutes to bring Martin's battery into position facing the woods, to reverse a battery of your corps, to detach some cavalry to stop runaways, and to secure more guns from our retreating forces. . . . Time was what we most wanted. Fortunately, I succeeded, before

THE GERMANNA PLANK ROAD IN 1864

"WHERE 'STONEWALL'S' CORPS, LIKE A BEAST OF PREY
TORE THROUGH WITH ANGRY TUSK"

the advancing columns of the enemy came in sight, in placing twenty-two pieces of artillery in position, double-shotted with canister, and bearing on the direction the rebels were pursuing. To support this force, I had two small squadrons of cavalry, ready to charge upon any attempt made to take the guns. My position was upon the extreme left of the line of the Eleventh Corps, and as it recoiled from the fierce onset of the rebels through and over my guns, it was soon apparent we must meet the shock. In rear of the Eleventh Corps the rebels came on rapidly, but now in silence. . . . I ordered all the guns to fire as they were advancing. This terrible discharge staggered them and threw the heads of their columns back on the woods, from which they opened a tremendous fire of musketry, bringing up fresh forces constantly, and striving to advance as fast as they we were swept back by our guns." In another place he adds: "Suspecting that they might play the trick of having their men lie down, draw the fire of artillery, then jump up and charge before the pieces could be reloaded, I poured in the canister for about twenty minutes, and the affair was over."

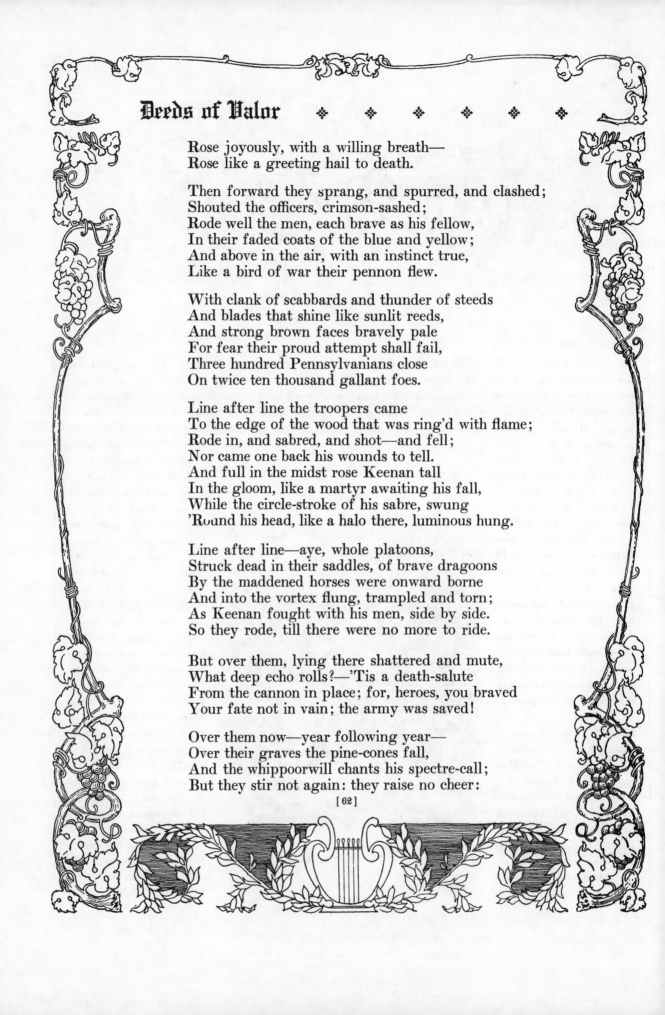

Deeds of Valor ✦ ✦ ✦ ✦ ✦ ✦

Rose joyously, with a willing breath—
Rose like a greeting hail to death.

Then forward they sprang, and spurred, and clashed;
Shouted the officers, crimson-sashed;
Rode well the men, each brave as his fellow,
In their faded coats of the blue and yellow;
And above in the air, with an instinct true,
Like a bird of war their pennon flew.

With clank of scabbards and thunder of steeds
And blades that shine like sunlit reeds,
And strong brown faces bravely pale
For fear their proud attempt shall fail,
Three hundred Pennsylvanians close
On twice ten thousand gallant foes.

Line after line the troopers came
To the edge of the wood that was ring'd with flame;
Rode in, and sabred, and shot—and fell;
Nor came one back his wounds to tell.
And full in the midst rose Keenan tall
In the gloom, like a martyr awaiting his fall,
While the circle-stroke of his sabre, swung
'Round his head, like a halo there, luminous hung.

Line after line—aye, whole platoons,
Struck dead in their saddles, of brave dragoons
By the maddened horses were onward borne
And into the vortex flung, trampled and torn;
As Keenan fought with his men, side by side.
So they rode, till there were no more to ride.

But over them, lying there shattered and mute,
What deep echo rolls?—'Tis a death-salute
From the cannon in place; for, heroes, you braved
Your fate not in vain; the army was saved!

Over them now—year following year—
Over their graves the pine-cones fall,
And the whippoorwill chants his spectre-call;
But they stir not again: they raise no cheer:

"SO THEY RODE, TILL THERE WERE NO MORE TO RIDE"

THE CHANCELLORSVILLE BATTLEFIELD, WHERE "KEENAN'S CHARGE" HAD SWEPT ON MAY 2, 1863

Across this spot swept the charge of the Eighth Pennsylvania Cavalry, celebrated in Lathrop's lines. Major Pennock Huey thus reported the affair: "We moved off briskly to the right, and found General Howard had fallen back, and the enemy's skirmish-line had crossed the road on which we were moving, throwing us between their skirmishers and battle-line. The whole regiment made a desperate charge on the main column of Jackson's corps, who were crossing the road in our front, completely checking the enemy, losing Major Keenan, Captain Arrowsmith, and Adjutant Haddock, with about 30 men and about 80 horses. I immediately re-formed the regiment to support the reserve artillery. We afterward moved back, and formed across the roads, to stop stragglers of the Eleventh Corps. Here we remained all night." But in the words of the poet, "The rush of their charge is resounding still."

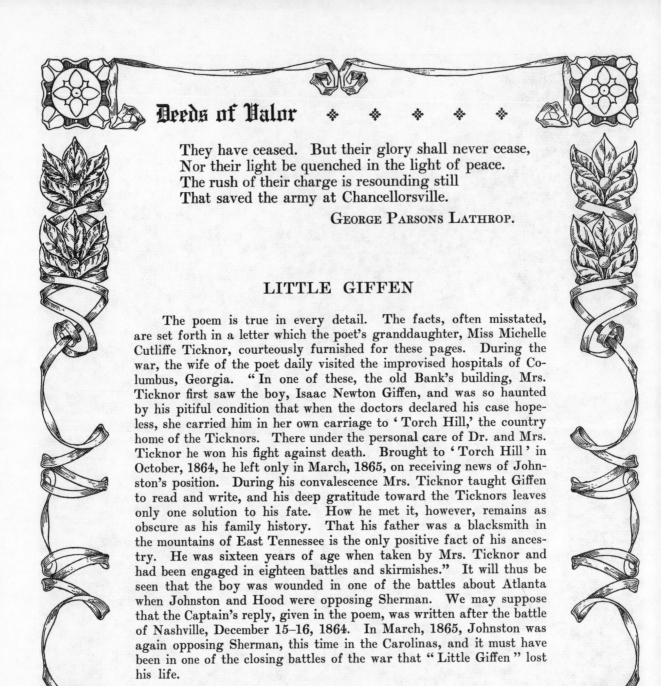

They have ceased. But their glory shall never cease,
Nor their light be quenched in the light of peace.
The rush of their charge is resounding still
That saved the army at Chancellorsville.

GEORGE PARSONS LATHROP.

LITTLE GIFFEN

The poem is true in every detail. The facts, often misstated, are set forth in a letter which the poet's granddaughter, Miss Michelle Cutliffe Ticknor, courteously furnished for these pages. During the war, the wife of the poet daily visited the improvised hospitals of Columbus, Georgia. "In one of these, the old Bank's building, Mrs. Ticknor first saw the boy, Isaac Newton Giffen, and was so haunted by his pitiful condition that when the doctors declared his case hopeless, she carried him in her own carriage to 'Torch Hill,' the country home of the Ticknors. There under the personal care of Dr. and Mrs. Ticknor he won his fight against death. Brought to 'Torch Hill' in October, 1864, he left only in March, 1865, on receiving news of Johnston's position. During his convalescence Mrs. Ticknor taught Giffen to read and write, and his deep gratitude toward the Ticknors leaves only one solution to his fate. How he met it, however, remains as obscure as his family history. That his father was a blacksmith in the mountains of East Tennessee is the only positive fact of his ancestry. He was sixteen years of age when taken by Mrs. Ticknor and had been engaged in eighteen battles and skirmishes." It will thus be seen that the boy was wounded in one of the battles about Atlanta when Johnston and Hood were opposing Sherman. We may suppose that the Captain's reply, given in the poem, was written after the battle of Nashville, December 15–16, 1864. In March, 1865, Johnston was again opposing Sherman, this time in the Carolinas, and it must have been in one of the closing battles of the war that "Little Giffen" lost his life.

Out of the focal and foremost fire,
Out of the hospital walls as dire,
Smitten of grape-shot and gangrene,
(Eighteenth battle, and *he* sixteen!)
Spectre! such as you seldom see,
Little Giffen, of Tennessee.

"TO THE EDGE OF THE WOOD THAT WAS RINGED WITH FLAME"

WILDERNESS TREES AFTER THE ARTILLERY FIRING THAT FOLLOWED THE CAVALRY CHARGE

Blasted by the artillery fire that saved the Federals at Chancellorsville, the Wilderness woods, only a couple of hundred yards south of the plank road, reveal the desperate nature of the conflict in the early evening of May 2, 1863. Of the close of the fight, the Union General Alfred Pleasonton reported: "It was now dark, and their presence could only be ascertained by the flash of their muskets, from which a continuous stream of fire was seen encircling us, and gradually extending to our right, to cut us off from the army. This was at last checked by our guns, and the rebels withdrew. Several guns and caissons were then recovered from the woods where the enemy had been posted. Such was the fight at the head of Scott's Run. Artillery against infantry at 300 yards; the infantry in the woods, the artillery in the clearing. War presents many anomalies, but few so curious and strange in its results."

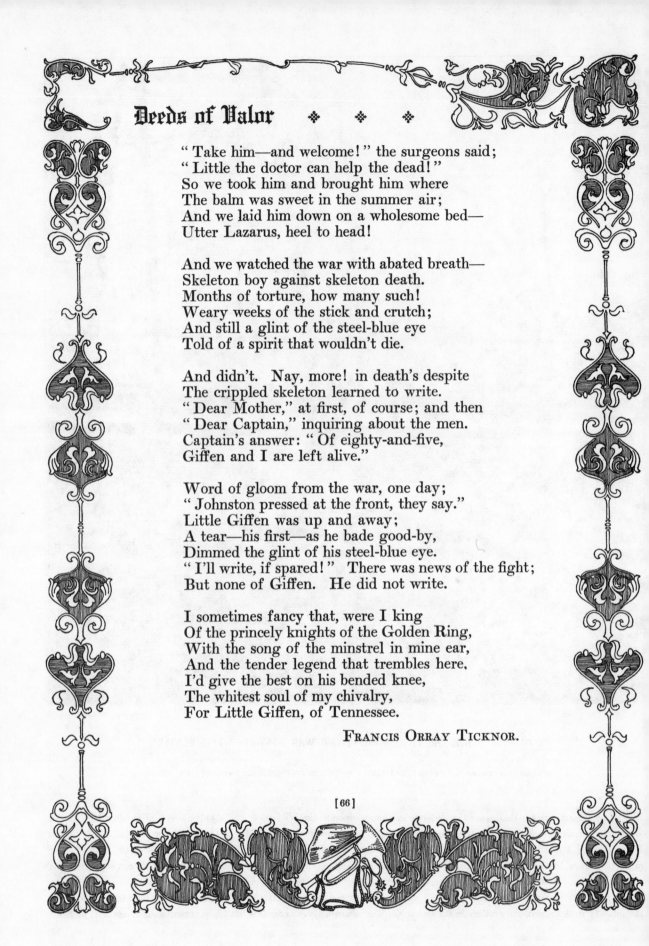

Deeds of Valor ❖ ❖ ❖

"Take him—and welcome!" the surgeons said;
"Little the doctor can help the dead!"
So we took him and brought him where
The balm was sweet in the summer air;
And we laid him down on a wholesome bed—
Utter Lazarus, heel to head!

And we watched the war with abated breath—
Skeleton boy against skeleton death.
Months of torture, how many such!
Weary weeks of the stick and crutch;
And still a glint of the steel-blue eye
Told of a spirit that wouldn't die.

And didn't. Nay, more! in death's despite
The crippled skeleton learned to write.
"Dear Mother," at first, of course; and then
"Dear Captain," inquiring about the men.
Captain's answer: "Of eighty-and-five,
Giffen and I are left alive."

Word of gloom from the war, one day;
"Johnston pressed at the front, they say."
Little Giffen was up and away;
A tear—his first—as he bade good-by,
Dimmed the glint of his steel-blue eye.
"I'll write, if spared!" There was news of the fight;
But none of Giffen. He did not write.

I sometimes fancy that, were I king
Of the princely knights of the Golden Ring,
With the song of the minstrel in mine ear,
And the tender legend that trembles here,
I'd give the best on his bended knee,
The whitest soul of my chivalry,
For Little Giffen, of Tennessee.

FRANCIS ORRAY TICKNOR.

WILLIAM BLACK, THE YOUNGEST WOUNDED SOLDIER REPORTED

Lest the instance of "Little Giffen" seem an uncommon one, there is presented here the winning face of little William Black. He was the youngest boy, it is true, to be reported "wounded." Yet General Charles King's researches on "Boys of the War Days" in Volume VIII brings out the fact that "over 800,000 lads of seventeen or less were found in the ranks of the Union army, that over 200,000 were no more than sixteen, that there were even 100,000 on the Union rolls who were no more than fifteen."

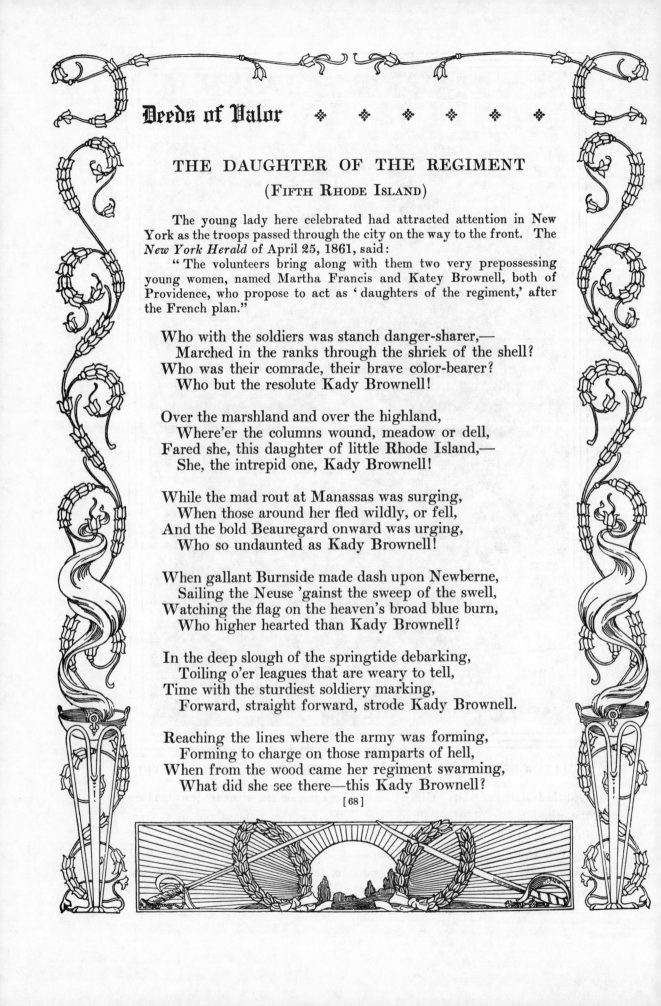

THE DAUGHTER OF THE REGIMENT
(Fifth Rhode Island)

The young lady here celebrated had attracted attention in New York as the troops passed through the city on the way to the front. The *New York Herald* of April 25, 1861, said:

" The volunteers bring along with them two very prepossessing young women, named Martha Francis and Katey Brownell, both of Providence, who propose to act as ' daughters of the regiment,' after the French plan."

Who with the soldiers was stanch danger-sharer,—
　　Marched in the ranks through the shriek of the shell?
Who was their comrade, their brave color-bearer?
　　Who but the resolute Kady Brownell!

Over the marshland and over the highland,
　　Where'er the columns wound, meadow or dell,
Fared she, this daughter of little Rhode Island,—
　　She, the intrepid one, Kady Brownell!

While the mad rout at Manassas was surging,
　　When those around her fled wildly, or fell,
And the bold Beauregard onward was urging,
　　Who so undaunted as Kady Brownell!

When gallant Burnside made dash upon Newberne,
　　Sailing the Neuse 'gainst the sweep of the swell,
Watching the flag on the heaven's broad blue burn,
　　Who higher hearted than Kady Brownell?

In the deep slough of the springtide debarking,
　　Toiling o'er leagues that are weary to tell,
Time with the sturdiest soldiery marking,
　　Forward, straight forward, strode Kady Brownell.

Reaching the lines where the army was forming,
　　Forming to charge on those ramparts of hell,
When from the wood came her regiment swarming,
　　What did she see there—this Kady Brownell?

"GALLANT BURNSIDE" AT THE HEIGHT OF HIS CAREER

PHOTOGRAPHED EIGHT MONTHS AFTER THE EVENTS OF SCOLLARD'S POEM; WHILE WITH HIS STAFF-OFFICERS AT WARRENTON, VIRGINIA, NOVEMBER 14, 1862

General Burnside entered the war in May, 1861, as colonel of the First Rhode Island Volunteers. At Bull Run, July 21, 1861, he at first commanded the brigade in which the regiment was serving, but was soon called upon to take charge of the Second (Hunter's) division in the presence of the opposing Confederates. Under his command, Kady Brownell showed herself "so undaunted"; the two Rhode Island regiments in the battle were in his brigade, the colonel of the Second losing his life early in the action. On August 6, 1861, Burnside was commissioned brigadier-general of volunteers, and from January to July, 1862, commanded the Department of North Carolina. He captured Roanoke Island, occupied New Berne in the manner alluded to in Scollard's poem, and forced the evacuation of Fort Macon, at Beaufort. In July. as major-general of volunteers, he was asked to take chief command of the Army of the Potomac, but he refused. In September the offer was renewed, and again refused. Finally, on November 9th, he accepted. His disastrous repulse a month later at Fredericksburg was followed by his resignation as chief, though he served no less faithfully, both as department and corps commander, to the end of the war.

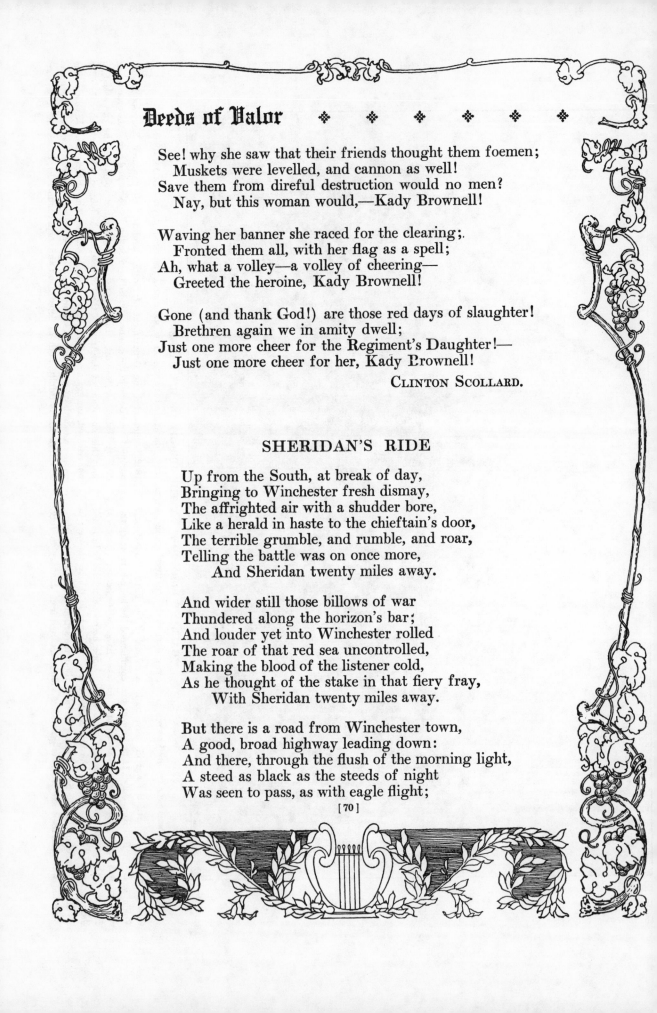

See! why she saw that their friends thought them foemen;
　　Muskets were levelled, and cannon as well!
Save them from direful destruction would no men?
　　Nay, but this woman would,—Kady Brownell!

Waving her banner she raced for the clearing;.
　　Fronted them all, with her flag as a spell;
Ah, what a volley—a volley of cheering—
　　Greeted the heroine, Kady Brownell!

Gone (and thank God!) are those red days of slaughter!
　　Brethren again we in amity dwell;
Just one more cheer for the Regiment's Daughter!—
　　Just one more cheer for her, Kady Prownell!

　　　　　　　　　　　CLINTON SCOLLARD.

SHERIDAN'S RIDE

Up from the South, at break of day,
Bringing to Winchester fresh dismay,
The affrighted air with a shudder bore,
Like a herald in haste to the chieftain's door,
The terrible grumble, and rumble, and roar,
Telling the battle was on once more,
　　And Sheridan twenty miles away.

And wider still those billows of war
Thundered along the horizon's bar;
And louder yet into Winchester rolled
The roar of that red sea uncontrolled,
Making the blood of the listener cold,
As he thought of the stake in that fiery fray,
　　With Sheridan twenty miles away.

But there is a road from Winchester town,
A good, broad highway leading down:
And there, through the flush of the morning light,
A steed as black as the steeds of night
Was seen to pass, as with eagle flight;

"OVER THE MARSHLAND AND OVER THE HIGHLAND"

FEDERAL FORTIFICATIONS NEAR THE RAILROAD, SOUTH OF NEW BERNE

This view recalls the incident of March 14, 1862, described by Clinton Scollard in "The Daughter of the Regiment." Burnside's attack on New Berne was part of the blockading movement which sought to close every port along the Southern coasts. The Fifth Rhode Island was in General John G. Parke's brigade. The soldiers were so eager to engage the enemy that many of them leaped from the ship into the water and waded waist-deep to the shore, and during the day often waded knee-deep in mud. The next morning little could be seen in the "open piney woods," owing to the dense fog. This condition accounts for the confusion that might have proved serious but for Kady Brownell. The brigade marched on out of the woods, and charged the Confederate works. Burnside himself reported: " Too much praise cannot be awarded to the officers and men for their untiring exertion and unceasing patience in accomplishing this work. The effecting of the landing and the approach to within a mile and a half of the enemy's work on the 13th I consider as great a victory as the engagement of the 14th. Owing to the difficult nature of the landing, our men were forced to wade ashore waist-deep, march through mud to a point twelve miles distant, bivouac in low, marshy ground in a rain-storm for the night, engage the enemy at daylight in the morning, fighting them for four hours amid a dense fog that prevented them from seeing the position of the enemy, and finally advancing rapidly over bad roads upon the city. In the midst of all this, not a complaint was heard; the men were only eager to accomplish their work." Burnside's success was rewarded by the rank of major-general of volunteers.

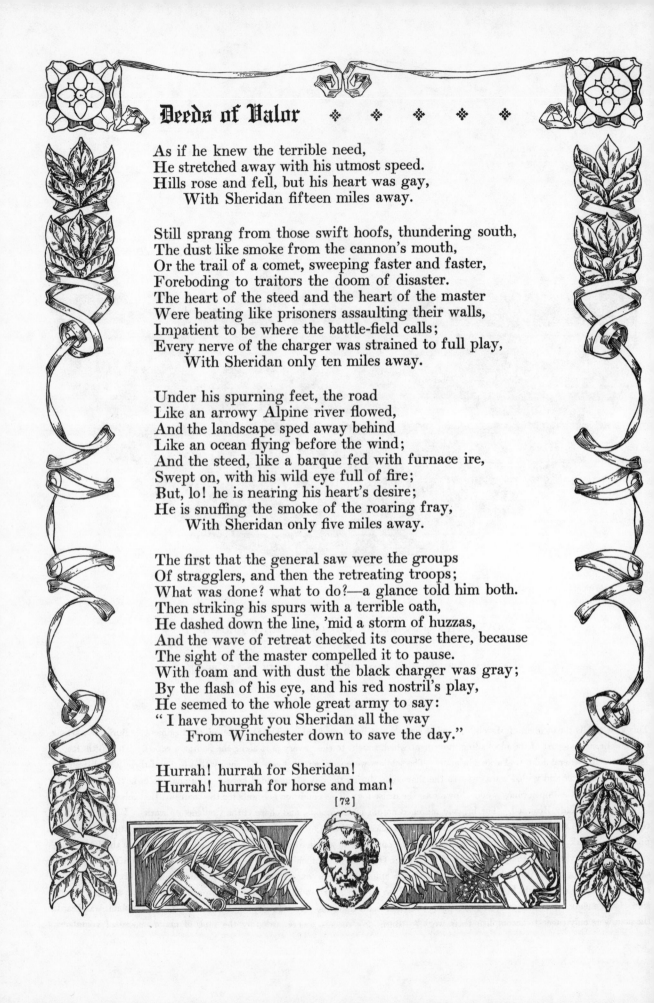

Deeds of Valor ✦ ✦ ✦ ✦ ✦

As if he knew the terrible need,
He stretched away with his utmost speed.
Hills rose and fell, but his heart was gay,
    With Sheridan fifteen miles away.

Still sprang from those swift hoofs, thundering south,
The dust like smoke from the cannon's mouth,
Or the trail of a comet, sweeping faster and faster,
Foreboding to traitors the doom of disaster.
The heart of the steed and the heart of the master
Were beating like prisoners assaulting their walls,
Impatient to be where the battle-field calls;
Every nerve of the charger was strained to full play,
    With Sheridan only ten miles away.

Under his spurning feet, the road
Like an arrowy Alpine river flowed,
And the landscape sped away behind
Like an ocean flying before the wind;
And the steed, like a barque fed with furnace ire,
Swept on, with his wild eye full of fire;
But, lo! he is nearing his heart's desire;
He is snuffing the smoke of the roaring fray,
    With Sheridan only five miles away.

The first that the general saw were the groups
Of stragglers, and then the retreating troops;
What was done? what to do?—a glance told him both.
Then striking his spurs with a terrible oath,
He dashed down the line, 'mid a storm of huzzas,
And the wave of retreat checked its course there, because
The sight of the master compelled it to pause.
With foam and with dust the black charger was gray;
By the flash of his eye, and his red nostril's play,
He seemed to the whole great army to say:
" I have brought you Sheridan all the way
    From Winchester down to save the day."

Hurrah! hurrah for Sheridan!
Hurrah! hurrah for horse and man!

[72]

GENERAL

P. H. SHERIDAN

IN 1864

WITH THE HAT

HE WORE ON HIS

FAMOUS "RIDE"

The most dramatic deed of a Federal general in the Valley of Virginia is recorded in Read's poem. In September, 1864, Sheridan had driven the Confederates up the Valley, and in early October had retreated northward. Early followed, but he was soon out of supplies. He was obliged to fight or fall back. At an early hour on the foggy morning of October 19th, he attacked the unsuspecting Union army encamped along Cedar Creek and drove it back in confusion. General Sheridan, who had made a flying visit to Washington, spent the night of the 18th at Winchester on his way back to the army. At Mill Creek, half a mile south of Winchester, he came in sight of the fugitives. An officer who was at the front gives this account: "Far away in the rear was heard cheer after cheer. What was the cause? Were reënforcements coming? Yes, Phil Sheridan was coming, and he was a host. . . . Dashing along the pike, he came upon the line of battle. 'What troops are those?' shouted Sheridan. 'The Sixth Corps,' was the response from a hundred voices. 'We are all right,' said Sheridan, as he swung his old hat and dashed along the line toward the right. 'Never mind, boys, we'll whip them yet; we'll whip them yet! We shall sleep in our old quarters to-night!' were the encouraging words of the chief, as he rode along, while the men threw their hats high in air, leaped and danced and cheered in wildest joy." The victory was so complete that the campaign was virtually at an end. Three weeks of occasional skirmishing and the last action in the Valley was over.

SHERIDAN'S WINCHESTER CHARGER, IN 1869

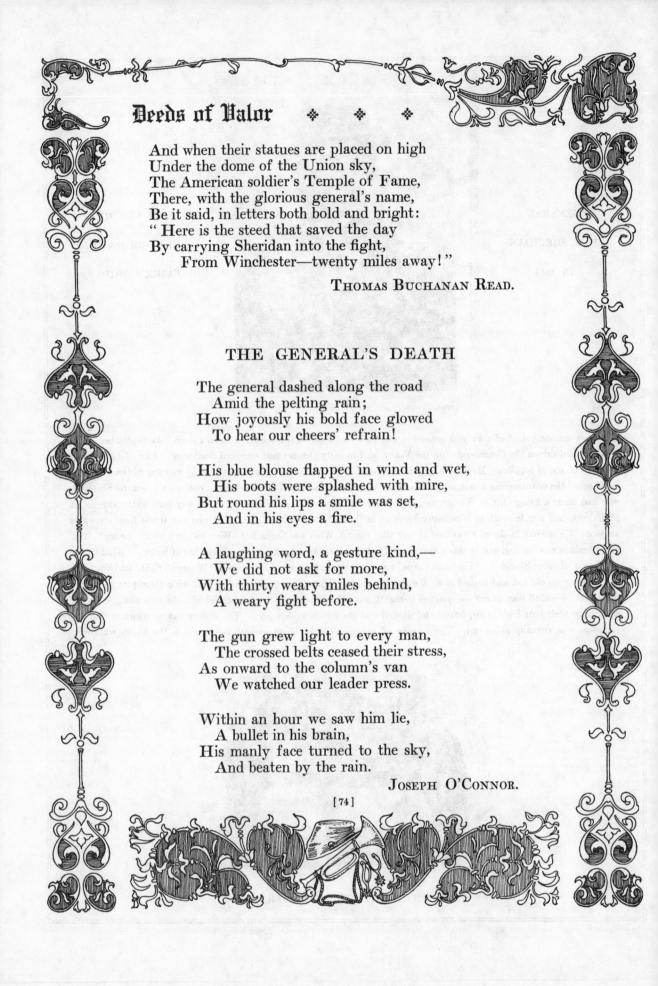

Deeds of Valor ❖ ❖ ❖

And when their statues are placed on high
Under the dome of the Union sky,
The American soldier's Temple of Fame,
There, with the glorious general's name,
Be it said, in letters both bold and bright:
"Here is the steed that saved the day
By carrying Sheridan into the fight,
    From Winchester—twenty miles away!"

THOMAS BUCHANAN READ.

THE GENERAL'S DEATH

The general dashed along the road
    Amid the pelting rain;
How joyously his bold face glowed
    To hear our cheers' refrain!

His blue blouse flapped in wind and wet,
    His boots were splashed with mire,
But round his lips a smile was set,
    And in his eyes a fire.

A laughing word, a gesture kind,—
    We did not ask for more,
With thirty weary miles behind,
    A weary fight before.

The gun grew light to every man,
    The crossed belts ceased their stress,
As onward to the column's van
    We watched our leader press.

Within an hour we saw him lie,
    A bullet in his brain,
His manly face turned to the sky,
    And beaten by the rain.

JOSEPH O'CONNOR.

[74]

"THE GENERAL'S DEATH"

This sylvan scene, as it looked a few months after the death of General George W. Taylor, on August 27, 1862, recalls Pope's Virginia campaign. "Stonewall" Jackson in a series of forced marches had swept round to the rear of Pope's army, seized the railroad, and then captured the immense depot of supplies at Manassas Station. To meet him, after an all-day's march from near Alexandria on August 26th, Union troops under General Taylor crossed Bull Run near the spot pictured above. They advanced about two miles to occupy the important point Taylor made all the dispositions for an attack on the Confederate force, which at once opened upon the advancing brigade with a heavy discharge of round-shot, shell, and grape. The men nevertheless moved forward undaunted and defiant. Within 300 yards of the earthworks Taylor discovered that he was greatly outnumbered. A force of cavalry was making for his rear. He stood in danger of being surrounded. Nothing was left but to regain the bridge. While directing the movement, Taylor received a wound from which he soon died. Assistance arrived, and he was carried across the stream, begging the officers to rally the men of his brigade and prevent another Bull Run.

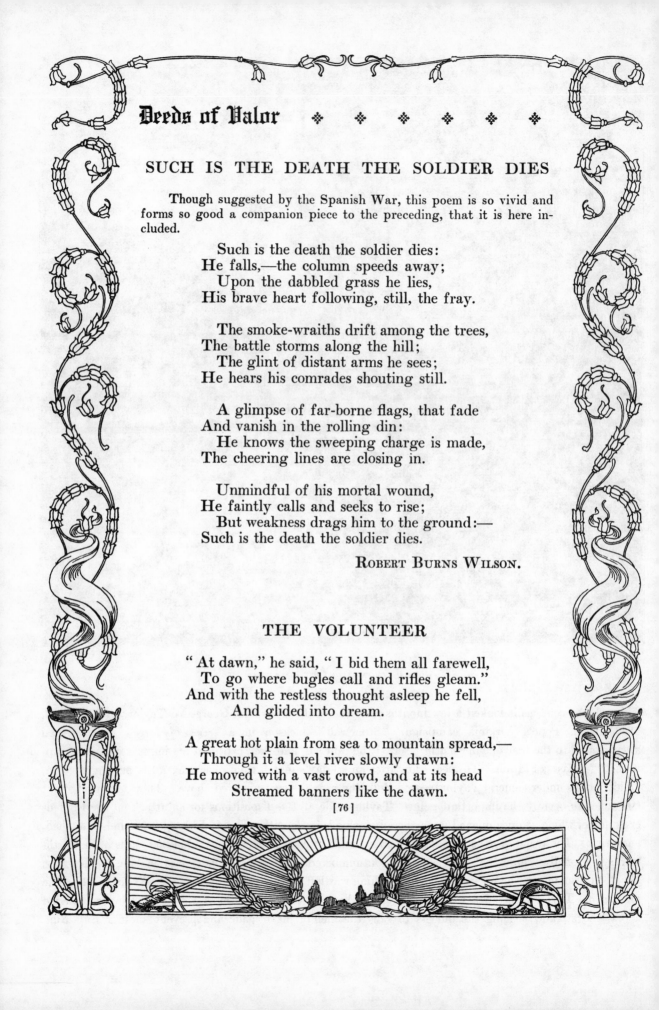

Deeds of Valor ❖ ❖ ❖ ❖ ❖ ❖

SUCH IS THE DEATH THE SOLDIER DIES

Though suggested by the Spanish War, this poem is so vivid and forms so good a companion piece to the preceding, that it is here included.

Such is the death the soldier dies:
He falls,—the column speeds away;
Upon the dabbled grass he lies,
His brave heart following, still, the fray.

The smoke-wraiths drift among the trees,
The battle storms along the hill;
The glint of distant arms he sees;
He hears his comrades shouting still.

A glimpse of far-borne flags, that fade
And vanish in the rolling din:
He knows the sweeping charge is made,
The cheering lines are closing in.

Unmindful of his mortal wound,
He faintly calls and seeks to rise;
But weakness drags him to the ground:—
Such is the death the soldier dies.

ROBERT BURNS WILSON.

THE VOLUNTEER

"At dawn," he said, "I bid them all farewell,
To go where bugles call and rifles gleam."
And with the restless thought asleep he fell,
And glided into dream.

A great hot plain from sea to mountain spread,—
Through it a level river slowly drawn:
He moved with a vast crowd, and at its head
Streamed banners like the dawn.

"SUCH IS THE DEATH
THE SOLDIER
DIES"

CONFEDERATES
WHO FELL IN EWELL'S
ATTACK ON MAY 19, 1864

His musket dropped across him as he fell, its hammer down as it had clicked in that last unavailing shot—here lies one of the 900 men in gray and behind him another comrade, left on the last Spotsylvania battlefield. In the actions about Spotsylvania Court House, of which this engagement was the close, the Union army lost about fifteen thousand. With sympathy for the last moments of each soldier, such as Robert Burns Wilson has put into his poem opposite, the horror of war becomes all too vivid. Ewell's attack illustrates the sudden facing of death that may come to every soldier. The desperate fighting about Spotsylvania had been prolonged ten days and more, when General Lee thought the Union army was withdrawing to his right. To ascertain whether this was true he directed Ewell to feel out the Federal position. After a long detour through roads nearly impassable, Ewell came upon the enemy ready to receive him. The object of his movement thus accomplished, he prepared to return, but found himself fiercely attacked. It was necessary then to make a stand, for no effective fighting can be done in retreat. The late afternoon and the early evening were filled with the fierce encounter. Only when darkness came was Ewell able in safety to withdraw.

"WHERE BUGLES CALL AND RIFLES GLEAM"

The men of the 74th New York Infantry, as they drill in their camp of 1861, exemplify the martial splendor of Cutler's poem; nor was its hero animated by a more unflinching resolve than they. The regiment's record tells the story. It was organized in New York and till August 20th was stationed at Camp Scott, on Staten Island, as the fifth in Sickles' "Excelsior Brigade." Barely a month after Bull Run, the first overwhelming Federal defeat, this regiment was on its way to Washington. The fall of the year, as the picture shows, was spent in the constant marching and drilling by which McClellan forged that fighting instrument known to fame as the Army of the Potomac. The volunteers were indeed where bugles called and rifles gleamed, but they were impatient for service on the "great hot plain" to hear the "dissonant cries of triumph and dismay." Marching about under the leafless trees over

[78]

ILLUSTRATION FOR "THE VOLUNTEER"

ground frequently covered with snow did not satisfy their notions of the glory of military service. The next year brought to both officers and men the long-wished-for opportunity. In April, 1862, they floated down the Potomac to take part in McClellan's Peninsula campaign. At the battle of Williamsburg, May 5th, the regiment performed distinguished service, fighting behind an abatis of felled timber and holding a position against the main force of the Confederate army. Of 36 of its number the regiment might report, "And with the dead he lay," and the total loss mounted to 143. Through the rest of the campaign, at Fair Oaks and during the Seven Days' Battles, it was in the hard fighting. At Chancellorsville it served under General Berry, who was killed on May 3, 1863. At Gettysburg it appeared with ranks thinned by two years of continuous service, yet sustained a loss of eighty-nine.

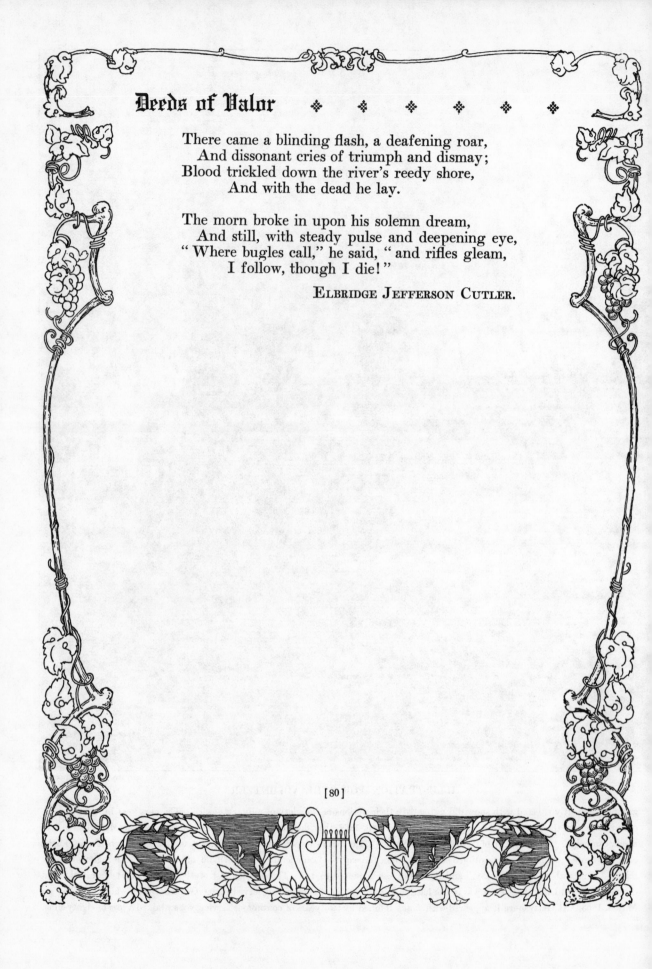

Deeds of Valor ❖ ❖ ❖ ❖ ❖ ❖

There came a blinding flash, a deafening roar,
   And dissonant cries of triumph and dismay;
Blood trickled down the river's reedy shore,
   And with the dead he lay.

The morn broke in upon his solemn dream,
   And still, with steady pulse and deepening eye,
"Where bugles call," he said, "and rifles gleam,
   I follow, though I die!"

ELBRIDGE JEFFERSON CUTLER.

III

IN

MEMORIAM

THE RUINED BRIDGE AT BULL RUN

ON THE HEIGHTS ABOVE, YOUNG PELHAM,
HERO OF RANDALL'S POEM FOLLOWING,
WON HIS FIRST LAURELS

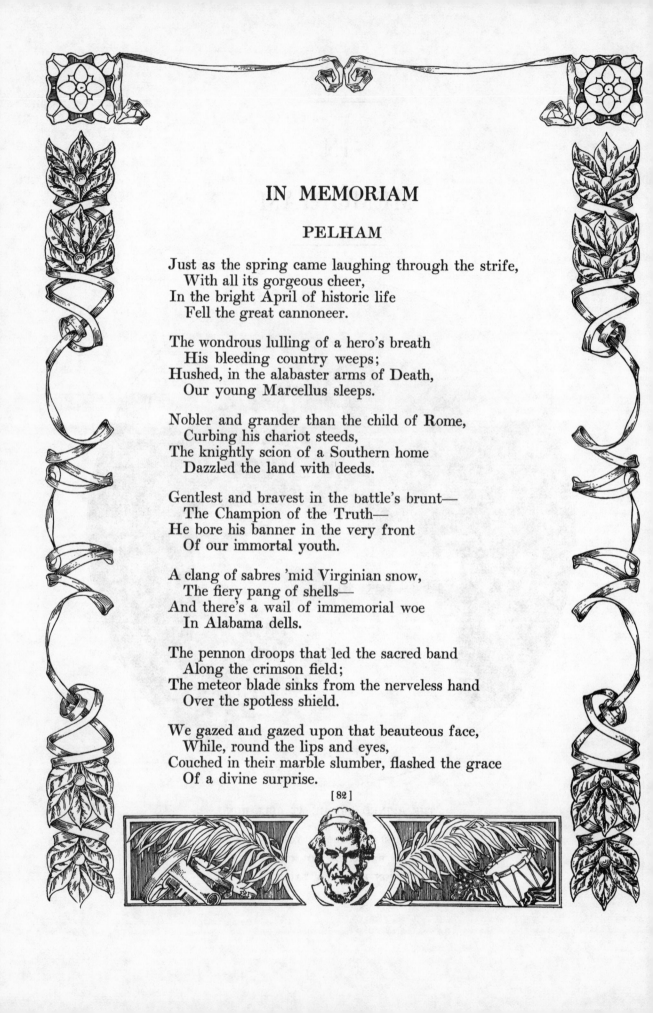

IN MEMORIAM

PELHAM

Just as the spring came laughing through the strife,
　With all its gorgeous cheer,
In the bright April of historic life
　Fell the great cannoneer.

The wondrous lulling of a hero's breath
　His bleeding country weeps;
Hushed, in the alabaster arms of Death,
　Our young Marcellus sleeps.

Nobler and grander than the child of Rome,
　Curbing his chariot steeds,
The knightly scion of a Southern home
　Dazzled the land with deeds.

Gentlest and bravest in the battle's brunt—
　The Champion of the Truth—
He bore his banner in the very front
　Of our immortal youth.

A clang of sabres 'mid Virginian snow,
　The fiery pang of shells—
And there's a wail of immemorial woe
　In Alabama dells.

The pennon droops that led the sacred band
　Along the crimson field;
The meteor blade sinks from the nerveless hand
　Over the spotless shield.

We gazed and gazed upon that beauteous face,
　While, round the lips and eyes,
Couched in their marble slumber, flashed the grace
　Of a divine surprise.

PELHAM, "THE GREAT CANNONEER"

Randall's poem was such a tribute as few young soldiers have ever received, and this is true also of General "Jeb" Stuart's order of March 20, 1863, after Pelham's death: "The major-general commanding approaches with reluctance the painful duty of announcing to the division its irreparable loss in the death of Major John Pelham, commanding the Horse Artillery. He fell mortally wounded in the battle of Kellysville, March 17, with the battle-cry on his lips and the light of victory beaming from his eye. To you, his comrades, it is needless to dwell upon what you have so often witnessed, his prowess in action, already proverbial. . . . His eye had glanced over every battle-field of this army from the First Manassas to the moment of his death, and he was, with a single exception, a brilliant actor in all. The memory of 'the gallant Pelham,' his many manly virtues, his noble nature and purity of character, are enshrined as a sacred legacy in the hearts of all who knew him. His record has been bright and spotless, his career brilliant and successful. He fell the noblest of sacrifices on the altar of his country, to whose glorious service he had dedicated his life from the beginning of the war." To this General Lee added an unusual endorsement: "Respectfully forwarded for the information of the department. I feel deeply the loss of the noble dead, and heartily concur in the commendation of the living. R. E. Lee, General." All Virginia concurred in these sentiments.

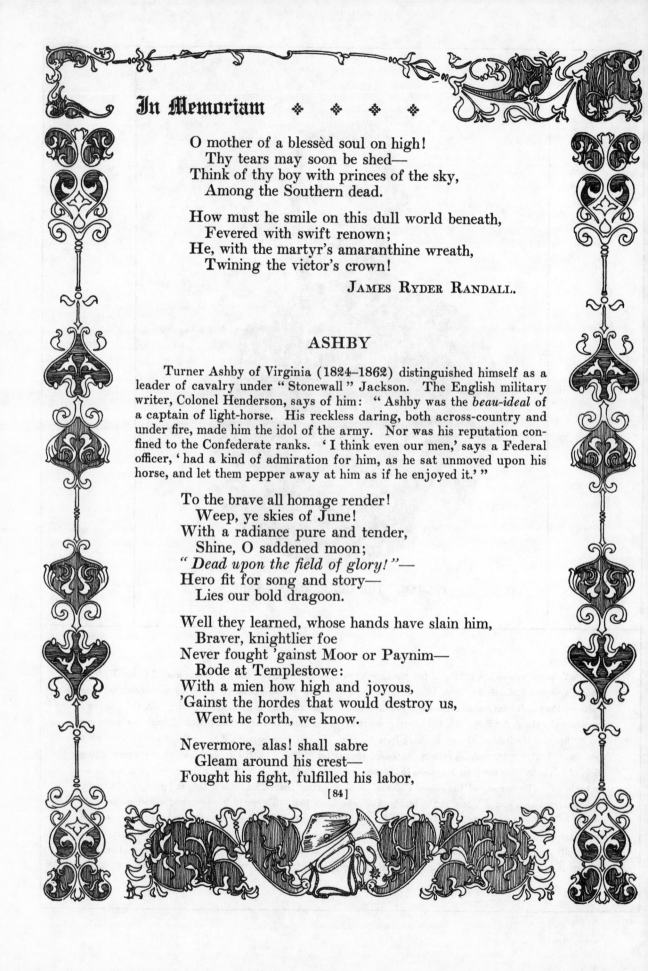

In Memoriam ❖ ❖ ❖ ❖

O mother of a blessèd soul on high!
    Thy tears may soon be shed—
Think of thy boy with princes of the sky,
    Among the Southern dead.

How must he smile on this dull world beneath,
    Fevered with swift renown;
He, with the martyr's amaranthine wreath,
    Twining the victor's crown!

JAMES RYDER RANDALL.

ASHBY

Turner Ashby of Virginia (1824–1862) distinguished himself as a leader of cavalry under "Stonewall" Jackson. The English military writer, Colonel Henderson, says of him: "Ashby was the *beau-ideal* of a captain of light-horse. His reckless daring, both across-country and under fire, made him the idol of the army. Nor was his reputation confined to the Confederate ranks. 'I think even our men,' says a Federal officer, 'had a kind of admiration for him, as he sat unmoved upon his horse, and let them pepper away at him as if he enjoyed it.'"

To the brave all homage render!
    Weep, ye skies of June!
With a radiance pure and tender,
    Shine, O saddened moon;
"Dead upon the field of glory!"—
Hero fit for song and story—
    Lies our bold dragoon.

Well they learned, whose hands have slain him,
    Braver, knightlier foe
Never fought 'gainst Moor or Paynim—
    Rode at Templestowe:
With a mien how high and joyous,
'Gainst the hordes that would destroy us,
    Went he forth, we know.

Nevermore, alas! shall sabre
    Gleam around his crest—
Fought his fight, fulfilled his labor,

WHERE PELHAM FIRST "DAZZLED THE LAND WITH DEEDS"

The Henry house on the Bull Run battlefield, the site of John Pelham's first effort. At that time he was only twenty, having been born in Calhoun County, Alabama, about 1841. At the outbreak of the war he had left West Point to enter the Southern army. Of his conduct near the ruins above, "Stonewall" Jackson reported: "Nobly did the artillery maintain its position for hours against the enemy's advancing thousands." Soon he won the command of a battery of horse artillery, to serve with General "Jeb" Stuart's cavalry. Stuart officially reported of the battle of Williamsburg, May 5, 1862: "I ordered the horse artillery at once into action; but before the order could be given, Pelham's battery was speaking to the enemy in thunder-tones of defiance, its maiden effort on the field, thus filling its function of unexpected arrival with instantaneous execution and sustaining in gallant style the fortunes of the day, keeping up a destructive fire upon the enemy until our infantry, having re-formed, rushed onward, masking the pieces. I directed Captain Pelham then to take a position farther to the left and open a cross-fire on the Telegraph Road, which he did as long as the presence of the enemy warranted the expenditure of ammunition." At Antietam, Stuart again reports: "The gallant Pelham displayed all those noble qualities which have made him immortal. He had under his command batteries from every portion of General Jackson's command. The batteries of Poague, Pegram, and Carrington (the only ones which now recur to me) did splendid service, as also did the Stuart horse artillery, all under Pelham. The hill held on the extreme left so long and so gallantly by artillery alone, was essential to the maintenance of our position." It is surprising to remember that these reports are not of a war-grimed veteran but of a youth of twenty.

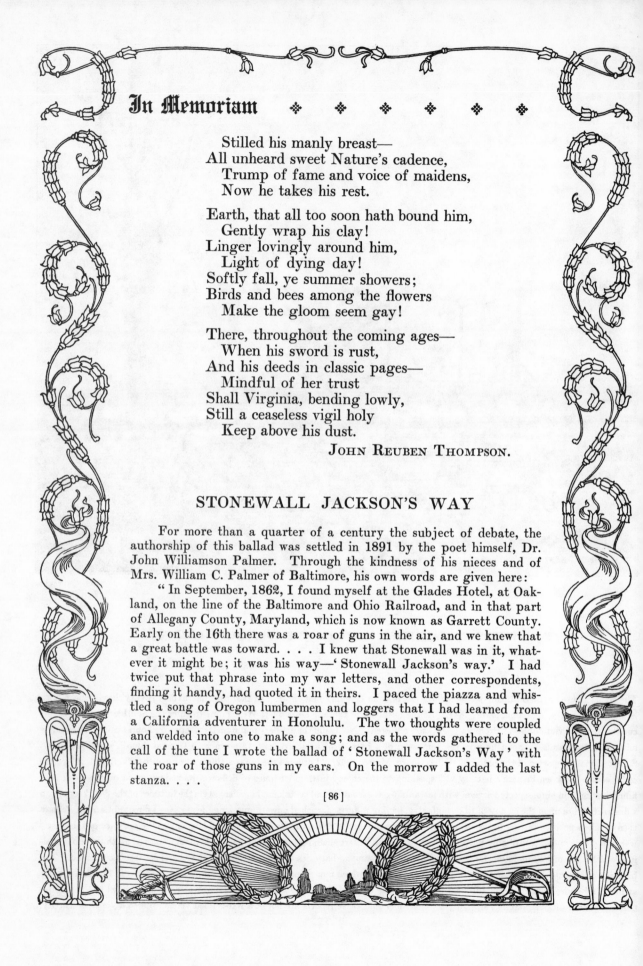

Stilled his manly breast—
All unheard sweet Nature's cadence,
   Trump of fame and voice of maidens,
   Now he takes his rest.

Earth, that all too soon hath bound him,
   Gently wrap his clay!
Linger lovingly around him,
   Light of dying day!
Softly fall, ye summer showers;
Birds and bees among the flowers
   Make the gloom seem gay!

There, throughout the coming ages—
   When his sword is rust,
And his deeds in classic pages—
   Mindful of her trust
Shall Virginia, bending lowly,
Still a ceaseless vigil holy
   Keep above his dust.

JOHN REUBEN THOMPSON.

STONEWALL JACKSON'S WAY

For more than a quarter of a century the subject of debate, the authorship of this ballad was settled in 1891 by the poet himself, Dr. John Williamson Palmer. Through the kindness of his nieces and of Mrs. William C. Palmer of Baltimore, his own words are given here:

"In September, 1862, I found myself at the Glades Hotel, at Oakland, on the line of the Baltimore and Ohio Railroad, and in that part of Allegany County, Maryland, which is now known as Garrett County. Early on the 16th there was a roar of guns in the air, and we knew that a great battle was toward. . . . I knew that Stonewall was in it, whatever it might be; it was his way—'Stonewall Jackson's way.' I had twice put that phrase into my war letters, and other correspondents, finding it handy, had quoted it in theirs. I paced the piazza and whistled a song of Oregon lumbermen and loggers that I had learned from a California adventurer in Honolulu. The two thoughts were coupled and welded into one to make a song; and as the words gathered to the call of the tune I wrote the ballad of 'Stonewall Jackson's Way' with the roar of those guns in my ears. On the morrow I added the last stanza. . . .

WHERE JACKSON PLAYED WITH FEDERAL ARMIES

THE MASSANNUTTEN MOUNTAINS, IN THE CENTER OF THE SHENANDOAH VALLEY, 1884

"Stonewall Jackson's Way" came to be known amid this fertile valley and noble range. The English military authority, Colonel Henderson, writes that "The Valley campaign saved Richmond. In a few short months the quiet gentleman of Lexington became, in the estimation of friend and foe, a very thunderbolt of war; and his name, which a year previous had hardly been known beyond the Valley, was already famous." Jackson had been in command of the Southern forces in the Valley since the beginning of 1862. For the Confederate Government the Shenandoah region was of the greatest importance; it afforded an easy avenue of advance into Maryland and the rear of Washington, and was the granary for all the Virginia armies. When McClellan with his hundred thousand men was advancing upon Richmond, which seemed certain to fall before superior numbers, Jackson prevented the junction of the Union armies by a series of startling achievements. On May 8th, by a forced march, he took the Federal force at McDowell by surprise, and despite a four hours' resistance drove it back in defeat. He followed up the retreating troops. In the early morning of May 23d, at Fort Royal, the clear notes of the bugle, followed by the crash of musketry, startled the Union camp. The hastily formed line was sturdily repelling the charge when the appearance of cavalry in its rear caused it to fall back. But Jackson was soon following the dust of the retreating column down the road to Winchester. There Banks, who was "fond of shell," was attacked with artillery on the morning of May 25th, after which ten thousand bayonets rushed forward to the ringing "rebel yell" in a charge that drove everything before them. Jackson, rising in his stirrups, shouted to his officers, "Press forward to the Potomac!" The troops that had marched thirty miles in thirty hours pressed forward; but, the cavalry not assisting, Banks made good his escape across the broad river. During the month of June, Jackson kept three armies busy in the Shenandoah; then, vanishing as by magic, he joined Lee in driving McClellan from within five miles of Richmond to his gunboats on the James. Henderson exclaims, "75,000 men absolutely paralyzed by 16,000! Only Napoleon's campaign of 1814 affords a parallel to this extraordinary spectacle." Jackson's death was like the loss of an army.

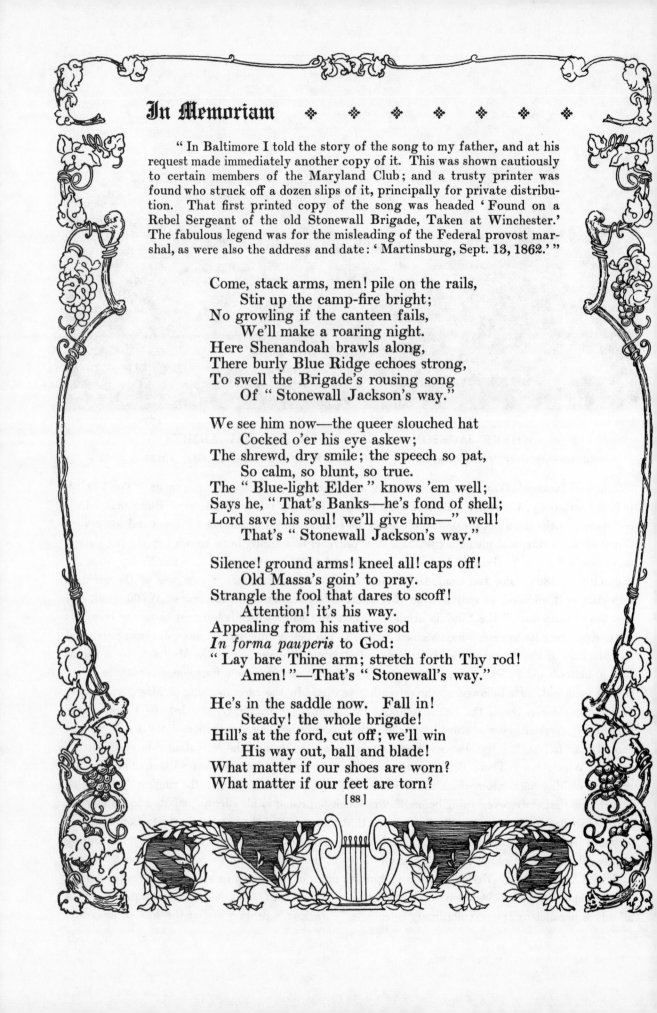

In Memoriam ✦ ✦ ✦ ✦ ✦ ✦

"In Baltimore I told the story of the song to my father, and at his request made immediately another copy of it. This was shown cautiously to certain members of the Maryland Club; and a trusty printer was found who struck off a dozen slips of it, principally for private distribution. That first printed copy of the song was headed 'Found on a Rebel Sergeant of the old Stonewall Brigade, Taken at Winchester.' The fabulous legend was for the misleading of the Federal provost marshal, as were also the address and date: 'Martinsburg, Sept. 13, 1862.'"

Come, stack arms, men! pile on the rails,
    Stir up the camp-fire bright;
No growling if the canteen fails,
    We'll make a roaring night.
Here Shenandoah brawls along,
There burly Blue Ridge echoes strong,
To swell the Brigade's rousing song
    Of "Stonewall Jackson's way."

We see him now—the queer slouched hat
    Cocked o'er his eye askew;
The shrewd, dry smile; the speech so pat,
    So calm, so blunt, so true.
The "Blue-light Elder" knows 'em well;
Says he, "That's Banks—he's fond of shell;
Lord save his soul! we'll give him—" well!
    That's "Stonewall Jackson's way."

Silence! ground arms! kneel all! caps off!
    Old Massa's goin' to pray.
Strangle the fool that dares to scoff!
    Attention! it's his way.
Appealing from his native sod
In forma pauperis to God:
"Lay bare Thine arm; stretch forth Thy rod!
    Amen!"—That's "Stonewall's way."

He's in the saddle now. Fall in!
    Steady! the whole brigade!
Hill's at the ford, cut off; we'll win
    His way out, ball and blade!
What matter if our shoes are worn?
What matter if our feet are torn?

[88]

WHERE "STONEWALL" JACKSON FELL

In this tangled nook Lee's right-hand man was shot through a terrible mistake of his own soldiers. It was the second of May, 1863. After his brilliant flank march, the evening attack on the rear of Hooker's army had just been driven home. About half-past eight, Jackson had ridden beyond his lines to reconnoiter for the final advance. A single rifle-shot rang out in the darkness. The outposts of the two armies were engaged. Jackson turned toward his own line, where the Eighteenth North Carolina was stationed. The regiment, keenly on the alert and startled by the group of strange horsemen riding through the gloom, fired a volley that brought several men and horses to the earth. Jackson was struck once in the right hand and twice in the left arm, a little below the shoulder. His horse dashed among the trees; but with his bleeding right hand Jackson succeeded in seizing the reins and turning the frantic animal back into the road. Only with difficulty was the general taken to the rear so that his wounds might be dressed. To his attendants he said, "Tell them simply that you have a wounded Confederate officer." To one who asked if he was seriously hurt, he replied: "Don't bother yourself about me. Win the battle first and attend to the wounded afterward." He was taken to Guiney's Station. At first it was hoped that he would recover, but pneumonia set in and his strength gradually ebbed. On Sunday evening, May 10th, he uttered the words which inspired the young poet, Sidney Lanier, to write his elegy, beautiful in its serene resignation.

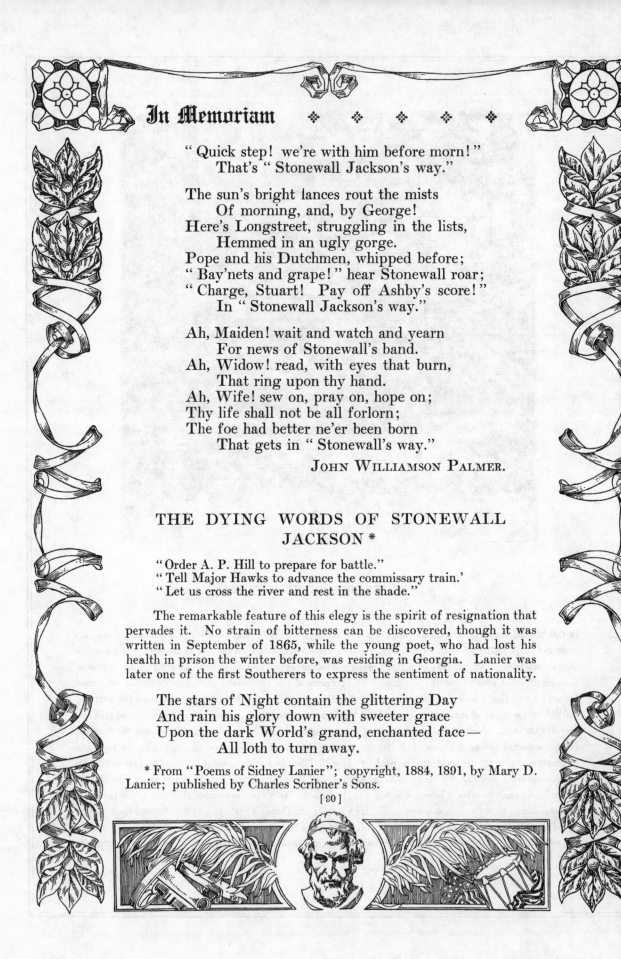

"Quick step! we're with him before morn!"
    That's "Stonewall Jackson's way."

The sun's bright lances rout the mists
    Of morning, and, by George!
Here's Longstreet, struggling in the lists,
    Hemmed in an ugly gorge.
Pope and his Dutchmen, whipped before;
"Bay'nets and grape!" hear Stonewall roar;
"Charge, Stuart! Pay off Ashby's score!"
    In "Stonewall Jackson's way."

Ah, Maiden! wait and watch and yearn
    For news of Stonewall's band.
Ah, Widow! read, with eyes that burn,
    That ring upon thy hand.
Ah, Wife! sew on, pray on, hope on;
Thy life shall not be all forlorn;
The foe had better ne'er been born
    That gets in "Stonewall's way."

JOHN WILLIAMSON PALMER.

THE DYING WORDS OF STONEWALL JACKSON *

"Order A. P. Hill to prepare for battle."
"Tell Major Hawks to advance the commissary train.'
"Let us cross the river and rest in the shade."

The remarkable feature of this elegy is the spirit of resignation that pervades it. No strain of bitterness can be discovered, though it was written in September of 1865, while the young poet, who had lost his health in prison the winter before, was residing in Georgia. Lanier was later one of the first Southerers to express the sentiment of nationality.

The stars of Night contain the glittering Day
And rain his glory down with sweeter grace
Upon the dark World's grand, enchanted face—
    All loth to turn away.

* From "Poems of Sidney Lanier"; copyright, 1884, 1891, by Mary D. Lanier; published by Charles Scribner's Sons.

From this humble grave on the green Virginia hillside, Jackson rises before the American people as one of the mightiest figures of a mighty conflict. When he died on May 10, 1863, in the little town of Guiney's Station, not far from the battlefield of Chancellorsville, his remains were taken to Richmond. In the Hall of Representatives the body lay in state while the sorrowing throngs passed by the open coffin in silence. In the Military Institute at Lexington, which Jackson had left two years before as an obscure professor, the remains of the illustrious leader were under the charge of the cadets, until his burial in the quiet cemetery above the town. The pure

"STONEWALL" JACKSON

"STILL SHINE THE WORDS
THAT MINIATURE
HIS DEEDS"

and noble words of Lanier need no comment. A few lines from an Englishman, Colonel G. F. R. Henderson, declare Jackson's life a message not for America alone. "The hero who lies buried at Lexington, in the Valley of Virginia, belongs to a race that is not confined to a single continent; and to those who speak the same tongue, and in whose veins the same blood flows, his words come home like an echo of all that is noblest in their history: 'What is life without honor? Degradation is worse than death. We must think of the living and of those who are to come after us, and see that by God's blessing we transmit to them the freedom we have ourselves inherited'"

JACKSON'S GRAVE AT LEXINGTON, VIRGINIA

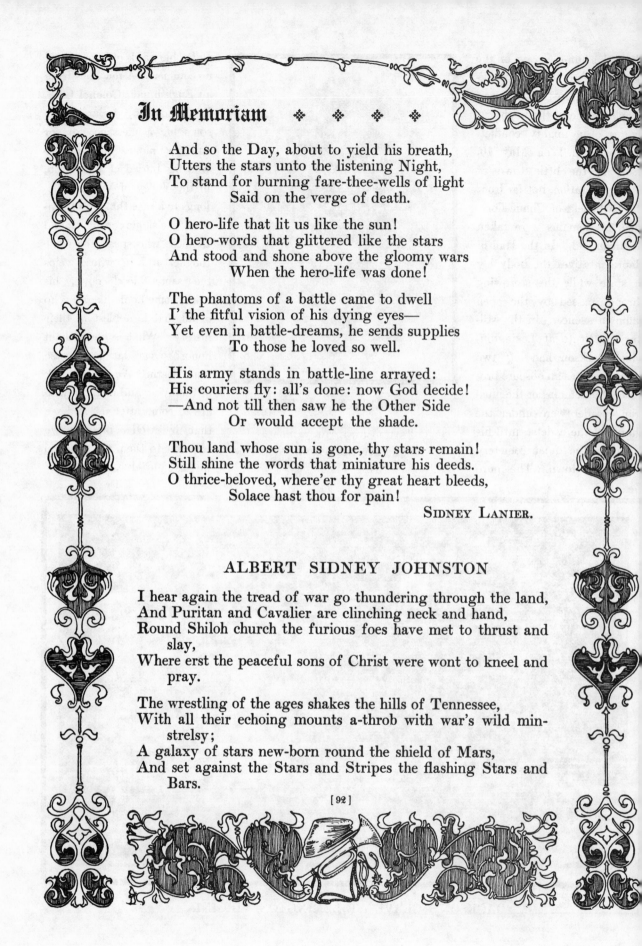

In Memoriam ❖ ❖ ❖ ❖

And so the Day, about to yield his breath,
Utters the stars unto the listening Night,
To stand for burning fare-thee-wells of light
    Said on the verge of death.

O hero-life that lit us like the sun!
O hero-words that glittered like the stars
And stood and shone above the gloomy wars
    When the hero-life was done!

The phantoms of a battle came to dwell
I' the fitful vision of his dying eyes—
Yet even in battle-dreams, he sends supplies
    To those he loved so well.

His army stands in battle-line arrayed:
His couriers fly: all's done: now God decide!
—And not till then saw he the Other Side
    Or would accept the shade.

Thou land whose sun is gone, thy stars remain!
Still shine the words that miniature his deeds.
O thrice-beloved, where'er thy great heart bleeds,
    Solace hast thou for pain!

                   SIDNEY LANIER.

ALBERT SIDNEY JOHNSTON

I hear again the tread of war go thundering through the land,
And Puritan and Cavalier are clinching neck and hand,
Round Shiloh church the furious foes have met to thrust and
    slay,
Where erst the peaceful sons of Christ were wont to kneel and
    pray.

The wrestling of the ages shakes the hills of Tennessee,
With all their echoing mounts a-throb with war's wild min-
    strelsy;
A galaxy of stars new-born round the shield of Mars,
And set against the Stars and Stripes the flashing Stars and
    Bars.

ALBERT SIDNEY JOHNSTON

The man who, at the opening of hostilities, was regarded as the most formidable general in the Confederacy is commemorated in the poem opposite by a woman long prominent in the relief work of the Grand Army of the Republic. Johnston, whose father was a Connecticut Yankee, won distinction in the Black Hawk War, entered the army of Texas in its struggle for independence, succeeded Sam Houston as commander-in-chief, fought in the War with Mexico, and was recommended for the grade of brigadier-general for his conduct at Monterey. When he heard that his adopted state, Texas, had passed the ordinance of secession, he resigned from the Department of the Pacific. He was assured that he might have the highest position in the Federal service. Sorrowfully he declined, writing at the time: "No one could feel more sensibly the calamitous condition of our country than myself, and whatever part I may take hereafter, it will always be a subject of gratulation with me that no act of mine ever contributed to bring it about. I suppose the difficulties now will only be adjusted by the sword. In my humble judgment, that was not the remedy." Johnston counted for more, said Jefferson Davis, than an army of 10,000.

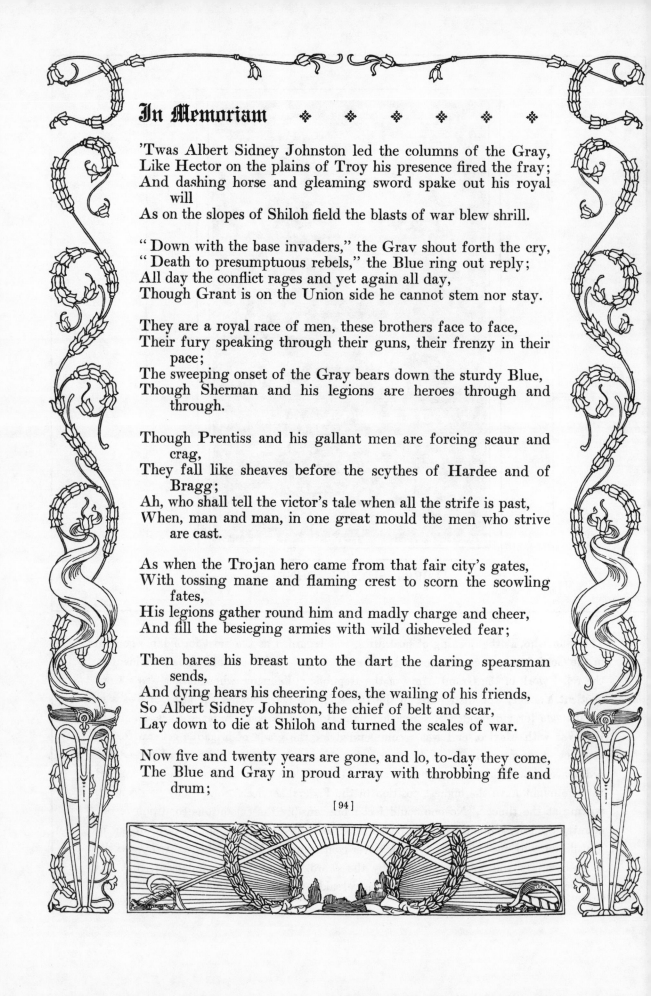

In Memoriam ❖ ❖ ❖ ❖ ❖ ❖

'Twas Albert Sidney Johnston led the columns of the Gray,
Like Hector on the plains of Troy his presence fired the fray;
And dashing horse and gleaming sword spake out his royal
    will
As on the slopes of Shiloh field the blasts of war blew shrill.

"Down with the base invaders," the Gray shout forth the cry,
"Death to presumptuous rebels," the Blue ring out reply;
All day the conflict rages and yet again all day,
Though Grant is on the Union side he cannot stem nor stay.

They are a royal race of men, these brothers face to face,
Their fury speaking through their guns, their frenzy in their
    pace;
The sweeping onset of the Gray bears down the sturdy Blue,
Though Sherman and his legions are heroes through and
    through.

Though Prentiss and his gallant men are forcing scaur and
    crag,
They fall like sheaves before the scythes of Hardee and of
    Bragg;
Ah, who shall tell the victor's tale when all the strife is past,
When, man and man, in one great mould the men who strive
    are cast.

As when the Trojan hero came from that fair city's gates,
With tossing mane and flaming crest to scorn the scowling
    fates,
His legions gather round him and madly charge and cheer,
And fill the besieging armies with wild disheveled fear;

Then bares his breast unto the dart the daring spearsman
    sends,
And dying hears his cheering foes, the wailing of his friends,
So Albert Sidney Johnston, the chief of belt and scar,
Lay down to die at Shiloh and turned the scales of war.

Now five and twenty years are gone, and lo, to-day they come,
The Blue and Gray in proud array with throbbing fife and
    drum;

"ON THE SLOPES OF SHILOH FIELD"

PITTSBURG LANDING—A FEW DAYS AFTER THE BATTLE

By the name of "Pittsburg Landing," this Tennessee River point, Southerners designate the conflict of April 6 and 7, 1862. The building upon the left and one farther up the bank were the only ones standing at the time of the battle. Of the six steamers, the name of the *Tycoon*, which brought hospital supplies from the Cincinnati branch of the Sanitary Commission, is visible. Johnston's plan in the attack on the Federal forces was to pound away on their left until they were driven away from the Landing and huddled in the angle between the Tennessee River and Snake Creek. The onset of the Confederates was full of dash. Sherman was at length driven from Shiloh Church, and the command of Prentiss was surrounded and forced to surrender. It looked as if Johnston would crush the left. Just at this point he was struck down by a minie-ball from the last line of a Federal force that he had victoriously driven back. The success of the day now begins to tell on the Confederate army. Many of the lines show great gaps. But the men in gray push vigorously toward the point where these boats lie anchored. Some heavy guns are massed near this point. Reënforcements are arriving across the river, but General Beauregard, who succeeds Johnston in command, suspends the battle till the morrow. During the night 24,000 fresh troops are taken across the river by the transports here pictured. They successfully withstand the attempt of Beauregard, and with the arrival of Lew Wallace from up the river victory shifts to the Stars and Stripes.

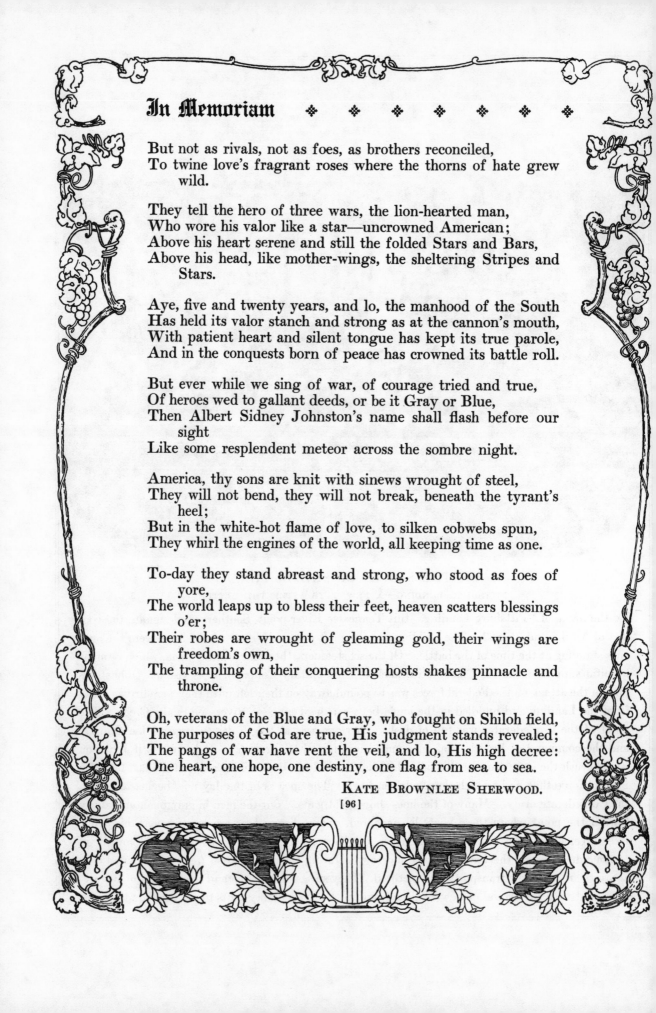

In Memoriam ✦ ✦ ✦ ✦ ✦ ✦ ✦

But not as rivals, not as foes, as brothers reconciled,
To twine love's fragrant roses where the thorns of hate grew
    wild.

They tell the hero of three wars, the lion-hearted man,
Who wore his valor like a star—uncrowned American;
Above his heart serene and still the folded Stars and Bars,
Above his head, like mother-wings, the sheltering Stripes and
    Stars.

Aye, five and twenty years, and lo, the manhood of the South
Has held its valor stanch and strong as at the cannon's mouth,
With patient heart and silent tongue has kept its true parole,
And in the conquests born of peace has crowned its battle roll.

But ever while we sing of war, of courage tried and true,
Of heroes wed to gallant deeds, or be it Gray or Blue,
Then Albert Sidney Johnston's name shall flash before our
    sight
Like some resplendent meteor across the sombre night.

America, thy sons are knit with sinews wrought of steel,
They will not bend, they will not break, beneath the tyrant's
    heel;
But in the white-hot flame of love, to silken cobwebs spun,
They whirl the engines of the world, all keeping time as one.

To-day they stand abreast and strong, who stood as foes of
    yore,
The world leaps up to bless their feet, heaven scatters blessings
    o'er;
Their robes are wrought of gleaming gold, their wings are
    freedom's own,
The trampling of their conquering hosts shakes pinnacle and
    throne.

Oh, veterans of the Blue and Gray, who fought on Shiloh field,
The purposes of God are true, His judgment stands revealed;
The pangs of war have rent the veil, and lo, His high decree:
One heart, one hope, one destiny, one flag from sea to sea.

KATE BROWNLEE SHERWOOD.

[96]

GRANT

HIS APPEARANCE AT SHILOH
—HIS EARLIEST PORTRAIT
AS MAJOR-GENERAL

"THOUGH GRANT IS ON
THE UNION SIDE HE CAN-
NOT STEM NOR STAY"

SHERMAN

SOON AFTER SHILOH—BEFORE
WAR HAD AGED AND
GRIZZLED HIM

"THOUGH SHERMAN AND
HIS LEGIONS ARE HEROES
THROUGH AND THROUGH"

These rare photographs preserve the grim determination that steeled both of these young leaders during their first great battle, while gallantly facing Albert Sidney Johnston, as celebrated by the poem opposite. Grant was already known to fame. His brilliant capture of Forts Henry and Donelson in February, 1862, had focussed the eyes of the Nation upon him. In executing a movement against Corinth the battle of April 6th–7th was fought. Grant arrived on the field about eight o'clock, and with the quick judgment of a soldier at once organized an ammunition train to supply the men on the firing-line. During the rest of the day he rode along the front, smoking a cigar and encouraging both officers and men at every point. The second day's battle was a complete victory for his army, but he was traduced by the press universally and came near terminating his military career by resigning from the service. The picture of Sherman in August, 1862, at Memphis, was the first to show the three stars on his shoulder straps. Sherman's troops plunged into the very heaviest of the fighting at Shiloh. Three horses were shot under him. He was himself wounded in two places. For his gallant services he was commissioned major-general of volunteers. The carnage produced a profound effect on both Sherman and Grant. It was then Grant first saw that the conflict would be long and bitter. Four days after the battle Sherman wrote his wife: "I still feel the horrid nature of this war, and the piles of dead and wounded and maimed makes me more anxious than ever for some hope of an end, but I know such a thing cannot be for a long, long time. Indeed I never expect it, or to survive it." But both survived in great honor.

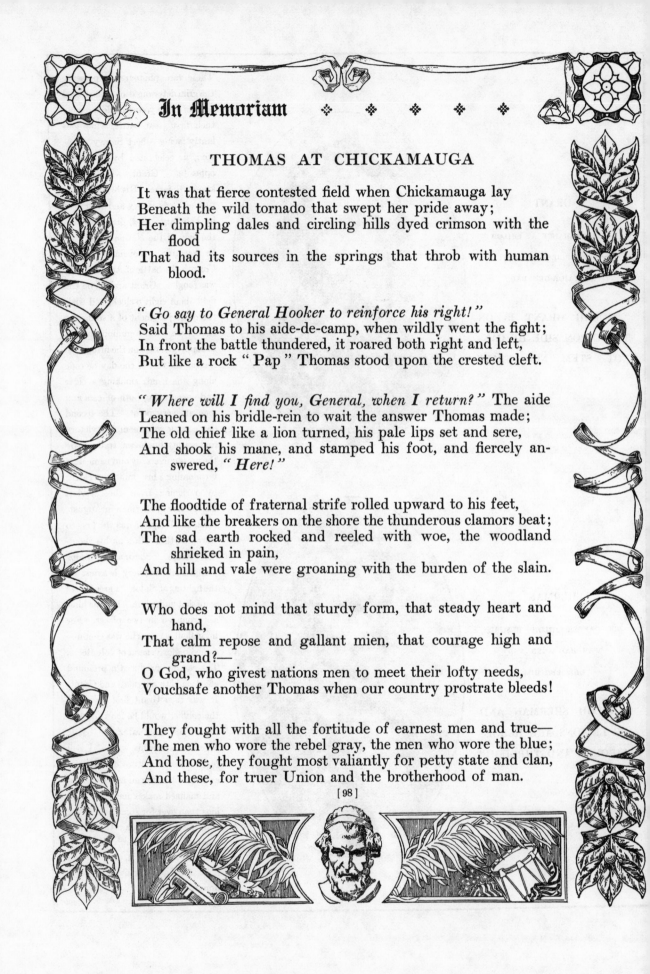

THOMAS AT CHICKAMAUGA

It was that fierce contested field when Chickamauga lay
Beneath the wild tornado that swept her pride away;
Her dimpling dales and circling hills dyed crimson with the
    flood
That had its sources in the springs that throb with human
    blood.

"Go say to General Hooker to reinforce his right!"
Said Thomas to his aide-de-camp, when wildly went the fight;
In front the battle thundered, it roared both right and left,
But like a rock "Pap" Thomas stood upon the crested cleft.

"Where will I find you, General, when I return?" The aide
Leaned on his bridle-rein to wait the answer Thomas made;
The old chief like a lion turned, his pale lips set and sere,
And shook his mane, and stamped his foot, and fiercely an-
    swered, *"Here!"*

The floodtide of fraternal strife rolled upward to his feet,
And like the breakers on the shore the thunderous clamors beat;
The sad earth rocked and reeled with woe, the woodland
    shrieked in pain,
And hill and vale were groaning with the burden of the slain.

Who does not mind that sturdy form, that steady heart and
    hand,
That calm repose and gallant mien, that courage high and
    grand?—
O God, who givest nations men to meet their lofty needs,
Vouchsafe another Thomas when our country prostrate bleeds!

They fought with all the fortitude of earnest men and true—
The men who wore the rebel gray, the men who wore the blue;
And those, they fought most valiantly for petty state and clan,
And these, for truer Union and the brotherhood of man.

[98]

BEFORE CHICKAMAUGA—IN THE RUSH OF EVENTS

Rarely does the camera afford such a perfectly contemporaneous record of the march of events so momentous. This photograph shows the hotel at Stevenson, Alabama, during the Union advance that ended in Chickamauga. Sentinels are parading the street in front of the hotel, several horses are tied to the hotel posts, and the officers evidently have gone into the hotel headquarters. General Alexander McDowell McCook, commanding the old Twentieth Army Corps, took possession of the hotel as temporary headquarters on the movement of the Army of the Cumberland from Tullahoma. On August 29, 1863, between Stevenson and Caperton's Ferry, on the Tennessee River, McCook gathered his boats and pontoons, hidden under the dense foliage of overhanging trees, and when ready for his crossing suddenly launched them into and across the river. Thence the troops marched over Sand Mountain and at length into Lookout Valley. During the movements the army was in extreme peril, for McCook was at one time three days' march from Thomas, so that Bragg might have annihilated the divisions in detail. Finally the scattered corps were concentrated along Chickamauga Creek, where the bloody struggle of September 19th and 20th was so bravely fought.

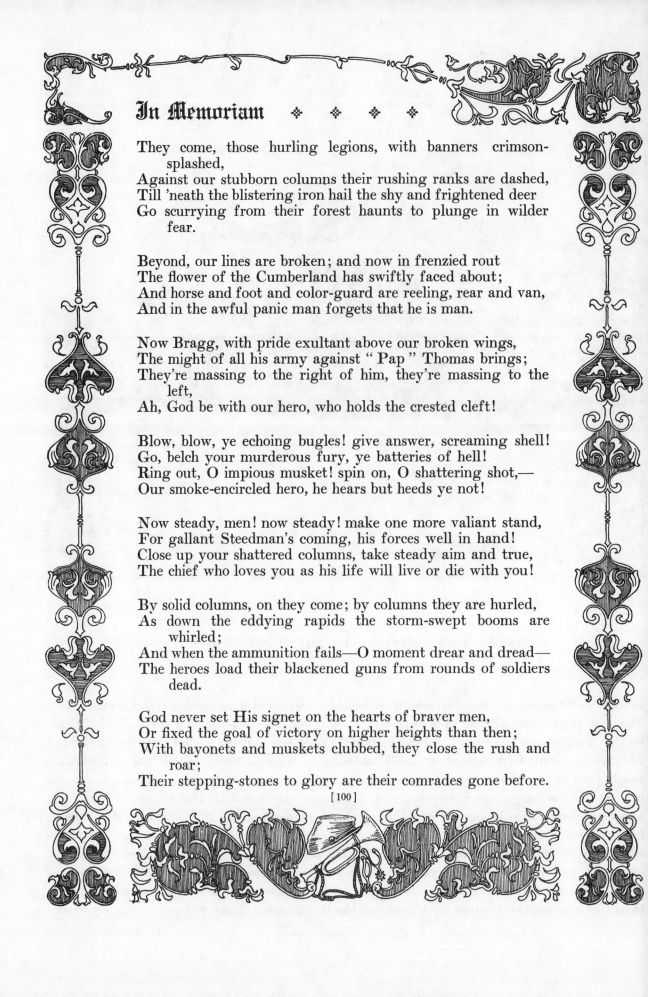

In Memoriam ❖ ❖ ❖ ❖

They come, those hurling legions, with banners crimson-
   splashed,
Against our stubborn columns their rushing ranks are dashed,
Till 'neath the blistering iron hail the shy and frightened deer
Go scurrying from their forest haunts to plunge in wilder
   fear.

Beyond, our lines are broken; and now in frenzied rout
The flower of the Cumberland has swiftly faced about;
And horse and foot and color-guard are reeling, rear and van,
And in the awful panic man forgets that he is man.

Now Bragg, with pride exultant above our broken wings,
The might of all his army against " Pap " Thomas brings;
They're massing to the right of him, they're massing to the
   left,
Ah, God be with our hero, who holds the crested cleft!

Blow, blow, ye echoing bugles! give answer, screaming shell!
Go, belch your murderous fury, ye batteries of hell!
Ring out, O impious musket! spin on, O shattering shot,—
Our smoke-encircled hero, he hears but heeds ye not!

Now steady, men! now steady! make one more valiant stand,
For gallant Steedman's coming, his forces well in hand!
Close up your shattered columns, take steady aim and true,
The chief who loves you as his life will live or die with you!

By solid columns, on they come; by columns they are hurled,
As down the eddying rapids the storm-swept booms are
   whirled;
And when the ammunition fails—O moment drear and dread—
The heroes load their blackened guns from rounds of soldiers
   dead.

God never set His signet on the hearts of braver men,
Or fixed the goal of victory on higher heights than then;
With bayonets and muskets clubbed, they close the rush and
   roar;
Their stepping-stones to glory are their comrades gone before.

[100]

ON THE WAY TO CHICKAMAUGA

This solitary observer, if he was standing here September 20, 1863, shortly before this was photographed, certainly gazed at the base of the hill to the left. For through the pass called Rossville Gap a column in blue was streaming—Steedman's Division of the Reserve Corps, rushing to aid Thomas, so sore pressed at Chickamauga. Those slopes by Chickamauga Creek witnessed the deadliest battle in the West and the highest in percentage of killed and wounded of the entire war. It was fought as a result of Rosecrans' attempt to maneuver Bragg out of Chattanooga. The Federal army crossed the Tennessee River west of the city, passed through the mountain-ranges, and came upon Bragg's line of communications. Finding his position untenable, the Southern leader moved southward and fell upon the united forces of Rosecrans along Chickamauga Creek. The vital point in the Federal line was the left, held by Thomas. Should that give way, the army would be cut off from Chattanooga, with no base to fall back on. The heavy fighting of September 19th showed that Bragg realized the situation. Brigades and regiments were shattered. For a time, the Union army was driven back. But at nightfall Thomas had regained the lost ground. He re-formed during the night in order to protect the road leading into Chattanooga. Since the second day was foggy till the middle of the forenoon, the fighting was not renewed till late. About noon a break was made in the right of the Federal battle-line, into which the eager Longstreet promptly hurled his men. Colonel Dodge writes: "Everything seems lost. The entire right of the army, with Rosecrans and his staff, is driven from the field in utter rout. But, unknown even to the commanding general, Thomas, the Rock of Chickamauga, stands there at bay, surrounded, facing two to one. Heedless of the wreck of one-half the army, he knows not how to yield."

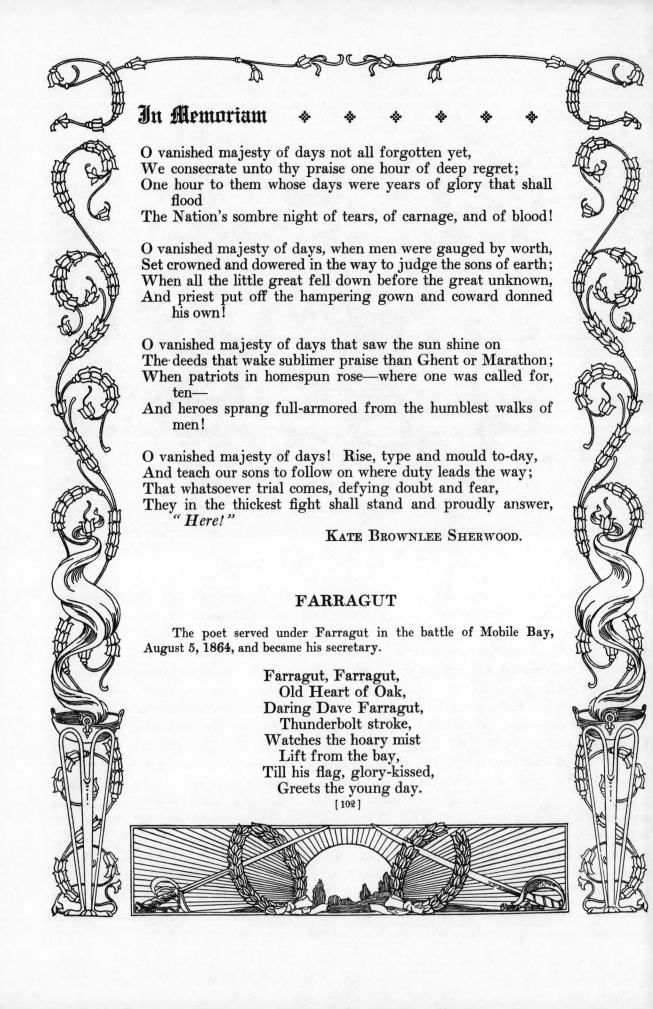

In Memoriam ✧ ✧ ✧ ✧ ✧ ✧

O vanished majesty of days not all forgotten yet,
We consecrate unto thy praise one hour of deep regret;
One hour to them whose days were years of glory that shall
    flood
The Nation's sombre night of tears, of carnage, and of blood!

O vanished majesty of days, when men were gauged by worth,
Set crowned and dowered in the way to judge the sons of earth;
When all the little great fell down before the great unknown,
And priest put off the hampering gown and coward donned
    his own!

O vanished majesty of days that saw the sun shine on
The deeds that wake sublimer praise than Ghent or Marathon;
When patriots in homespun rose—where one was called for,
    ten—
And heroes sprang full-armored from the humblest walks of
    men!

O vanished majesty of days! Rise, type and mould to-day,
And teach our sons to follow on where duty leads the way;
That whatsoever trial comes, defying doubt and fear,
They in the thickest fight shall stand and proudly answer,
" Here!"

KATE BROWNLEE SHERWOOD.

FARRAGUT

The poet served under Farragut in the battle of Mobile Bay,
August 5, 1864, and became his secretary.

Farragut, Farragut,
  Old Heart of Oak,
Daring Dave Farragut,
  Thunderbolt stroke,
Watches the hoary mist
  Lift from the bay,
Till his flag, glory-kissed,
  Greets the young day.

GENERAL GEORGE H. THOMAS

"Pap" Thomas is the name Sherwood's poem gives this massive, stern warrior; for thus he was affectionately known among his devoted soldiers. Colonel T. F. Dodge has written of him: "He was essentially cast in a large mold, in mind and body; so modest that he shrunk from command, to which he was peculiarly fitted; with courage of the stamp that ignores self; possessing steadfastness in greater measure than audacity, he yet lacked none of that ability which can deal heavy blows; while no antagonist was ever able to shake his foothold. Honesty in thought, word, and deed was constitutional with him. A thorough military training, added to a passionate love of his profession and great natural powers, made him peer of any soldier. Sedate in mind and physically slow in movement, he yet aroused great enthusiasm."

In Memoriam ❖ ❖ ❖ ❖ ❖ ❖ ❖ ❖

Far, by gray Morgan's walls,
  Looms the black fleet.
Hark, deck to rampart calls
  With the drums' beat!
Buoy your chains overboard,
  While the steam hums;
Men! to the battlement,
  Farragut comes.

See, as the hurricane
  Hurtles in wrath
Squadrons of clouds amain
  Back from its path!
Back to the parapet,
  To the guns' lips,
Thunderbolt Farragut
  Hurls the black ships.

Now through the battle's roar
  Clear the boy sings,
" By the mark fathoms four,"
  While his lead swings.
Steady the wheelmen five
  " Nor' by East keep her."
" Steady," but two alive:
  How the shells sweep her!

Lashed to the mast that sways
  Over red decks,
Over the flame that plays
  Round the torn wrecks,
Over the dying lips
  Framed for a cheer,
Farragut leads his ships,
  Guides the line clear.

On by heights cannon-browed,
  While the spars quiver;
Onward still flames the cloud
  Where the hulks shiver.

THE MOST FAMOUS OF AMERICAN NAVAL OFFICERS AND ONE OF HIS MOST DARING FEATS

In his admiral's uniform, "Dave" Farragut might contrast with pride his start in life, in an obscure Tennessee town at the opening of the century. The son of a veteran of the Revolutionary War, he early entered the navy, and while yet a lad of thirteen took distinguished part in the battle between the *Essex* and the British vessels, *Phœbe* and *Cherub*. After cruising all over the world, he was stationed, at the opening of the Civil War, in the navy-yard in Norfolk, Virginia. Though bound to the South by birth and strong family ties, he remained in the national service without wavering. His capture of New Orleans in April, 1862, when he ran by two forts

"DARING DAVE FARRAGUT"

TO ILLUSTRATE MEREDITH'S POEM OPPOSITE

under terrific fire and worked havoc in a Confederate fleet of thirteen vessels, is one of the most thrilling actions in naval warfare. Its importance to the Federal cause lay in the opening of the port of New Orleans and securing control of the lower Mississippi. Farragut was of service to the army in opening the whole river and thus cutting the Confederacy in two. The closing of Mobile Bay in August, 1864, was another daring exploit. He had long planned to attack the forts at the entrance of the bay, but not till August was the necessary fleet ready. The battery pictured below was one of the features to be reckoned with. Here at the water's edge the Confederates mounted seven guns. During the engagement the gunners were driven from their posts again and again by the broadsides of the fleet, only to return with fresh men—but in vain.

THE CAPTURED WATER BATTERY AT FORT MORGAN, 1864

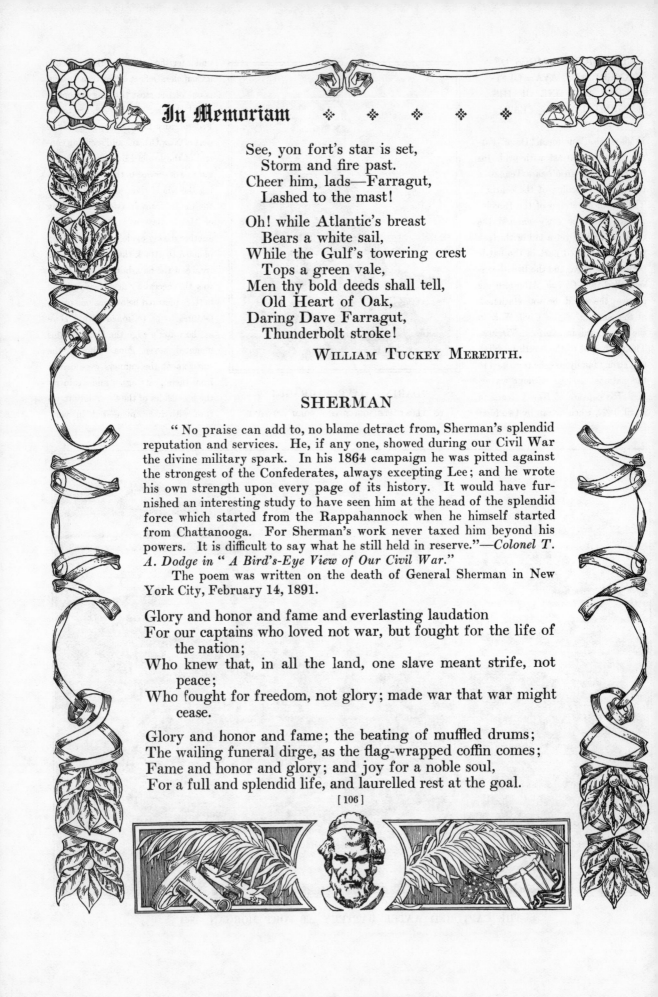

See, yon fort's star is set,
   Storm and fire past.
Cheer him, lads—Farragut,
   Lashed to the mast!

Oh! while Atlantic's breast
   Bears a white sail,
While the Gulf's towering crest
   Tops a green vale,
Men thy bold deeds shall tell,
   Old Heart of Oak,
Daring Dave Farragut,
   Thunderbolt stroke!

WILLIAM TUCKEY MEREDITH.

SHERMAN

"No praise can add to, no blame detract from, Sherman's splendid reputation and services. He, if any one, showed during our Civil War the divine military spark. In his 1864 campaign he was pitted against the strongest of the Confederates, always excepting Lee; and he wrote his own strength upon every page of its history. It would have furnished an interesting study to have seen him at the head of the splendid force which started from the Rappahannock when he himself started from Chattanooga. For Sherman's work never taxed him beyond his powers. It is difficult to say what he still held in reserve."—*Colonel T. A. Dodge in " A Bird's-Eye View of Our Civil War."*

The poem was written on the death of General Sherman in New York City, February 14, 1891.

Glory and honor and fame and everlasting laudation
For our captains who loved not war, but fought for the life of
   the nation;
Who knew that, in all the land, one slave meant strife, not
   peace;
Who fought for freedom, not glory; made war that war might
   cease.

Glory and honor and fame; the beating of muffled drums;
The wailing funeral dirge, as the flag-wrapped coffin comes;
Fame and honor and glory; and joy for a noble soul,
For a full and splendid life, and laurelled rest at the goal.

"FAR BY GRAY MORGAN'S WALLS"—THE MOBILE BAY FORT, BATTERED BY FARRAGUT'S GUNS

How formidable was Farragut's undertaking in forcing his way into Mobile Bay is apparent from these photographs. For wooden vessels to pass Morgan and Gaines, two of the strongest forts on the coast, was pronounced by experts most foolhardy. Besides, the channel was planted with torpedoes that might blow the ships to atoms, and within the bay was the Confederate ram *Tennessee*, thought to be the most powerful ironclad ever put afloat. In the arrangements for the attack, Farragut's flagship, the *Hartford*, was placed second, the *Brooklyn* leading the line of battleships, which were preceded by four monitors. At a quarter before six, on the morning of August 5th, the fleet moved. Half an hour later it came within range of Fort Morgan. The whole undertaking was then threatened with disaster. The monitor *Tecumseh*, eager to engage the Confederate ram *Tennessee* behind the line of torpedoes, ran straight ahead, struck a torpedo, and in a few minutes went down with most of the crew. As the monitor sank, the *Brooklyn* recoiled. Farragut signaled: "What's the trouble?" "Torpedoes," was the answer.

WHERE BROADSIDES STRUCK

"Damn the torpedoes!" shouted Farragut. "Go ahead, Captain Drayton. Four bells." Finding that the smoke from the guns obstructed the view from the deck, Farragut ascended to the rigging of the main mast, where he was in great danger of being struck and of falling to the deck. The captain accordingly ordered a quartermaster to tie him in the shrouds. The *Hartford*, under a full head of steam, rushed over the torpedo ground far in advance of the fleet. The battle was not yet over. The Confederate ram, invulnerable to the broadsides of the Union guns, steamed alone for the ships, while the ramparts of the two forts were crowded with spectators of the coming conflict. The ironclad monster made straight for the flagship, attempting to ram it and paying no attention to the fire or the ramming of the other vessels. Its first effort was unsuccessful, but a second came near proving fatal. It then became a target for the whole Union fleet; finally its rudder-chain was shot away and it became unmanageable; in a few minutes it raised the white flag. No wonder Americans call Farragut the greatest of naval commanders.

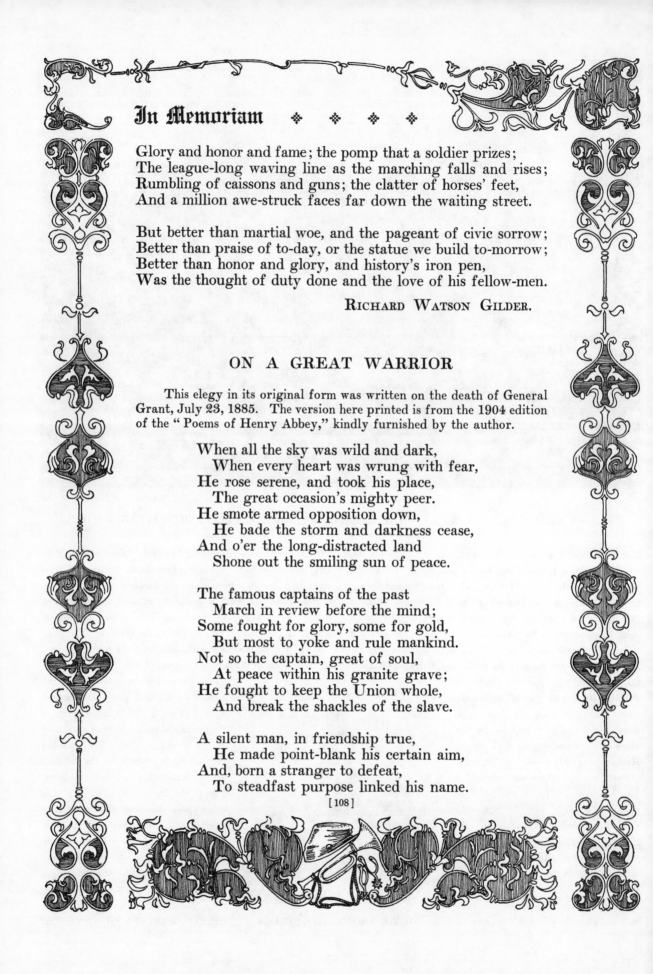

In Memoriam ❖ ❖ ❖

Glory and honor and fame; the pomp that a soldier prizes;
The league-long waving line as the marching falls and rises;
Rumbling of caissons and guns; the clatter of horses' feet,
And a million awe-struck faces far down the waiting street.

But better than martial woe, and the pageant of civic sorrow;
Better than praise of to-day, or the statue we build to-morrow;
Better than honor and glory, and history's iron pen,
Was the thought of duty done and the love of his fellow-men.

RICHARD WATSON GILDER.

ON A GREAT WARRIOR

This elegy in its original form was written on the death of General
Grant, July 23, 1885. The version here printed is from the 1904 edition
of the "Poems of Henry Abbey," kindly furnished by the author.

When all the sky was wild and dark,
    When every heart was wrung with fear,
He rose serene, and took his place,
    The great occasion's mighty peer.
He smote armed opposition down,
    He bade the storm and darkness cease,
And o'er the long-distracted land
    Shone out the smiling sun of peace.

The famous captains of the past
    March in review before the mind;
Some fought for glory, some for gold,
    But most to yoke and rule mankind.
Not so the captain, great of soul,
    At peace within his granite grave;
He fought to keep the Union whole,
    And break the shackles of the slave.

A silent man, in friendship true,
    He made point-blank his certain aim,
And, born a stranger to defeat,
    To steadfast purpose linked his name.

[108]

"THE LEAGUE–LONG WAVING LINE AS THE MARCHING FALLS AND RISES"

AN ILLUSTRATION FOR GILDER'S ELEGY ON THE DEATH OF

GENERAL WILLIAM TECUMSEH SHERMAN

Veterans of the Sixth Corps, Army of the Potomac, are here seen marching down Pennsylvania Avenue in the National Capital on June 8, 1865. In the immediate foreground, at the left, the very sway and swing of the leading files is recorded on the glass plate as the column executes "platoons, right wheel." The masses in the advancing column almost seem to fall and rise. Up the long street the eye sweeps to catch the dim outlines of the Capitol. Here are no "awe-struck faces," for this is the moment of the nation's rejoicing. But twenty-six years later, when General Sherman died, some of the same men who passed when this picture was taken marched in the solemn procession that attended the last rites of the distinguished chieftain, Sherman.

In Memoriam ❖ ❖ ❖ ❖ ❖ ❖

He followed duty with the mien
   Of but a soldier in the ranks,
This God-sent man that saved the State,
   And conquered its victorious thanks.

How well he wore white honor's flower,
   The gratitude and praise of men,
As General, as President,
   And then as simple citizen!
He was a hero to the end!
   The dark rebellion raised by death
Against the powers of life and light,
   He battled hard, with failing breath.

O hero of Fort Donelson,
   And wooded Shiloh's frightful strife!
Sleep on! for honor loves the tomb
   More than the garish ways of life.
Sleep on! sleep on! Thy wondrous days
   Fill freedom's most illustrious page.
Long-mem'ried Fame shall sound thy praise
   In every clime, in every age.

HENRY ABBEY.

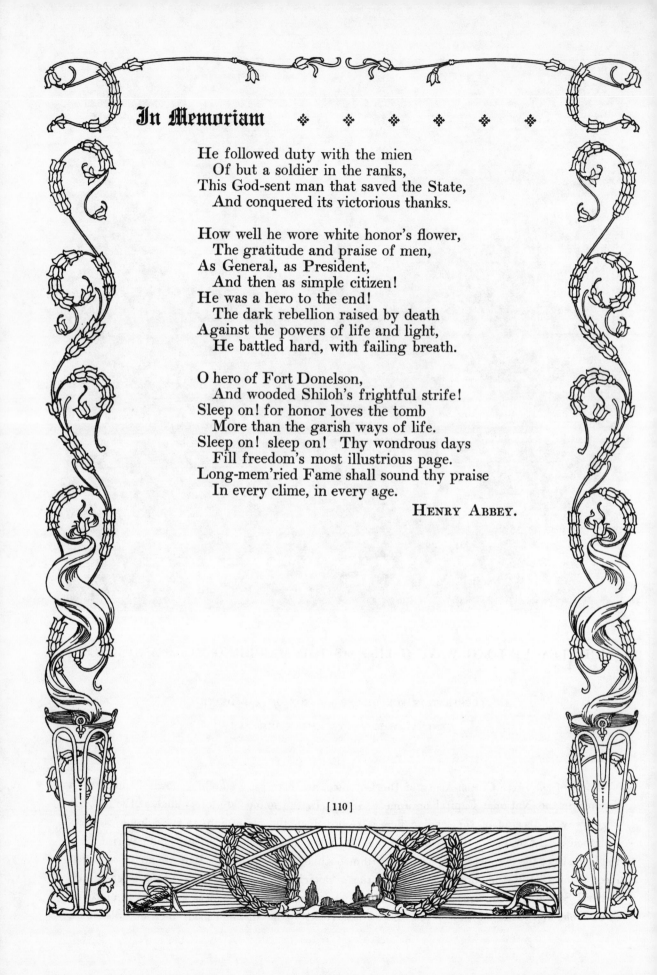

"WITH THE MIEN
OF BUT
A SOLDIER
IN THE RANKS"

THE COMMANDER
OF THE ARMIES
GRANT
IN JULY, 1864

Here Grant's dress is nearer uniform than usual. A veteran recalls that it consisted ordinarily of a plain old army hat—"slouch," as it was called—and fatigue coat, pretty well worn, with very little insignia of rank for outward show. Thus he was frequently taken by the soldiers along the line for some old cavalryman who was investigating affairs he knew nothing about. In his tours General Grant was often stopped by the guards around the camps and compelled to identify himself before the men would permit him to pass. It sometimes happened that the sentries knew the General well enough by sight, but since he was not in full uniform and bore no insignia of rank, they would solemnly compel him to halt until they could call for the officer of the guard, who would formally examine the general as to his identity.

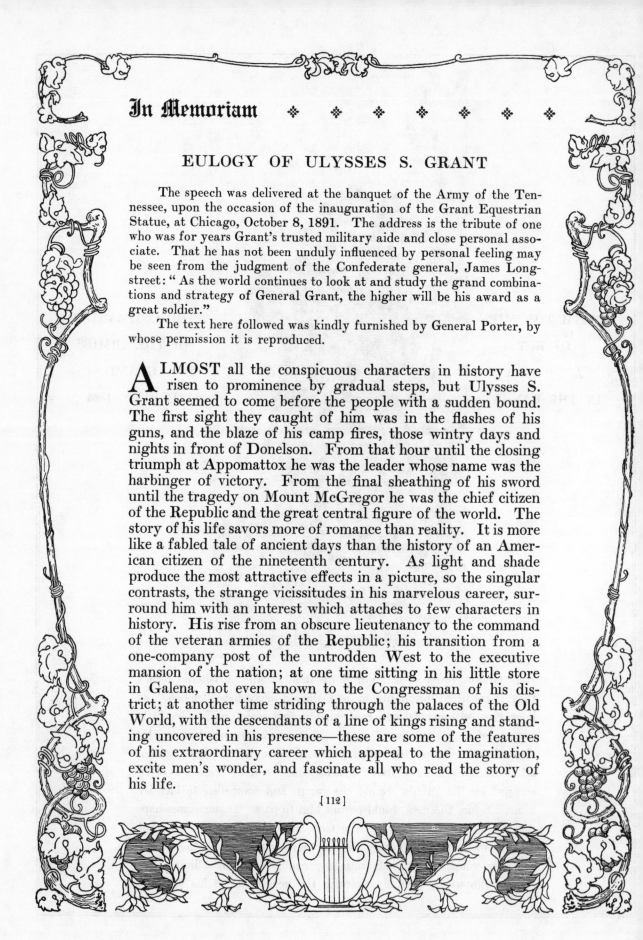

In Memoriam ✦ ✦ ✦ ✦ ✦ ✦

EULOGY OF ULYSSES S. GRANT

The speech was delivered at the banquet of the Army of the Tennessee, upon the occasion of the inauguration of the Grant Equestrian Statue, at Chicago, October 8, 1891. The address is the tribute of one who was for years Grant's trusted military aide and close personal associate. That he has not been unduly influenced by personal feeling may be seen from the judgment of the Confederate general, James Longstreet: "As the world continues to look at and study the grand combinations and strategy of General Grant, the higher will be his award as a great soldier."

The text here followed was kindly furnished by General Porter, by whose permission it is reproduced.

ALMOST all the conspicuous characters in history have risen to prominence by gradual steps, but Ulysses S. Grant seemed to come before the people with a sudden bound. The first sight they caught of him was in the flashes of his guns, and the blaze of his camp fires, those wintry days and nights in front of Donelson. From that hour until the closing triumph at Appomattox he was the leader whose name was the harbinger of victory. From the final sheathing of his sword until the tragedy on Mount McGregor he was the chief citizen of the Republic and the great central figure of the world. The story of his life savors more of romance than reality. It is more like a fabled tale of ancient days than the history of an American citizen of the nineteenth century. As light and shade produce the most attractive effects in a picture, so the singular contrasts, the strange vicissitudes in his marvelous career, surround him with an interest which attaches to few characters in history. His rise from an obscure lieutenancy to the command of the veteran armies of the Republic; his transition from a one-company post of the untrodden West to the executive mansion of the nation; at one time sitting in his little store in Galena, not even known to the Congressman of his district; at another time striding through the palaces of the Old World, with the descendants of a line of kings rising and standing uncovered in his presence—these are some of the features of his extraordinary career which appeal to the imagination, excite men's wonder, and fascinate all who read the story of his life.

"FRIENDS WHO LOVED HIM FOR HIS OWN SAKE"

GRANT AND HIS STAFF IN 1864—BY THE TENT POLE SITS HORACE PORTER,
AUTHOR OF THE ADDRESS REPRODUCED OPPOSITE

The roll-call of those present at City Point in June, 1864, is impressive. Sitting on the bench at the left is Lieutenant-General Grant, with his familiar slouch hat on his knee, By him is Brigadier-General J. A. Rawlins, his chief-of-staff. To the left of the latter sits Lieutenant-Colonel W. L. Duff, assistant inspector-general. By the tent-pole is Lieutenant-Colonel Horace Porter, the author of the address here reprinted. At the right is Captain Ely S. Parker, a full-blooded Indian. Standing behind Grant is one of his secretaries, Lieutenant-Colonel Adam Badeau, who later wrote a military biography of the general. Behind Rawlins is Lieutenant-Colonel C. B. Comstock, noted as an engineer. By Duff stands Lieutenant-Colonel F. T. Dent. Between Porter and Parker is Lieutenant-Colonel O. E. Babcock. All were faithful, in the war and later.

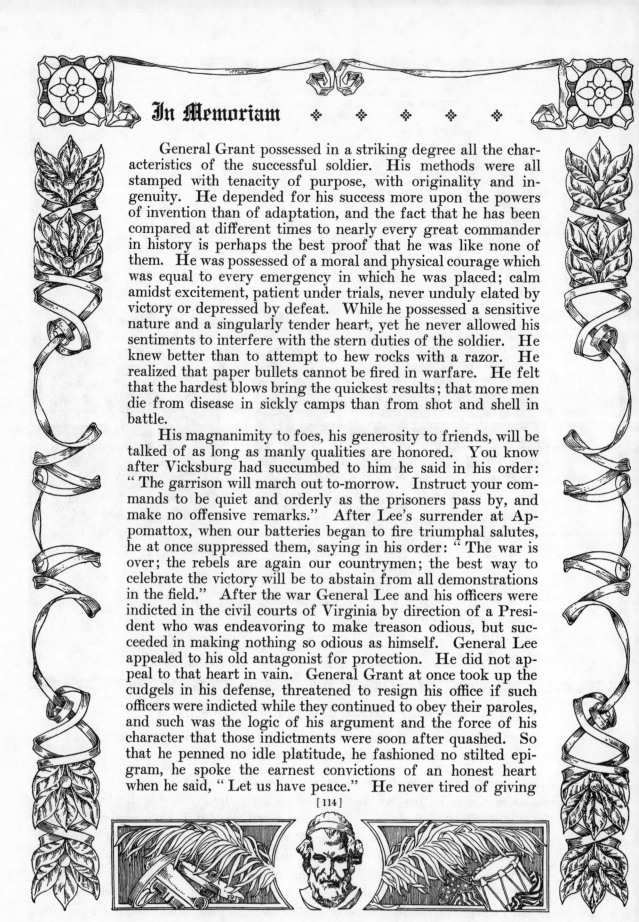

General Grant possessed in a striking degree all the characteristics of the successful soldier. His methods were all stamped with tenacity of purpose, with originality and ingenuity. He depended for his success more upon the powers of invention than of adaptation, and the fact that he has been compared at different times to nearly every great commander in history is perhaps the best proof that he was like none of them. He was possessed of a moral and physical courage which was equal to every emergency in which he was placed; calm amidst excitement, patient under trials, never unduly elated by victory or depressed by defeat. While he possessed a sensitive nature and a singularly tender heart, yet he never allowed his sentiments to interfere with the stern duties of the soldier. He knew better than to attempt to hew rocks with a razor. He realized that paper bullets cannot be fired in warfare. He felt that the hardest blows bring the quickest results; that more men die from disease in sickly camps than from shot and shell in battle.

His magnanimity to foes, his generosity to friends, will be talked of as long as manly qualities are honored. You know after Vicksburg had succumbed to him he said in his order: "The garrison will march out to-morrow. Instruct your commands to be quiet and orderly as the prisoners pass by, and make no offensive remarks." After Lee's surrender at Appomattox, when our batteries began to fire triumphal salutes, he at once suppressed them, saying in his order: "The war is over; the rebels are again our countrymen; the best way to celebrate the victory will be to abstain from all demonstrations in the field." After the war General Lee and his officers were indicted in the civil courts of Virginia by direction of a President who was endeavoring to make treason odious, but succeeded in making nothing so odious as himself. General Lee appealed to his old antagonist for protection. He did not appeal to that heart in vain. General Grant at once took up the cudgels in his defense, threatened to resign his office if such officers were indicted while they continued to obey their paroles, and such was the logic of his argument and the force of his character that those indictments were soon after quashed. So that he penned no idle platitude, he fashioned no stilted epigram, he spoke the earnest convictions of an honest heart when he said, "Let us have peace." He never tired of giving

"ON THE HEIGHTS OF CHATTANOOGA"—A LANDMARK IN GRANT'S RISE TO FAME

The view from Lookout Mountain, showing the very ground over which the Federal soldiers scrambled in their charge, illustrates Porter's reference to the battle of November 23–25, 1863. Grant's own account thus describes the concluding charge: "Discovering that the enemy in his desperation to defeat or resist the progress of Sherman was weakening his center on Missionary Ridge, determined me to order the advance at once. Thomas was accordingly directed to move forward his troops, constituting our center, Baird's division (Fourteenth Corps), Wood's and Sheridan's divisions (Fourth Corps), and Johnston's division (Fourteenth Corps), with a double line of skirmishers thrown out, followed in easy supporting distance by the whole force, and carry the rifle-pits at the foot of Missionary Ridge, and, when carried, to re-form his lines on the rifle-pits with a view to carrying the top of the ridge. These troops moved forward, drove the enemy from the rifle-pits at the base of the ridge like bees from a hive—stopped but a moment until the whole were in line—and commenced the ascent of the mountain from right to left almost simultaneously, following closely the retreating enemy, without further orders. They encountered a fearful volley of grape and canister from near thirty pieces of artillery and musketry from still well-filled rifle-pits, on the summit of the ridge. Not a waver, however, was seen in all that long line of brave men. Their progress was steadily onward until the summit was in their possession." Three months later Grant became the first lieutenant-general since Washington.

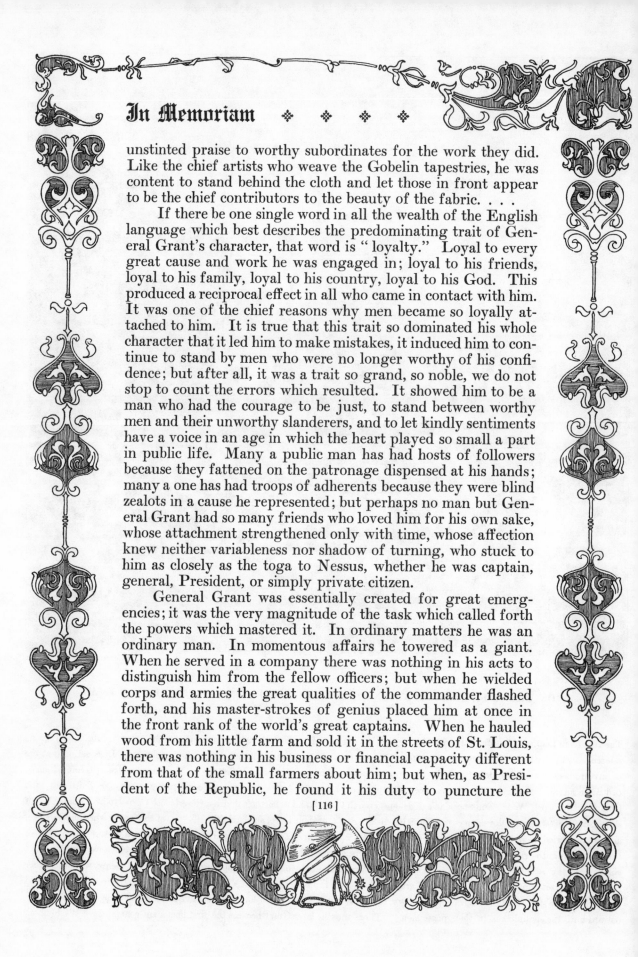

unstinted praise to worthy subordinates for the work they did. Like the chief artists who weave the Gobelin tapestries, he was content to stand behind the cloth and let those in front appear to be the chief contributors to the beauty of the fabric. . . .

If there be one single word in all the wealth of the English language which best describes the predominating trait of General Grant's character, that word is "loyalty." Loyal to every great cause and work he was engaged in; loyal to his friends, loyal to his family, loyal to his country, loyal to his God. This produced a reciprocal effect in all who came in contact with him. It was one of the chief reasons why men became so loyally attached to him. It is true that this trait so dominated his whole character that it led him to make mistakes, it induced him to continue to stand by men who were no longer worthy of his confidence; but after all, it was a trait so grand, so noble, we do not stop to count the errors which resulted. It showed him to be a man who had the courage to be just, to stand between worthy men and their unworthy slanderers, and to let kindly sentiments have a voice in an age in which the heart played so small a part in public life. Many a public man has had hosts of followers because they fattened on the patronage dispensed at his hands; many a one has had troops of adherents because they were blind zealots in a cause he represented; but perhaps no man but General Grant had so many friends who loved him for his own sake, whose attachment strengthened only with time, whose affection knew neither variableness nor shadow of turning, who stuck to him as closely as the toga to Nessus, whether he was captain, general, President, or simply private citizen.

General Grant was essentially created for great emergencies; it was the very magnitude of the task which called forth the powers which mastered it. In ordinary matters he was an ordinary man. In momentous affairs he towered as a giant. When he served in a company there was nothing in his acts to distinguish him from the fellow officers; but when he wielded corps and armies the great qualities of the commander flashed forth, and his master-strokes of genius placed him at once in the front rank of the world's great captains. When he hauled wood from his little farm and sold it in the streets of St. Louis, there was nothing in his business or financial capacity different from that of the small farmers about him; but when, as President of the Republic, he found it his duty to puncture the

"TO THE EXECUTIVE MANSION OF THE NATION"

GRANT'S INAUGURATION AS PRESIDENT—MARCH 4, 1869

The inauguration of Ulysses S. Grant was a particularly impressive ceremony.   When he was nominated in May, 1868, his letter of acceptance had closed with the phrase, "Let us have peace," which became the slogan of the campaign.   The ceremonies on March 4th were marked by intense enthusiasm.   The recent contest between the President and Congress had made the people more than responsive to the prayer, "Let us have peace"; they looked forward with eagerness for this hero of war, the youngest of their Presidents, to allay the bitterness of partisan strife and sectional animosity.   This was so much the purpose of Grant's own heart that, out of all his public utterances, this was chosen for inscription on his tomb on Riverside Drive in New York.   Grant is one of the few captains in the history of the world who "made war that war might cease."   The story of his career forms more than military history; it is an example for all ages.

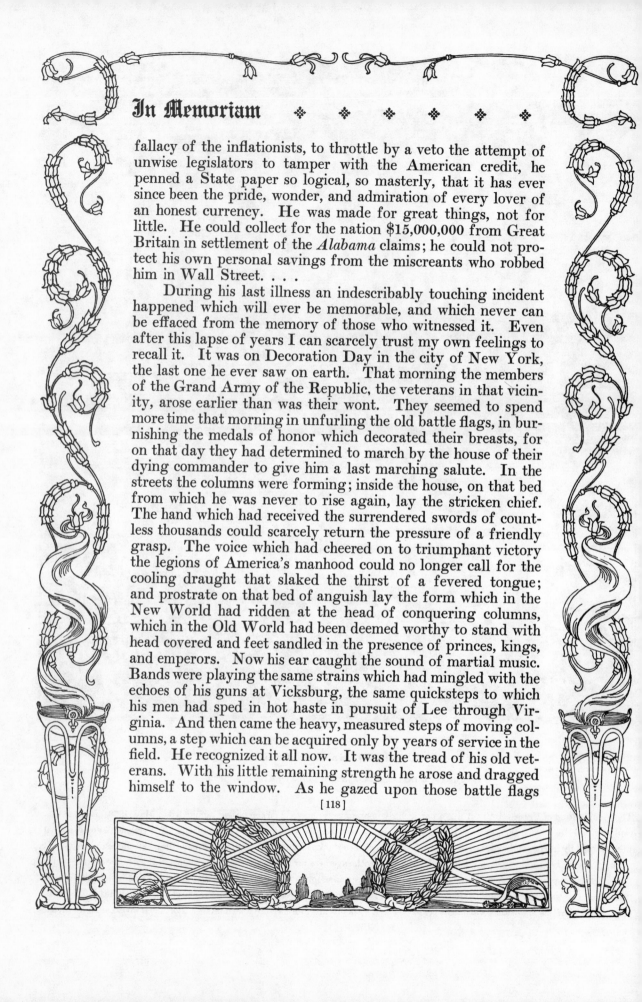

fallacy of the inflationists, to throttle by a veto the attempt of unwise legislators to tamper with the American credit, he penned a State paper so logical, so masterly, that it has ever since been the pride, wonder, and admiration of every lover of an honest currency. He was made for great things, not for little. He could collect for the nation $15,000,000 from Great Britain in settlement of the *Alabama* claims; he could not protect his own personal savings from the miscreants who robbed him in Wall Street. . . .

During his last illness an indescribably touching incident happened which will ever be memorable, and which never can be effaced from the memory of those who witnessed it. Even after this lapse of years I can scarcely trust my own feelings to recall it. It was on Decoration Day in the city of New York, the last one he ever saw on earth. That morning the members of the Grand Army of the Republic, the veterans in that vicinity, arose earlier than was their wont. They seemed to spend more time that morning in unfurling the old battle flags, in burnishing the medals of honor which decorated their breasts, for on that day they had determined to march by the house of their dying commander to give him a last marching salute. In the streets the columns were forming; inside the house, on that bed from which he was never to rise again, lay the stricken chief. The hand which had received the surrendered swords of countless thousands could scarcely return the pressure of a friendly grasp. The voice which had cheered on to triumphant victory the legions of America's manhood could no longer call for the cooling draught that slaked the thirst of a fevered tongue; and prostrate on that bed of anguish lay the form which in the New World had ridden at the head of conquering columns, which in the Old World had been deemed worthy to stand with head covered and feet sandled in the presence of princes, kings, and emperors. Now his ear caught the sound of martial music. Bands were playing the same strains which had mingled with the echoes of his guns at Vicksburg, the same quicksteps to which his men had sped in hot haste in pursuit of Lee through Virginia. And then came the heavy, measured steps of moving columns, a step which can be acquired only by years of service in the field. He recognized it all now. It was the tread of his old veterans. With his little remaining strength he arose and dragged himself to the window. As he gazed upon those battle flags

Top labels:

MRS. U. S. GRANT — MRS. NELLIE GRANT SARTORIS — GENERAL U. S. GRANT — COLONEL FREDERICK D. GRANT, ELDEST SON — JESSE R. GRANT, YOUNGEST SON

Bottom labels:

U. S. GRANT, JR., THE SECOND SON — JULIA GRANT, DAUGHTER OF F. D. GRANT — ULYSSES S. GRANT, THIRD SON OF F. D. GRANT — IDA HONORÉ GRANT, WIFE OF F. D. GRANT — NELLIE GRANT, DAUGHTER OF JESSE R. GRANT — MRS. ELIZABETH C. GRANT, WIFE OF JESSE R. GRANT

"THE TRAGEDY AT MOUNT McGREGOR"—GRANT AND HIS FAMILY, JULY 19, 1885

On July 16th, three days before this photograph was taken, the general was removed to a summer cottage on Mount McGregor, near Saratoga Springs. Exactly a week later, July 23, 1885, he breathed his last amid the family here assembled. No period of Ulysses S. Grant's life was more heroic than its closing months. He had remained in excellent health up to Christmas of 1883. In the summer of 1884 he was annoyed by unpleasant sensations in his throat. He paid little attention to the symptoms until autumn. A physician, calling one day in October, made an examination that alarmed him. He advised that a specialist be·called at once. Cancer of the throat had set in. The annoying sensations at length became painful, and in December the disease had so far advanced that to drink even liquid food was torture. General Badeau says: "He was in no way dismayed, but the sight was to me the most appalling I had ever witnessed—the conqueror looking at his own inevitable conqueror; the stern soldier to whom so many armies had surrendered, watching the approach of that enemy before whom even he must yield." Yet the stricken chief continued work upon his "Memoirs." He could not now dictate to an amanuensis, so he wrote with a hand quivering with pain upon pads placed in his lap. There is something peculiarly noble in this determination to provide by his own efforts a competence for his family. What effect his departure had on the country is told in the Introduction to this volume, but the demonstrations were not confined to America. On August 4th a memorial service was held in the English temple of fame, Westminster Abbey. No less a dignitary than Canon Farrar delivered the funeral address. The civilized world joined in the mourning. Tributes to his memory extended over many years. In 1896, the Chinese statesman, Li Hung Chang, left a memorial at his tomb on Riverside Drive, New York City. Grant's fame is a secure American possession.

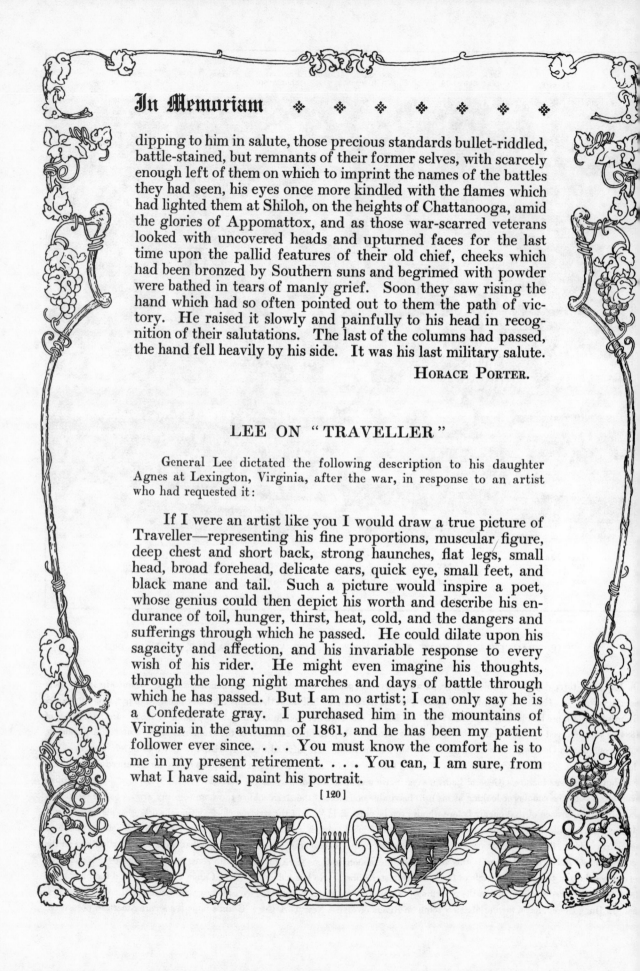

dipping to him in salute, those precious standards bullet-riddled, battle-stained, but remnants of their former selves, with scarcely enough left of them on which to imprint the names of the battles they had seen, his eyes once more kindled with the flames which had lighted them at Shiloh, on the heights of Chattanooga, amid the glories of Appomattox, and as those war-scarred veterans looked with uncovered heads and upturned faces for the last time upon the pallid features of their old chief, cheeks which had been bronzed by Southern suns and begrimed with powder were bathed in tears of manly grief. Soon they saw rising the hand which had so often pointed out to them the path of victory. He raised it slowly and painfully to his head in recognition of their salutations. The last of the columns had passed, the hand fell heavily by his side. It was his last military salute.

HORACE PORTER.

LEE ON "TRAVELLER"

General Lee dictated the following description to his daughter Agnes at Lexington, Virginia, after the war, in response to an artist who had requested it:

If I were an artist like you I would draw a true picture of Traveller—representing his fine proportions, muscular figure, deep chest and short back, strong haunches, flat legs, small head, broad forehead, delicate ears, quick eye, small feet, and black mane and tail. Such a picture would inspire a poet, whose genius could then depict his worth and describe his endurance of toil, hunger, thirst, heat, cold, and the dangers and sufferings through which he passed. He could dilate upon his sagacity and affection, and his invariable response to every wish of his rider. He might even imagine his thoughts, through the long night marches and days of battle through which he has passed. But I am no artist; I can only say he is a Confederate gray. I purchased him in the mountains of Virginia in the autumn of 1861, and he has been my patient follower ever since. . . . You must know the comfort he is to me in my present retirement. . . . You can, I am sure, from what I have said, paint his portrait.

COPYRIGHT, 1911, REVIEW OF REVIEWS CO.

"I CAN ONLY SAY HE IS A CONFEDERATE GRAY"—LEE ON "TRAVELLER"

This famous photograph of Lee on "Traveller" was taken by Miley, of Lexington, in September, 1866. In July of that year Brady, Gardner, and Miley had tried to get a photograph of the general on his horse, but the weather was so hot and the flies accordingly so annoying that the pictures were very poor. But the September picture has become probably the most popular photograph in the South. In the Army of Northern Virginia the horse was almost as well known as his master. It was foaled near the White Sulphur Springs in West Virginia, and attracted the notice of General Lee in 1861. Lee's affection for it was very deep and strong. On it he rode from Richmond to Lexington to assume his duties as president of Washington College. During the remainder of his life "Traveller" was his constant companion. His son records that the general enjoyed nothing more than a long ride, which gave him renewed energy for his work. In one of his letters while away from home he said: "How is Traveller? Tell him I miss him dreadfully, and have repented of our separation but once—and that is the whole time since we parted."

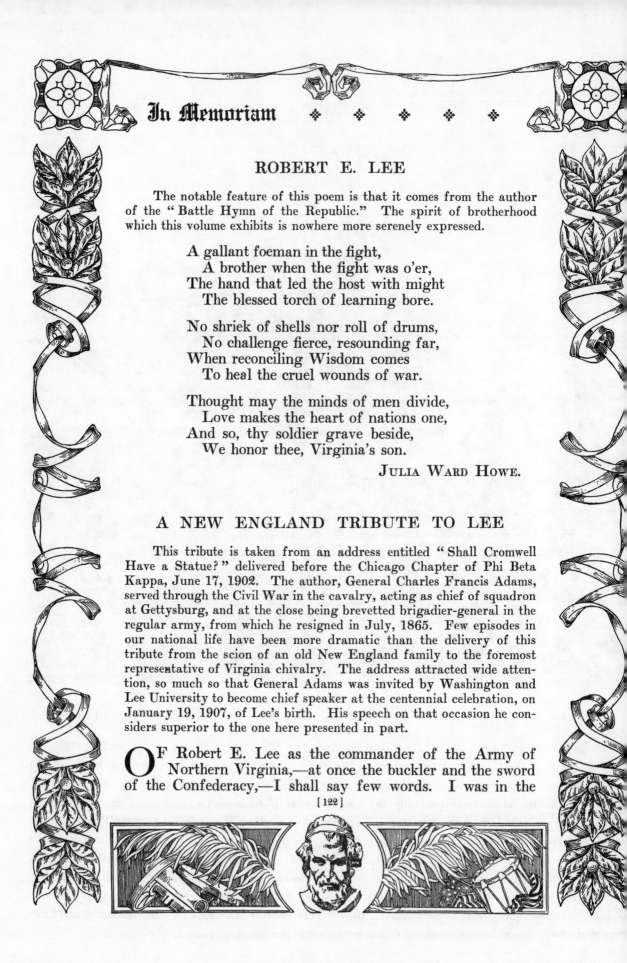

ROBERT E. LEE

The notable feature of this poem is that it comes from the author of the "Battle Hymn of the Republic." The spirit of brotherhood which this volume exhibits is nowhere more serenely expressed.

A gallant foeman in the fight,
    A brother when the fight was o'er,
The hand that led the host with might
    The blessed torch of learning bore.

No shriek of shells nor roll of drums,
    No challenge fierce, resounding far,
When reconciling Wisdom comes
    To heal the cruel wounds of war.

Thought may the minds of men divide,
    Love makes the heart of nations one,
And so, thy soldier grave beside,
    We honor thee, Virginia's son.

JULIA WARD HOWE.

A NEW ENGLAND TRIBUTE TO LEE

This tribute is taken from an address entitled "Shall Cromwell Have a Statue?" delivered before the Chicago Chapter of Phi Beta Kappa, June 17, 1902. The author, General Charles Francis Adams, served through the Civil War in the cavalry, acting as chief of squadron at Gettysburg, and at the close being brevetted brigadier-general in the regular army, from which he resigned in July, 1865. Few episodes in our national life have been more dramatic than the delivery of this tribute from the scion of an old New England family to the foremost representative of Virginia chivalry. The address attracted wide attention, so much so that General Adams was invited by Washington and Lee University to become chief speaker at the centennial celebration, on January 19, 1907, of Lee's birth. His speech on that occasion he considers superior to the one here presented in part.

OF Robert E. Lee as the commander of the Army of Northern Virginia,—at once the buckler and the sword of the Confederacy,—I shall say few words. I was in the

LEE IN '63—"EVERY INCH A SOLDIER"

The words of General Charles Francis Adams are fittingly borne out by this magnificent likeness, taken by Vannerson of Richmond in 1863, when Lee was at the height of his military power. He wears a handsome sword and sash presented to him by ladies of Baltimore just previously. Some of the ladies of Richmond had made a set of shirts for their hero, and asked him for his portrait on one of his visits to Richmond. Out of compliment to the ladies, General Lee wore one here; the turnover collar, high in the neck, clearly identifies this portrait.

ranks of those opposed to him. For years I was face to face with some fragment of the Army of Northern Virginia, and intent to do it harm; and during those years there was not a day when I would not have drawn a deep breath of relief and satisfaction at hearing of the death of Lee, even as I did draw it at hearing of the death of Jackson. But now, looking back through a perspective of nearly forty years, I glory in it, and in them as foes,—they were worthy of the best of steel. I am proud now to say that I was their countryman. Whatever differences of opinion may exist as to the course of Lee when his choice was made, of Lee as a foe and the commander of an army, but one opinion can be entertained. Every inch a soldier, he was an opponent not less generous and humane than formidable, a type of highest martial character; cautious, magnanimous and bold, a very thunderbolt in war, he was self-contained in victory, but greatest in defeat. To that escutcheon attaches no stain.

I now come to what I have always regarded—shall ever regard—as the most creditable episode in all American history, —an episode without a blemish,—imposing, dignified, simple, heroic. I refer to Appomattox. Two men met that day, representative of American civilization, the whole world looking on. The two were Grant and Lee,—types each. Both rose, and rose unconsciously, to the full height of the occasion,— and than that occasion there has been none greater. About it, and them, there was no theatrical display, no self-consciousness, no effort at effect. A great crisis was to be met; and they met that crisis as great countrymen should. Consider the possibilities; think for a moment of what that day might have been; you will then see cause to thank God for much.

That month of April saw the close of exactly four years of persistent strife,—a strife which the whole civilized world had been watching intently. Democracy—the capacity of man in his present stage of development for self-government—was believed to be on trial. The wish the father to the thought, the prophets of evil had been liberal in prediction. It so chances that my attention has been especially drawn to the European utterances of that time; and, read in the clear light of subsequent history, I use words of moderation when I say that they are now both inconceivable and ludicrous. Staid journals, grave public men seemed to take what was little less than

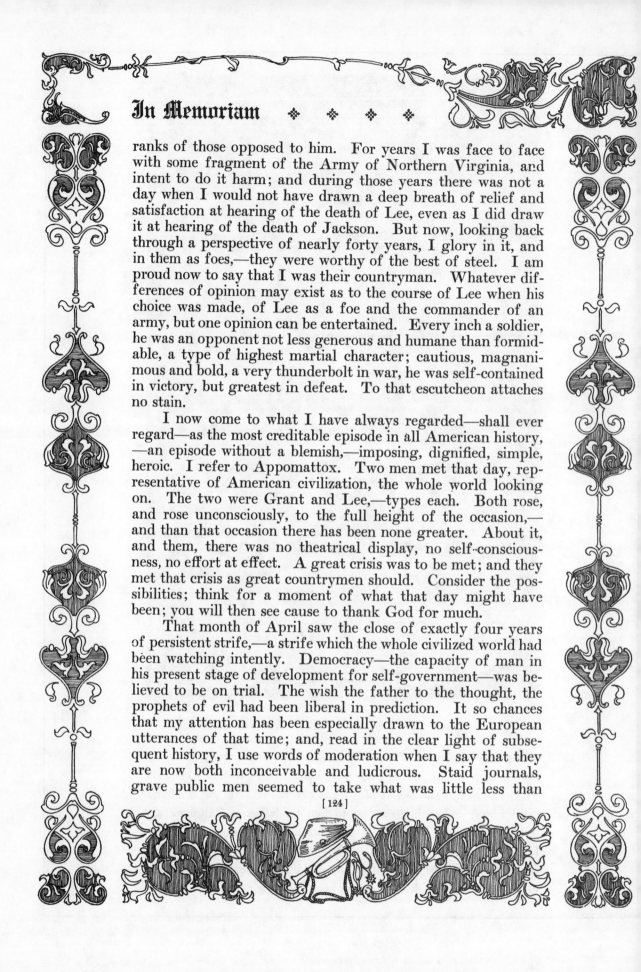

"WITH A HOME NO LONGER HIS"

The massive Doric pillars of the home of Robert E. Lee are, in June, 1864, the background for a group of Federal soldiers. Around this splendid colonial mansion cluster memories of the whole course of American history. It was built by the adopted son of Washington, George Washington Parke Custis, grandson of his wife Martha Custis. On the death of Martha Washington in 1802, he erected this lordly mansion with the front in imitation of the Temple of Theseus at Athens. Within were stored memorials brought from Mount Vernon—pictures, silver-service, and furniture. Here Custis entertained with a lavish hospitality. Lafayette was a guest of honor on his visit to this country. In 1831, in the room to the left of the main hall, the only daughter of the house was married to Lieutenant Robert E. Lee. In 1861 the estate was confiscated and occupied by Federal troops. The family heirlooms were removed, many of them eventually finding their way to the National Museum in Washington and others to their original abiding-place, Mount Vernon. The grounds became a national cemetery; the first person buried there being a Confederate soldier. In 1864 the estate was sold at auction for delinquent taxes for $26,100 to the National Government. After the war General Lee made small effort to recover the property, but in 1877 George Washington Custis Lee, the heir under the law, established his title to the place and received therefor $150,000. Thus the resting-place of some 20,000 American soldiers passed permanently into the possession of the American nation.

pleasure in pronouncing that impossible of occurrence which was destined soon to occur, and in committing themselves to readings of the book of fate in exact opposition to what the muse of history was wetting the pen to record. Volumes of unmerited abuse and false vaticination—and volumes hardly less amusing now than instructive—could be garnered from the columns of the London *Times,*—volumes in which the spirit of contemptuous and patronizing dislike sought expression in the profoundest ignorance of facts, set down in bitterest words. Not only were republican institutions and man's capacity for self-government on trial, but the severest of sentences was imposed in advance of the adverse verdict, assumed to be inevitable. Then, suddenly, came the dramatic climax at Appomattox,—dramatic, I say, not theatrical,—severe in its simple, sober, matter-of-fact majesty. The world, I again assert, has seen nothing like it; and the world, instinctively, was at the time conscious of the fact. I like to dwell on the familiar circumstances of the day; on its momentous outcome; on its far-reaching results. It affords one of the greatest educational object-lessons to be found in history; and the actors were worthy of the theater, the auditory, and the play.

A mighty tragedy was drawing to a close. The breathless world was the audience. It was a bright, balmy April Sunday in a quiet Virginia landscape, with two veteran armies confronting each other; one, game to the death, completely in the grasp of the other. The future was at stake. What might ensue? What might not ensue? Would the strife end then and there? Would it die in a death-grapple, only to reappear in that chronic form of a vanquished but indomitable people writhing and struggling in the grasp of an insatiate but only nominal victor? Such a struggle as all European authorities united in confidently predicting?

The answer depended on two men,—the captains of the contending forces. Grant that day had Lee at his mercy. He had but to close his hand, and his opponent was crushed. Think what then might have resulted had those two men been other than what they were,—had the one been stern and aggressive, the other sullen and unyielding. Most fortunately for us, they were what and who they were,—Grant and Lee. More, I need not, could not say; this only let me add,—a people has good right to be proud of the past and self-confident of its future

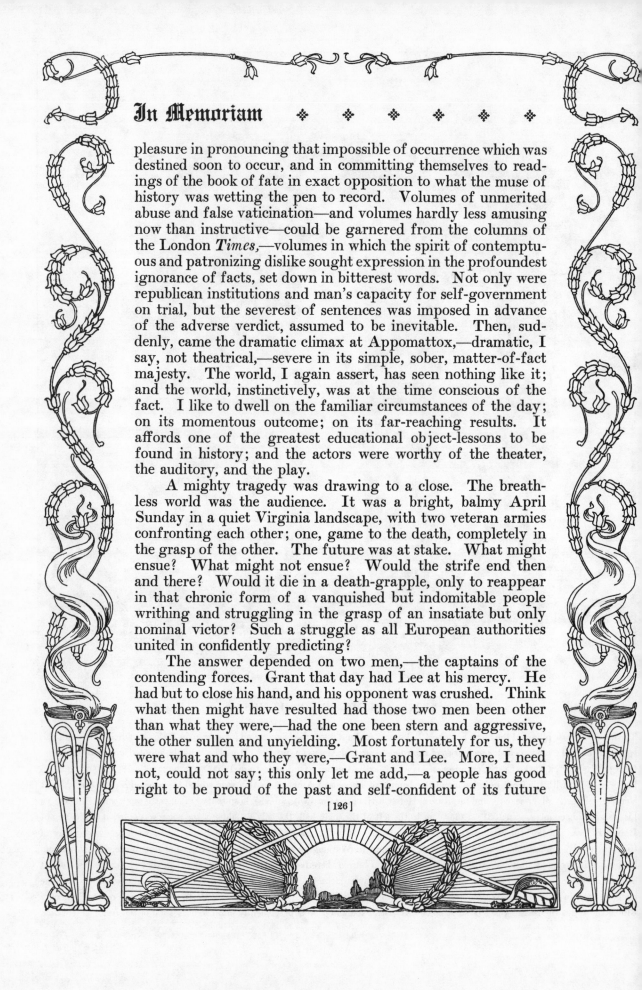

SOLDIER AND CITIZEN BEFORE THE APPOMATTOX COURT HOUSE

This picture and the next one reveal contrasting scenes at the close of the greatest civil conflict of modern times—the soldiers of the Union army after Lee's surrender grouped before Appomattox Court House, and citizens of the hitherto quiet village gathered in front of the village inn. Grant himself did not remain long after the negotiations were concluded. As he left the McLean house a little after four in the afternoon he heard the firing of salutes in the Union camp in celebration of the news of surrender. He at once issued orders to discontinue it. "The war is over," he said, "the rebels are our countrymen again, and the best sign of rejoicing after the victory will be to abstain from all demonstrations." The next morning he rode to the Confederate lines and held a last interview with Lee, after which he returned to the McLean house before setting out for Washington. Many of his staff were disappointed, but Grant had no curiosity to look upon the conquered army. He was much more eager to restore harmony and prosperity to the reunited nation.

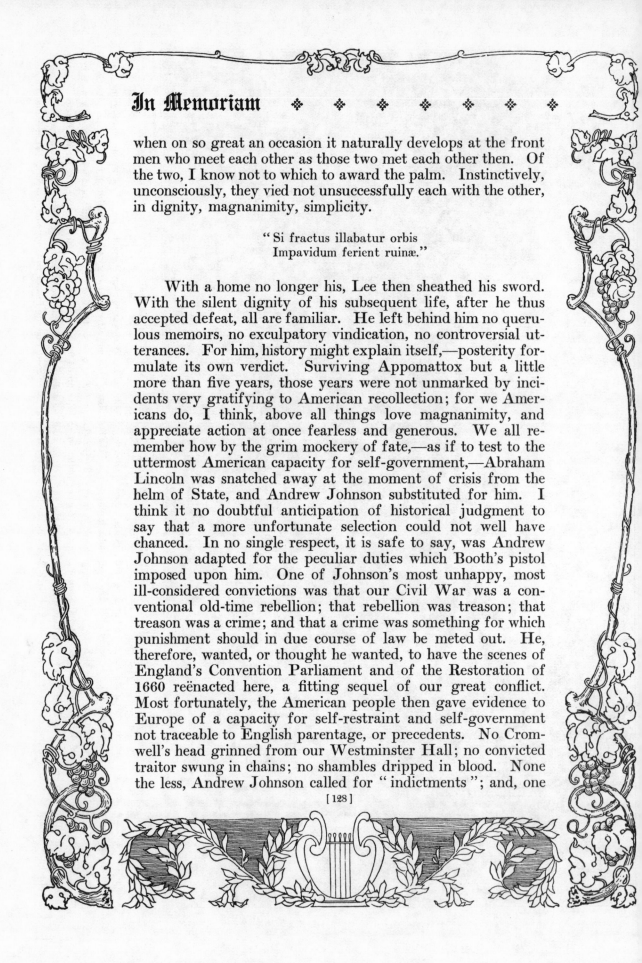

when on so great an occasion it naturally develops at the front men who meet each other as those two met each other then. Of the two, I know not to which to award the palm. Instinctively, unconsciously, they vied not unsuccessfully each with the other, in dignity, magnanimity, simplicity.

> "Si fractus illabatur orbis
> Impavidum ferient ruinæ."

With a home no longer his, Lee then sheathed his sword. With the silent dignity of his subsequent life, after he thus accepted defeat, all are familiar. He left behind him no querulous memoirs, no exculpatory vindication, no controversial utterances. For him, history might explain itself,—posterity formulate its own verdict. Surviving Appomattox but a little more than five years, those years were not unmarked by incidents very gratifying to American recollection; for we Americans do, I think, above all things love magnanimity, and appreciate action at once fearless and generous. We all remember how by the grim mockery of fate,—as if to test to the uttermost American capacity for self-government,—Abraham Lincoln was snatched away at the moment of crisis from the helm of State, and Andrew Johnson substituted for him. I think it no doubtful anticipation of historical judgment to say that a more unfortunate selection could not well have chanced. In no single respect, it is safe to say, was Andrew Johnson adapted for the peculiar duties which Booth's pistol imposed upon him. One of Johnson's most unhappy, most ill-considered convictions was that our Civil War was a conventional old-time rebellion; that rebellion was treason; that treason was a crime; and that a crime was something for which punishment should in due course of law be meted out. He, therefore, wanted, or thought he wanted, to have the scenes of England's Convention Parliament and of the Restoration of 1660 reënacted here, a fitting sequel of our great conflict. Most fortunately, the American people then gave evidence to Europe of a capacity for self-restraint and self-government not traceable to English parentage, or precedents. No Cromwell's head grinned from our Westminster Hall; no convicted traitor swung in chains; no shambles dripped in blood. None the less, Andrew Johnson called for "indictments"; and, one

APPOMATTOX—IN THE SUNSHINE OF PEACE

The quaint costumes of the groups before the village inn—the flaring skirt of the woman by the gate and the queer pinafores and roundabouts of the children standing by their father near the tree—all mark the year of 1865. These spectators cannot realize the immensity of the event they have witnessed. But the wisest heads are thankful that peace has returned to their land. They are ready to become once more citizens of the United States of America, and to contribute by their industry and loyalty to the future of a common country. The record of the South since Appomattox shows how faithfully its sons have kept the terms accepted there by Robert E. Lee, and turned defeat into victory.

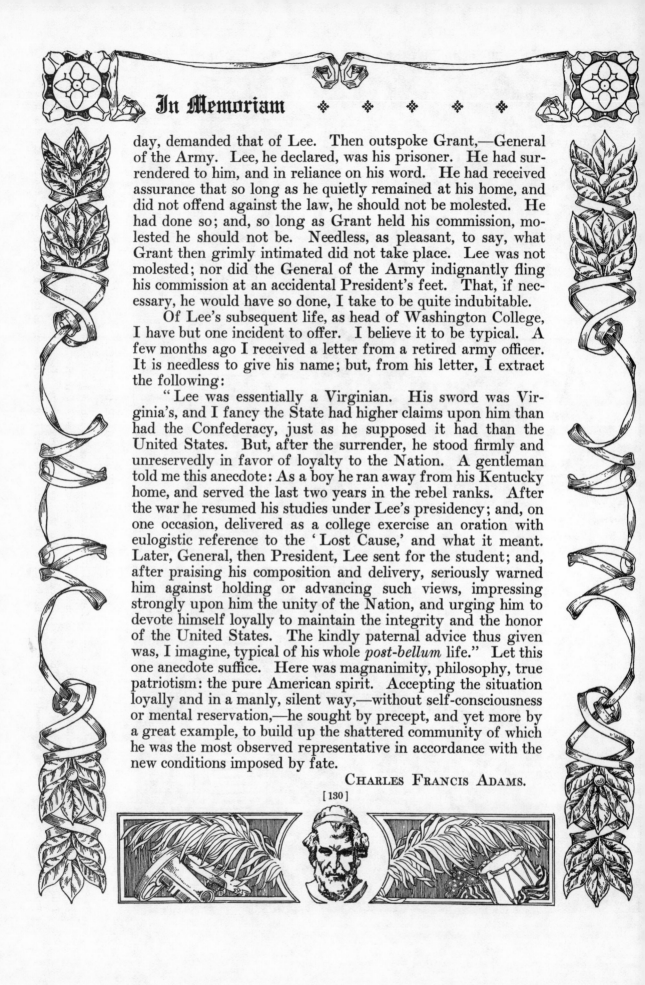

day, demanded that of Lee. Then outspoke Grant,—General of the Army. Lee, he declared, was his prisoner. He had surrendered to him, and in reliance on his word. He had received assurance that so long as he quietly remained at his home, and did not offend against the law, he should not be molested. He had done so; and, so long as Grant held his commission, molested he should not be. Needless, as pleasant, to say, what Grant then grimly intimated did not take place. Lee was not molested; nor did the General of the Army indignantly fling his commission at an accidental President's feet. That, if necessary, he would have so done, I take to be quite indubitable.

Of Lee's subsequent life, as head of Washington College, I have but one incident to offer. I believe it to be typical. A few months ago I received a letter from a retired army officer. It is needless to give his name; but, from his letter, I extract the following:

"Lee was essentially a Virginian. His sword was Virginia's, and I fancy the State had higher claims upon him than had the Confederacy, just as he supposed it had than the United States. But, after the surrender, he stood firmly and unreservedly in favor of loyalty to the Nation. A gentleman told me this anecdote: As a boy he ran away from his Kentucky home, and served the last two years in the rebel ranks. After the war he resumed his studies under Lee's presidency; and, on one occasion, delivered as a college exercise an oration with eulogistic reference to the 'Lost Cause,' and what it meant. Later, General, then President, Lee sent for the student; and, after praising his composition and delivery, seriously warned him against holding or advancing such views, impressing strongly upon him the unity of the Nation, and urging him to devote himself loyally to maintain the integrity and the honor of the United States. The kindly paternal advice thus given was, I imagine, typical of his whole *post-bellum* life." Let this one anecdote suffice. Here was magnanimity, philosophy, true patriotism: the pure American spirit. Accepting the situation loyally and in a manly, silent way,—without self-consciousness or mental reservation,—he sought by precept, and yet more by a great example, to build up the shattered community of which he was the most observed representative in accordance with the new conditions imposed by fate.

CHARLES FRANCIS ADAMS.

IV

SCENES FROM
SOLDIER
LIFE

SCENES FROM SOLDIER LIFE

BIVOUAC ON A MOUNTAINSIDE

This picture, aside from the beautiful touches at the close, is to be prized for the record it affords of the large soul of Walt Whitman. He witnessed little of life at the front, but he saw all of the horror of war in the hospitals at Washington, and exhausted his splendid vitality in comforting and aiding the wounded and dying. Yet into his poetry crept no word of bitterness or sectionalism.

I see before me now a traveling army halting,
Below, a fertile valley spread, with barns and the orchards of
    summer,
Behind, the terraced sides of a mountain, abrupt, in places ris-
    ing high,
Broken, with rocks, with clinging cedars, with tall shapes din-
    gily seen,
The numerous camp-fires scattered near and far, some away up
    on the mountain,
The shadowy forms of men and horses, looming, large-sized,
    flickering,
And over all the sky—the sky! far, far out of reach, studded,
    breaking out, the eternal stars.

WALT WHITMAN.

THE BIVOUAC IN THE SNOW

The representative woman singer of the Confederacy here furnishes a picture in full contrast with the preceding. She was the daughter of the eminent Presbyterian clergyman, Dr. George Junkin, who was from 1848 to 1861 president of Washington College. On the outbreak of the war he resigned and returned North, but his daughter, who in 1857 had married Professor J. T. L. Preston, founder of the Virginia Military Institute, warmly championed the cause of her husband and of the South.

Halt!—the march is over,
Day is almost done;

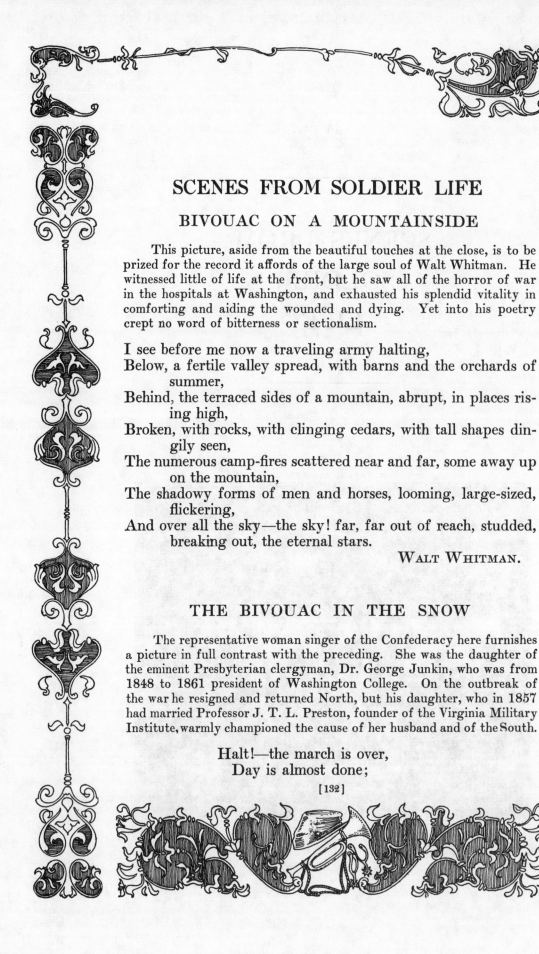

"BIVOUAC"

TO ILLUSTRATE
THE POEM BY
WHITMAN

The encampment of the Army of the Potomac at Cumberland Landing is a scene strikingly similar to that described by Whitman. With the shadowy soldiers in the foreground one can gaze upon the camp that fills the plain. The ascending smoke from the camp-fires drifts about in the still air, while the horses stand at their fodder and the men await the evening meal. Away to the left the low ground is covered with a pool of water formed by the rain that has fallen most of that day. To-morrow the wagon-trains in the distance will again move slowly along the heavy roads, and the soldiers will trudge forward toward Richmond. This picture shows a scene in the famous Peninsula campaign, when the boys in blue were jubilantly responding to the demand of the North, "On to Richmond." When this view was taken the army had covered more than half the distance. The soldiers' hopes rise with the smoke of the camp-fires all over the peaceful plain.

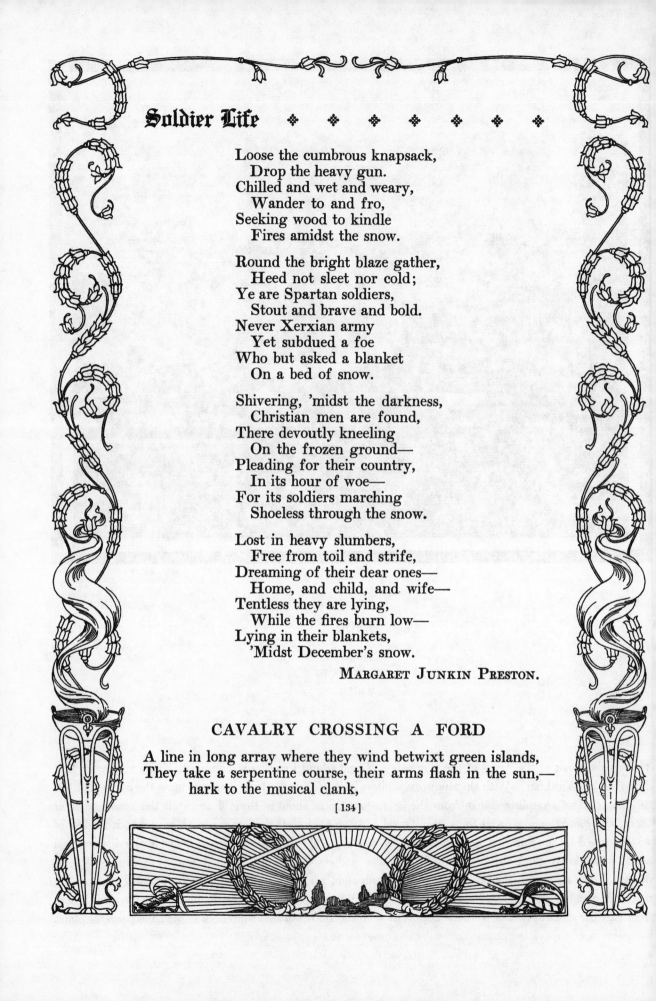

Soldier Life ❖ ❖ ❖ ❖ ❖ ❖

Loose the cumbrous knapsack,
  Drop the heavy gun.
Chilled and wet and weary,
  Wander to and fro,
Seeking wood to kindle
  Fires amidst the snow.

Round the bright blaze gather,
  Heed not sleet nor cold;
Ye are Spartan soldiers,
  Stout and brave and bold.
Never Xerxian army
  Yet subdued a foe
Who but asked a blanket
  On a bed of snow.

Shivering, 'midst the darkness,
  Christian men are found,
There devoutly kneeling
  On the frozen ground—
Pleading for their country,
  In its hour of woe—
For its soldiers marching
  Shoeless through the snow.

Lost in heavy slumbers,
  Free from toil and strife,
Dreaming of their dear ones—
  Home, and child, and wife—
Tentless they are lying,
  While the fires burn low—
Lying in their blankets,
  'Midst December's snow.

MARGARET JUNKIN PRESTON.

CAVALRY CROSSING A FORD

A line in long array where they wind betwixt green islands,
They take a serpentine course, their arms flash in the sun,—
  hark to the musical clank,

[134]

"THE SHADOWY FORMS OF HORSES"

These scenes from a bivouac of McClellan's army, in 1862, reveal, in much the same spirit as Whitman's poem, the actual life of the soldier. At the end of a hard day's march, officers and men were tired, and horses and mules were willing to be unhitched and to nibble on the fodder by the wagon-tongue, or in the rear of the vehicle. The teamsters, meanwhile, were gathered about the twinkling camp-fires that Whitman brings before our eyes. Night will soon fall, and the army will pass into the land of dreams. Little it realizes the dangers of the road to Richmond.

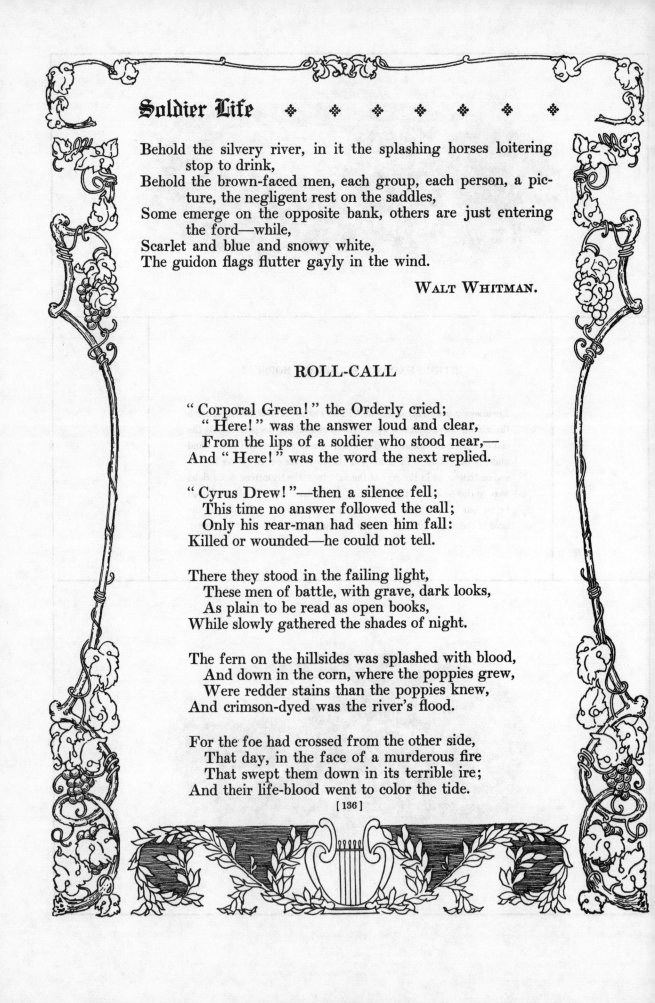

Soldier Life ✦ ✦ ✦ ✦ ✦ ✦ ✦

Behold the silvery river, in it the splashing horses loitering
    stop to drink,
Behold the brown-faced men, each group, each person, a pic-
    ture, the negligent rest on the saddles,
Some emerge on the opposite bank, others are just entering
    the ford—while,
Scarlet and blue and snowy white,
The guidon flags flutter gayly in the wind.

WALT WHITMAN.

ROLL-CALL

"Corporal Green!" the Orderly cried;
  "Here!" was the answer loud and clear,
  From the lips of a soldier who stood near,—
And "Here!" was the word the next replied.

"Cyrus Drew!"—then a silence fell;
  This time no answer followed the call;
  Only his rear-man had seen him fall:
Killed or wounded—he could not tell.

There they stood in the failing light,
  These men of battle, with grave, dark looks,
  As plain to be read as open books,
While slowly gathered the shades of night.

The fern on the hillsides was splashed with blood,
  And down in the corn, where the poppies grew,
  Were redder stains than the poppies knew,
And crimson-dyed was the river's flood.

For the foe had crossed from the other side,
  That day, in the face of a murderous fire
  That swept them down in its terrible ire;
And their life-blood went to color the tide.

"KILLED OR WOUNDED—HE COULD NOT TELL"

As a companion to the sad lines of the poem "Roll Call," this Confederate soldier, fallen on the field of Spotsylvania, speaks more clearly than words. He is but one of 200,000 "killed and died of wounds" during the war; yet there is a whole world of pitifulness in his useless trappings, his crumpled hat, his loosened straps and haversack. Here the young soldier lies in the gathering twilight, while his companions far away answer to their names. The empty canteen will never more wet the lips of the upturned face, nor shall the long musket dropped in the moment of falling speak again to the foe.

"THERE THEY STOOD
IN THE FAILING LIGHT
THESE MEN OF BATTLE, WITH GRAVE DARK LOOKS"

The spirit of Shepherd's somber poem, "Roll Call," lives in this group—from the spadesmen whose last services to their comrades have been performed, to the solemn bearers of the muffled drums. Many more such occasions were to arise; for these soldiers belonged to the brigade that suffered the greatest loss of life of any one brigade during the war; 1,172 of its men were either killed in battle or died of wounds. The same five regiments that lay in Camp Griffin when this picture was taken in 1861 marched together in the Grand Review on Pennsylvania Avenue in Washington, in 1865. When their term of enlistment expired in 1864, they had all re-enlisted and preserved the existence of the brigade. It was famous also for being composed entirely of troops from one State. It contained the Second, Third, Fourth, Fifth and Sixth Vermont Infantry, and later the First Vermont Heavy Artillery. It was in this respect conspicuous in the Union army, which did not adopt the Confederate policy of grouping regiments from the same

BURIAL PARTY,
OLD VERMONT BRIGADE,
CAMP GRIFFIN, NEAR WASHINGTON, 1861

State in brigades.   The gallant record of the Vermont brigade was nowhere more conspicuous than in the Wilderness campaign.   The first five regiments lost in the battle of the Wilderness, May 5–6, 1864, 195 killed, 1,017 wounded, and 57 missing, making a total of 1,269.   Within a week its loss had amounted to 58 per cent. of the number engaged.   The words of the poet are therefore no merely fanciful picture of frightful loss in battle.   There were a dozen battles in which the Federal armies alone lost more than 10,000 men, enough in each case to populate a city, and it has been estimated that the totals on both sides amounted to more than 700,000 killed and wounded.   When it is recalled that most of these were young men, who in the natural course of events had many years of usefulness yet to live for their country, the cost to the American nation is simply appalling.   This is entirely aside from the many sorrowing mourners for the heroes of the Old Vermont Brigade and for many others who failed on any battlefield to answer "Here" at roll-call.

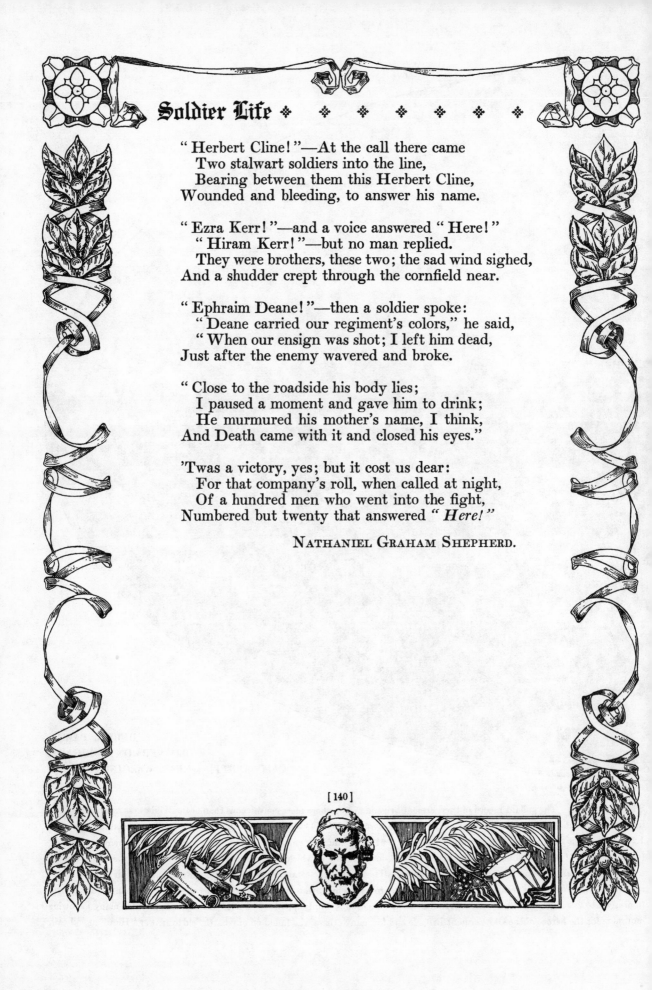

Soldier Life ❖ ❖ ❖ ❖ ❖ ❖

" Herbert Cline! "—At the call there came
  Two stalwart soldiers into the line,
  Bearing between them this Herbert Cline,
Wounded and bleeding, to answer his name.

" Ezra Kerr! "—and a voice answered " Here! "
  " Hiram Kerr! "—but no man replied.
  They were brothers, these two; the sad wind sighed,
And a shudder crept through the cornfield near.

" Ephraim Deane! "—then a soldier spoke:
  " Deane carried our regiment's colors," he said,
  " When our ensign was shot; I left him dead,
Just after the enemy wavered and broke.

" Close to the roadside his body lies;
  I paused a moment and gave him to drink;
  He murmured his mother's name, I think,
And Death came with it and closed his eyes."

'Twas a victory, yes; but it cost us dear:
  For that company's roll, when called at night,
  Of a hundred men who went into the fight,
Numbered but twenty that answered " *Here!* "

NATHANIEL GRAHAM SHEPHERD.

[140]

V

WIVES
AND
SWEETHEARTS

AT ANTIETAM BRIDGE

A UNION SOLDIER AFTER THE BATTLE, IN SEPTEM-
BER, 1862, OCCUPIED WITH DIFFERENT "DUTIES"

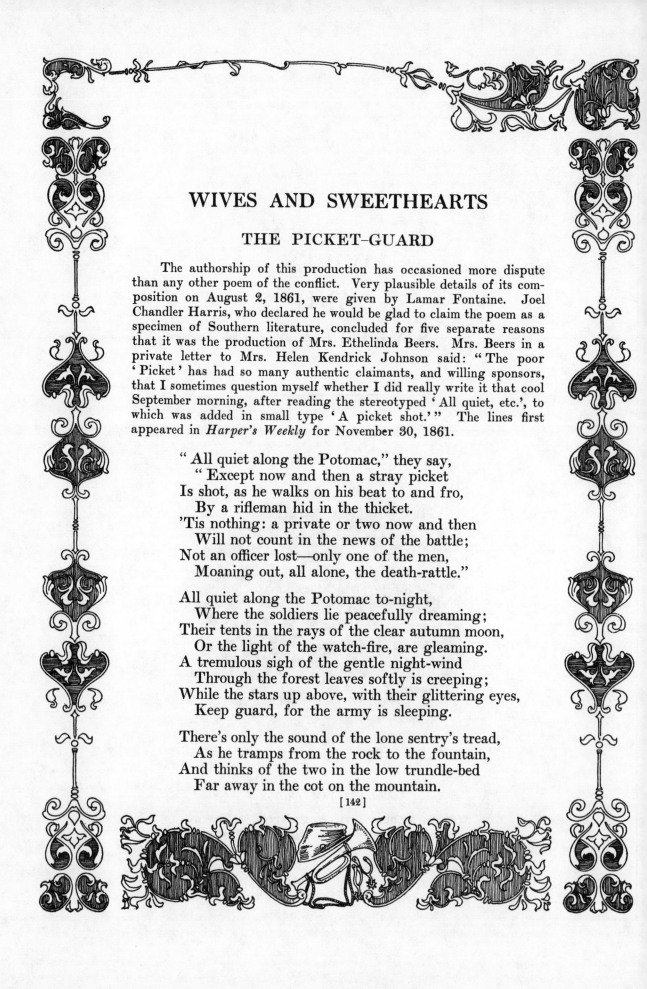

WIVES AND SWEETHEARTS

THE PICKET–GUARD

The authorship of this production has occasioned more dispute than any other poem of the conflict. Very plausible details of its composition on August 2, 1861, were given by Lamar Fontaine. Joel Chandler Harris, who declared he would be glad to claim the poem as a specimen of Southern literature, concluded for five separate reasons that it was the production of Mrs. Ethelinda Beers. Mrs. Beers in a private letter to Mrs. Helen Kendrick Johnson said: "The poor 'Picket' has had so many authentic claimants, and willing sponsors, that I sometimes question myself whether I did really write it that cool September morning, after reading the stereotyped 'All quiet, etc.', to which was added in small type 'A picket shot.'" The lines first appeared in *Harper's Weekly* for November 30, 1861.

" All quiet along the Potomac," they say,
  " Except now and then a stray picket
Is shot, as he walks on his beat to and fro,
  By a rifleman hid in the thicket.
'Tis nothing: a private or two now and then
  Will not count in the news of the battle;
Not an officer lost—only one of the men,
  Moaning out, all alone, the death-rattle."

All quiet along the Potomac to-night,
  Where the soldiers lie peacefully dreaming;
Their tents in the rays of the clear autumn moon,
  Or the light of the watch-fire, are gleaming.
A tremulous sigh of the gentle night-wind
  Through the forest leaves softly is creeping;
While the stars up above, with their glittering eyes,
  Keep guard, for the army is sleeping.

There's only the sound of the lone sentry's tread,
  As he tramps from the rock to the fountain,
And thinks of the two in the low trundle-bed
  Far away in the cot on the mountain.

"ALL QUIET

ALONG

THE POTOMAC"

A CIVIL-WAR

SENTRY

ON HIS BEAT

This Union picket by the Potomac River bank, clasping his musket in the chilling blast as he tramps his beat, conjures up the original of Ethel Beers' historic poem.   The sympathy of the poet was not misplaced.   Picket duty was an experience in every soldier's life.   Regiments were detailed at stated intervals to march from their camps to the outer lines and there disposition would be made of the men in the following order: about one half of the regiment would be placed in what was known as the "reserve," while the balance of the men would be taken, by the officer of the guard designated for that purpose, to the extreme outpost, either relieving another regiment or forming new outposts, according to the necessities or changes of position.   The period of the poem is the fall of 1861.   The battle of Bull Run had been fought in the summer, and thereafter there was very little military activity along the Potomac. McClellan was doing what was absolutely necessary to effective operations—he was drilling the raw recruits into professional soldiers.   The public at large, whose impatience had brought on the disaster of Bull Run before either side was prepared for battle, was naturally exasperated.   But the author—a woman—was more impressed by the fate of the lonely sentinel.

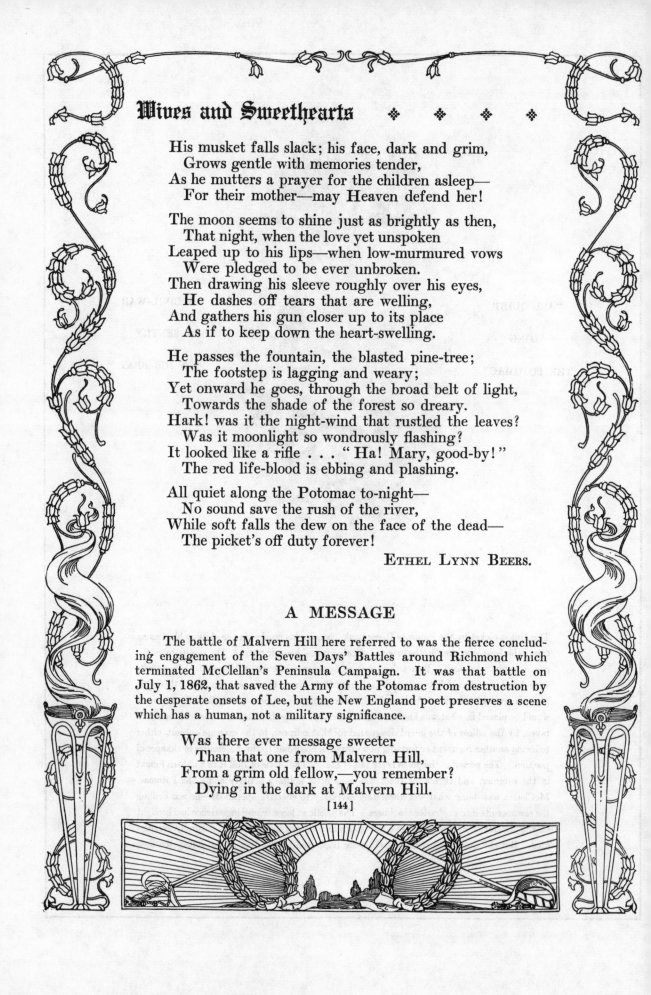

Wives and Sweethearts ❖ ❖ ❖ ❖

His musket falls slack; his face, dark and grim,
    Grows gentle with memories tender,
As he mutters a prayer for the children asleep—
    For their mother—may Heaven defend her!

The moon seems to shine just as brightly as then,
    That night, when the love yet unspoken
Leaped up to his lips—when low-murmured vows
    Were pledged to be ever unbroken.
Then drawing his sleeve roughly over his eyes,
    He dashes off tears that are welling,
And gathers his gun closer up to its place
    As if to keep down the heart-swelling.

He passes the fountain, the blasted pine-tree;
    The footstep is lagging and weary;
Yet onward he goes, through the broad belt of light,
    Towards the shade of the forest so dreary.
Hark! was it the night-wind that rustled the leaves?
    Was it moonlight so wondrously flashing?
It looked like a rifle . . . "Ha! Mary, good-by!"
    The red life-blood is ebbing and plashing.

All quiet along the Potomac to-night—
    No sound save the rush of the river,
While soft falls the dew on the face of the dead—
    The picket's off duty forever!

ETHEL LYNN BEERS.

A MESSAGE

The battle of Malvern Hill here referred to was the fierce concluding engagement of the Seven Days' Battles around Richmond which
terminated McClellan's Peninsula Campaign. It was that battle on
July 1, 1862, that saved the Army of the Potomac from destruction by
the desperate onsets of Lee, but the New England poet preserves a scene
which has a human, not a military significance.

Was there ever message sweeter
    Than that one from Malvern Hill,
From a grim old fellow,—you remember?
    Dying in the dark at Malvern Hill.

"THEIR SEARCHING MESSAGE FROM THOSE DISTANT HOURS"

OFF TO THE WAR—EMBARKATION OF NINTH ARMY CORPS AT AQUIA CREEK LANDING, IN FEBRUARY, 1863

Elizabeth Stuart Phelps' poem "A Message" breathes a faith that inspired the mothers of many men who stand expectantly in this picture, and of many thousands more who, like them, were "off to the war" in '61–'65. Proud, indeed, were the sweethearts and wives of their "heroes" marching away to the big camps or floating down the stream on the transports. Honor and glory awaited these sons and brothers who were helping to serve their cause. To each fond heart came the hope: "Soon the nation will be ringing with my boy's praise, and his name will be repeated with blessings by unnumbered tongues." But there was also the sickening dread that he might never again be heard of, that stalking disease might single him out in the camp, that he might fall unnoticed when on lonely picket service, that in the wild tumult of the cannonading or the panting rush of the bayonet charge he might be forgotten by his comrades. Mrs. Ward voiced the desire of all true women, both North and South. Though the hero in Blue or in Gray was not to fill the pages of history with deathless deeds, these women believed that at least he would find an honored grave and rise to a higher bliss than this world gives.

Wives and Sweethearts ✦ ✦ ✦ ✦ ✦

With his rough face turned a little,
　On a heap of scarlet sand,
They found him, just within the thicket,
　With a picture in his hand,—

With a stained and crumpled picture
　Of a woman's aged face;
Yet there seemed to leap a wild entreaty,
　Young and living—tender—from the face
When they flashed the lantern on it,
　Gilding all the purple shade,
And stooped to raise him softly,—
　"That's my mother, sir," he said.

"Tell her"—but he wandered, slipping
　Into tangled words and cries,—
Something about Mac and Hooker,
　Something dropping through the cries
About the kitten by the fire,
　And mother's cranberry-pies; and there
The words fell, and an utter
　Silence brooded in the air.

Just as he was drifting from them,
　Out into the dark, alone
(Poor old mother, waiting for your message,
　Waiting with the kitten, all alone!),
Through the hush his voice broke,—"Tell her—
　Thank you, Doctor—when you can,—
Tell her that I kissed her picture,
　And wished I'd been a better man."

Ah, I wonder if the red feet
　Of departed battle-hours
May not leave for us their searching
　Message from those distant hours.
Sisters, daughters, mothers, think you,
　Would your heroes now or then,
Dying, kiss your pictured faces,
　Wishing they'd been better men?

ELIZABETH STUART PHELPS WARD.

"THE WINTRY BLAST GOES WAILING BY"

Like a vision evoked by Gordon McCabe's verse rises this encampment of the Forty-fourth New York on the Virginia plains. The snow that covers the foreground suggests of itself the faint smoke that rises from the camp and hovers like a veil over the hillside beyond. One may suppose that "the owl, for all his feathers is a-cold," and that hares go limping through the frozen grass.   Yet it is not so much the effort to keep warm amid the bleak surroundings that brings gloom to the soldier's heart. It is rather the emotions which the Southern poet has expressed in Tennysonian stanzas. Distant from home, or with no home to return to, the soldier feels the loss of those domestic relations which fill life with warmth and hope. The patriotism that leads to enlistment, or the ardor that springs from war's wild alarms, must sooner or later give way for a time to the simple human emotions that even a child can share and understand.   "East, west, home's best."

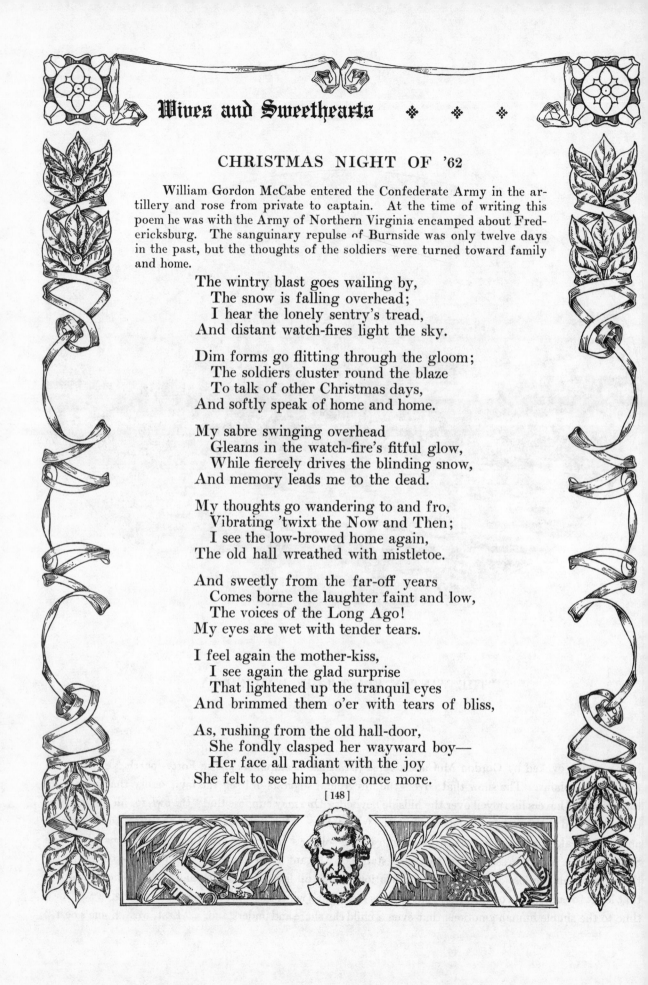

CHRISTMAS NIGHT OF '62

William Gordon McCabe entered the Confederate Army in the artillery and rose from private to captain. At the time of writing this poem he was with the Army of Northern Virginia encamped about Fredericksburg. The sanguinary repulse of Burnside was only twelve days in the past, but the thoughts of the soldiers were turned toward family and home.

The wintry blast goes wailing by,
  The snow is falling overhead;
  I hear the lonely sentry's tread,
And distant watch-fires light the sky.

Dim forms go flitting through the gloom;
  The soldiers cluster round the blaze
  To talk of other Christmas days,
And softly speak of home and home.

My sabre swinging overhead
  Gleams in the watch-fire's fitful glow,
  While fiercely drives the blinding snow,
And memory leads me to the dead.

My thoughts go wandering to and fro,
  Vibrating 'twixt the Now and Then;
  I see the low-browed home again,
The old hall wreathed with mistletoe.

And sweetly from the far-off years
  Comes borne the laughter faint and low,
  The voices of the Long Ago!
My eyes are wet with tender tears.

I feel again the mother-kiss,
  I see again the glad surprise
  That lightened up the tranquil eyes
And brimmed them o'er with tears of bliss,

As, rushing from the old hall-door,
  She fondly clasped her wayward boy—
  Her face all radiant with the joy
She felt to see him home once more.

[148]

"THE SOLDIERS CLUSTER ROUND THE BLAZE"

As if made for Gorden McCabe's poem, this photograph shows vividly a group of pickets in winter. Pickets were the "eyes" of the army, to observe all movements made by the enemy and to give warning of the approach of any force from the direction of his lines. The particular picket here is a soldier who, after lonely outpost duty on the hilltop just beyond his companions, has returned to warm his hands over their fire. "It was fortunate for these boys," remarked a veteran, "that they had a little hill between themselves and the enemy so that a fire might be made without observation." In general, when facing the foe, pickets upon the outer lines were allowed no fires of any kind. The utmost vigilance was required, no matter what the state of the weather. In many instances during the war soldiers were found frozen to death at their posts of duty, leaning against trees, or as they had fallen while marching on their beats.

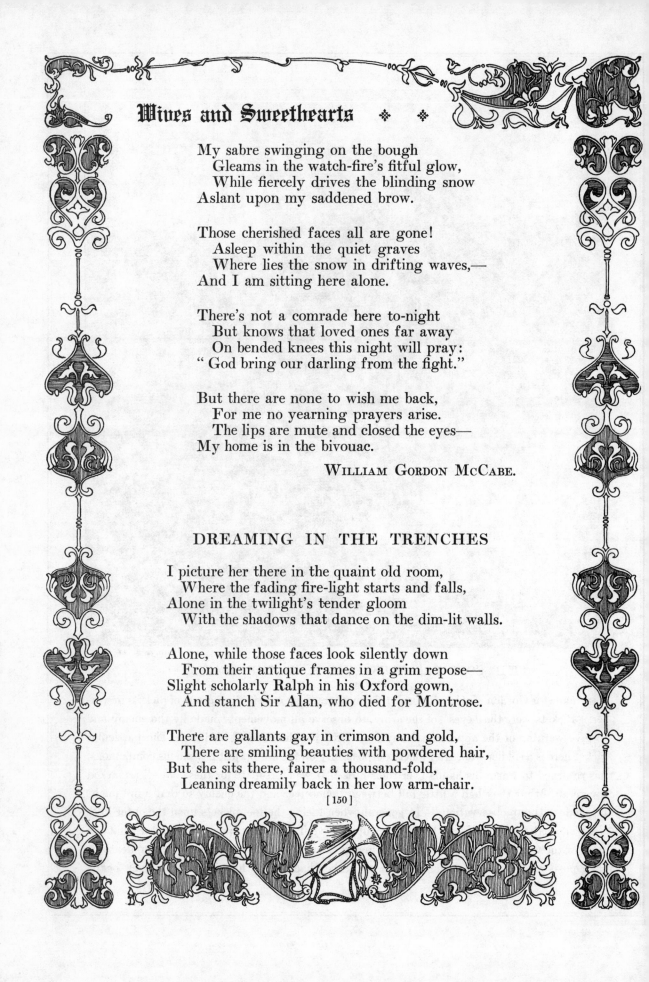

Wives and Sweethearts ❖ ❖

My sabre swinging on the bough
  Gleams in the watch-fire's fitful glow,
  While fiercely drives the blinding snow
Aslant upon my saddened brow.

Those cherished faces all are gone!
  Asleep within the quiet graves
  Where lies the snow in drifting waves,—
And I am sitting here alone.

There's not a comrade here to-night
  But knows that loved ones far away
  On bended knees this night will pray:
" God bring our darling from the fight."

But there are none to wish me back,
  For me no yearning prayers arise.
  The lips are mute and closed the eyes—
My home is in the bivouac.

           WILLIAM GORDON MCCABE.

DREAMING IN THE TRENCHES

I picture her there in the quaint old room,
  Where the fading fire-light starts and falls,
Alone in the twilight's tender gloom
  With the shadows that dance on the dim-lit walls.

Alone, while those faces look silently down
  From their antique frames in a grim repose—
Slight scholarly Ralph in his Oxford gown,
  And stanch Sir Alan, who died for Montrose.

There are gallants gay in crimson and gold,
  There are smiling beauties with powdered hair,
But she sits there, fairer a thousand-fold,
  Leaning dreamily back in her low arm-chair.

[150]

"THE VOICES OF THE LONG AGO"

The war-time home scene from Virginia gives McCabe's line a more touching pathos. The old-fashioned croquet on the lawn, where the little girl has sat down and delayed the game, is in keeping with the quaint hats and crinoline skirts. The house and its vine-clad arbor have the "home" feeling that emphasizes one of the sorest deprivations of a soldier's life. All the poems in this section record some phase of the loneliness of the tented field, where thousands are gathered from many sections. Differ as much as they may in age, previous occupation, and whole manner of life, they are all moved by the recollection of loved ones afar, who will give a joyous welcome on their return. McCabe's verses on this theme are classic.

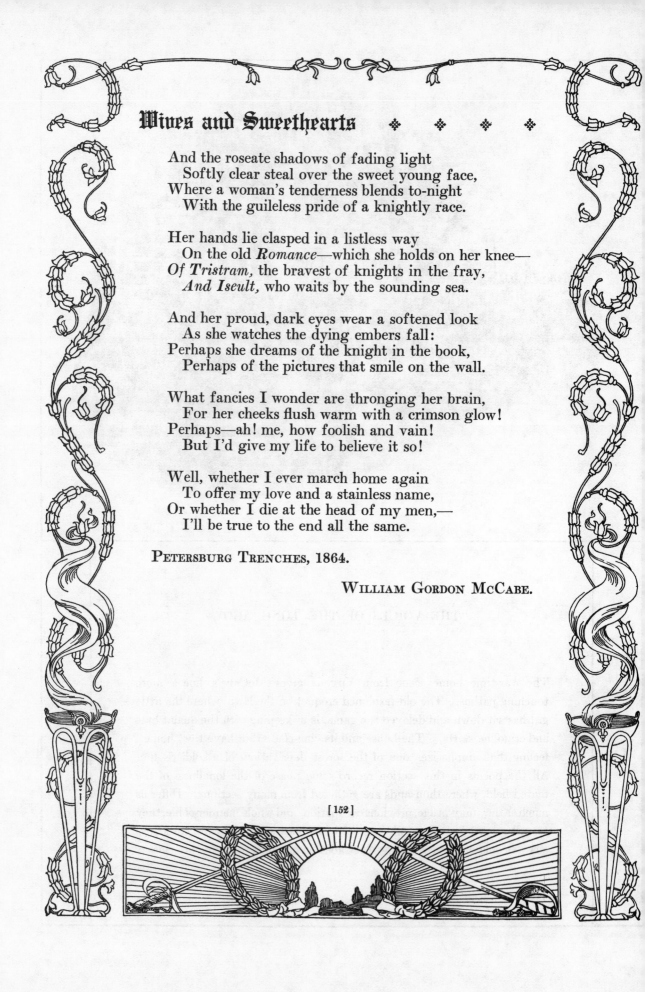

Wives and Sweethearts ❖ ❖ ❖ ❖

And the roseate shadows of fading light
   Softly clear steal over the sweet young face,
Where a woman's tenderness blends to-night
   With the guileless pride of a knightly race.

Her hands lie clasped in a listless way
   On the old *Romance*—which she holds on her knee—
Of Tristram, the bravest of knights in the fray,
   And Iseult, who waits by the sounding sea.

And her proud, dark eyes wear a softened look
   As she watches the dying embers fall:
Perhaps she dreams of the knight in the book,
   Perhaps of the pictures that smile on the wall.

What fancies I wonder are thronging her brain,
   For her cheeks flush warm with a crimson glow!
Perhaps—ah! me, how foolish and vain!
   But I'd give my life to believe it so!

Well, whether I ever march home again
   To offer my love and a stainless name,
Or whether I die at the head of my men,—
   I'll be true to the end all the same.

PETERSBURG TRENCHES, 1864.

WILLIAM GORDON McCABE.

VI

LYRICS

A SOLDIER GROUP IN A MOMENT FIT FOR SONG—THE 170TH NEW YORK
ON RESERVE PICKET DUTY

THE BATTLE HYMN OF THE REPUBLIC—"A HUNDRED CIRCLING CAMPS"

The time of this photograph and its actors connect directly with Julia Ward Howe's inspiration for her "Battle Hymn." The author, in the late fall of 1861, had made her first visit to Washington in company with her pastor, James Freeman Clarke, Governor Andrew of Massachusetts, and her husband, Dr. Howe, who, already past the age of military service, rendered valuable aid as an officer of the Sanitary Commission. Of her visit she writes in her "Reminiscences": "On the return from the review of troops near the city, to beguile the rather tedious drive, we sang from time to time snatches of the army songs so popular at that time, concluding, I think, with 'John Brown's body.' The soldiers . . . answered back, 'Good for you!' Mr. Clarke said, 'Mrs. Howe, why do you not write some good words for that stirring tune?' I replied that I had often wished to do this, but had not as yet found in my mind any leading toward it. I went to bed that night as usual, and slept, according to my wont, quite soundly. I awoke in the gray of the morning twilight; and as I lay waiting for the dawn, the long lines of the desired poem began to twine themselves in my mind. Having thought out all the stanzas, I said to myself, 'I must get up and write those verses down, lest I fall asleep and forget them.' So, with a sudden effort, I sprang out of bed, and found in the dimness an old stump of a pen which I remembered to have used the day before. I scrawled the verses almost without looking at the paper. I had learned to do this when, on previous occasions, attacks of versification had visited me in the night, and I feared to have recourse to a light lest I should wake the baby, who slept near me. I was always obliged to decipher my scrawl before another night should intervene, as it was only legible while the matter was fresh in my mind. At this

THE FIFTH VERMONT IN 1861, WITH THEIR COLONEL, L. A. GRANT

time, having completed my writing, I returned to bed and fell asleep, saying to myself, 'I like this better than most things that I have written.'" In 1861 the Fifth Vermont lay near Camp Griffin. It was on the outskirts of the encampments in Virginia, near Washington, and consequently subject to attacks by the Confederates. Its career throughout the war is proof that the spirit of the "Battle-Hymn" animated these boys in blue. Its Lieutenant-Colonel, L. A. Grant, who sits on his charger to the right, became famous later as the general commanding the "Vermont Brigade." To the left is Major Redfield Proctor. Leaving Camp Griffin on March 10, 1862, the regiment moved to the Peninsula. Its name became known at Yorktown and Savage's Station, at Antietam, Fredericksburg, and Gettysburg. In the Wilderness campaign, in the battle of May 5th, it assisted in checking the advance of the Confederates along the plank road in time for the Second Corps to take a strong position. It was in the heavy fighting of the succeeding day, and at the "Bloody Angle" at Spotsylvania was engaged for eight hours in the desperate and determined contest. The brigade commander reported: "It was empathically a hand-to-hand fight. Scores were shot down within a few feet of the death-dealing muskets." After battling all the way down to Petersburg, the Fifth Vermont was suddenly rushed to Washington to repel Early's attack. It then engaged in the thrilling victories of Sheridan in the Valley. In December, it returned to Petersburg and ended its active service only with the surrender at Appomattox. During these four years of service, the regiment lost eleven officers and 202 enlisted men killed and mortally wounded, and one officer and 124 enlisted men by disease. Its total loss was therefore 338, worthy of the famous "Vermont Brigade."

LYRICS

BATTLE-HYMN OF THE REPUBLIC

The unusual circumstances under which this national classic was written are recounted under the picture of the Fifth Vermont in '61, with their Colonel, L. A. Grant, on the immediately preceding page.

Mine eyes have seen the glory of the coming of the Lord:
He is trampling out the vintage where the grapes of wrath are
    stored;
He hath loosed the fateful lightning of his terrible swift sword:
    His truth is marching on.

I have seen Him in the watch-fires of a hundred circling camps;
They have builded Him an altar in the evening dews and
    damps;
I can read His righteous sentence by the dim and flaring
    lamps.
    His day is marching on.

I have read a fiery gospel, writ in burnished rows of steel:
"As ye deal with my contemners, so with you my grace shall
    deal;
Let the Hero, born of woman, crush the serpent with his heel,
    Since God is marching on."

He has sounded forth the trumpet that shall never call retreat;
He is sifting out the hearts of men before his judgment-seat:
Oh! be swift, my soul, to answer Him! be jubilant, my feet!
    Our God is marching on.

In the beauty of the lilies Christ was born across the sea,
With a glory in his bosom that transfigures you and me:
As He died to make men holy, let us die to make men free,
    While God is marching on.

JULIA WARD HOWE.

"IN BURNISHED ROWS OF STEEL"

As pictured above, the Seventeenth New York Infantry at Minor's Hill marches along the rolling Virginia fields to the inspiring music of the military band. This regiment, with its bright array, lives up to its spirited name, "Westchester Chasseurs." Well might such a pageant have inspired Mrs. Howe to write the resonant war-song to which her name is forever linked. But these New Yorkers saw much severe service. They went with McClellan on the Peninsula campaign in 1862, and back toward Washington in time to fight in the second battle of Bull Run and to see service in the bloody conflict at Antietam, September 16–17, 1862. They were in the sanguinary repulse at Fredericksburg, December 13, 1862. They remained at Falmouth, across the river from Fredericksburg, till Chancellorsville. Its three-years men then went to the 146th New York.

In the earnest spirit of Mrs. Howe's poem, the Ninth Vermont Infantry, as pictured vividly below, marches out of camp in North Carolina, 1863. Its career of only a year has been unusual. It had barely entered active service in 1862 when it was transferred to Harper's Ferry. There it was captured by "Stonewall" Jackson on September 15, 1862, and was paroled the next day. Its military career was apparently cut short. It was used, however, to guard Confederate prisoners at Camp Douglas, Chicago, until March 28, 1863. In January of that year, it had been declared exchanged and in the fall was at length sent to New Berne, North Carolina, where it was on duty in the Newport Barracks till July, 1864. There it engaged in various expeditions into the vicinity, destroying salt-works and capturing turpentine. There the photograph here reproduced was taken.

MY MARYLAND

This famous Confederate lyric had a striking origin. While James Ryder Randall was teaching in Poydras College he became acquainted with Mr. D. C. Jenkins, editor of the New Orleans *Delta*, who published some of his verse. In April, 1861, he sent the young professor a copy of the poems of James Clarence Mangan. Randall was warm in his admiration of the " gifted Irish poet," and especially enthusiastic about that passionate outburst, the " Karamanian Exile." One stanza begins:

" I see thee ever in my dreams,
    Karaman!
Thy hundred hills, thy thousand streams,
    Karaman, O Karaman!

His dreamy existence at Pointe Coupée was rudely broken on April 23, 1861, by the news in the New Orleans *Delta* of the attack on the troops of the Sixth Massachusetts as they passed through Baltimore on April 19th. The first citizen to fall was a friend and college mate of the poet. Randall's own account of the effect of this news appears in a letter printed in Professor Brander Matthews' " Pen and Ink ":

" This account excited me greatly. I had long been absent from my native city, and the startling event there inflamed my mind. That night I could not sleep, for my nerves were all unstrung, and I could not dismiss what I had read in the paper from my mind. About midnight I rose, lit a candle, and went to my desk. Some powerful spirit appeared to possess me, and almost involuntarily I proceeded to write the song of ' My Maryland.' I remember that the idea appeared to first take shape as music in the brain—some wild air that I cannot now recall. The whole poem was dashed off rapidly when once begun. It was not composed in cold blood, but under what may be called a conflagration of the senses, if not an inspiration of the intellect. I was stirred to a desire for some way linking my name with that of my native State, if not ' with my land's language.' But I never expected to do this with one single supreme effort, and no one was more surprised than I was at the widespread and instantaneous popularity of the lyric I had been so strangely stimulated to write." Randall was always free to acknowledge that Mangan's poem " solved the meter " of his famous lyric.

The college boys to whom he read the poem the next morning were so enthusiastic that he at once forwarded it to the *Delta*, in which it was printed on April 26th. Nearly every Southern journal at once copied it. Mr. Randall says: " I did not concern myself much about it, but very soon, from all parts of the country, there was borne to me, in my remote place of residence, evidence that I had made a great hit, and that, whatever might be the fate of the Confederacy, the song would survive it."

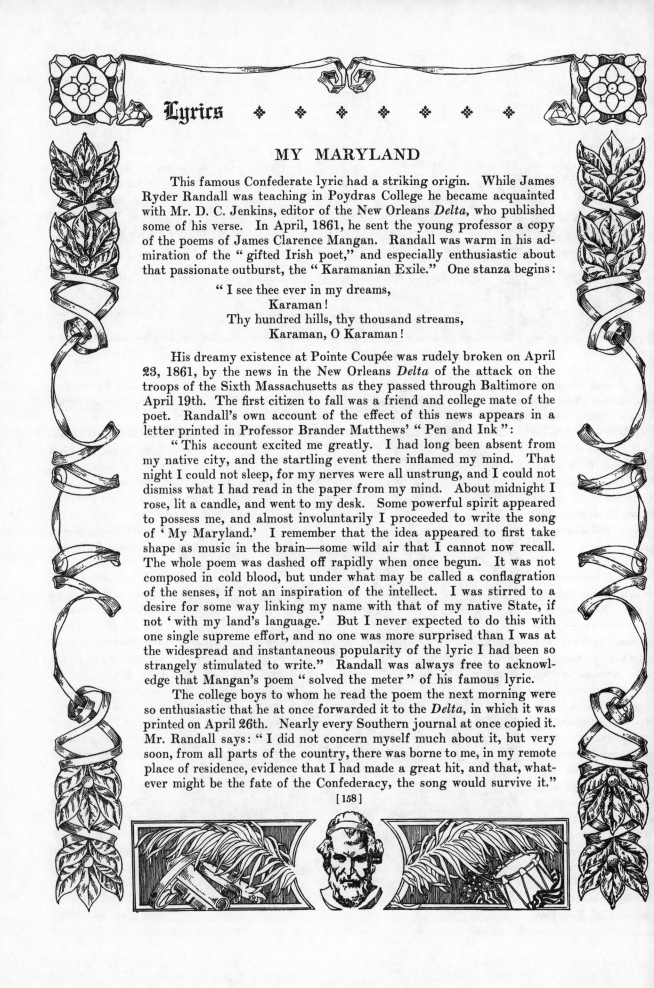

"THE
DESPOT'S
HEEL IS
ON THY
SHORE"

THE
NEW YORK
"SEVENTH"
IN
MARYLAND

These Union soldiers at Federal Hill, Maryland, in 1862, are the Gun Squad of the Fifth Company in New York's representative "Seventh" regiment. Sergeant-Major Rathbone is handing an order to Captain Spaight. Personally, the invaders were far from "despots," as Southerners soon ascertained. In the picture below are veterans of this same "Seventh" regiment, as they appeared seventeen years later in a different rôle—hosts and escorts of the Gate City Guard. In 1861, this had been the first body of troops to enter Confederate service from Atlanta. In 1879, its neighborly call upon New York City was met by one courtesy after another, under the auspices of the "Seventh." The *New York Sun* said: "The visit among us of the Gate City Guard will do more to bring about an understanding between North and South than the legislation of a century." Other newspapers commented on the event in a similar cordial spirit of friendship.

Lyrics ❖ ❖ ❖ ❖

The despot's heel is on thy shore,
    Maryland!
His torch is at thy temple door,
    Maryland!
Avenge the patriotic gore
That flecked the streets of Baltimore,
And be the battle-queen of yore,
    Maryland, my Maryland!

Hark to an exiled son's appeal,
    Maryland!
My Mother State, to thee I kneel,
    Maryland!
For life and death, for woe and weal,
Thy peerless chivalry reveal,
And gird thy beauteous limbs with steel,
    Maryland, my Maryland!

Thou wilt not cower in the dust,
    Maryland!
Thy beaming sword shall never rust,
    Maryland!
Remember Carroll's sacred trust,
Remember Howard's warlike thrust,
And all thy slumberers with the just,
    Maryland, my Maryland!

Come! 'tis the red dawn of the day,
    Maryland!
Come with thy panoplied array,
    Maryland!
With Ringgold's spirit for the fray,
With Watson's blood at Monterey,
With fearless Lowe and dashing May,
    Maryland, my Maryland!

Come! for thy shield is bright and strong,
    Maryland!
Come! for thy dalliance does thee wrong,
    Maryland!

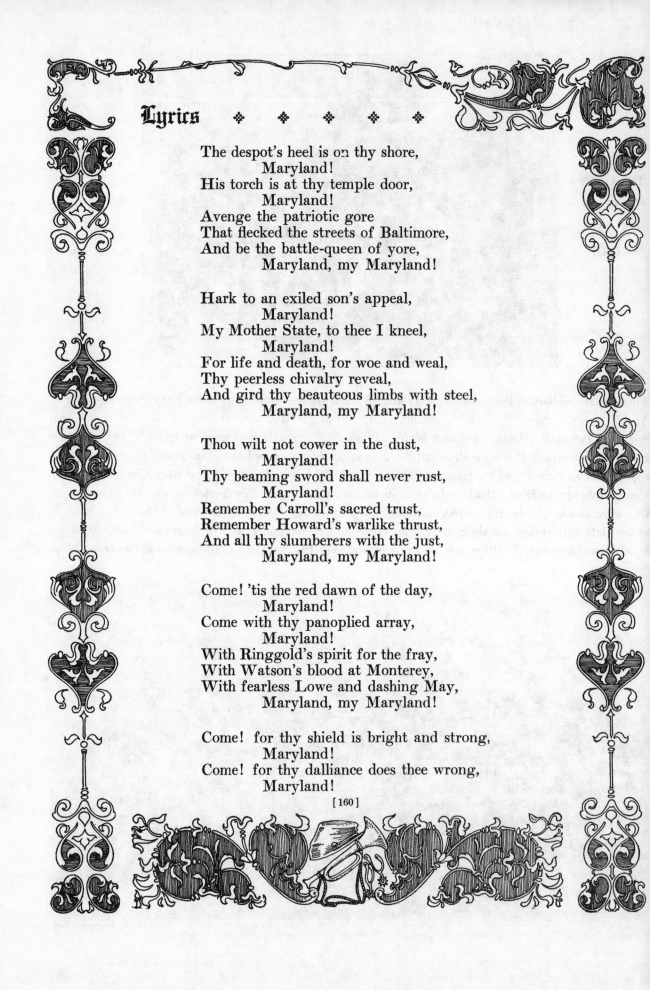

"BURST THE TYRANT'S CHAIN"

NORTHERN OFFICERS AT A MARYLAND HOME IN PLEASANT VALLEY, AFTER THE BATTLE OF ANTIETAM

The young Maryland girl with the charming ruffles has evidently discovered at least one Northerner not a "tyrant" or otherwise disagreeable. The scene is at the Lee homestead near the battlefield of Antietam; the time, October, 1862. Two members of General Burnside's staff and one of General McClellan's are here seen talking with the family, who were furnishing a temporary home for Mrs. McClellan after Antietam. One would never surmise that, a short time before, the fiercest single day's action of the war had been fought. Many another hospitable home among the beautiful rolling hills of Maryland entertained the same kindly feelings for the "despots" of whom Randall sang. Many another young lady, like the one sitting in her crinoline and ruffles opposite the handsome young officer, held a similar admiration for some leader in blue. Maryland, even in war-time, was always conscious of the bond of brotherhood that linked its people with the American Union. The group on the vine-shadowed veranda was but a prophecy of a day when all can admire the martial ring of "My Maryland" without losing pride in the greatness of the American Republic.

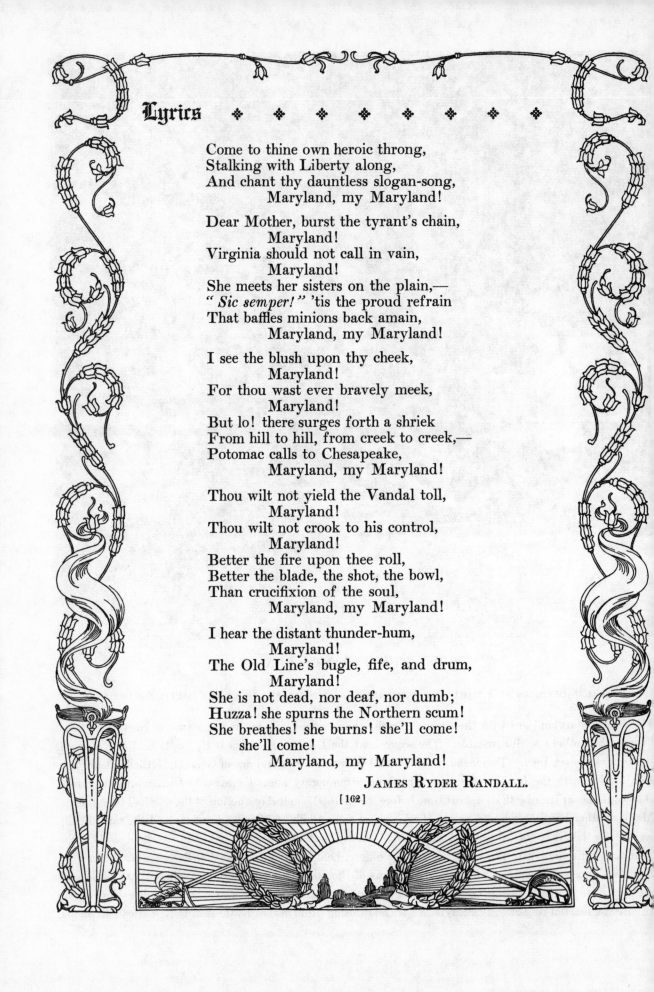

Come to thine own heroic throng,
Stalking with Liberty along,
And chant thy dauntless slogan-song,
    Maryland, my Maryland!

Dear Mother, burst the tyrant's chain,
    Maryland!
Virginia should not call in vain,
    Maryland!
She meets her sisters on the plain,—
" *Sic semper!* " 'tis the proud refrain
That baffles minions back amain,
    Maryland, my Maryland!

I see the blush upon thy cheek,
    Maryland!
For thou wast ever bravely meek,
    Maryland!
But lo! there surges forth a shriek
From hill to hill, from creek to creek,—
Potomac calls to Chesapeake,
    Maryland, my Maryland!

Thou wilt not yield the Vandal toll,
    Maryland!
Thou wilt not crook to his control,
    Maryland!
Better the fire upon thee roll,
Better the blade, the shot, the bowl,
Than crucifixion of the soul,
    Maryland, my Maryland!

I hear the distant thunder-hum,
    Maryland!
The Old Line's bugle, fife, and drum,
    Maryland!
She is not dead, nor deaf, nor dumb;
Huzza! she spurns the Northern scum!
She breathes! she burns! she'll come!
    she'll come!
    Maryland, my Maryland!
                JAMES RYDER RANDALL.

"ADVANCE

THE FLAG

OF

DIXIE"

A HOPEFUL

CONFEDERATE

GROUP

OF '61

Actual photographs of the Confederate flags raised within the Confederate fortifications are rare indeed. This photograph was taken by Edwards, the New Orleans artist, inside the Confederate lines at Pensacola, Florida. The cannon, at whose "ringing voices" Pike sang "The South's great heart rejoices," are shining in the warm Southern sunlight that brightens the flag in the color-bearer's hands. All is youth and hope.

DIXIE

Southrons, hear your country call you!
Up, lest worse than death befall you!
    To arms! To arms! To arms, in Dixie!
Lo! all the beacon-fires are lighted,—
Let all hearts be now united!
    To arms! To arms! To arms, in Dixie!
      Advance the flag of Dixie!
        Hurrah! hurrah!
For Dixie's land we take our stand,
    And live or die for Dixie!
      To arms! To arms!
    And conquer peace for Dixie!
      To arms! To arms!
    And conquer peace for Dixie!

Hear the Northern thunders mutter!
Northern flags in South winds flutter!
Send them back your fierce defiance!
Stamp upon the accursed alliance!

Fear no danger! Shun no labor!
Lift up rifle, pike, and sabre!
Shoulder pressing close to shoulder,
Let the odds make each heart bolder!

How the South's great heart rejoices
At your cannons' ringing voices!
For faith betrayed, and pledges broken,
Wrongs inflicted, insults spoken.

Strong as lions, swift as eagles,
Back to their kennels hunt these beagles!
Cut the unequal bonds asunder!
Let them hence each other plunder!

Swear upon your country's altar
Never to submit or falter,
Till the spoilers are defeated,
Till the Lord's work is completed!

"NORTHERN FLAGS

IN

SOUTH WINDS

FLUTTER"

UNION GUNBOATS

ON THE

MISSISSIPPI

AND THE JAMES

These views of Federal gunboats flying the Stars and Stripes preserve such scenes as inspired Albert Pike's stanzas to the tune of "Dixie." The ram *Vindicator* above is particularly apt, since "Dixie" first appeared in a "River" town, being printed in the *Natchez Courier* on April 30, 1862. It is a curious fact that the author was born in Boston and attended Harvard. The tune itself had a Northern origin. Daniel Decatur Emmet, who had traveled a great deal with circus bands and a minstrel company of his own, and was already known as the composer of "Old Dan Tucker," joined the famous Bryant's Minstrels in 1857. He not only appeared in the performances, but composed airs for the entertainments. The closing number on each occasion was known as a "walk-around," in which all members of the company would appear. One Saturday night, September 17, 1859, Emmet was told to prepare a new walk-around for the following Monday rehearsal. Sunday was gloomy, with a cold rain falling. As Emmet looked out the window an expression with which he had become familiar in his circus experience flashed across his memory,—"I wish I was in Dixie." Dixie referred to the South, where many companies

spent the winter on the road. Emmet at once took up his fiddle and began to work out the melody along with the words. The melody which he used is supposed to have been an old Northern Negro air, associated with the name of one Dix or Dixy, who had a large plantation, some say on Manhattan Island, others on Staten Island. When the progress of abolition sentiment obliged him to migrate southward, his slaves looked back to their old home as a paradise. But with years the term Dixie's Land was transferred to their new home and was taken up by both white and black as a name for the South. Emmet's production was sung for the first time on Monday night, September 19, 1859, at 472 Broadway, New York City, where Bryant's Minstrels were then showing. It enjoyed instant popularity. Its vogue in the South was begun in New Orleans in the Spring of 1861. Mrs. John Woods was then playing at the New Orleans Varieties Theater in John Brougham's burlesque of "Pocahontas." In the last scene was a zouave march. At the first performance the zouaves were led by Miss Susan Denin, singing "Dixie," and reappearing seven times in answer to the persistent applause. The whole South took it up.

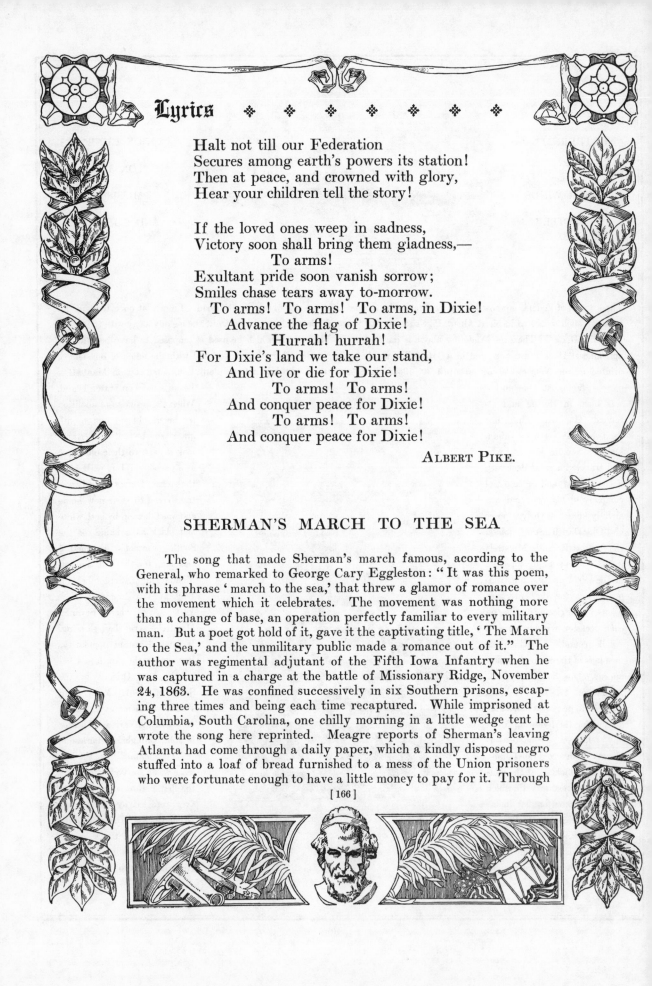

Halt not till our Federation
Secures among earth's powers its station!
Then at peace, and crowned with glory,
Hear your children tell the story!

If the loved ones weep in sadness,
Victory soon shall bring them gladness,—
    To arms!
Exultant pride soon vanish sorrow;
Smiles chase tears away to-morrow.
    To arms! To arms! To arms, in Dixie!
        Advance the flag of Dixie!
            Hurrah! hurrah!
For Dixie's land we take our stand,
    And live or die for Dixie!
        To arms! To arms!
    And conquer peace for Dixie!
        To arms! To arms!
    And conquer peace for Dixie!

ALBERT PIKE.

SHERMAN'S MARCH TO THE SEA

The song that made Sherman's march famous, acording to the General, who remarked to George Cary Eggleston: "It was this poem, with its phrase 'march to the sea,' that threw a glamor of romance over the movement which it celebrates. The movement was nothing more than a change of base, an operation perfectly familiar to every military man. But a poet got hold of it, gave it the captivating title, 'The March to the Sea,' and the unmilitary public made a romance out of it." The author was regimental adjutant of the Fifth Iowa Infantry when he was captured in a charge at the battle of Missionary Ridge, November 24, 1863. He was confined successively in six Southern prisons, escaping three times and being each time recaptured. While imprisoned at Columbia, South Carolina, one chilly morning in a little wedge tent he wrote the song here reprinted. Meagre reports of Sherman's leaving Atlanta had come through a daily paper, which a kindly disposed negro stuffed into a loaf of bread furnished to a mess of the Union prisoners who were fortunate enough to have a little money to pay for it. Through

"AND WE STORMED THE WILD HILLS OF RESACA"

A SCENE AFTER SHERMAN'S MARCH

This freshly turned earth on the entrenchments at Resaca, over which the weeds have shot up in the spring weather of 1864, witnessed the even-handed struggle of May 14–15th, to which Byers refers. The heavy timber made the movement of troops very difficult, but it was of advantage to the Confederates behind their fortifications. In one case the attackers under General Henry M. Judah were moving up a valley to storm a salient, when they were met by a murderous fire from the edge of the woods in front as well as from the right. The bluffs proved too steep for even their dash and courage. At another point General J. D. Cox's men charged directly upon the entrenchments and drove the opposing force out after a fierce struggle. Artillery from higher up the slope then opened upon the Federals, so that they had to use the reverse of the work just captured, strengthening it with small timber, like that in the picture, till reënforcements came. All the fighting was of this nature. As soon as Sherman got into position to march across the river to Johnston's rear, that wary general retreated, leaving all the "wild hills" in the possession of the Federals.

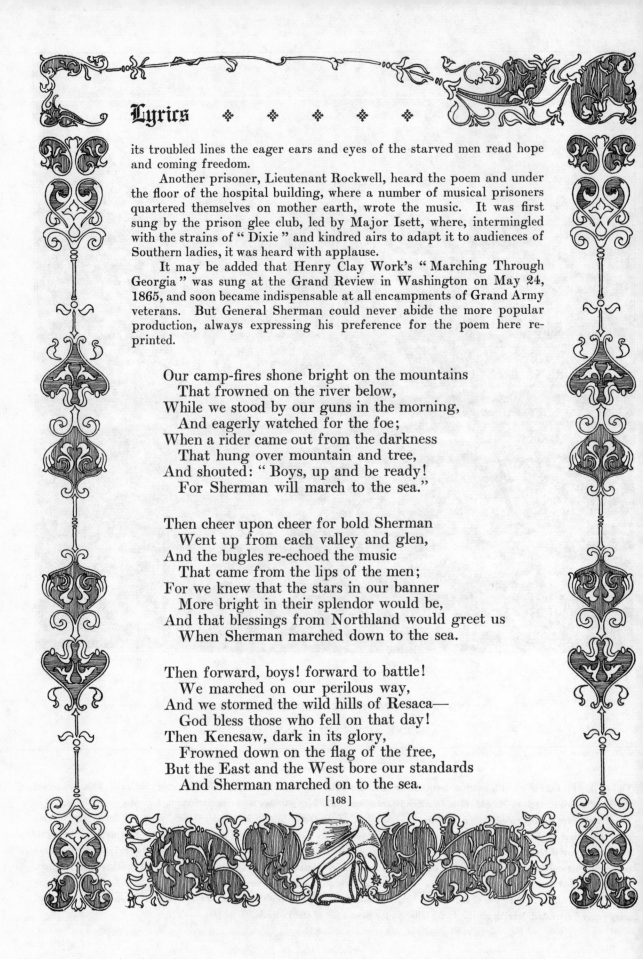

its troubled lines the eager ears and eyes of the starved men read hope and coming freedom.

Another prisoner, Lieutenant Rockwell, heard the poem and under the floor of the hospital building, where a number of musical prisoners quartered themselves on mother earth, wrote the music. It was first sung by the prison glee club, led by Major Isett, where, intermingled with the strains of "Dixie" and kindred airs to adapt it to audiences of Southern ladies, it was heard with applause.

It may be added that Henry Clay Work's "Marching Through Georgia" was sung at the Grand Review in Washington on May 24, 1865, and soon became indispensable at all encampments of Grand Army veterans. But General Sherman could never abide the more popular production, always expressing his preference for the poem here reprinted.

Our camp-fires shone bright on the mountains
    That frowned on the river below,
While we stood by our guns in the morning,
    And eagerly watched for the foe;
When a rider came out from the darkness
    That hung over mountain and tree,
And shouted: "Boys, up and be ready!
    For Sherman will march to the sea."

Then cheer upon cheer for bold Sherman
    Went up from each valley and glen,
And the bugles re-echoed the music
    That came from the lips of the men;
For we knew that the stars in our banner
    More bright in their splendor would be,
And that blessings from Northland would greet us
    When Sherman marched down to the sea.

Then forward, boys! forward to battle!
    We marched on our perilous way,
And we stormed the wild hills of Resaca—
    God bless those who fell on that day!
Then Kenesaw, dark in its glory,
    Frowned down on the flag of the free,
But the East and the West bore our standards
    And Sherman marched on to the sea.

"WHEN SHERMAN MARCHED DOWN TO THE SEA"

This somber view of Fort McAllister, on the Great Ogeechee River, was taken soon after the termination of Sherman's famous march. As Byers sings of the achievement, the movement began in May, 1864, with the advance against Johnston, but the usual understanding is of the march from Atlanta, which began on November 15th. On December 10th, Sherman's army had closed in on the works around Savannah. The general's first move was to make connections with the fleet and its supplies. The country about Savannah afforded nothing but rice, which did not satisfy an army that for a month had been living on pigs, chickens, and turkeys. But the only convenient channel of communication was the Great Ogeechee, guarded by the fort that had defied the navy for two years. Its storming by Hazen, on December 17th, was welcome to Sherman's men above most victories. A foraging party had rowed down the river into Ossabaw Sound and met a steamer coming in, the crew of which said that it was the *Nemeha* and had Major-General Foster on board. The party answered: "Oh, we've got twenty-seven major-generals up at camp. What we want is hardtack!" On December 21st, the army entered Savannah. Sherman's achievement was world-famous.

"OUR CAMP-FIRES SHONE BRIGHT ON THE MOUNTAIN"

The war-time view of the Chattanooga River, from Lookout Mountain, gives a good notion of the country through which Sherman advanced on the first half of his "march to the sea." Byers reckons this famous military operation as beginning with the campaign against Joseph E. Johnston. Sherman's forces were centered at Ringgold, a little south of the point here pictured. The fighting in this campaign was of the most picturesque variety. Johnston was a master of defensive warfare. The mountainous nature of the country enabled him to entrench his forces at every step. He could always wait to be attacked, could always be sure of having the advantage in position, and could retreat through the passes to a new stand before the Federal forces could arrive. The Union troops, on the other hand, must advance along the railway to keep in touch with their base of supplies in the rear, must fight their way through forests, over boulders, across torrents and broad rivers, ever in the face of a vigilant foe. Thus from May 6th to September 2d, 1864, Sherman fought every foot of his way into the city of Atlanta. "Each valley and glen" had seen some of his sturdy followers fall, but his victorious banners fluttered in the breeze on every mountain side

"BUT TO–DAY FAIR SAVANNAH IS OURS"

Byers' line celebrates a triumph fresh when this charming view of the Savannah River was taken. Drooping live-oaks and tangled vines give the scene an air of almost tropical luxuriance. The far gleam of the river from across the level marshes adds just the picture to accompany the song "that echoed o'er river and lea." The march from Atlanta to Savannah is the operation usually thought of when the famous phrase, "March to the Sea" is uttered. It was November 15, 1864, when Sherman's army "swept out from Atlanta's grim walls" after the total destruction of the military resources of the city. The undertaking was considered one of unparalleled daring. For more than a month the North heard not a word of Sherman and his men. Conjectures as to his whereabouts and activities were of the wildest. But, as a matter of fact, the undertaking was proving one long holiday. There were no Confederate troops sufficient to check the Northern forces. Their foraging parties provided all the soldiers could desire. Indeed, Sherman wrote his wife, "We have lived sumptuously,—turkeys, chickens, and sweet potatoes all the way." Yet the greatness of the expedition grew on him. Before the end of the year he wrote, "Like one who has walked a narrow plank, I look back and wonder if I really did it." He did well to wonder. The journals of the civilized world were loud in his praise. Scores of poems heralded him. Byers' song gave additional fame by its captivatingly romantic title.

Lyrics ✦ ✦ ✦ ✦ ✦ ✦ ✦ ✦ ✦

Still onward we pressed till our banners
   Swept out from Atlanta's grim walls,
And the blood of the patriot dampened
   The soil where the traitor flag falls.
We paused not to weep for the fallen,
   Who sleep by each river and tree,
But we twined them a wreath of the laurel,
   And Sherman marched on to the sea.

Oh, proud was our army that morning,
   That stood where the pine darkly towers,
When Sherman said, "Boys, you are weary,
   But to-day fair Savannah is ours."
Then sang we a song for our chieftain,
   That echoed o'er river and lea,
And the stars in our banner shone brighter
   When Sherman marched down to the sea.

SAMUEL HAWKINS MARSHALL BYERS.

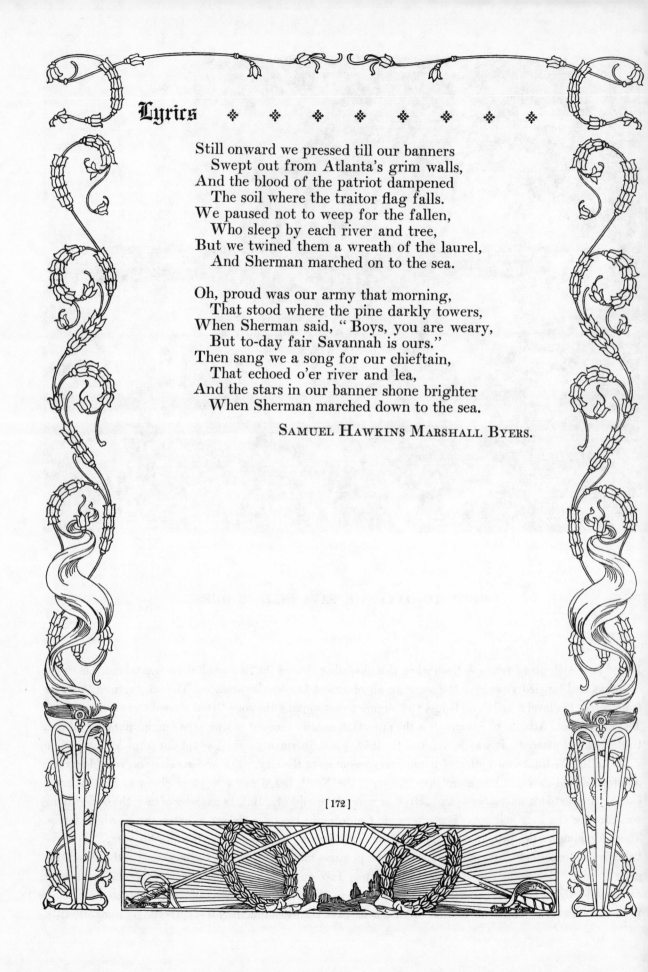

VII

THE

LIGHTER

SIDE

"SAMBO'S RIGHT TO BE KILT"

COLORED TROOPS AT DRILL—VICKSBURG, 1864

TO ILLUSTRATE "SAMBO'S RIGHT TO BE KILT"

A beautiful Southern mansion stands in flickering shadows of walnut and elm and white oak, and in front are some of the negro troops that have been formed from "contrabands." The passions of the period waxed particularly bitter over the question of employing Negroes in warfare. Charles Graham Halpine comes to the rescue, in his poem that follows on page 176, with a saving sense of Irish humor. He suggests that "men who object to Sambo should take his place and fight." As for himself, he will object not at all "if Sambo's body

GUARD OF COLORED TROOPS AT THE PROVOST–MARSHAL'S—BEAUFORT, NORTH CAROLINA, 1864

should stop a ball that was coming for me direct." This recalls Artemas Ward's announcement of his own patriotism, which he said he had carried so far that he was willing for all his wife's relatives to go to the front! The human side of this problem helps to solve it, as with others. Certainly, the line above presents a firm and soldierly front. Many of the colored regiments came to be well-disciplined and serviceable. Their bravery is attested by the loss of life at Battery Wagner and in the charges at the Petersburg crater.

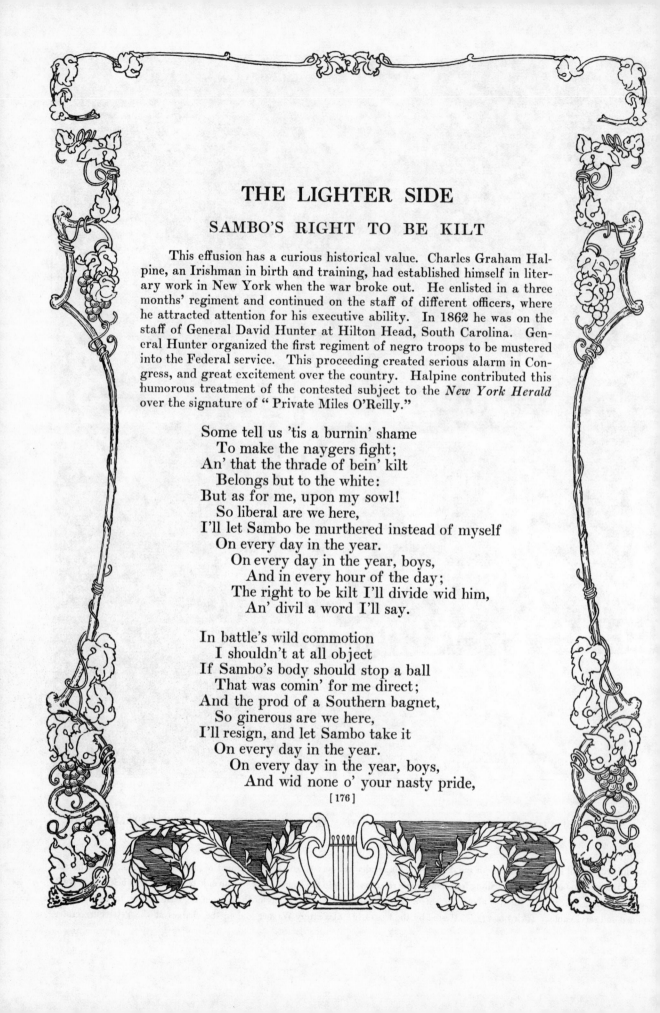

THE LIGHTER SIDE

SAMBO'S RIGHT TO BE KILT

This effusion has a curious historical value. Charles Graham Halpine, an Irishman in birth and training, had established himself in literary work in New York when the war broke out. He enlisted in a three months' regiment and continued on the staff of different officers, where he attracted attention for his executive ability. In 1862 he was on the staff of General David Hunter at Hilton Head, South Carolina. General Hunter organized the first regiment of negro troops to be mustered into the Federal service. This proceeding created serious alarm in Congress, and great excitement over the country. Halpine contributed this humorous treatment of the contested subject to the *New York Herald* over the signature of "Private Miles O'Reilly."

Some tell us 'tis a burnin' shame
    To make the naygers fight;
An' that the thrade of bein' kilt
    Belongs but to the white:
But as for me, upon my sowl!
    So liberal are we here,
I'll let Sambo be murthered instead of myself
    On every day in the year.
        On every day in the year, boys,
            And in every hour of the day;
        The right to be kilt I'll divide wid him,
            An' divil a word I'll say.

In battle's wild commotion
    I shouldn't at all object
If Sambo's body should stop a ball
    That was comin' for me direct;
And the prod of a Southern bagnet,
    So ginerous are we here,
I'll resign, and let Sambo take it
    On every day in the year.
        On every day in the year, boys,
            And wid none o' your nasty pride,

"I'LL LET SAMBO BE MURTHERED INSTEAD OF MYSELF"
COLORED INFANTRY AT FORT LINCOLN, 1862

This picture possesses especial interest as the subject of the following comment by Major George Haven Putnam (a contributor to Volume I of this HISTORY) from his experience as a Federal officer in charge of colored troops: Late in the war, when the Confederacy was sadly in need of fresh supplies of men, the proposition was more than once brought up in the Confederate Congress and elsewhere for the arming of the slaves or of a selection of the slaves. But such a step was never ventured upon. On the Northern side, as early as 1862, regiments were formed of the colored residents of the North, the first two being the famous Fifty-fourth and Fifty-fifth Massachusetts. These men represented, of course, a fairly high average of intelligence and of education, and they did brilliant fighting. In the course of the succeeding two years many regiments were organized out of the plantation negroes as they made their way across into Federal lines, or as Federal control extended over plantation country. These men also rendered earnest, faithful, and usually effective service. They lacked, as was quite natural, individual initiative. They did not do good fighting in a skirmish-line. They wanted to be in touch, shoulder to shoulder, and within immediate reach of the commander's word; but there is hardly an instance in which, when once under fire, they did not fulfil their duty pluckily and persistently. The army rosters show that more than 150,000 colored men fought under the Stars and Stripes.

All my right in a Southern bagnet prod
 Wid Sambo I'll divide!

The men who object to Sambo
 Should take his place and fight;
And it's betther to have a nayger's hue
 Than a liver that's wake an' white.
Though Sambo's black as the ace of spades,
 His finger a thrigger can pull,
And his eye runs sthraight on the barrel-sights
 From undher its thatch of wool.
 So hear me all, boys darlin',
  Don't think I'm tippin' you chaff,
 The right to be kilt we'll divide wid him,
  And give him the largest half!

CHARLES GRAHAM HALPINE.

THE YEAR OF JUBILEE

  According to common report a body of negro troops sang these words as they entered Richmond on the morning of April 3, 1865. George Cary Eggleston adds a special interest to the song: " It is an interesting fact, illustrative of the elasticity of spirit shown by the losers in the great contest, that the song, which might have been supposed to be peculiarly offensive to their wounded pride and completely out of harmony with their deep depression and chagrin, became at once a favorite among them, and was sung with applause by young men and maidens in well nigh every house in Virginia."

Say, darkeys, hab you seen de massa,
 Wid de muffstash on he face,
Go long de road some time dis mornin',
 Like he gwine leabe de place?
He see de smoke way up de ribber
 Whar de Lincum gunboats lay;
He took he hat an' leff berry sudden,
 And I spose he's runned away.
  De massa run, ha, ha!
  De darkey stay, ho, ho!
  It mus' be now de kingdum comin',
  An' de yar ob jubilo.

"AND HIS EYE RUNS STHRAIGHT ON THE BARREL SIGHTS"

These Negro pickets near Dutch Gap Canal in 1864 were posing proudly for their photograph, unconscious that they were illustrating Halpine's line so closely. The natural love of the Negro for imitating the white folks was not the only trait that distinguished the colored troops at Dutch Gap. Work on the canal proved to be very dangerous. The Confederate sharpshooters in the vicinity were continually firing at the men from tree-tops, and several mortars were continually dropping bombs among the squads, who had to seek refuge in dug-outs. In the fall of 1864 most of the labor was performed by colored troops. General P. S. Michie reports that they "displayed the greatest courage and fortitude, and maintained under the most trying circumstances their usual good humor and cheerful disposition." Such a record may encourage their well-wishers.

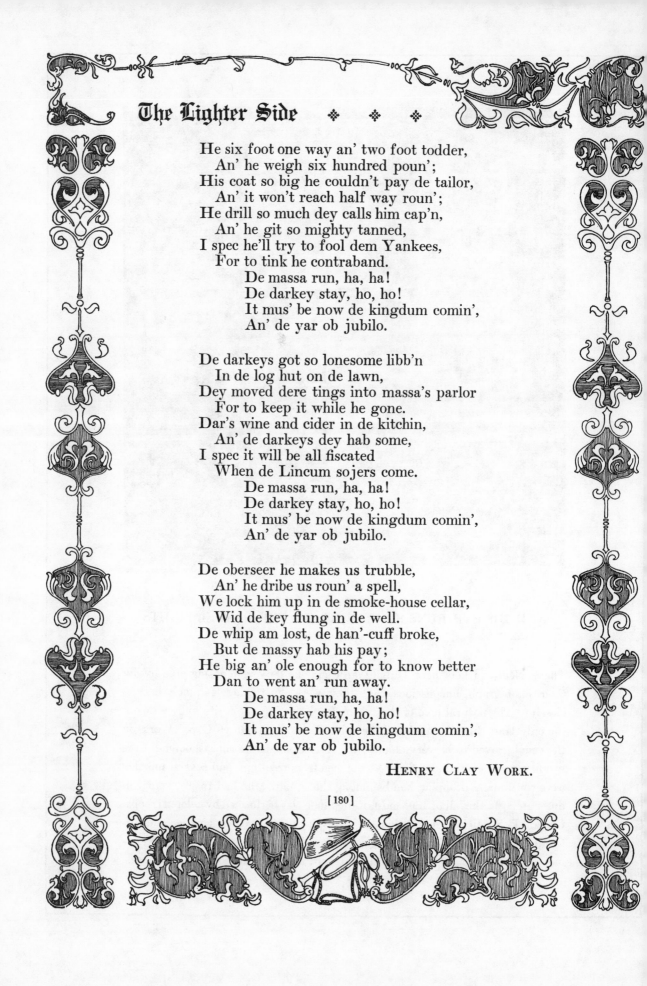

The Lighter Side ❖ ❖ ❖

He six foot one way an' two foot todder,
 An' he weigh six hundred poun';
His coat so big he couldn't pay de tailor,
 An' it won't reach half way roun';
He drill so much dey calls him cap'n,
 An' he git so mighty tanned,
I spec he'll try to fool dem Yankees,
 For to tink he contraband.
  De massa run, ha, ha!
  De darkey stay, ho, ho!
  It mus' be now de kingdum comin',
  An' de yar ob jubilo.

De darkeys got so lonesome libb'n
 In de log hut on de lawn,
Dey moved dere tings into massa's parlor
 For to keep it while he gone.
Dar's wine and cider in de kitchin,
 An' de darkeys dey hab some,
I spec it will be all fiscated
 When de Lincum sojers come.
  De massa run, ha, ha!
  De darkey stay, ho, ho!
  It mus' be now de kingdum comin',
  An' de yar ob jubilo.

De oberseer he makes us trubble,
 An' he dribe us roun' a spell,
We lock him up in de smoke-house cellar,
 Wid de key flung in de well.
De whip am lost, de han'-cuff broke,
 But de massy hab his pay;
He big an' ole enough for to know better
 Dan to went an' run away.
  De massa run, ha, ha!
  De darkey stay, ho, ho!
  It mus' be now de kingdum comin',
  An' de yar ob jubilo.

HENRY CLAY WORK.

[180]

"CONTRABAN"

NEGRO TEAMSTERS NEAR BUTLER'S SIGNAL TOWER, BERMUDA HUNDRED, 1864

The history and nature of "contraband of war," so expressively illustrated by this photograph, are thus explained by George Haven Putnam: Early in the war, General Benjamin F. Butler invented the term "contraband," which came to be accepted as the most convenient classification for the colored refugee who had made his way within the Federal lines and who, while no longer a slave or a piece of property, was not yet accepted as a person. It was the legal theory of Butler that the property rights in the refugee who had been a slave had, under war conditions, been annulled. Throughout the war, the information of happenings within the enemy's lines was frequently enough brought to our headquarters by the (more or less) "intelligent contraband." As far as my experience goes, the colored reporter was always willing and eager to help. I know of no single instance on record in which false or misleading information was knowingly given by the colored man; but this information was, nevertheless, in a large number of cases by no means trustworthy. The darkey had no capacity for accuracy of observation or for precision of statement. An enormous allowance had to be made for his imagination when he was describing to us the number of the enemy's troops that were in position or that possibly were advancing to the attack. His imagination worked most frequently on the apprehensive side. His experience had made hopefulness somewhat difficult for him.

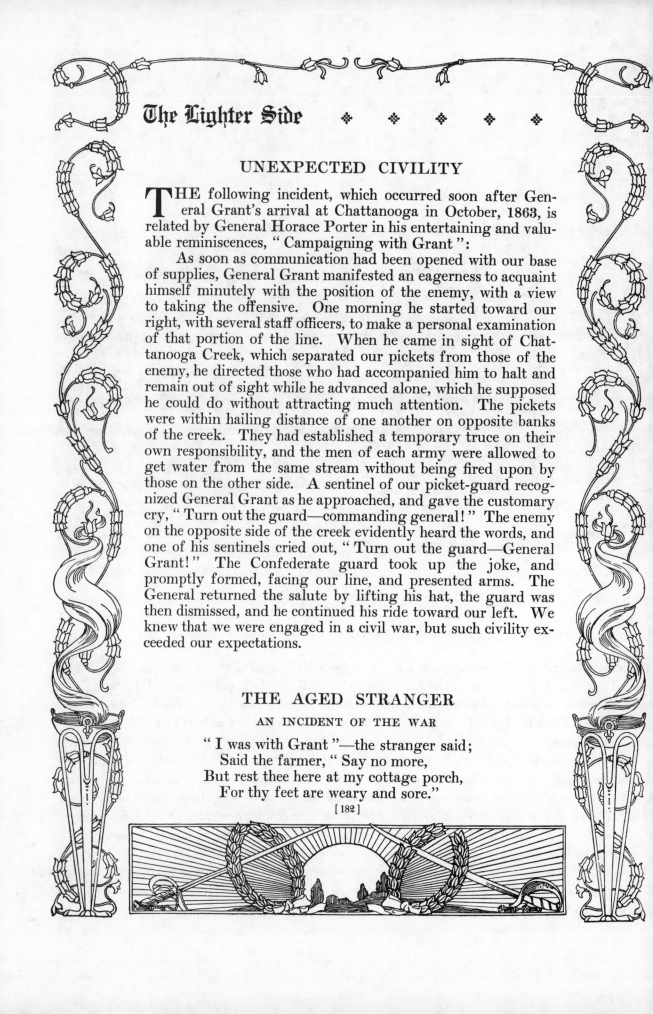

UNEXPECTED CIVILITY

THE following incident, which occurred soon after General Grant's arrival at Chattanooga in October, 1863, is related by General Horace Porter in his entertaining and valuable reminiscences, "Campaigning with Grant":

As soon as communication had been opened with our base of supplies, General Grant manifested an eagerness to acquaint himself minutely with the position of the enemy, with a view to taking the offensive. One morning he started toward our right, with several staff officers, to make a personal examination of that portion of the line. When he came in sight of Chattanooga Creek, which separated our pickets from those of the enemy, he directed those who had accompanied him to halt and remain out of sight while he advanced alone, which he supposed he could do without attracting much attention. The pickets were within hailing distance of one another on opposite banks of the creek. They had established a temporary truce on their own responsibility, and the men of each army were allowed to get water from the same stream without being fired upon by those on the other side. A sentinel of our picket-guard recognized General Grant as he approached, and gave the customary cry, "Turn out the guard—commanding general!" The enemy on the opposite side of the creek evidently heard the words, and one of his sentinels cried out, "Turn out the guard—General Grant!" The Confederate guard took up the joke, and promptly formed, facing our line, and presented arms. The General returned the salute by lifting his hat, the guard was then dismissed, and he continued his ride toward our left. We knew that we were engaged in a civil war, but such civility exceeded our expectations.

THE AGED STRANGER

AN INCIDENT OF THE WAR

"I was with Grant"—the stranger said;
Said the farmer, "Say no more,
But rest thee here at my cottage porch,
For thy feet are weary and sore."

"DE DARKEYS GOT SO LONESOME"

ILLUSTRATION FOR "THE YEAR OF JUBILEE"

The crinoline of the old "auntie" in the center and the quaint sunbonnets of her companions are distinguish-
ing marks of the war-time scene—a Mississippi plantation, where the darkies have gathered to relieve
some of the lonesomeness of which Work writes. It was one of the noteworthy features of the war that the
people who, before the conflict, had been supposed to be on the point of rising and inaugurating a race-war,
remained quietly at work on the large plantations. Frequently only women were left to direct the labor
of the slaves. Several diaries from various parts of the South tell of the continued affection and even devotion of these colored people. It is only of the close of the war that the scenes in "The Year of Jubilee" can
be imagined. But the picture above is typical of all the four years of the conflict and of later negro life.

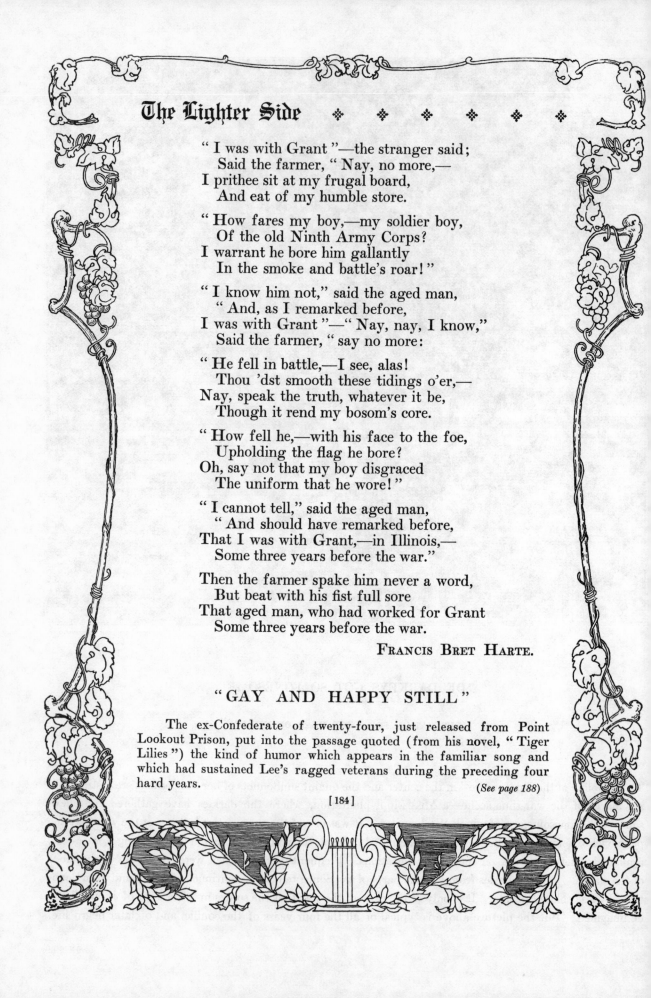

The Lighter Side ❖ ❖ ❖ ❖ ❖ ❖

" I was with Grant "—the stranger said;
　　Said the farmer, " Nay, no more,—
I prithee sit at my frugal board,
　　And eat of my humble store.

" How fares my boy,—my soldier boy,
　　Of the old Ninth Army Corps?
I warrant he bore him gallantly
　　In the smoke and battle's roar! "

" I know him not," said the aged man,
　　" And, as I remarked before,
I was with Grant "—" Nay, nay, I know,"
　　Said the farmer, " say no more:

" He fell in battle,—I see, alas!
　　Thou 'dst smooth these tidings o'er,—
Nay, speak the truth, whatever it be,
　　Though it rend my bosom's core.

" How fell he,—with his face to the foe,
　　Upholding the flag he bore?
Oh, say not that my boy disgraced
　　The uniform that he wore! "

" I cannot tell," said the aged man,
　　" And should have remarked before,
That I was with Grant,—in Illinois,—
　　Some three years before the war."

Then the farmer spake him never a word,
　　But beat with his fist full sore
That aged man, who had worked for Grant
　　Some three years before the war.

　　　　　　　FRANCIS BRET HARTE.

"GAY AND HAPPY STILL"

The ex-Confederate of twenty-four, just released from Point Lookout Prison, put into the passage quoted (from his novel, " Tiger Lilies ") the kind of humor which appears in the familiar song and which had sustained Lee's ragged veterans during the preceding four hard years. (See page 188)

IMPOSING OFFICERS AND FOREIGN ATTACHÉS—

WHO UNBEND BETWEEN BATTLES—FALMOUTH, VIRGINIA, APRIL, 1863

Lest the reader suppose the life of the Civil War soldier was unrelieved by any sallies of playfulness, these photographs of 1863 are reproduced. No schoolboys in their wildest larks could engage in a struggle of more mock-desperate nature than that waged by these officers of the Army of the Potomac, with the English, French, and Austrian attachés come to report to their Governments how Americans made war. Boxes and chairs have been scattered hither and yon; swords are slashing in deadly combat; bottles are wielded by some in the hand-to-hand mêlée. The burly attaché at the right is even preparing to dig a grave for the unfortunate slain in the combat.

AT THE SUTLER'S STORE

A LIFELIKE GROUP

A high degree of artistic feeling and skill was shown by the war photographer who preserved this band of joking soldiers beside a sutler's store. Few photographic feats are as difficult, even to-day, as the successful portraying of such a number of different subjects, in poses so remarkably diversified, and under such abrupt color contrasts of light and shadow. Evidently, the army was in a permanent camp when this picture was taken; for it was then that the sutlers would open up their stocks of canned goods, soft drinks, playing cards, handkerchiefs, paper collars, and such luxuries, enjoyed by the boys of '61 only at infrequent intervals. Sometimes the soldiers rebelled against the storekeeper's extortionate prices, and once in a while, on the eve of a forward movement, they would sack the little shanty of its contents by way of reprisal.

CAMP HUMOR

FACETIOUSNESS OF A SUTLER WITH THE WESTERN ARMIES

The signs about this sutler's store in Tennessee display the rude wit of the soldier in camp. The name over the little shanty contains an affectation of French elegance that is amusing even to-day. The misspelling in the announcement, "Meels at all Ours," may not have appealed to all the frequenters as strongly as to us, but the imposing declaration that it was kept on the European plan came to be understood by everyone. There was no humor at all in some of the signs, such as the warning over the door "No Tick," as many a lad with empty pockets must have found when he felt very thirsty for "XXXX Ale." No one can be so sure of the other sign "No Licker Sold to Soljers." Probably the arrangements could be made in the dark of the moon for suspension of this grim regulation. The sutler's store was a center of the social life of the squad in off hours. Here they would gather to chat over the events of the last campaign, to compare notes on the various leaders, to discuss the probabilities of the next advance, and to swap yarns from all possible sources.

Lieutenant Flemington spurred his horse forward and turned him round full-face to the party.

"Gentlemen, there's some mistake about all this!" said he, as the men stopped, laughing at a puzzled expression which overspread his face: "for whereas, this honorable company of six has been for three years or more toilsomely marching on foot with an infantry regiment—but now rides good horses: and whereas, this honorable company of six has been for three years feeding upon hard-tack and bacon which grew continually harder and also less and wormier—but now devours Virginia biscuit and spring-chickens and ham and eggs and—and all the other things that came on, and went off, the table at mine host's of the Court House this morning . . . and whereas, we have hitherto draggled along in pantaloons that we could put on a dozen ways by as many holes, have worn coats that afforded no protection to anything but the insects congregated in the seams of the same, have had shirts that—shirts that—that—at any rate we *have* had shirts—but now do fare forth prankt in all manner of gorgeous array, such as gray jackets with fillima-gree on the sleeves of 'em, and hussar-breeches, and cavalry-boots, and O shade of Jones of Georgia! with spurs to boot and clean white collars to neck: and whereas, we have been accustomed to think a mud-hole a luxury in the way of beds, and have been wont to beg Heaven as its greatest boon to man, not to let the cavalry ride over us without waking us up to see 'em do it—but now do sleep between white sheets without fear of aught but losing our senses from sleeping so intensely: and whereas, finally, all these things are contrary to the ordinary course of nature and are not known save as dim recollections of a previous state of existence in itself extremely hypothetical, therefore, be it resolved and it is hereby resolved:

"Unanimously," from the five.

"That this—figure—at present on this horse and clothed with these sumptuous paraphernalia of pompous war, is *not* B. Chauncey Flemington, that is to say (to borrow a term from the German metaphysics) is Not-Me, that this horse is not *my* horse, this paraphernalia not *my* paraphernalia, that para-ditto not *your* para-ditto, that this road is *no* road, and the whole affair a dream or phantasmagory of the Devil for no purpose but to embitter the waking from it."

SIDNEY LANIER.

VIII

BETWEEN
BATTLES

"THE SCREAMING MISSILES FELL"

THIS LINE FROM "THE PRIDE OF BATTERY B," AN EPISODE OF ANTIETAM (PAGE 196), IS ILLUSTRATED BY THE HUMBLE DUNKER CHURCH AROUND WHICH RAGED THE CENTER OF THE CONFLICT — THE PHOTOGRAPH FOLLOWED SOON, BEFORE THE SHOT HOLES HAD BEEN REPAIRED

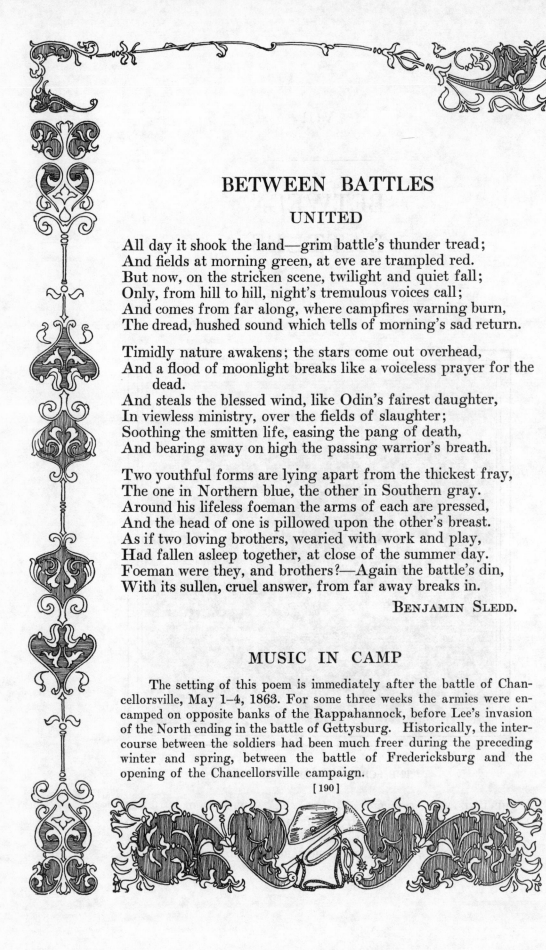

BETWEEN BATTLES

UNITED

All day it shook the land—grim battle's thunder tread;
And fields at morning green, at eve are trampled red.
But now, on the stricken scene, twilight and quiet fall;
Only, from hill to hill, night's tremulous voices call;
And comes from far along, where campfires warning burn,
The dread, hushed sound which tells of morning's sad return.

Timidly nature awakens; the stars come out overhead,
And a flood of moonlight breaks like a voiceless prayer for the
 dead.
And steals the blessed wind, like Odin's fairest daughter,
In viewless ministry, over the fields of slaughter;
Soothing the smitten life, easing the pang of death,
And bearing away on high the passing warrior's breath.

Two youthful forms are lying apart from the thickest fray,
The one in Northern blue, the other in Southern gray.
Around his lifeless foeman the arms of each are pressed,
And the head of one is pillowed upon the other's breast.
As if two loving brothers, wearied with work and play,
Had fallen asleep together, at close of the summer day.
Foeman were they, and brothers?—Again the battle's din,
With its sullen, cruel answer, from far away breaks in.

Benjamin Sledd.

MUSIC IN CAMP

  The setting of this poem is immediately after the battle of Chancellorsville, May 1–4, 1863. For some three weeks the armies were encamped on opposite banks of the Rappahannock, before Lee's invasion of the North ending in the battle of Gettysburg. Historically, the intercourse between the soldiers had been much freer during the preceding winter and spring, between the battle of Fredericksburg and the opening of the Chancellorsville campaign.

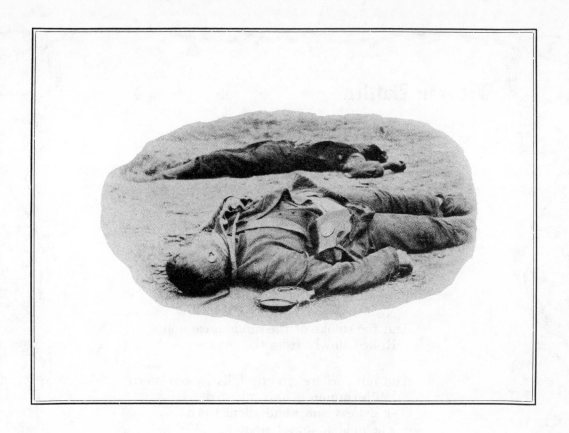

"APART FROM THE THICKEST FRAY"—A SCENE OF '65

CONFEDERATE AND UNION DEAD, SIDE BY SIDE, IN THE TRENCHES AT FORT MAHONE

This spectacle of April 3d, the day after Grant's army stormed the Petersburg defenses, is a strikingly real illustration for the poem "United." With "U. S." on his haversack lies a Union soldier; beyond, a booted Confederate. Every field of the war was a reminder of the brotherhood of the opponents. The same cast of features indicated their common descent. The commands heard above the roar of cannonading or in the midst of desperate charges revealed the identity of their language and heritage from a heroic past. The unyielding fortitude and unhesitating fidelity displayed by the private in the ranks as he followed his appointed leaders was merely additional proof of the Anglo-Saxon blood that flowed in the veins of the embattled countrymen. During the conflict there was, naturally, a great deal of hostility. The ranks opposed were the ranks of the enemy, no matter how close the bonds of relationship, and against the enemy the utmost destruction must be hurled. Yet in the Eastern and Western armies, friendly relations were established whenever the camps of opposing forces were stationed near each other for any length of time. Since the war this feeling has grown until the saddest feature of the irrepressible conflict is that it was waged between brothers, that every battlefield furnished many a spot like the one above.

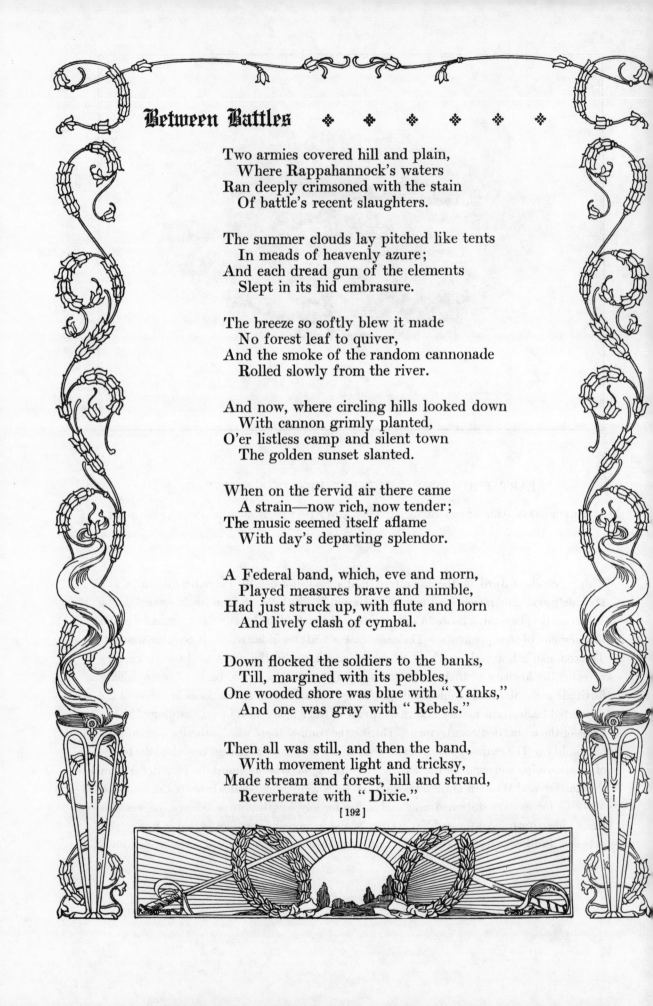

Between Battles ❖ ❖ ❖ ❖ ❖ ❖ ❖

Two armies covered hill and plain,
   Where Rappahannock's waters
Ran deeply crimsoned with the stain
   Of battle's recent slaughters.

The summer clouds lay pitched like tents
   In meads of heavenly azure;
And each dread gun of the elements
   Slept in its hid embrasure.

The breeze so softly blew it made
   No forest leaf to quiver,
And the smoke of the random cannonade
   Rolled slowly from the river.

And now, where circling hills looked down
   With cannon grimly planted,
O'er listless camp and silent town
   The golden sunset slanted.

When on the fervid air there came
   A strain—now rich, now tender;
The music seemed itself aflame
   With day's departing splendor.

A Federal band, which, eve and morn,
   Played measures brave and nimble,
Had just struck up, with flute and horn
   And lively clash of cymbal.

Down flocked the soldiers to the banks,
   Till, margined with its pebbles,
One wooded shore was blue with " Yanks,"
   And one was gray with " Rebels."

Then all was still, and then the band,
   With movement light and tricksy,
Made stream and forest, hill and strand,
   Reverberate with " Dixie."

"WHERE RAPPAHANNOCK'S WATERS RAN DEEPLY CRIMSONED"

hese two views, the lower being the right half of the panorama, are a truly remarkable illustration of Thompson's lines. "Taken uring the battle of May 3, 1863" is the legend written on the print by the Government photographer, Captain A. J. Russell. In the early orning of that day, Gibbon had encrimsoned the stream at this point in crossing the river to cooperate with Sedgwick to attack the onfederate positions on the heights of Fredericksburg. When this picture was taken, Sedgwick was some nine miles away, fighting sperately along a crest near Salem Chapel, from which he was at length driven slowly back through the woods. Sedgwick held his ound through the next day; but on the night of May 4th he recrossed the Rappahannock, this time above Fredericksburg, while the onfederate batteries shelled the bridges over which his troops were marching. The waters were indeed "crimsoned by battle's recent aughters." To the right in the lower half of the panorama are the stone piers of the bridge in the telephoto picture on the next page.

PANORAMA (WITH PICTURE ABOVE) OF FREDERICKSBURG FROM LACY HOUSE

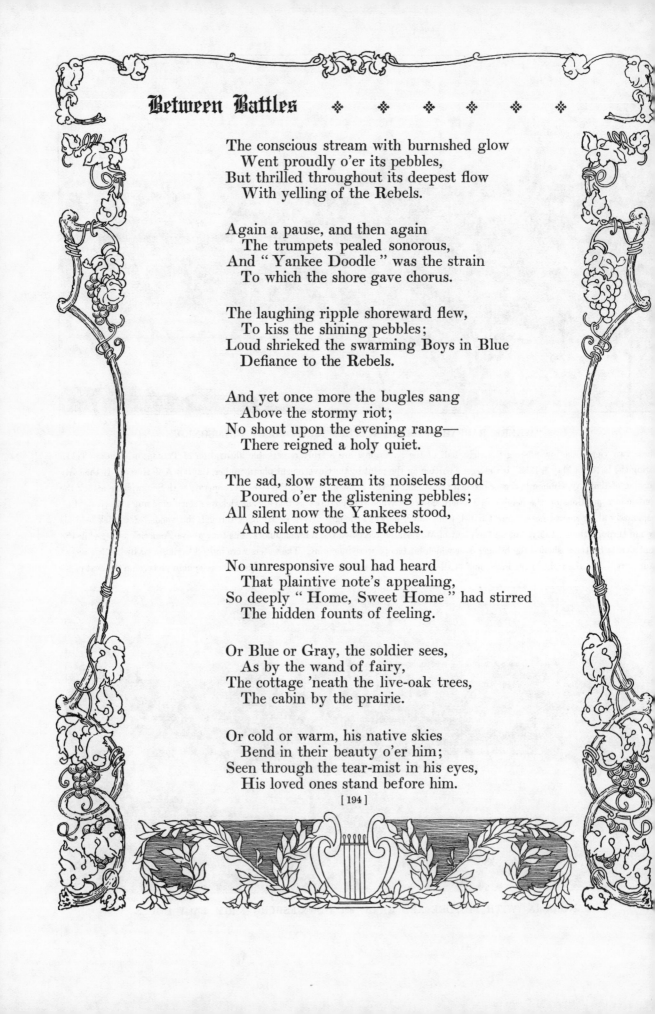

Between Battles

The conscious stream with burnished glow
　Went proudly o'er its pebbles,
But thrilled throughout its deepest flow
　With yelling of the Rebels.

Again a pause, and then again
　The trumpets pealed sonorous,
And " Yankee Doodle " was the strain
　To which the shore gave chorus.

The laughing ripple shoreward flew,
　To kiss the shining pebbles;
Loud shrieked the swarming Boys in Blue
　Defiance to the Rebels.

And yet once more the bugles sang
　Above the stormy riot;
No shout upon the evening rang—
　There reigned a holy quiet.

The sad, slow stream its noiseless flood
　Poured o'er the glistening pebbles;
All silent now the Yankees stood,
　And silent stood the Rebels.

No unresponsive soul had heard
　That plaintive note's appealing,
So deeply " Home, Sweet Home " had stirred
　The hidden founts of feeling.

Or Blue or Gray, the soldier sees,
　As by the wand of fairy,
The cottage 'neath the live-oak trees,
　The cabin by the prairie.

Or cold or warm, his native skies
　Bend in their beauty o'er him;
Seen through the tear-mist in his eyes,
　His loved ones stand before him.

[194]

"AND ONE WAS GRAY WITH REBELS"

The photograph of Confederates on the Fredericksburg end of the ruined railroad bridge is one of the first telephoto photographs anywhere taken. On page 26, Volume I, of this HISTORY is reproduced a photograph made by climbing out along the portion of the bridge standing on the eastern bank of the river. At the left of this picture, the end of a bridge-beam is seen roughly projected against the brick wall. The photograph is proof of the friendly relations existing between the two armies encamped on opposite banks of the Rappahannock. Men in gray, both officer and private, are actually posing before the Federal camera. General Gordon says: "This rollicking sort of intercourse would have been alarming in its intimacy, but for the perfect confidence which the officers of both sides had in their men. Even officers on the opposite banks of this narrow stream would now and then declare a truce among themselves, in order that they might bathe in the little river. Where the water was shallow they would wade in and meet each other in the center and shake hands and 'swap' newspapers and barter Southern tobacco for Yankee coffee. Where the water was deep so that they could not wade in and 'swap,' they sent the articles of traffic across in miniature boats, laden on the southern shore with tobacco and sailed across to the Union side. These little boats were unloaded by the Union soldiers, reloaded, and sent back with Yankee coffee for the Confederates." He then tells of finding a Union soldier lying in the weeds, who said that he came across the river see the Johnnies for a little while, since there was no battle in progress. When General Gordon threatened to send the scantily clad visitor to prison, his own soldiers protested so stoutly that he allowed the "Yank" to swim back to his camp.

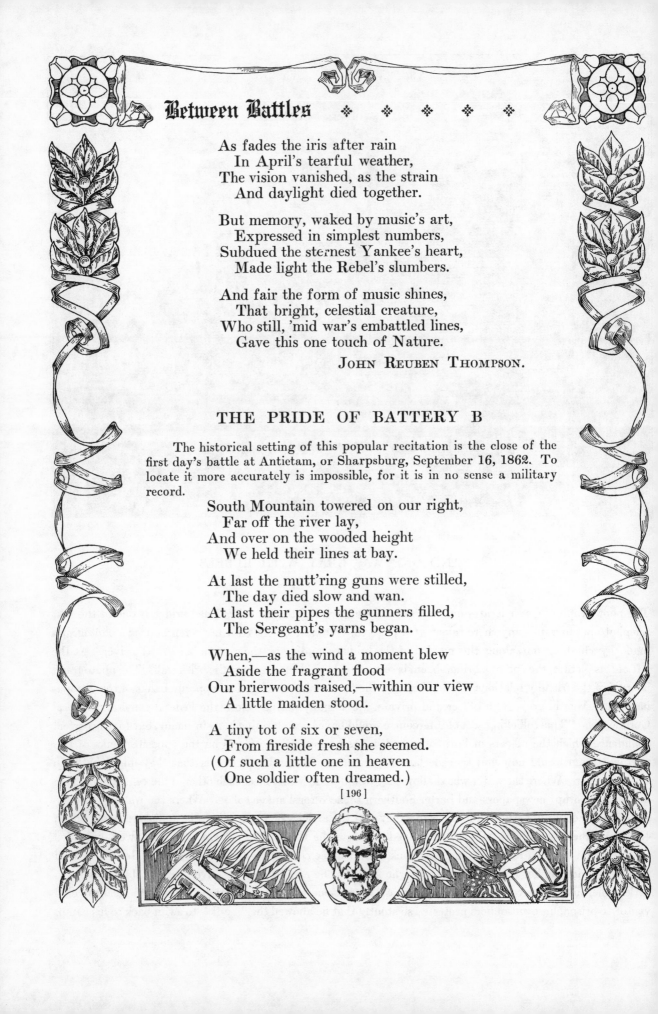

As fades the iris after rain
  In April's tearful weather,
The vision vanished, as the strain
  And daylight died together.

But memory, waked by music's art,
  Expressed in simplest numbers,
Subdued the sternest Yankee's heart,
  Made light the Rebel's slumbers.

And fair the form of music shines,
  That bright, celestial creature,
Who still, 'mid war's embattled lines,
  Gave this one touch of Nature.

JOHN REUBEN THOMPSON.

THE PRIDE OF BATTERY B

The historical setting of this popular recitation is the close of the first day's battle at Antietam, or Sharpsburg, September 16, 1862. To locate it more accurately is impossible, for it is in no sense a military record.

South Mountain towered on our right,
  Far off the river lay,
And over on the wooded height
  We held their lines at bay.

At last the mutt'ring guns were stilled,
  The day died slow and wan.
At last their pipes the gunners filled,
  The Sergeant's yarns began.

When,—as the wind a moment blew
  Aside the fragrant flood
Our brierwoods raised,—within our view
  A little maiden stood.

A tiny tot of six or seven,
  From fireside fresh she seemed.
(Of such a little one in heaven
  One soldier often dreamed.)

[196]

UNION SOLDIERS IN THE JUST DESERTED CONFEDERATE CAMP AT FREDERICKSBURG

The camera has caught a dramatic moment in the period of Thompson's "Music in Camp." It is May 3, 1863, and Sedgwick has carried the heights of Fredericksburg, impregnable to six assaults in December. One who was present reported: "Upon reaching the summit of the sharp hill, after passing through the extensive and well-wooded grounds of the Marye house, an exciting scene met the eye. A single glance exhibited to view the broad plateau alive with fleeing soldiers, riderless horses, and artillery and wagon-trains on a gallop." As no cavalry was at hand, the troops that carried the heights, "exhausted by the night march, the weight of several days' rations and sixty rounds of ammunition, and by the heat, fatigue, and excitement of battle, were allowed to halt for a short time. Many were soon asleep, while others made coffee and partook of their first meal that day." Captain A. J. Russell, the Government photographer who followed the army in its movements, dated this picture, May 3d, the very same day. The soldiers so confident in the picture were obliged to retreat across the Rappahannock, where, in a week or so, Thompson imagines the events of "Music in Camp" to take place. In a month these men were to fight the decisive battle of the war—Gettysburg.

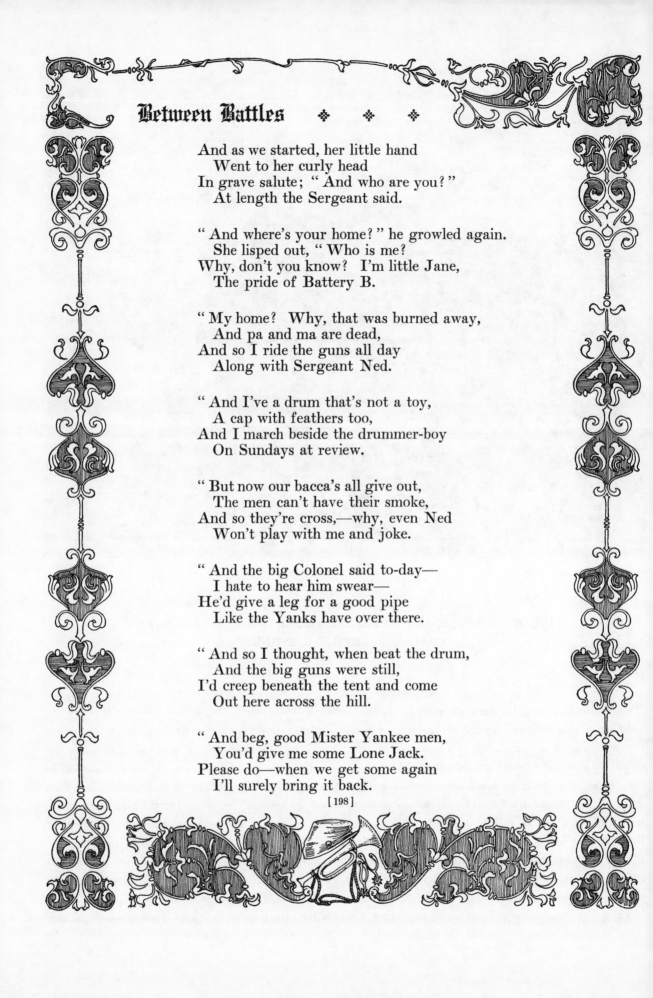

Between Battles ❖ ❖ ❖

And as we started, her little hand
    Went to her curly head
In grave salute; "And who are you?"
    At length the Sergeant said.

"And where's your home?" he growled again.
    She lisped out, "Who is me?
Why, don't you know? I'm little Jane,
    The pride of Battery B.

"My home? Why, that was burned away,
    And pa and ma are dead,
And so I ride the guns all day
    Along with Sergeant Ned.

"And I've a drum that's not a toy,
    A cap with feathers too,
And I march beside the drummer-boy
    On Sundays at review.

"But now our bacca's all give out,
    The men can't have their smoke,
And so they're cross,—why, even Ned
    Won't play with me and joke.

"And the big Colonel said to-day—
    I hate to hear him swear—
He'd give a leg for a good pipe
    Like the Yanks have over there.

"And so I thought, when beat the drum,
    And the big guns were still,
I'd creep beneath the tent and come
    Out here across the hill.

"And beg, good Mister Yankee men,
    You'd give me some Lone Jack.
Please do—when we get some again
    I'll surely bring it back.

"FAR OFF
THE RIVER LAY"
ANTIETAM CREEK IN 1862

BURNSIDE'S
BRIDGE—WHERE
THE FIGHTING RAGED

Thus the placid stream flowed on to join the far Potomac after the sanguinary battle sung by Gass-away in "The Pride of Battery B." In neither the white sunlight falling upon the pillars nor the cool reflection of the foliage is there a suggestion of the death and wounds suffered by nearly 25,000 men in Blue and Gray. Around this very spot some of the hottest fighting raged. Along the hills on either side of the stream were ranged hundreds of guns. All through the first day of the battle, September 16, 1862, they volleyed and thundered at each other across the narrow valley. Both Union and Confederate armies were well supplied with artillery, which was so well served that every one tried to keep behind the crests of the ridges. At the termination of this long-continued duel, the incident of little Jane's visit to the Union battery is described by Gassaway as occurring in the vicin-ity of the peaceful scene here reproduced, from a photograph taken a few days after the battle.

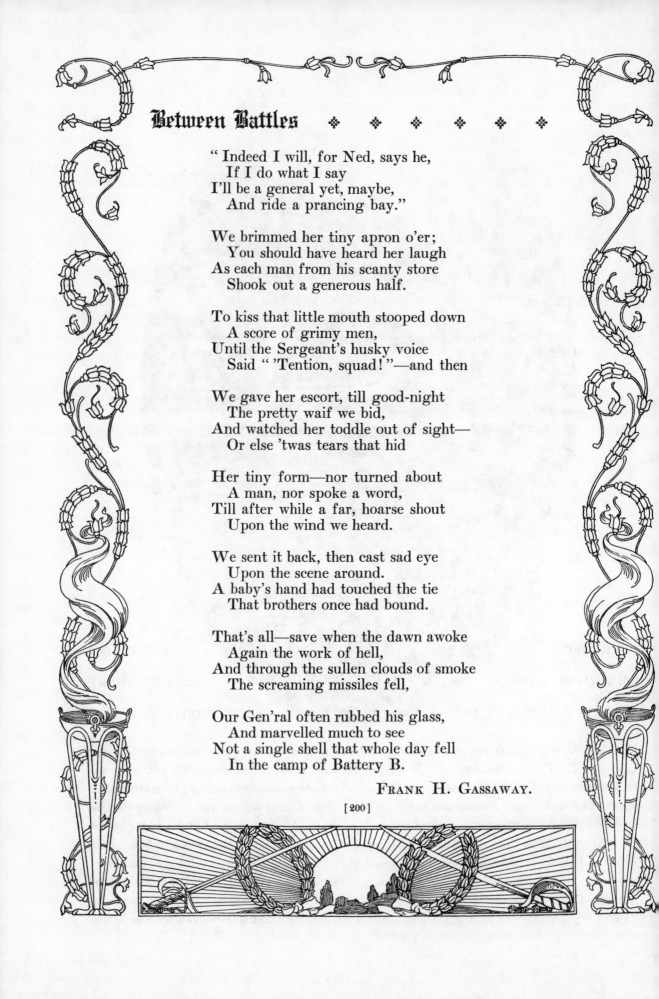

Between Battles ❖ ❖ ❖ ❖ ❖ ❖

"Indeed I will, for Ned, says he,
  If I do what I say
I'll be a general yet, maybe,
  And ride a prancing bay."

We brimmed her tiny apron o'er;
  You should have heard her laugh
As each man from his scanty store
  Shook out a generous half.

To kiss that little mouth stooped down
  A score of grimy men,
Until the Sergeant's husky voice
  Said "'Tention, squad!"—and then

We gave her escort, till good-night
  The pretty waif we bid,
And watched her toddle out of sight—
  Or else 'twas tears that hid

Her tiny form—nor turned about
  A man, nor spoke a word,
Till after while a far, hoarse shout
  Upon the wind we heard.

We sent it back, then cast sad eye
  Upon the scene around.
A baby's hand had touched the tie
  That brothers once had bound.

That's all—save when the dawn awoke
  Again the work of hell,
And through the sullen clouds of smoke
  The screaming missiles fell,

Our Gen'ral often rubbed his glass,
  And marvelled much to see
Not a single shell that whole day fell
  In the camp of Battery B.

FRANK H. GASSAWAY.

"AGAIN THE WORK OF HELL"

With painful realism the camera has furnished an illustration for Gassaway's line in "The Pride of Battery B." But even the horror of this view fails to give a true idea of the fearful slaughter at this point of the battlefield. About nine o'clock the Confederates fighting in the vicinity of the little Dunker Church heard the shout, "They are flanking us!" "This cry spread like an electric shock along the ranks. In a moment they broke and fell to the rear," says General D. H. Hill. In the rear of the fleeing companies General Rodes immediately formed a line along an old sunken road. The soldiers rendered the position more secure by piling rails upon the ridge. Some of these rails are seen scattered along the edge of the ditch. General Hill continues: "It was now apparent that the grand attack would be made upon my position, which was the center of the line. Before reenforcements arrived a heavy force advanced in three parallel lines, with all the precision of a parade day, upon my two brigades. They met with a galling fire, however, recoiled, and fell back; again advanced and again fell back, and finally lay down behind the crest of the hill and kept up an irregular fire." Owing to an unfortunate blunder, Rodes's men retreated, whereupon the Federal troops charged and after a fierce struggle drove the Confederate force from its position. General Hill concludes: "The unparalleled loss of the division shows that, spite of hunger and fatigue, the officers and men fought most heroically." The "Bloody Lane" was full of the men who had defended their position to the bitter end.

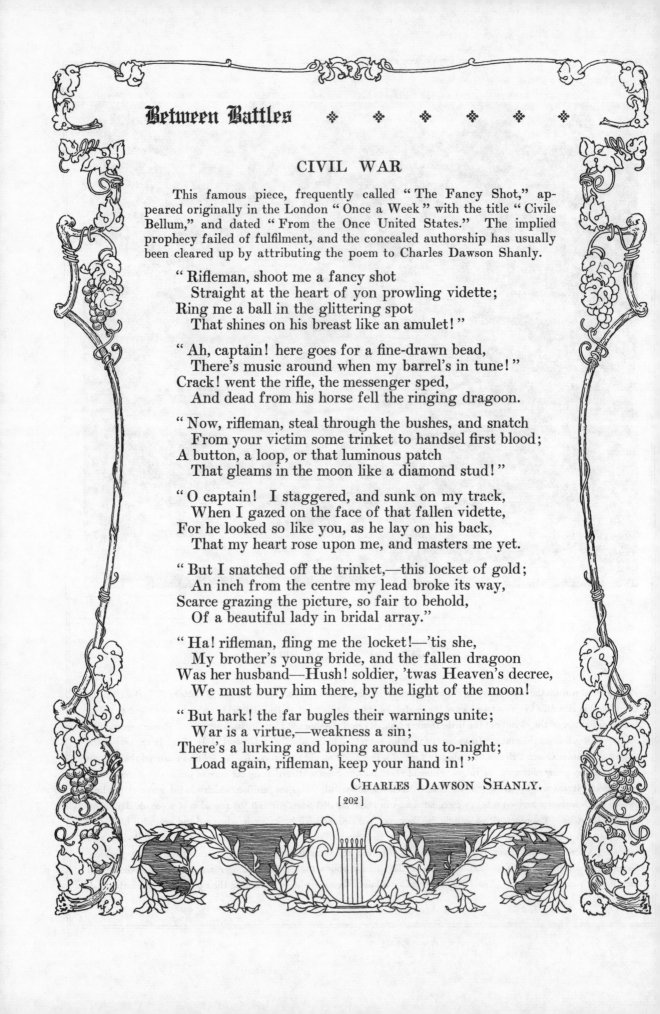

CIVIL WAR

This famous piece, frequently called "The Fancy Shot," appeared originally in the London "Once a Week" with the title "Civile Bellum," and dated "From the Once United States." The implied prophecy failed of fulfilment, and the concealed authorship has usually been cleared up by attributing the poem to Charles Dawson Shanly.

"Rifleman, shoot me a fancy shot
   Straight at the heart of yon prowling vidette;
Ring me a ball in the glittering spot
   That shines on his breast like an amulet!"

"Ah, captain! here goes for a fine-drawn bead,
   There's music around when my barrel's in tune!"
Crack! went the rifle, the messenger sped,
   And dead from his horse fell the ringing dragoon.

"Now, rifleman, steal through the bushes, and snatch
   From your victim some trinket to handsel first blood;
A button, a loop, or that luminous patch
   That gleams in the moon like a diamond stud!"

"O captain! I staggered, and sunk on my track,
   When I gazed on the face of that fallen vidette,
For he looked so like you, as he lay on his back,
   That my heart rose upon me, and masters me yet.

"But I snatched off the trinket,—this locket of gold;
   An inch from the centre my lead broke its way,
Scarce grazing the picture, so fair to behold,
   Of a beautiful lady in bridal array."

"Ha! rifleman, fling me the locket!—'tis she,
   My brother's young bride, and the fallen dragoon
Was her husband—Hush! soldier, 'twas Heaven's decree,
   We must bury him there, by the light of the moon!

"But hark! the far bugles their warnings unite;
   War is a virtue,—weakness a sin;
There's a lurking and loping around us to-night;
   Load again, rifleman, keep your hand in!"

CHARLES DAWSON SHANLY.

X

GETTYSBURG

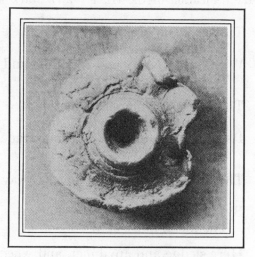

GETTYSBURG
THE HIGH–WATER MARK OF THE WAR

TWO HOSTILE BULLETS IN MID-AIR
TOGETHER SHOCKED
AND SWIFT WERE LOCKED
FOREVER IN A FIRM EMBRACE
—*Lathrop*

This is a picture of which Captain Gordon McCabe of Richmond, Virginia, writes: "I send photographs of two bullets, one Federal, the other Confederate, that met in mid-air and flattened out against each other. The bullets were picked up in 1865 between the 'lines' immediately after the evacuation of Petersburg."

GETTYSBURG

GETTYSBURG

Military critics have generally settled upon the battle of Gettysburg, July 1–3, 1863, as the decisive battle of the war, and the greatest battle in American history. It ended Lee's second invasion of the North, and, together with the fall of Vicksburg, threw the Confederacy upon the defensive and shut out hope of foreign intervention. The poem was written for the dedication of the High Water Mark Monument, July 2, 1892.

There was no union in the land,
   Though wise men labored long
With links of clay and ropes of sand
   To bind the right and wrong.

There was no temper in the blade
   That once could cleave a chain;
Its edge was dull with touch of trade
   And clogged with rust of gain.

The sand and clay must shrink away
   Before the lava tide:
By blows and blood and fire assay
   The metal must be tried.

Here sledge and anvil met, and when
   The furnace fiercest roared,
God's undiscerning workingmen
   Reforged His people's sword.

Enough for them to ask and know
   The moment's duty clear—
The bayonets flashed it there below,
   The guns proclaimed it here:

To do and dare, and die at need,
   But while life lasts, to fight—
For right or wrong a simple creed,
   But simplest for the right.

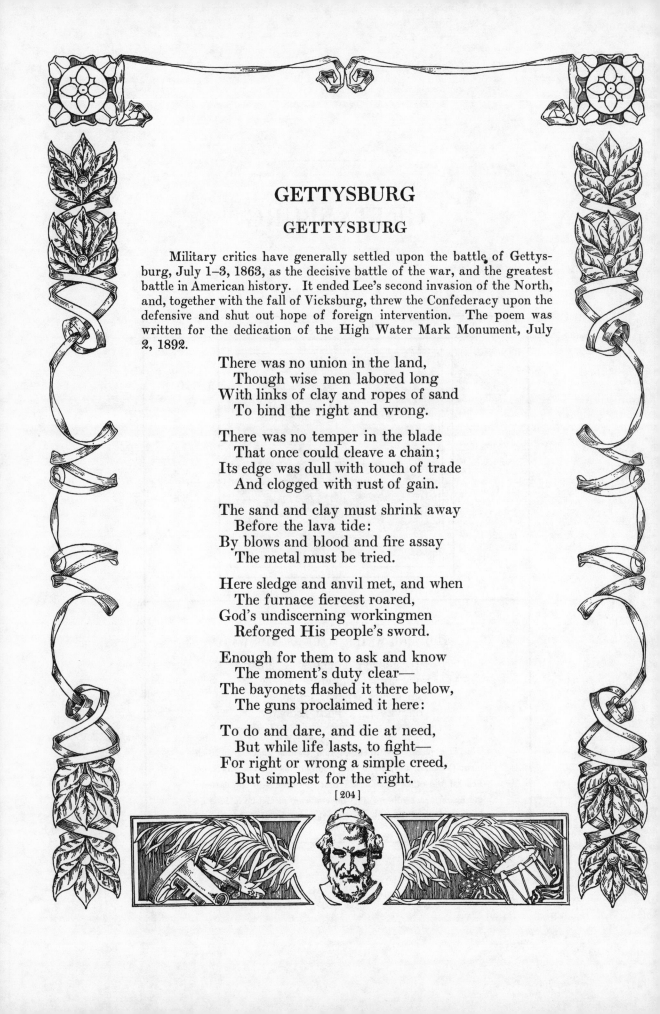

"BUT WHILE LIFE LASTS, TO FIGHT"

Such was the fate of many of the 5,000 and more Confederates of whom no returns were made after the fighting at Gettysburg. This young soldier was one of the sharpshooters posted in the "Devil's Den," the only position captured and held by the Confederates in the fighting at the Round Tops. In their lonely fastness these boys in gray sent many a swift messenger of death into the Federal lines that were fighting on the near-by crest. Then at last a Federal shell, bursting over this lad, wounded him in the head, but was not merciful enough to kill him outright. He was evidently able to spread his blanket and must have lain there alone for hours in his death agony. The photographer who took this picture, just after the battle in July, attended the dedication of the National Cemetery at Gettysburg, in November, and again penetrated to this rocky spot. The musket, rusted by many storms, still leaned against the rock; the remains of the boy soldier lay undisturbed within the mouldering uniform. No burial party had found him. The only news that his loved ones got was the single word, "Missing." A tale like this is true for 5,000 more.

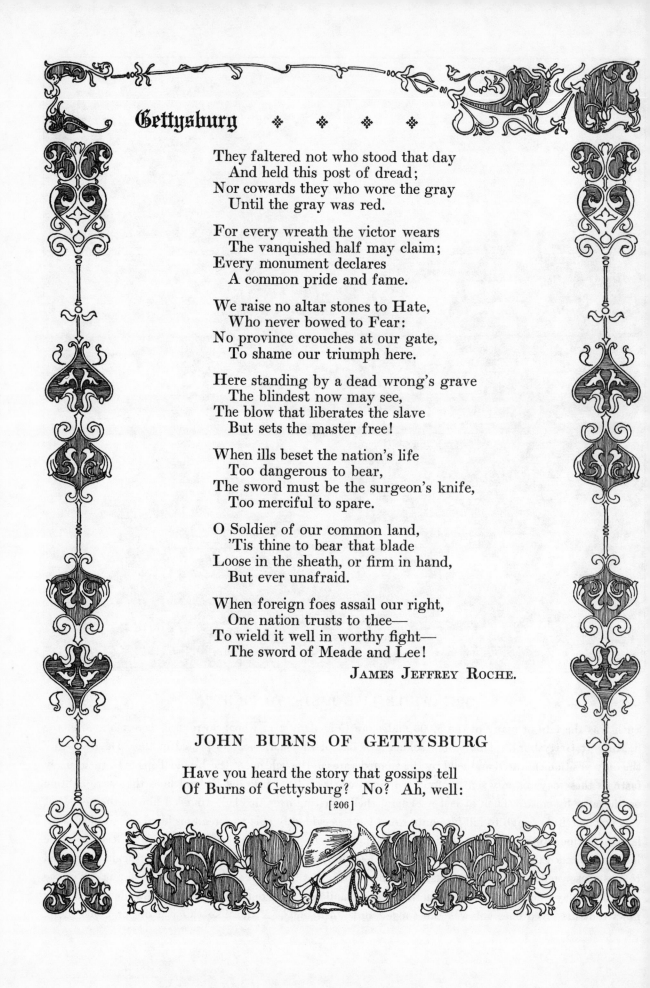

Gettysburg ✦ ✦ ✦❖ ✦ ✦

They faltered not who stood that day
    And held this post of dread;
Nor cowards they who wore the gray
    Until the gray was red.

For every wreath the victor wears
    The vanquished half may claim;
Every monument declares
    A common pride and fame.

We raise no altar stones to Hate,
    Who never bowed to Fear:
No province crouches at our gate,
    To shame our triumph here.

Here standing by a dead wrong's grave
    The blindest now may see,
The blow that liberates the slave
    But sets the master free!

When ills beset the nation's life
    Too dangerous to bear,
The sword must be the surgeon's knife,
    Too merciful to spare.

O Soldier of our common land,
    'Tis thine to bear that blade
Loose in the sheath, or firm in hand,
    But ever unafraid.

When foreign foes assail our right,
    One nation trusts to thee—
To wield it well in worthy fight—
    The sword of Meade and Lee!

                    JAMES JEFFREY ROCHE.

JOHN BURNS OF GETTYSBURG

Have you heard the story that gossips tell
Of Burns of Gettysburg? No? Ah, well:

"TO DO AND DARE, AND DIE AT NEED"

These sharpshooters, prone beside the mossy boulders and scrub trees of "Devil's Den" are among the most daring of those who fought at Gettysburg. They have paid the penalty so often attending such duty. At the beginning of the war it was argued that individual and unattached riflemen should be regarded as murderers and shot if captured; but this was never done, since sharpshooters came to play an important part on both sides. In the Confederate ranks they were men from Alabama, Mississippi, and Texas—men whose outdoor life made them experts with the rifle. Seeing the value of such a force, the Federals early organized a regiment of sharpshooters, enlisting men from each of the Federal States. These brought their own rifles, and most of them could snuff out a candle at a hundred yards. Often far in advance of the line, the sharpshooters chose their own positions, sometimes climbing into trees and lashing themselves to the branches to avoid a fall in case they should be wounded. Thousands paid the price of their daring.

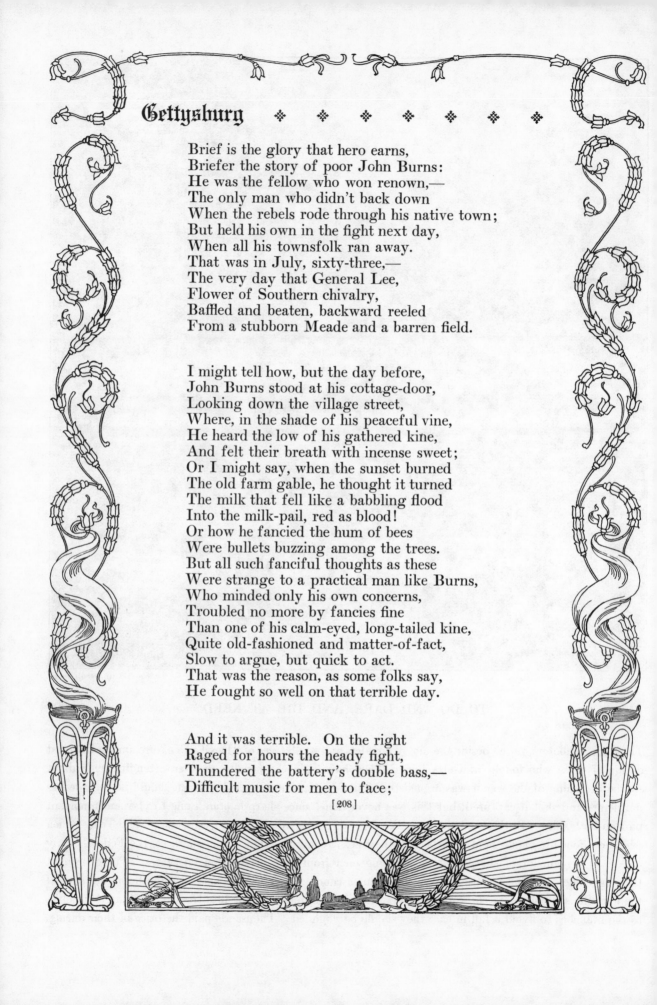

Gettysburg ✦ ✦ ✦ ✦ ✦ ✦

Brief is the glory that hero earns,
Briefer the story of poor John Burns:
He was the fellow who won renown,—
The only man who didn't back down
When the rebels rode through his native town;
But held his own in the fight next day,
When all his townsfolk ran away.
That was in July, sixty-three,—
The very day that General Lee,
Flower of Southern chivalry,
Baffled and beaten, backward reeled
From a stubborn Meade and a barren field.

I might tell how, but the day before,
John Burns stood at his cottage-door,
Looking down the village street,
Where, in the shade of his peaceful vine,
He heard the low of his gathered kine,
And felt their breath with incense sweet;
Or I might say, when the sunset burned
The old farm gable, he thought it turned
The milk that fell like a babbling flood
Into the milk-pail, red as blood!
Or how he fancied the hum of bees
Were bullets buzzing among the trees.
But all such fanciful thoughts as these
Were strange to a practical man like Burns,
Who minded only his own concerns,
Troubled no more by fancies fine
Than one of his calm-eyed, long-tailed kine,
Quite old-fashioned and matter-of-fact,
Slow to argue, but quick to act.
That was the reason, as some folks say,
He fought so well on that terrible day.

And it was terrible. On the right
Raged for hours the heady fight,
Thundered the battery's double bass,—
Difficult music for men to face;

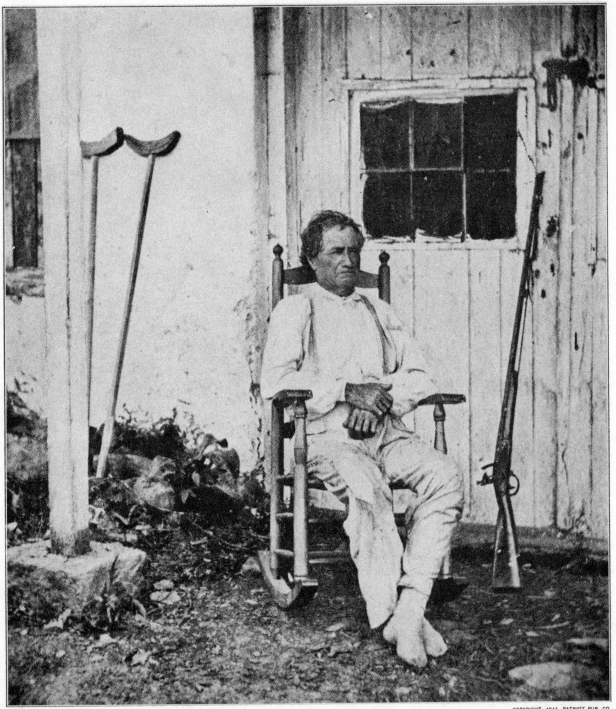

"WITH HIS LONG BROWN RIFLE"—JOHN BURNS OF GETTYSBURG

The old hero of Gettysburg sits here by his cottage. On one side is the old-fashioned gun Harte speaks of, on the other, the crutches he needed after the battle. Sergeant George Eustice, of Company F, Seventh Wisconsin Volunteers, in "Battles and Leaders" describes John Burns' action in the ranks of that regiment: "It must have been about noon when I saw a little old man coming up in the rear of Company F. In regard to the peculiarities of his dress, I remember he wore a swallow-tailed coat with smooth brass buttons. He had a rifle on his shoulder. We boys began to poke fun at him as soon as he came amongst us, as we thought no civilian in his senses would show himself in such a place. . . . Bullets were flying thicker and faster, and we hugged the ground about us as close as we could. Burns got behind a tree and surprised us all by not taking a double-quick to the rear. He was as calm and collected as any veteran."

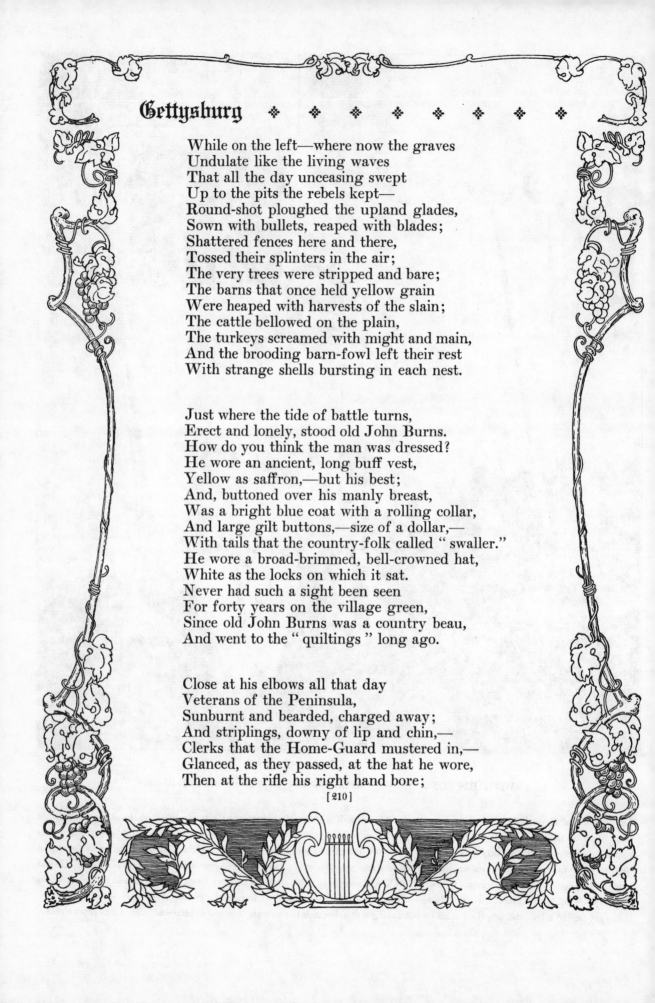

Gettysburg ✦ ✦ ✦ ✦ ✦ ✦

While on the left—where now the graves
Undulate like the living waves
That all the day unceasing swept
Up to the pits the rebels kept—
Round-shot ploughed the upland glades,
Sown with bullets, reaped with blades;
Shattered fences here and there,
Tossed their splinters in the air;
The very trees were stripped and bare;
The barns that once held yellow grain
Were heaped with harvests of the slain;
The cattle bellowed on the plain,
The turkeys screamed with might and main,
And the brooding barn-fowl left their rest
With strange shells bursting in each nest.

Just where the tide of battle turns,
Erect and lonely, stood old John Burns.
How do you think the man was dressed?
He wore an ancient, long buff vest,
Yellow as saffron,—but his best;
And, buttoned over his manly breast,
Was a bright blue coat with a rolling collar,
And large gilt buttons,—size of a dollar,—
With tails that the country-folk called " swaller."
He wore a broad-brimmed, bell-crowned hat,
White as the locks on which it sat.
Never had such a sight been seen
For forty years on the village green,
Since old John Burns was a country beau,
And went to the " quiltings " long ago.

Close at his elbows all that day
Veterans of the Peninsula,
Sunburnt and bearded, charged away;
And striplings, downy of lip and chin,—
Clerks that the Home-Guard mustered in,—
Glanced, as they passed, at the hat he wore,
Then at the rifle his right hand bore;

"JOHN BURNS STOOD AT HIS COTTAGE DOOR"

These photographs present at his home the man of whom Harte wrote the half-humorous poem. According to common report, Burns was seventy years old when the battle was fought. In the war of 1812, though still a youth, he had been among the first to volunteer; and he took part in the battles of Plattsburg, Queenstown, and Lundy's Lane. In 1846 he again volunteered for service in the American armies, and served through the Mexican War. At the beginning of the Civil War he tried to enlist once more, but the officer told him that a man of sixty-seven was not acceptable for active service. He did, however, secure employment for a time as a teamster but was finally sent home to Gettysburg. To keep him contented his townsmen elected him constable of the then obscure village. He took his duties very seriously. When General Lee's troops entered the place in June, 1863, Burns asserted his authority in opposition to that of the Confederate provost-guard and was accordingly locked up. But no sooner had the troops left the town than he began to arrest the stragglers of the army. On July 1st, the first day of the battle of Gettysburg, the old man borrowed a rifle and ammunition from a Federal soldier who had been wounded, went west of the town to the point of heaviest fighting, and asked to be given a place in the line. The colonel of the Seventh Wisconsin handed him a long-range rifle and allowed him to join the other troops. There he fought like a veteran. When the Union forces were driven back by superior numbers, Burns fell into the hands of the Confederates and came very near being executed as an ununiformed combatant. Though wounded in three places, he recovered and lived here until his death in 1872.

WITH HIS WIFE AFTER THE BATTLE

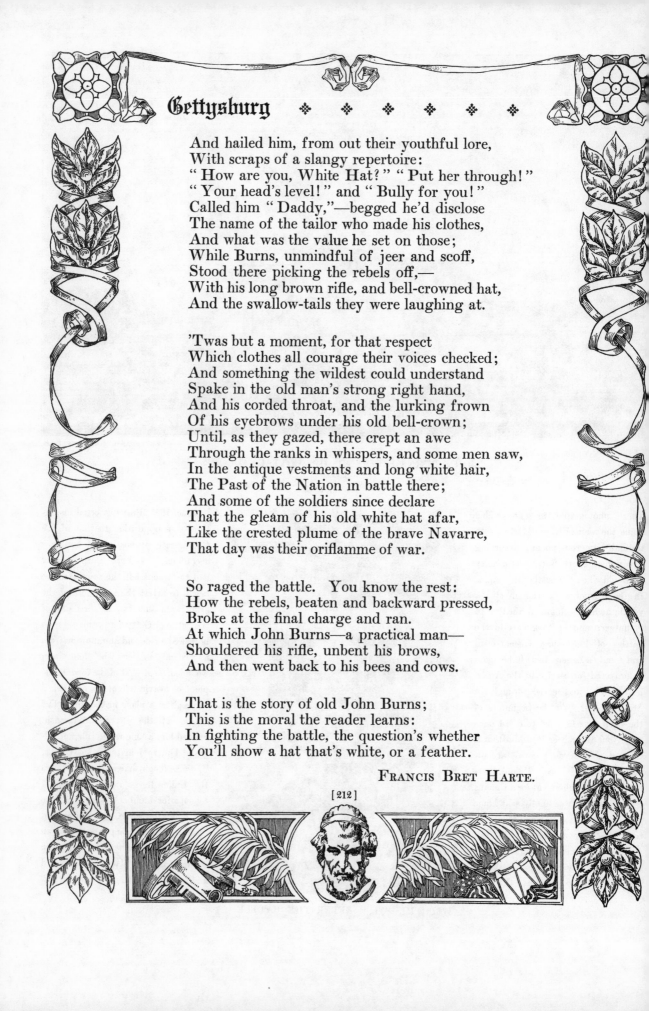

And hailed him, from out their youthful lore,
With scraps of a slangy repertoire:
" How are you, White Hat? " " Put her through! "
" Your head's level! " and " Bully for you! "
Called him " Daddy,"—begged he'd disclose
The name of the tailor who made his clothes,
And what was the value he set on those;
While Burns, unmindful of jeer and scoff,
Stood there picking the rebels off,—
With his long brown rifle, and bell-crowned hat,
And the swallow-tails they were laughing at.

'Twas but a moment, for that respect
Which clothes all courage their voices checked;
And something the wildest could understand
Spake in the old man's strong right hand,
And his corded throat, and the lurking frown
Of his eyebrows under his old bell-crown;
Until, as they gazed, there crept an awe
Through the ranks in whispers, and some men saw,
In the antique vestments and long white hair,
The Past of the Nation in battle there;
And some of the soldiers since declare
That the gleam of his old white hat afar,
Like the crested plume of the brave Navarre,
That day was their oriflamme of war.

So raged the battle. You know the rest:
How the rebels, beaten and backward pressed,
Broke at the final charge and ran.
At which John Burns—a practical man—
Shouldered his rifle, unbent his brows,
And then went back to his bees and cows.

That is the story of old John Burns;
This is the moral the reader learns:
In fighting the battle, the question's whether
You'll show a hat that's white, or a feather.

FRANCIS BRET HARTE.

[212]

"THE VERY TREES WERE STRIPPED AND BARE"

This picture of cannonaded trees on Culp's Hill, and the views herewith of Round Top and Cemetery Ridge, carry the reader across the whole battlefield. Culp's Hill was the scene of a contest on the second day. Lee's plan on that day was to attack the right and left flanks of the Union army at the same time. Longstreet's attack on the left, at Little Round Top, approached a victory. Ewell's attack on the right at Culp's Hill, although made later than intended, came near complete success. His cannonading, the effects of which appear in the picture, was soon silenced, but the infantry forces that assaulted the positions on the extreme right found them nearly defenseless because the troops had been sent to reënforce the left. About sunset General Edward Johnson led this attack, which was repulsed by the thin but well fortified line under command of General George S. Greene. About nine o'clock Johnson walked into the undefended works of the extreme right. The next morning he was soon driven out, but the Union peril had been great.

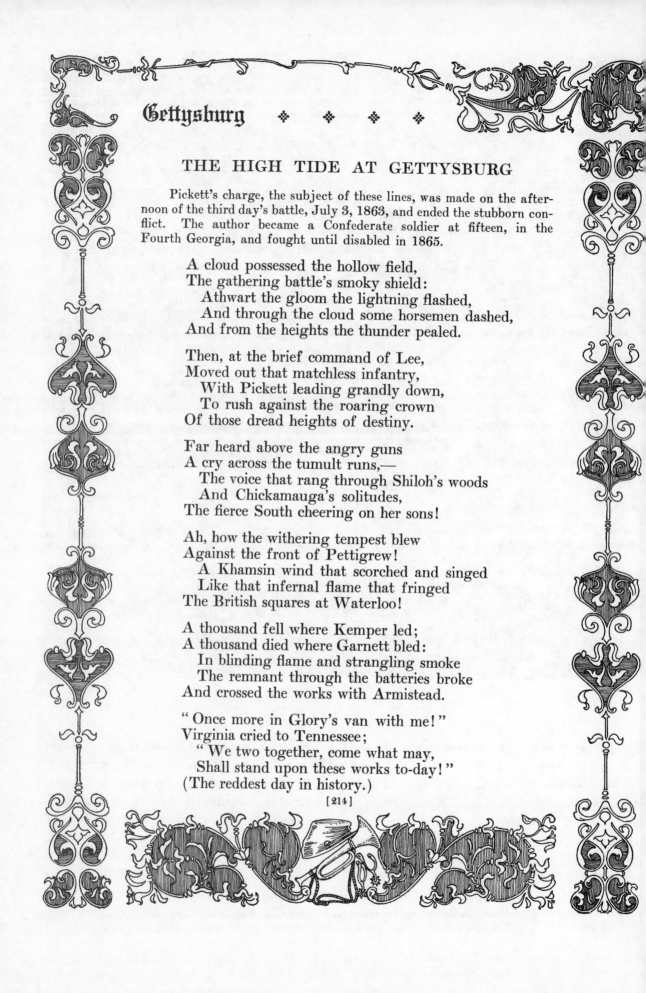

Gettysburg ❖ ❖ ❖

THE HIGH TIDE AT GETTYSBURG

Pickett's charge, the subject of these lines, was made on the afternoon of the third day's battle, July 3, 1863, and ended the stubborn conflict. The author became a Confederate soldier at fifteen, in the Fourth Georgia, and fought until disabled in 1865.

A cloud possessed the hollow field,
The gathering battle's smoky shield:
    Athwart the gloom the lightning flashed,
    And through the cloud some horsemen dashed,
And from the heights the thunder pealed.

Then, at the brief command of Lee,
Moved out that matchless infantry,
    With Pickett leading grandly down,
    To rush against the roaring crown
Of those dread heights of destiny.

Far heard above the angry guns
A cry across the tumult runs,—
    The voice that rang through Shiloh's woods
    And Chickamauga's solitudes,
The fierce South cheering on her sons!

Ah, how the withering tempest blew
Against the front of Pettigrew!
    A Khamsin wind that scorched and singed
    Like that infernal flame that fringed
The British squares at Waterloo!

A thousand fell where Kemper led;
A thousand died where Garnett bled:
    In blinding flame and strangling smoke
    The remnant through the batteries broke
And crossed the works with Armistead.

"Once more in Glory's van with me!"
Virginia cried to Tennessee;
    "We two together, come what may,
    Shall stand upon these works to-day!"
(The reddest day in history.)

"WITH PICKETT LEADING GRANDLY DOWN"

Thompson's description of Pickett's charge, with this martial portrait, calls for little explanation. A few words from an English army officer who was present, Arthur J. Fremantle, will describe Lee's share in the record of nobility. General Lee's conduct after the charge, writes the English colonel, "was perfectly sublime. He was engaged in rallying and in encouraging the broken troops, and was riding about a little in front of the wood, quite alone, the whole of his staff being engaged in a similar manner further to the rear. His face, which is always placid and cheerful, did not show signs of the slightest disappointment, care, or annoyance; and he was addressing to every soldier he met a few words of encouragement, such as, 'All this will come right in the end—we'll talk it over afterward; but, in the mean time, all good men must rally—we want all good and true men just now,' etc. He spoke to all the wounded men that passed him, and the slightly wounded he exhorted 'to bind up their hurts and take up a musket' in this emergency. Very few failed to answer his appeal, and I saw many badly wounded men take off their hats and cheer him. He said to me, 'This has been a very sad day for us, Colonel, a sad day; but we can't expect always to gain victories.' . . . I saw General Wilcox come up to him, and explain, almost crying, the state of his brigade. General Lee immediately shook hands with him and said, cheerfully, 'Never mind, General, all this has been *my* fault; it is *I* that have lost this fight, and you must help me out of it in the best way you can.'"

Gettysburg ✦ ✦ ✦ ✦ ✦ ✦

Brave Tennessee! In reckless way
Virginia heard her comrade say:
   " Close round this rent and riddled rag! "
   What time she set her battle-flag
Amid the guns of Doubleday.

But who shall break the guards that wait
Before the awful face of Fate?
   The tattered standards of the South
   Were shrivelled at the cannon's mouth,
And all her hopes were desolate.

In vain the Tennesseean set
His breast against the bayonet;
   In vain Virginia charged and raged,
   A tigress in her wrath uncaged,
Till all the hill was red and wet!

Above the bayonets, mixed and crossed,
Men saw a gray, gigantic ghost
   Receding through the battle-cloud,
   And heard across the tempest loud
The death-cry of a nation lost!

The brave went down! Without disgrace
They leaped to Ruin's red embrace;
   They only heard Fame's thunders wake,
   And saw the dazzling sun-burst break
In smiles on Glory's bloody face!

They fell, who lifted up a hand
And bade the sun in heaven to stand;
   They smote and fell, who set the bars
   Against the progress of the stars,
And stayed the march of Motherland!

They stood, who saw the future come
On through the fight's delirium;
   They smote and stood, who held the hope
   Of nations on that slippery slope
Amid the cheers of Christendom.

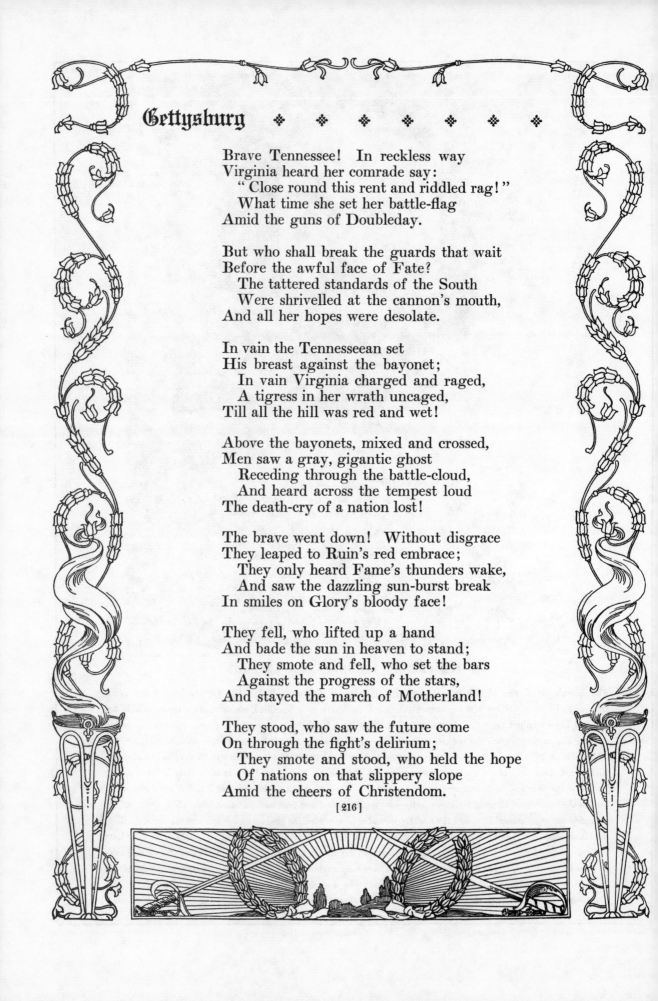

A GUN AND GUNNERS THAT REPULSED PICKETT'S CHARGE

FROM A PHOTOGRAPH TREASURED NEARLY HALF A CENTURY BY THE CAPTAIN OF THIS BATTERY

This photograph of a gun and cannoneers that helped to check Pickett's charge at Gettysburg was preserved for nearly fifty years by Andrew Cowan, captain of the battery containing this gun. From that bloody angle on Cemetery Ridge his life was spared, although the commanders of the batteries to right and left of him, Lieutenant Alonzo H. Cushing and Captain James Rorty, both were killed. At the very height of the action, General Henry J. Hunt, chief of artillery of the army, rode into the battery and fired his revolver at the oncoming gray line, exclaiming: "See 'em! See 'em! See 'em!" A moment later, Cowan ordered his guns to cease firing, for fear of injuring the men of the Sixty-ninth Pennsylvania at the wall in their front. The Sixty-ninth suddenly swung to the right, leaving the guns uncovered. The Confederates came rushing on from behind a slight elevation, covered with bushes and rocks, where they had crouched. A Confederate officer shouted, "Take the guns!" They were double-loaded, with canister. Some of the brave assailants were within 10 yards of the muzzles when Captain Cowan shouted, "Fire!" Two hundred and twenty chunks of lead burst from the muzzles of each of the five guns. Before the deadly storm, the line in gray withered and was no more. "We buried that officer with honor," wrote Captain Cowan, to whom readers are indebted for both the photograph and this account. "I returned his sword to survivors of Pickett's division on the same ground, twenty-five years afterward." At Cedar Creek, six months after this photograph, Sergeant William E. Uhlster (A) was crippled and Corporal Henry J. Tucker (B) was killed.

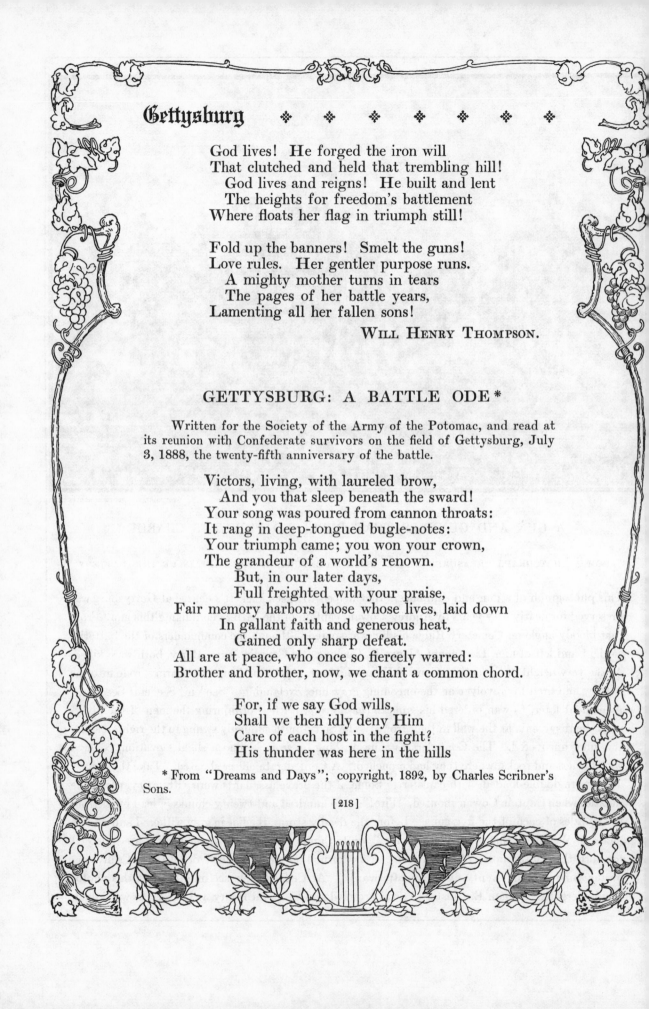

Gettysburg ❖ ❖ ❖ ❖ ❖ ❖

God lives! He forged the iron will
That clutched and held that trembling hill!
  God lives and reigns! He built and lent
  The heights for freedom's battlement
Where floats her flag in triumph still!

Fold up the banners! Smelt the guns!
Love rules. Her gentler purpose runs.
  A mighty mother turns in tears
  The pages of her battle years,
Lamenting all her fallen sons!

WILL HENRY THOMPSON.

GETTYSBURG: A BATTLE ODE *

Written for the Society of the Army of the Potomac, and read at
its reunion with Confederate survivors on the field of Gettysburg, July
3, 1888, the twenty-fifth anniversary of the battle.

Victors, living, with laureled brow,
  And you that sleep beneath the sward!
Your song was poured from cannon throats:
It rang in deep-tongued bugle-notes:
Your triumph came; you won your crown,
The grandeur of a world's renown.
  But, in our later days,
  Full freighted with your praise,
Fair memory harbors those whose lives, laid down
  In gallant faith and generous heat,
  Gained only sharp defeat.
All are at peace, who once so fiercely warred:
Brother and brother, now, we chant a common chord.

  For, if we say God wills,
  Shall we then idly deny Him
  Care of each host in the fight?
  His thunder was here in the hills

* From "Dreams and Days"; copyright, 1892, by Charles Scribner's
Sons.

"FOLD UP THE BANNERS, SMELT THE GUNS"

The tangled heap is all that remains of hundreds of captured Confederate artillery carriages, gathered at the Watervliet Arsenal in Troy, New York, and burned for the iron. A more impressive illustration of the line quoted from the stirring battle-ballad could hardly exist. But Thompson's words were used in a higher sense. Never more shall Americans level artillery or musketry upon their fellow-countrymen. Gettysburg virtually decided that. Not only so, but the people shall be bound together by active pride in their common blood and common traditions which finds expression in common hopes and aspirations for the future. America has become a single country, with a central Government wielding sovereign power and holding among the nations of the earth a position of world-wide honor and influence. One of the foremost New England historians, Professor Albert Bushnell Hart of Harvard, declares: "The keynote to which intelligent spirits respond most quickly in the United States is Americanism; no nation is more conscious of its own existence and its importance in the universe, more interested in the greatness, the strength, the pride, the influence, and the future of the common country."

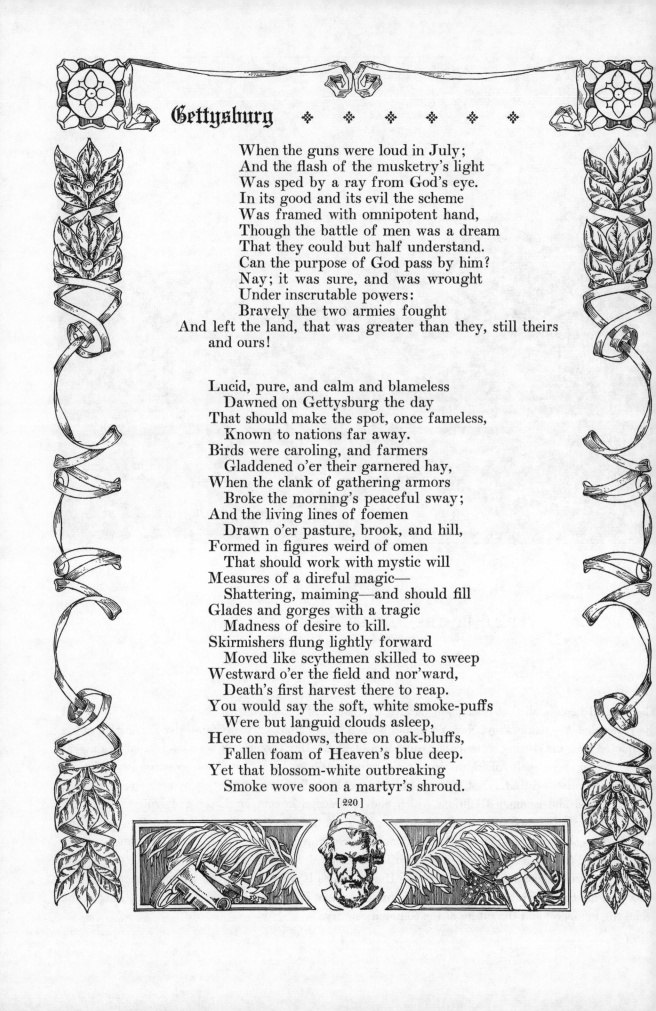

Gettysburg ✦ ✦ ✦ ✦ ✦

When the guns were loud in July;
And the flash of the musketry's light
Was sped by a ray from God's eye.
In its good and its evil the scheme
Was framed with omnipotent hand,
Though the battle of men was a dream
That they could but half understand.
Can the purpose of God pass by him?
Nay; it was sure, and was wrought
Under inscrutable powers:
Bravely the two armies fought
And left the land, that was greater than they, still theirs
and ours!

Lucid, pure, and calm and blameless
   Dawned on Gettysburg the day
That should make the spot, once fameless,
   Known to nations far away.
Birds were caroling, and farmers
   Gladdened o'er their garnered hay,
When the clank of gathering armors
   Broke the morning's peaceful sway;
And the living lines of foemen
   Drawn o'er pasture, brook, and hill,
Formed in figures weird of omen
   That should work with mystic will
Measures of a direful magic—
   Shattering, maiming—and should fill
Glades and gorges with a tragic
   Madness of desire to kill.
Skirmishers flung lightly forward
   Moved like scythemen skilled to sweep
Westward o'er the field and nor'ward,
   Death's first harvest there to reap.
You would say the soft, white smoke-puffs
   Were but languid clouds asleep,
Here on meadows, there on oak-bluffs,
   Fallen foam of Heaven's blue deep.
Yet that blossom-white outbreaking
   Smoke wove soon a martyr's shroud.

[220]

AFTER THE BATTLE—ROUND TOP, SOUTHERN END OF THE FEDERAL LINE

From these rocks of Round Top, as seen from Little Round Top, echoed the cannonading at Gettysburg—the heaviest ever heard on this continent, and seldom equaled anywhere. For two miles the Confederate line was planted thick with cannon. General Hancock's official account gives a clear notion of this part of the battle: "From 11 A.M. until 1 P.M. there was an ominous stillness. About 1 o'clock, apparently by a given signal, the enemy opened upon our front with the heaviest artillery fire I have ever known. Their guns were in position at an average distance of about 1,400 yards from my line, and ran in a semicircle from the town of Gettysburg to a point opposite Round Top Mountain. Their number is variously estimated at from one hundred and fif-

ABNER DOUBLEDAY

DEFENDER OF CEMETERY RIDGE, THE NORTHERN END
OF MEADE'S LINE

teen to one hundred and fifty. The air was filled with projectiles, there being scarcely an instant but that several were seen bursting at once. No irregularity of ground afforded much protection, and the plain in rear of the line of battle was soon swept of everything movable. The infantry troops maintained their position with great steadiness, covering themselves as best they might by the temporary but trifling defenses they had erected and the accidents of the ground. Scarcely a straggler was seen, but all waited the cessation of the fierce cannonade, knowing well what it foreshadowed. The artillery of the corps, imperfectly supplied with ammunition, replied to the enemy most gallantly, maintaining the unequal contest in a manner that reflected the highest honor on this arm."

Gettysburg ✦ ✦ ✦

Reynolds fell, with soul unquaking,
  Ardent-eyed and open-browed:
Noble men in humbler raiment
  Fell where shot their graves had plowed,
Dying not for paltry payment:
  Proud of home, of honor proud.

.   .   .   .

Dear are the dead we weep for;
  Dear are the strong hearts broken!
Proudly their memory we keep for
  Our help and hope; a token
Of sacred thought too deep for
  Words that leave it unspoken.
All that we know of fairest,
  All that we have of meetest,
Here we lay down for the rarest
  Doers whose souls rose fleetest
And in their homes of air rest,
  Ranked with the truest and sweetest.

Days, with fiery-hearted, bold advances;
  Nights in dim and shadowy, swift retreat;
Rains that rush with bright, embattled lances;
  Thunder, booming round your stirless feet;—
Winds that set the orchard with sweet fancies
  All abloom, or ripple the ripening wheat;
Moonlight, starlight, on your mute graves falling;
  Dew, distilled as tears unbidden flow;—
Dust of drought in drifts and layers crawling;
  Lulling dreams of softly whispering snow;
Happy birds, from leafy coverts calling;—
  These go on, yet none of these you know:
    Hearing not our human voices
    Speaking to you all in vain,
    Nor the psalm of a land that rejoices,
Ringing from churches and cities and foundries a mighty
      refrain!
But we, and the sun and the birds, and the breezes that
      blow
When tempests are striving and lightnings of heaven are
      spent,

"REYNOLDS FELL, WITH SOUL UNQUAKING"

MCPHERSON'S WOODS AT GETTYSBURG—ILLUSTRATION FOR LATHROP'S "ODE"

Matthew Brady, the wizard who preserved so many war scenes, is here gazing across the field toward the woods where Reynolds fell. About ten o'clock in the morning, July 1st, the brigade of the Confederate General Archer and the Federal "Iron Brigade," directed by General Reynolds, were both trying to secure control of this strip. Reynolds was on horseback in the edge of the woods, impatient for the troops to come up so that he could make the advance. As he turned once to see how close they were, a Confederate sharpshooter from the depths of the thicket hit him in the back of the head. He fell dead without a word. General Hunt says of him: "He had opened brilliantly a battle which required three days of hard fighting to close with a victory. To him may be applied in a wider sense than in its original one, Napier's happy eulogium on Ridge: 'No man died on that field with more glory than he, yet many died, and there was much glory.'" Thus his name is inseparably linked with the history of his country at a turning-point in its course.

Gettysburg ✦ ✦ ✦ ✦ ✦ ✦

With one consent
Make unto them
Who died for us eternal requiem.

Lovely to look on, O South,
    No longer stately-scornful
But beautiful still in pride,
Our hearts go out to you as toward a bride!
    Garmented soft in white,
Haughty, and yet how love-imbuing and tender!
You stand before us with your gently mournful
Memory-haunted eyes and flower-like mouth,
    Where clinging thoughts—as bees a-cluster
    Murmur through the leafy gloom,
    Musical in monotone—
Whisper sadly. Yet a lustre
As of glowing gold-gray light
    Shines upon the orient bloom,
    Sweet with orange-blossoms, thrown
Round the jasmine-starred, deep night
Crowning with dark hair your brow.
Ruthless, once, we came to slay,
    And you met us then with hate.
Rough was the wooing of war: we won you,
    Won you at last, though late!
    Dear South, to-day,
As our country's altar made us
    One forever, so we vow
Unto yours our love to render:
Strength with strength we here endow,
And we make your honor ours.
Happiness and hope shall sun you:
All the wiles that half betrayed us
    Vanish from us like spent showers.

Two hostile bullets in mid-air
    Together shocked,
    And swift were locked
Forever in a firm embrace.
Then let us men have so much grace

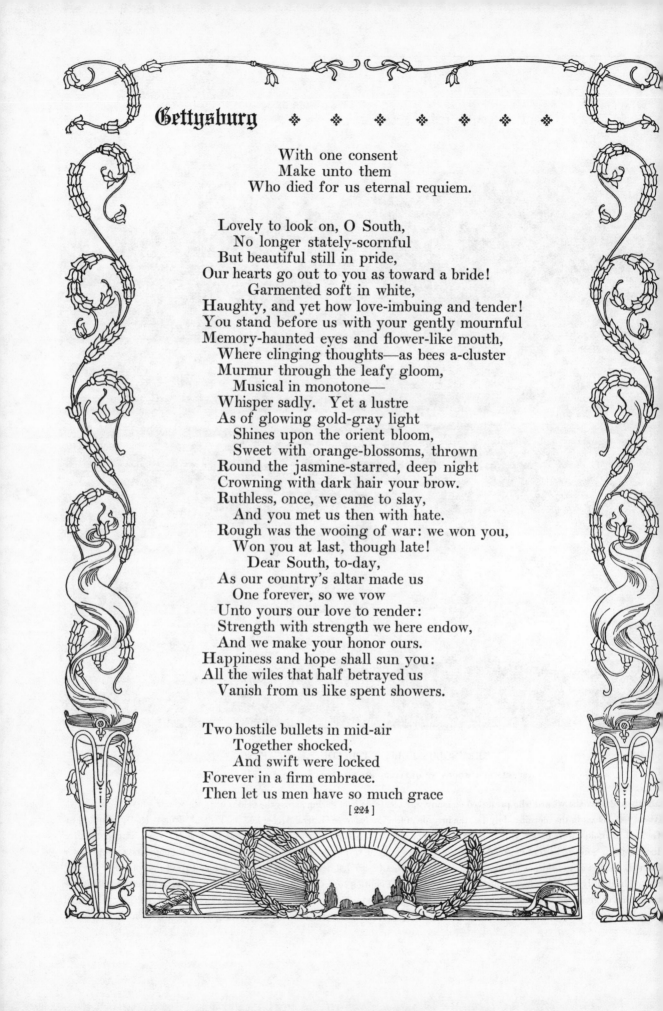

' NOBLE MEN IN HUMBLER RAIMENT FELL"

A CONFEDERATE SHARPSHOOTER KILLED AT THE BATTLE OF GETTYSBURG

The words from Lathrop's poem on "Gettysburg" apply to the 7,058 soldiers who fell in this deadliest of American battles.   The point photographed is "Devil's Den," a rocky height rising sharply on the east and sloping gradually to the plain on the west.   Its northern point was composed of huge rocks and boulders with numberless crevices and holes such as the one that yawns at the left of the picture. The whole region is covered with similar boulders, which afforded retreats for sharpshooters on both sides.   Five hundred yards east, and a hundred feet higher than "Devil's Den," was Little Round Top, the key to the entire Federal position along Cemetery Ridge.   Lee's tactics on the second day were to drive back a Federal force on the plain near "Devil's Den" and secure Little Round Top and the whole Union position.   His troops formed in the woods, far outflanking the opposing troops on the plain.   They were almost at Little Round Top before General G. K. Warren discovered that a single signal-man was there to defend the height.   Only by marvelous exertions were defenders secured in time to meet the attack.   Longstreet's men, however, gained possession of "Devil's Den."   A multitude of sharp-shooters clambered into the lurking-places among the boulders, whence they could not be dislodged by artillery fire or by sharpshooting. These men were especially successful in picking off the cannoneers on Little Round Top.   At one time three were shot down in quick succession, and only the fourth succeeded in firing the piece.   When night closed on the scene the Confederates still held the "Den" and the ground at the foot of Little Round Top, but many of the defenders were dead or dying.   And yet another day of carnage was to come.

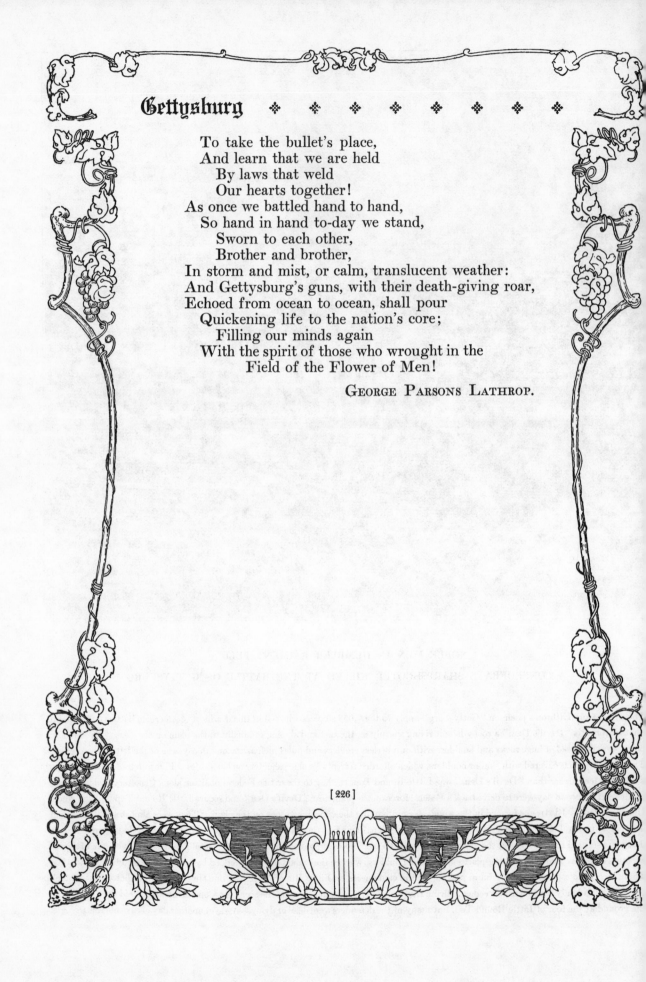

Gettysburg ❖ ❖ ❖ ❖ ❖ ❖ ❖

To take the bullet's place,
And learn that we are held
By laws that weld
Our hearts together!
As once we battled hand to hand,
So hand in hand to-day we stand,
Sworn to each other,
Brother and brother,
In storm and mist, or calm, translucent weather:
And Gettysburg's guns, with their death-giving roar,
Echoed from ocean to ocean, shall pour
Quickening life to the nation's core;
Filling our minds again
With the spirit of those who wrought in the
Field of the Flower of Men!

GEORGE PARSONS LATHROP.

X

THE END
OF THE STRUGGLE

HISTORIC FORT MOULTRIE AT CHARLESTON IN RUINS—1865

ILLUSTRATIONS FOR MARGARET PRESTON'S LINES "A PAST WHOSE MEMORY MAKES US THRILL"—THIS STRONGHOLD, NAMED FOR WILLIAM MOULTRIE, THE YOUNG SOUTH CAROLINIAN WHO DEFENDED IT IN 1776 AGAINST THE BRITISH, WAS 85 YEARS LATER HELD BY SOUTH CAROLINIANS AGAINST FELLOW-AMERICANS —IN THE PICTURE IT IS ONCE MORE UNDER THE FLAG OF A UNITED LAND.

"A PAST WHOSE MEM—ORY MAKES US THRILL"

WAR-TIME SCENES IN VIRGINIA ASSOCIATED WITH THE FATHER OF HIS COUNTRY

The picture below of Washington's headquarters recalls his advance to fame. He had proceeded with Braddock as aide-de-camp on the ill-fated expedition ending in the battle of the Monongahela, July 9, 1755. Owing to Washington's conspicuous gallantry in that engagement, he was assigned the duty of reorganizing the provincial troops. During this period his headquarters were in the little stone house by the tree. In the church below, a second period of his life was inaugurated. Here he was married on January 6, 1759, to

THE RICHMOND STATUE

Mrs. Martha Custis, a young widow with two children. Already a member of the House of Burgesses of Virginia, he soon came to be recognized as one of the leading men in the colony. Important trusts were frequently laid upon him, and he was often chosen as an arbitrator. The statue at the top of the page, standing in Capitol Square in Richmond, commemorates Washington as leader of the colonial forces in the Revolution. With a few ill-trained and ill-equipped troops he maintained a long struggle against one of the great military powers of the day and won American Independence. Every Virginian has a right to thrill at the honored name of Washington, be he Southerner or Northerner.

SAINT PETER'S CHURCH—UNION SOLDIERS

WASHINGTON'S HEADQUARTERS IN RICHMOND

"A PAST WHOSE MEMORY MAKES US THRILL"—THE JAMESTOWN CHURCH

The pictures on this page bring back vividly the history of Virginia. First is the ruins of the church at Jamestown, the first permanent English settlement within the limits of the United States. The church was built about a century before the Declaration of Independence, while the little village on the James was still the capital of Virginia. Below it appears St. John's Church, Richmond, the scene of Patrick Henry's immortal oration. The First Continental Congress had met in Philadelphia in September, 1774, and the colonies were drifting toward war. But many were very timid about taking such a step. Some were directly opposed to any break with Great Britain. Patrick Henry was far in advance of his fellow-colonists, when the Second Revolutionary Convention of Virginia met in this church on March 20, 1775. The event of the week was a set of resolutions offered on March 23d "for embodying, arming, and disciplining such a number of men as may be sufficient" to put the colony in a posture of defense. This was Henry's opportunity.

WHERE PATRICK HENRY SPOKE

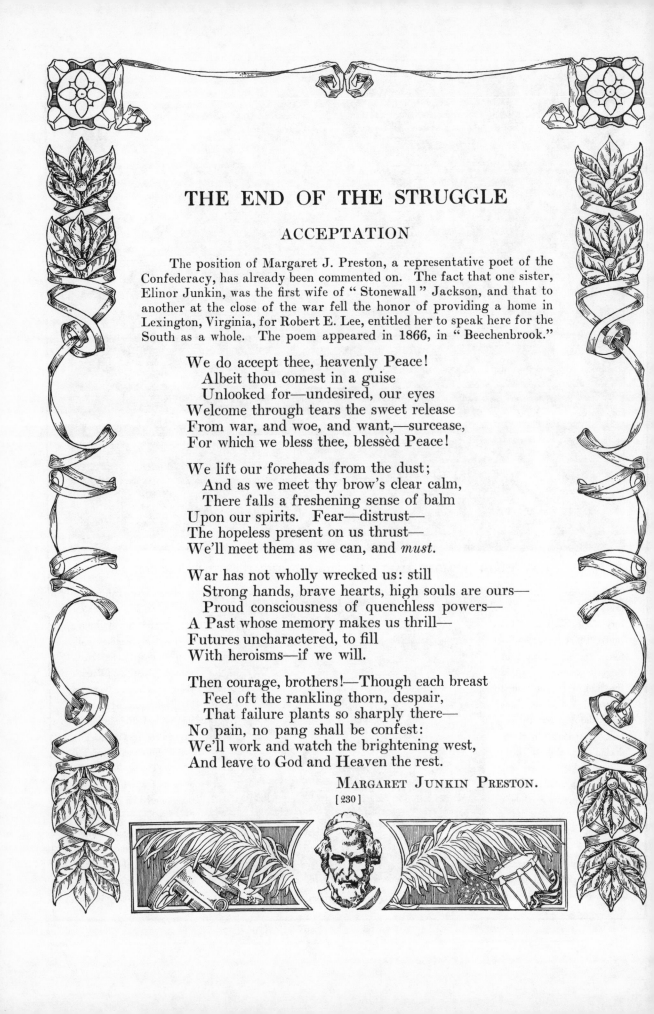

THE END OF THE STRUGGLE

ACCEPTATION

The position of Margaret J. Preston, a representative poet of the Confederacy, has already been commented on. The fact that one sister, Elinor Junkin, was the first wife of " Stonewall " Jackson, and that to another at the close of the war fell the honor of providing a home in Lexington, Virginia, for Robert E. Lee, entitled her to speak here for the South as a whole. The poem appeared in 1866, in " Beechenbrook."

We do accept thee, heavenly Peace!
    Albeit thou comest in a guise
    Unlooked for—undesired, our eyes
Welcome through tears the sweet release
From war, and woe, and want,—surcease,
For which we bless thee, blessèd Peace!

We lift our foreheads from the dust;
    And as we meet thy brow's clear calm,
    There falls a freshening sense of balm
Upon our spirits. Fear—distrust—
The hopeless present on us thrust—
We'll meet them as we can, and *must*.

War has not wholly wrecked us: still
    Strong hands, brave hearts, high souls are ours—
    Proud consciousness of quenchless powers—
A Past whose memory makes us thrill—
Futures uncharactered, to fill
With heroisms—if we will.

Then courage, brothers!—Though each breast
    Feel oft the rankling thorn, despair,
    That failure plants so sharply there—
No pain, no pang shall be confest:
We'll work and watch the brightening west,
And leave to God and Heaven the rest.

MARGARET JUNKIN PRESTON.

[230]

MOURNING WOMEN AMONG THE RICHMOND RUINS—APRIL, 1865

A SOMBER PICTURE THAT VISUALIZES MARGARET PRESTON'S POEM "ACCEPTATION"

". . . Our Eyes
Welcome Through Tears the Sweet Release
From War."

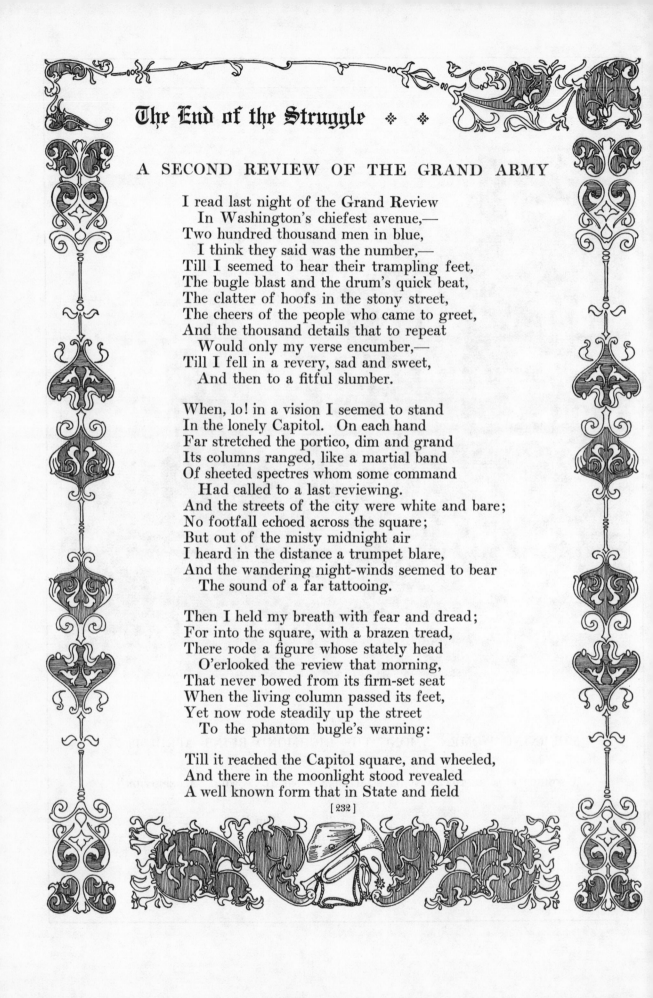

The End of the Struggle ❖ ❖

A SECOND REVIEW OF THE GRAND ARMY

I read last night of the Grand Review
  In Washington's chiefest avenue,—
Two hundred thousand men in blue,
  I think they said was the number,—
Till I seemed to hear their trampling feet,
The bugle blast and the drum's quick beat,
The clatter of hoofs in the stony street,
The cheers of the people who came to greet,
And the thousand details that to repeat
  Would only my verse encumber,—
Till I fell in a revery, sad and sweet,
  And then to a fitful slumber.

When, lo! in a vision I seemed to stand
In the lonely Capitol. On each hand
Far stretched the portico, dim and grand
Its columns ranged, like a martial band
Of sheeted spectres whom some command
  Had called to a last reviewing.
And the streets of the city were white and bare;
No footfall echoed across the square;
But out of the misty midnight air
I heard in the distance a trumpet blare,
And the wandering night-winds seemed to bear
  The sound of a far tattooing.

Then I held my breath with fear and dread;
For into the square, with a brazen tread,
There rode a figure whose stately head
  O'erlooked the review that morning,
That never bowed from its firm-set seat
When the living column passed its feet,
Yet now rode steadily up the street
  To the phantom bugle's warning:

Till it reached the Capitol square, and wheeled,
And there in the moonlight stood revealed
A well known form that in State and field

[232]

"TWO HUNDRED THOUSAND MEN IN BLUE"

MARCHING UP PENNSYLVANIA AVENUE, IN MAY, 1865

Bret Harte's poem sounds the note of sorrow amid the national rejoicing at the splendor of the Grand Review. Those who never returned from the field of battle, or returned only to die of their wounds, formed a greater host than that which marched from the recently completed Capitol to the reviewing stand in front of the Executive Mansion.   In the Federal army 110,070 were killed in battle or died of their wounds; 199,720 died of disease; 24,866 died in Confederate prisons; other causes of mortality bring the total up to 359,528.   The estimates for the Confederate losses are less definite; but probably 94,000 were killed in action, 59,297 died of disease, 4,000 died in prison, and other causes would probably bring the total up to 250,000.   Over 600,000 lives were therefore lost to the country by the necessities of warfare.   When it is remembered that not only thousands of homes were cast in gloom but that most of these men were young, the cost of the war is apparent.

The End of the Struggle ❖ ❖ ❖ ❖

Had led our patriot sires:
Whose face was turned to the sleeping camp,
Afar through the river's fog and damp,
That showed no flicker, nor waning lamp,
   Nor wasted bivouac fires.

And I saw a phantom army come,
With never a sound of fife or drum,
But keeping time to a throbbing hum
   Of wailing and lamentation:
The martyred heroes of Malvern Hill,
Of Gettysburg and Chancellorsville,
The men whose wasted figures fill
   The patriot graves of the nation.

And there came the nameless dead,—the men
Who perished in fever-swamp and fen,
The slowly-starved of the prison-pen;
   And marching beside the others,
Came the dusky martyrs of Pillow's fight,
With limbs enfranchised and bearing bright:
I thought—perhaps 'twas the pale moonlight—
   They looked as white as their brothers!

And so all night marched the Nation's dead,
With never a banner above them spread,
Nor a badge, nor a motto brandishèd;
No mark—save the bare uncovered head
   Of the silent bronze Reviewer;
With never an arch save the vaulted sky;
With never a flower save those that lie
On the distant graves—for love could buy
   No gift that was purer or truer.

So all night long swept the strange array;
So all night long, till the morning gray,
I watch'd for one who had passed away,
   With a reverent awe and wonder,—
Till a blue cap waved in the lengthening line,

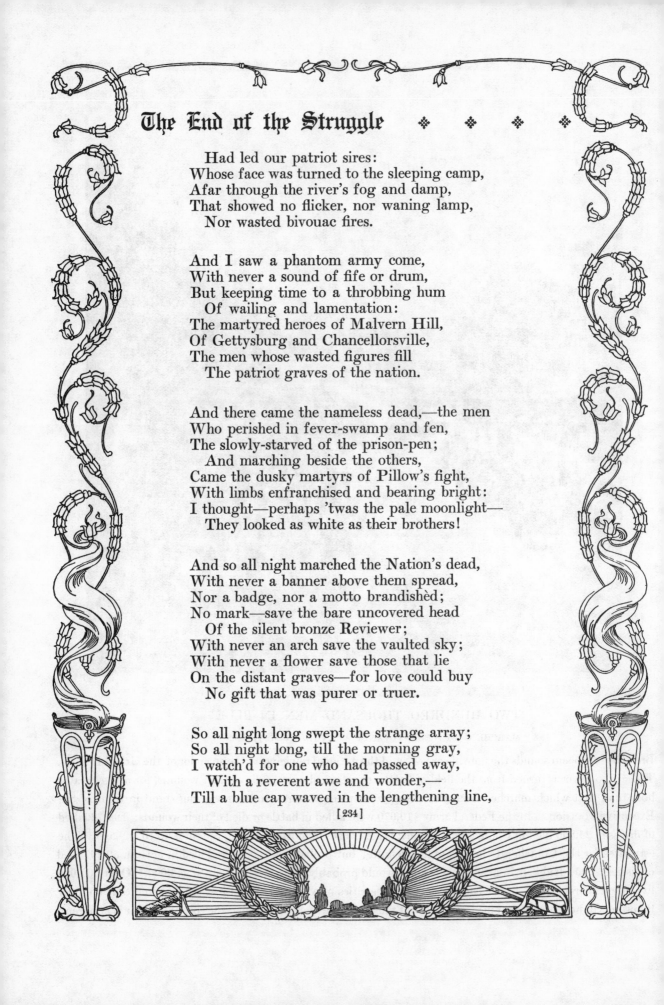

These shifting crowds on Pennsylvania Avenue, watching the Grand Review on May 23–24, 1865, seem like visions evoked by Bret Harte's lines. Part of the multitude of visitors to this most imposing fête day in American history are gathered near the reviewing-stand, before which the lines of men in blue are marching with military precision. Below the majestic elms and horse-chestnuts cavalrymen are trotting to the martial music of the band on the double-quick in the rear. The weather was perfect. Scores of bands filled the air with familiar tunes, and the choruses of "When this cruel war is over," "When Johnny comes marching home," and "Tramp, tramp, tramp, the boys are marching," were sung

"THE CHEERS OF THE PEOPLE WHO CAME TO GREET"

"I SEEMED TO HEAR THEIR TRAMPLING FEET"

lustily by the enthusiastic onlookers. Popular leaders were received with the most boisterous demonstrations. When Meade appeared at the head of the column, his pathway was strewn with flowers, and garlands were placed upon him and his horse. On the second day, Sherman was eagerly waited for, and he had advanced but a little way when flowers and wreaths almost covered him and his horse. When the bands at the reviewing stand struck up "Marching through Georgia," the people cheered wildly with delight. This was no Roman triumph. It was the rejoicing over the return of peace and the saving of the nation's life.

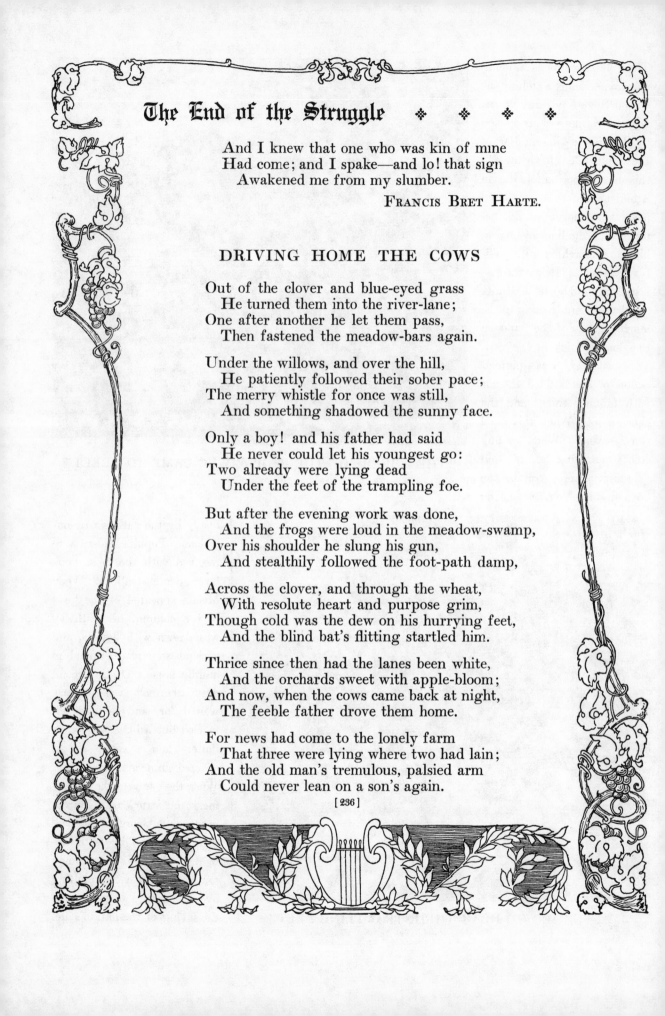

The End of the Struggle ❖ ❖ ❖ ❖

And I knew that one who was kin of mine
Had come; and I spake—and lo! that sign
Awakened me from my slumber.

FRANCIS BRET HARTE.

DRIVING HOME THE COWS

Out of the clover and blue-eyed grass
  He turned them into the river-lane;
One after another he let them pass,
  Then fastened the meadow-bars again.

Under the willows, and over the hill,
  He patiently followed their sober pace;
The merry whistle for once was still,
  And something shadowed the sunny face.

Only a boy! and his father had said
  He never could let his youngest go:
Two already were lying dead
  Under the feet of the trampling foe.

But after the evening work was done,
  And the frogs were loud in the meadow-swamp,
Over his shoulder he slung his gun,
  And stealthily followed the foot-path damp,

Across the clover, and through the wheat,
  With resolute heart and purpose grim,
Though cold was the dew on his hurrying feet,
  And the blind bat's flitting startled him.

Thrice since then had the lanes been white,
  And the orchards sweet with apple-bloom;
And now, when the cows came back at night,
  The feeble father drove them home.

For news had come to the lonely farm
  That three were lying where two had lain;
And the old man's tremulous, palsied arm
  Could never lean on a son's again.

"IN WASHINGTON'S CHIEFEST AVENUE"

Thus appeared the crowds that greeted the army whose home-coming inspired Bret Harte's poem. From the steps of the Treasury building the impatient people gaze down Pennsylvania Avenue on the morning of June 8, 1865, awaiting the march of the Sixth Corps of the Army of the Potomac, which had been prevented by duty in Virginia from participating in the Grand Review of May 23rd. The scene is similar. The women and children in the foreground, the senators and important citizens in silk hats, the throng surging far out into the street beneath the fluttering banners, the general restlessness and impatience are the same as on the earlier and more famous gala occasion. The pomp and panoply of war are here in the parades and the blare of trumpets and the admiring hosts that line the street—not in the actual service in the field. Harte writes of actual warfare as a sad business, which only the preservation of a nation's existence or honor can justify.

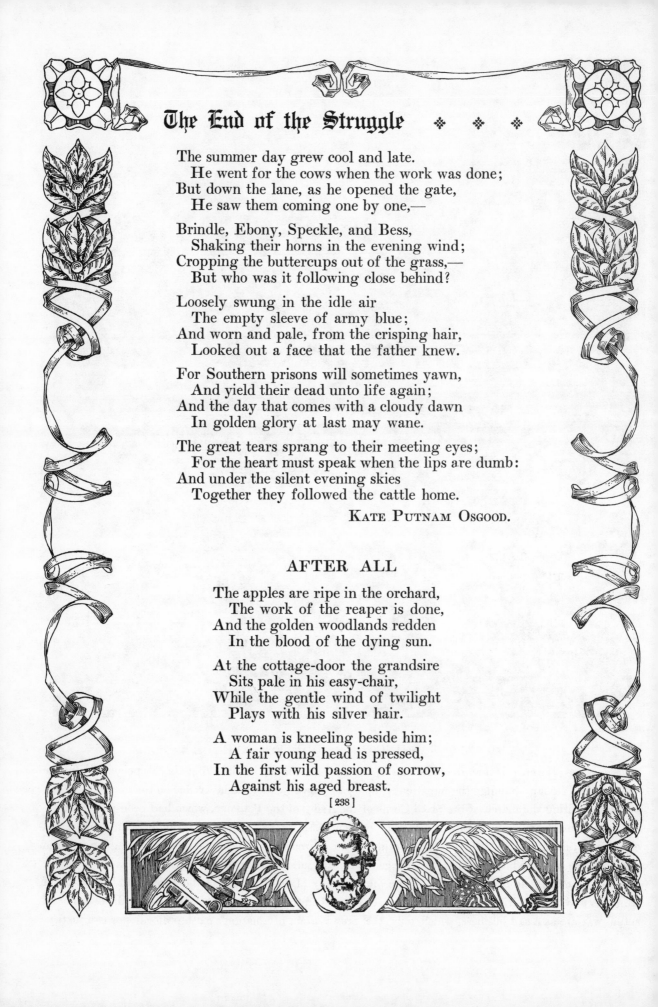

The End of the Struggle ✦ ✦ ✦

The summer day grew cool and late.
   He went for the cows when the work was done;
But down the lane, as he opened the gate,
   He saw them coming one by one,—

Brindle, Ebony, Speckle, and Bess,
   Shaking their horns in the evening wind;
Cropping the buttercups out of the grass,—
   But who was it following close behind?

Loosely swung in the idle air
   The empty sleeve of army blue;
And worn and pale, from the crisping hair,
   Looked out a face that the father knew.

For Southern prisons will sometimes yawn,
   And yield their dead unto life again;
And the day that comes with a cloudy dawn
   In golden glory at last may wane.

The great tears sprang to their meeting eyes;
   For the heart must speak when the lips are dumb:
And under the silent evening skies
   Together they followed the cattle home.

                KATE PUTNAM OSGOOD.

AFTER ALL

The apples are ripe in the orchard,
   The work of the reaper is done,
And the golden woodlands redden
   In the blood of the dying sun.

At the cottage-door the grandsire
   Sits pale in his easy-chair,
While the gentle wind of twilight
   Plays with his silver hair.

A woman is kneeling beside him;
   A fair young head is pressed,
In the first wild passion of sorrow,
   Against his aged breast.

[238]

WAITING FOR NEWS OF THE BATTLE

WAR-TIME GROUPS NEAR RICHMOND

AT HANOVER JUNCTION A BATTLE GROUND FOUGHT OVER MANY TIMES

These views of the station at Hanover Junction, in Virginia, bring back in pictorial form the emotions of war-time, much as do the accompanying poems of Kate Putnam Osgood and William Winter. The shabby building with the crowd about it, the queer little engine drawing old-fashioned coaches, on the last of which a man leans out from the steps, and behind, in the chilly gray atmosphere of autumn, the wooded Virginia hills—these details make more real the men and women who suffered in the days of 1861. On the platform, at the left, stands an old soldier whose white beard and venerable face contrast with the hearty content of the man whose hands are in the pockets of his conspicuously checked trousers. At the other end, on the steps, is a wounded officer painfully making his way with the aid of two canes. Grouped by the doorway stand some mothers, wives, and sweethearts, dressed in the ancient poke-bonnets and rustling crinoline of fifty years ago. Some poems in this chapter express phases of the anguish that came to many a fond heart in those four endless years. But the women in the picture are more fortunate than most. They can go to the front to be with the wounded son or brother. Thousands had to wait on the hillside farm, or in the cabin on the prairie, or near the cottage by the live-oaks, while weeks and months of dread uncertainty brought no solace to eyes that watched through the darkness and hearts that suffered on in silence until the news arrived.

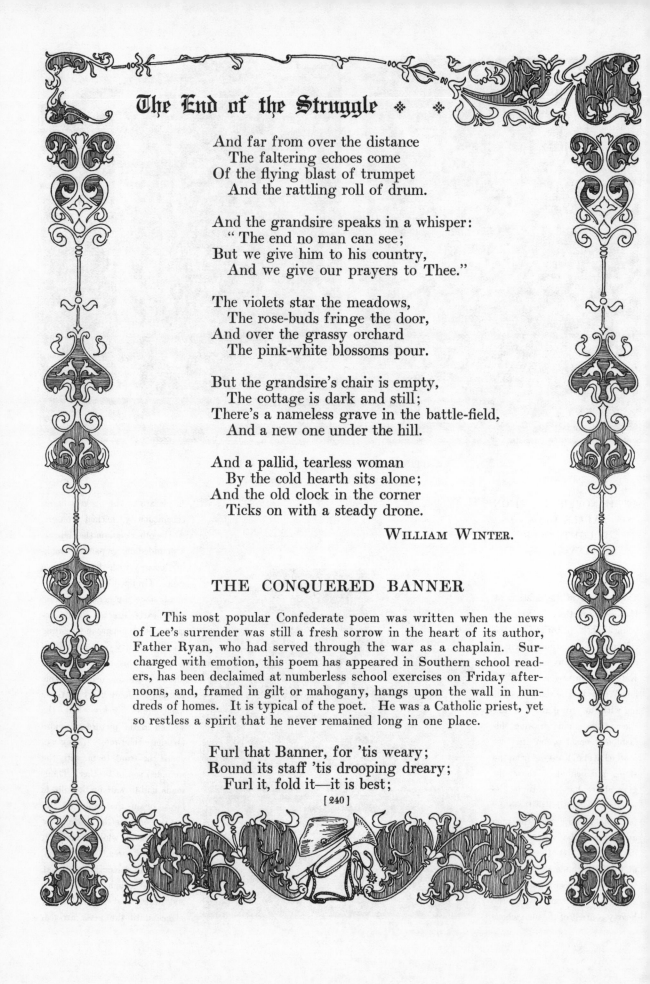

The End of the Struggle ❖ ❖

And far from over the distance
    The faltering echoes come
Of the flying blast of trumpet
    And the rattling roll of drum.

And the grandsire speaks in a whisper:
    " The end no man can see;
But we give him to his country,
    And we give our prayers to Thee."

The violets star the meadows,
    The rose-buds fringe the door,
And over the grassy orchard
    The pink-white blossoms pour.

But the grandsire's chair is empty,
    The cottage is dark and still;
There's a nameless grave in the battle-field,
    And a new one under the hill.

And a pallid, tearless woman
    By the cold hearth sits alone;
And the old clock in the corner
    Ticks on with a steady drone.

WILLIAM WINTER.

THE CONQUERED BANNER

This most popular Confederate poem was written when the news of Lee's surrender was still a fresh sorrow in the heart of its author, Father Ryan, who had served through the war as a chaplain. Surcharged with emotion, this poem has appeared in Southern school readers, has been declaimed at numberless school exercises on Friday afternoons, and, framed in gilt or mahogany, hangs upon the wall in hundreds of homes. It is typical of the poet. He was a Catholic priest, yet so restless a spirit that he never remained long in one place.

Furl that Banner, for 'tis weary;
Round its staff 'tis drooping dreary;
    Furl it, fold it—it is best;

"THERE'S A NAMELESS GRAVE IN THE BATTLEFIELD"

This mute reminder of Antietam's awful cost suggests how many thousand homes were sunk in grief such as the poem "After All" describes. The soldiers themselves shared this grief. One of their saddest duties was the burial of comrades. When the graves had been dug, if there was found on their person any means of identifying them or if any one knew who they were, little pieces of board were secured and placed at the head of each. On these little boards, pieces of cracker-box, generally, would be placed the name and regiment of the deceased comrade written in pencil. Under the rain and the snows the writing would be obliterated or the boards themselves tumble down, and those lying in their graves on the battlefield would pass into the number of the great "unknown." There were no opportunities afforded in these burial details to go through any religious forms. The numbers forbade. Yet the lads who formed burial parties always gave their meed of reverence.

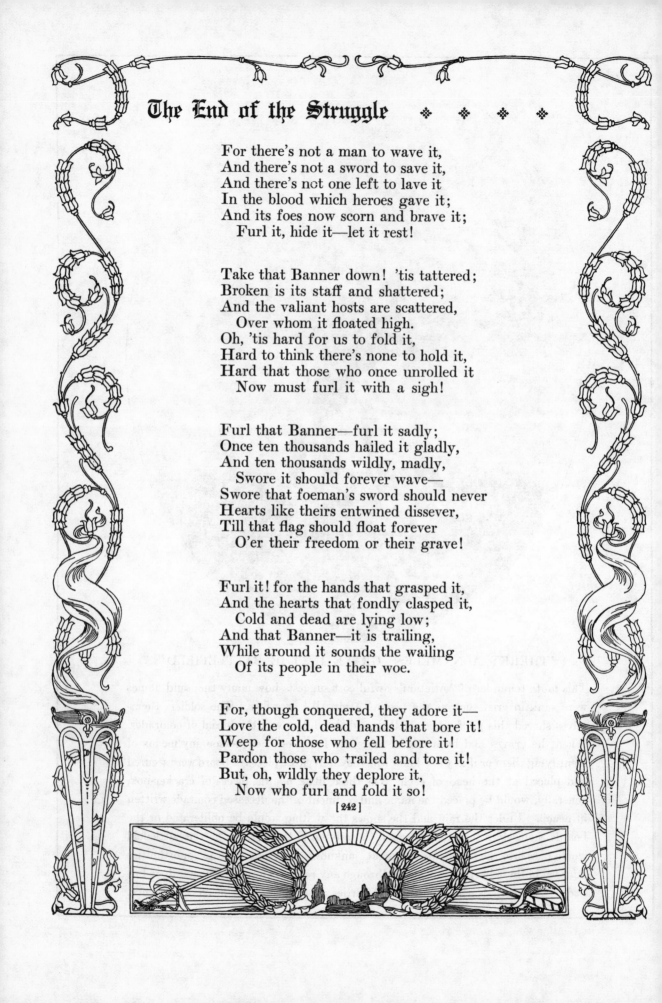

The End of the Struggle ❖ ❖ ❖ ❖

For there's not a man to wave it,
And there's not a sword to save it,
And there's not one left to lave it
In the blood which heroes gave it;
And its foes now scorn and brave it;
   Furl it, hide it—let it rest!

Take that Banner down! 'tis tattered;
Broken is its staff and shattered;
And the valiant hosts are scattered,
   Over whom it floated high.
Oh, 'tis hard for us to fold it,
Hard to think there's none to hold it,
Hard that those who once unrolled it
   Now must furl it with a sigh!

Furl that Banner—furl it sadly;
Once ten thousands hailed it gladly,
And ten thousands wildly, madly,
   Swore it should forever wave—
Swore that foeman's sword should never
Hearts like theirs entwined dissever,
Till that flag should float forever
   O'er their freedom or their grave!

Furl it! for the hands that grasped it,
And the hearts that fondly clasped it,
   Cold and dead are lying low;
And that Banner—it is trailing,
While around it sounds the wailing
   Of its people in their woe.

For, though conquered, they adore it—
Love the cold, dead hands that bore it!
Weep for those who fell before it!
Pardon those who trailed and tore it!
But, oh, wildly they deplore it,
   Now who furl and fold it so!

"THE VALIANT HOSTS ARE SCATTERED"

HERE PASSED THE MOST FAMOUS ARMY OF ALL THAT HAD FOUGHT FOR "THE CONQUERED BANNER"

This tragic still-life near Stony Creek, Virginia, is a witness to the turmoil of Lee's retreat. The caisson of a gun that tumbled into Chamberlain's Run on March 31, 1865, and was there abandoned, remains to tell of the last great battle. Through March Lee recognized that his only hope was to join Johnston in the Carolinas. Grant had spent many a sleepless night, fearing always that the next morning would bring him a report of Lee's retreat. To prevent this, he ordered Sheridan to destroy the railroads west of Petersburg. But on March 30th Sheridan was met at Five Forks by the Confederates under command of Fitzhugh Lee, and the next day was driven back southward to within half a mile of Dinwiddie Court House. In this engagement, W. H. F. Lee was sent along a wooded road leading south from Five Forks west of Chamberlain Bed, a creek running into Stony Creek near Dinwiddie Court House. After failing at one crossing, he succeeded in reaching the east bank at Danse's Crossing. All of Sheridan's cavalry corps then fell back on Dinwiddie Court House. Of this attack the single wheel of a caisson is the silent reminder. That night Sheridan was reënforced by the Fifth Corps; the next day, April 1st, he carried the Confederate position at Five Forks, and took nearly five thousand prisoners. The next morning, April 2d, the Petersburg entrenchments were carried by storm. The day after, the whole Confederate army was hastening westward. Seven days after this engagement came Appomattox. Lee's valiant hosts were indeed scattered, returning to their homes in a land that was once more united.

THE CONQUERED BANNER—WAVING FREE IN '61

The first Confederate flag made in Augusta, Georgia, swells in the May breeze of 1861. It has two red bars, with a white in the middle, and a union of blue with seven stars. The men who so proudly stand before it near the armory at Macon are the Clinch Rifles, forming Company A of the Fifth Georgia Infantry. The organization was completed on the next day—May 11th. It first went to Pensacola. From after the battle of Shiloh to July, 1864, it served in the Army of Tennessee, when it was sent to the Georgia coast, later serving under General Joseph E. Johnston in the final campaign in the Carolinas. It was conspicuous at Chickamauga, where its colonel commanded a brigade. His account of the action on September 20, 1863, is well worth quoting: "The brigade, with the battery in the center, moved forward in splendid style about 100 yards, when the enemy opened a galling fire from the front and left flank, enfilading the entire

"ONCE TEN THOUSANDS HAILED IT GLADLY"

line with canister and small-arms. The engagement now became terrific and the position of my brigade extremely critical. The troops, however, stood nobly to the work before them, and, steadily advancing, surmounted the hill on which the enemy's breastworks were, the battery moving with the line, and rendering effective service. The enemy were driven from their breastworks, and Brigadier-General Maney's brigade coming up at this opportune moment, charged them, and the contest was over. At daylight on Monday morning the enemy was found to have sought safety in flight under the cover of darkness." During the battle the regiment lost 194 men, a percentage of 54.95. The next highest recorded loss was 42.78. Ryan's words, "Those who once unrolled it," can appropriately be quoted under this spirited scene. And another phrase, "Cold and dead are lying now," fits too sadly well the careers of these volunteers from Georgia.

THE CONQUERED BANNER—"THERE'S NOT A SWORD TO SAVE IT"

As these rows and rows of cannon stretch across the arsenal grounds at Baton Rouge, soon after their surrender on May 4, 1865, by the Confederate general, Richard Taylor, a dramatic illustration appears of "The Conquered Banner" in war and in peace.   The large building at the right, the arsenal of war times, was transformed, 45 years later, into dormitories for the Louisiana State University.   It had been a military center under no less than five flags.   The smaller buildings at the left, formerly used as powderhouses, later became model dairies in the agricultural department of the university work.   Thus destruction gave place to training for citizenship and service.   As soon as General Taylor heard of the capitulation of General Joseph E. Johnston in North Carolina, he surrendered, on May 4, 1865, at Citronelle, Alabama, not far from Mobile, all the remaining forces of the Confederacy east of the Mississippi River to the Federal General E. R. S. Canby.   Canby had advanced from Dauphine Island, at the entrance to Mobile Bay, to the

THE GUNS OF THE LARGEST CONFEDERATE ARMY THAT SURRENDERED

Spanish Fort across from Mobile and had reduced it on April 8th, marching into the deserted works on the day that General Lee sur-rendered at Appomattox. At the same time, General Frederick Steele had advanced from Pensacola against Blakely, a little farther north than the Spanish Fort, and had captured it on the afternoon of Lee's surrender. On the morning of May 12th the Union forces under General Gordon Granger crossed the bay and found that the Confederate General Dabney H. Maury had marched out with his whole force. Maury succeeded in reaching Meridian in safety. During these operations the celebrated Confederate cavalry General Nathan B. Forrest had been defeated by the Federal cavalry under General James H. Wilson, and Selma, Alabama, with its fortifica-tions, foundries, and workshops, had fallen into his hands. He entered Montgomery the same day that Granger entered Mobile. Tay-lor surrendered 42,293 men, the largest aggregation anywhere laying down their arms at the close of the war.

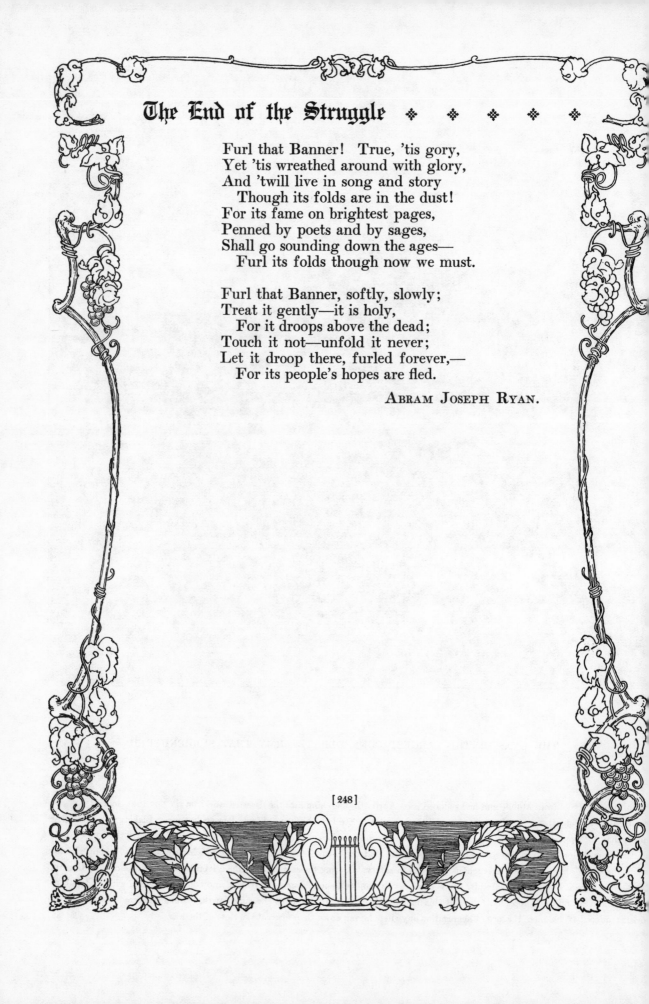

The End of the Struggle ✦ ✦ ✦ ✦ ✦

Furl that Banner! True, 'tis gory,
Yet 'tis wreathed around with glory,
And 'twill live in song and story
 Though its folds are in the dust!
For its fame on brightest pages,
Penned by poets and by sages,
Shall go sounding down the ages—
 Furl its folds though now we must.

Furl that Banner, softly, slowly;
Treat it gently—it is holy,
 For it droops above the dead;
Touch it not—unfold it never;
Let it droop there, furled forever,—
 For its people's hopes are fled.

ABRAM JOSEPH RYAN.

XI

LINCOLN

THE FUNERAL PROCESSION OF THE MARTYRED PRESIDENT
IN NEW YORK CITY, APRIL 25TH, 1865

LINCOLN

ON THE LIFE-MASK OF ABRAHAM LINCOLN

This bronze doth keep the very form and mould
Of our great martyr's face.   Yes, this is he:
That brow all wisdom, all benignity;
That human, humorous mouth; those cheeks that hold
Like some harsh landscape all the summer's gold;
That spirit fit for sorrow, as the sea
For storms to beat on; the lone agony
Those silent, patient lips too well foretold.
Yes, this is he who ruled a world of men
As might some prophet of the elder day—
Brooding above the tempest and the fray
With deep-eyed thought and more than mortal ken,
A power was his beyond the touch of art
Or armëd strength—his pure and mighty heart.

RICHARD WATSON GILDER.

THE SECOND INAUGURAL ADDRESS

Delivered by Abraham Lincoln, March 4, 1864. This, the greatest
of presidential inaugurals and one of the noblest papers ever penned by
an American statesman, expresses well the largeness of soul which held a
whole warring nation within his love, and has won for him the homage
of a reunited people. Though delivered little more than a month before
the closing scene at Appomattox, it voices no exultation in the triumph
of a cause dear to his heart, but with infinite pity and a truly sublime
magnanimity enters into the feelings of those who have lost.

FELLOW-COUNTRYMEN: At this second appearing to take
the oath of the presidential office, there is less occasion
for an extended address than there was at the first.   Then
a statement, somewhat in detail, of a course to be pursued,
seemed fitting and proper.   Now, at the expiration of four
years, during which public declarations have been constantly
called forth on every point and phase of the great contest

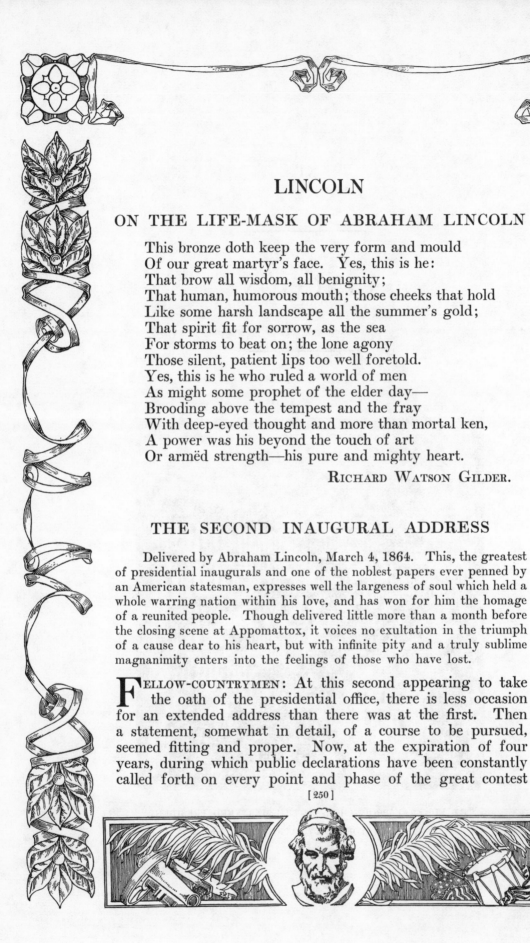

LINCOLN IN JUNE, 1860—TWO MONTHS AFTER VOLK MADE THE LIFE MASK

GILDER, WHOSE POEM OPPOSITE WAS INSPIRED BY THE MASK, WAS ALWAYS PARTICULARY ATTRACTED TO IT, AND KEPT A COPY OF IT IN HIS EDITORIAL SANCTUM AT THE *Century Magazine* OFFICES

In 1860, Lincoln had been a national figure only two years, since his campaign against Stephen A. Douglas for the Senate in Illinois. Indeed, his name meant little in the East till the early months of this very year. In February, he had appeared before a New York audience at Cooper Union to explain the purposes of the recently organized Republican party. The larger part of those present expected something "wild and woolly"—certainly nothing of much moment for the cultivated citizens of the East. When they saw the gaunt figure, six feet four inches tall, the large feet and clumsy hands, the jutting eyebrows and small blue eyes, the narrow forehead surmounted by the shock of unkempt hair—in a word, the man of the photograph on this page—the audience put him down for anything but a statesman. But he had not spoken long before it was plain that here stood a leader of the people indeed. The speech shaped the presidential campaign of that year. It resulted in giving Lincoln the Republican nomination at Chicago on May 16th, about a month before this photograph was made. When the ballot-boxes were opened on the first Tuesday of the following November, it was found that Abraham Lincoln was elected President of the United States. That meant war—and eventual Union of the warring elements.

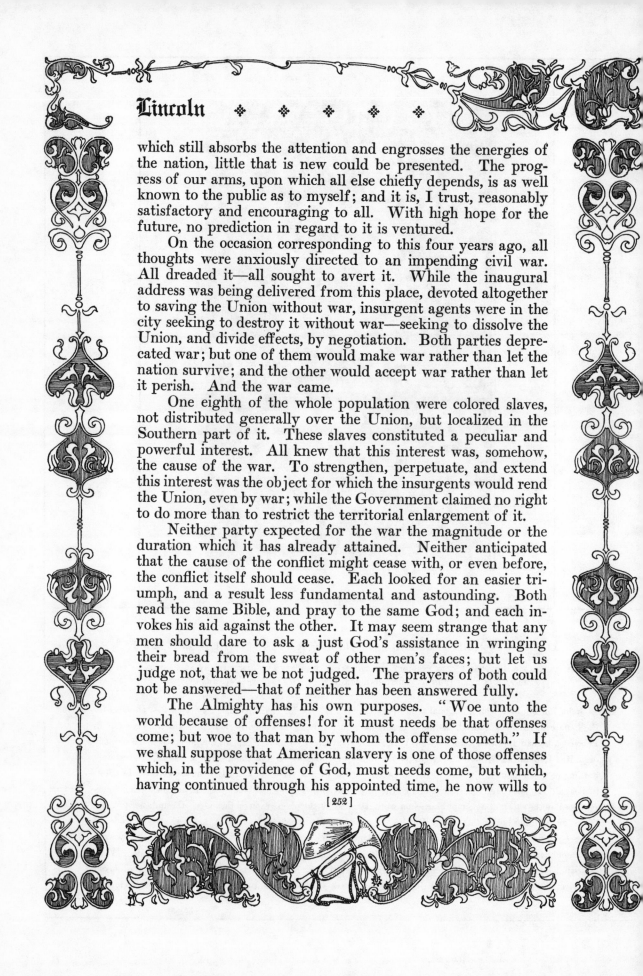

which still absorbs the attention and engrosses the energies of the nation, little that is new could be presented. The progress of our arms, upon which all else chiefly depends, is as well known to the public as to myself; and it is, I trust, reasonably satisfactory and encouraging to all. With high hope for the future, no prediction in regard to it is ventured.

On the occasion corresponding to this four years ago, all thoughts were anxiously directed to an impending civil war. All dreaded it—all sought to avert it. While the inaugural address was being delivered from this place, devoted altogether to saving the Union without war, insurgent agents were in the city seeking to destroy it without war—seeking to dissolve the Union, and divide effects, by negotiation. Both parties deprecated war; but one of them would make war rather than let the nation survive; and the other would accept war rather than let it perish. And the war came.

One eighth of the whole population were colored slaves, not distributed generally over the Union, but localized in the Southern part of it. These slaves constituted a peculiar and powerful interest. All knew that this interest was, somehow, the cause of the war. To strengthen, perpetuate, and extend this interest was the object for which the insurgents would rend the Union, even by war; while the Government claimed no right to do more than to restrict the territorial enlargement of it.

Neither party expected for the war the magnitude or the duration which it has already attained. Neither anticipated that the cause of the conflict might cease with, or even before, the conflict itself should cease. Each looked for an easier triumph, and a result less fundamental and astounding. Both read the same Bible, and pray to the same God; and each invokes his aid against the other. It may seem strange that any men should dare to ask a just God's assistance in wringing their bread from the sweat of other men's faces; but let us judge not, that we be not judged. The prayers of both could not be answered—that of neither has been answered fully.

The Almighty has his own purposes. "Woe unto the world because of offenses! for it must needs be that offenses come; but woe to that man by whom the offense cometh." If we shall suppose that American slavery is one of those offenses which, in the providence of God, must needs come, but which, having continued through his appointed time, he now wills to

LINCOLN AND HIS SON "TAD"

This photograph of Lincoln and little "Tad" was taken in 1861, when the four years of war were yet to burden the heart of the great President. In 1865, only a few days before his assassination, Lincoln for the last time entered the Brady gallery in Washington, and again sat for his picture with "Tad." The scene is touching beyond words.

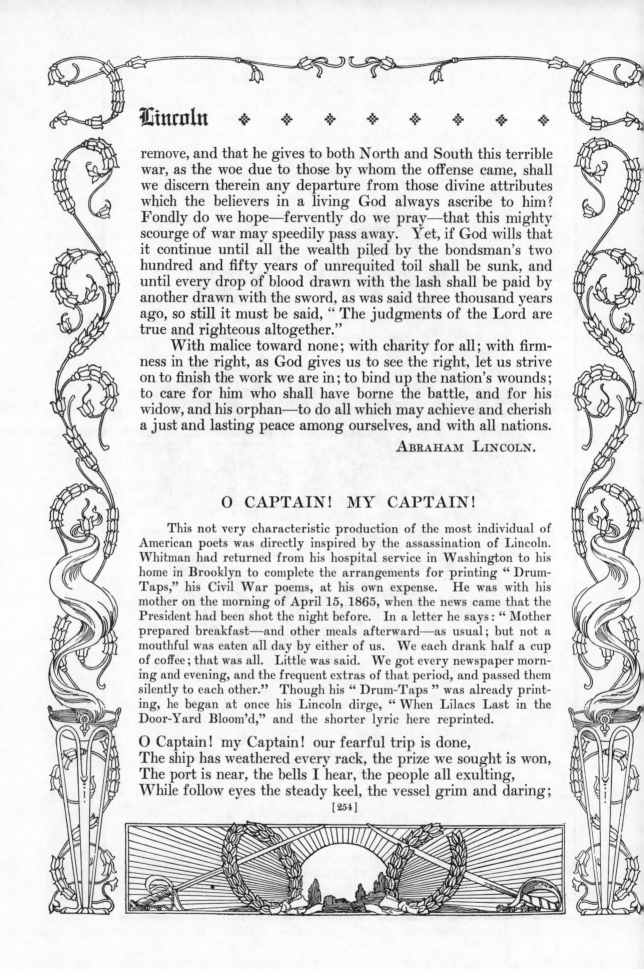

remove, and that he gives to both North and South this terrible war, as the woe due to those by whom the offense came, shall we discern therein any departure from those divine attributes which the believers in a living God always ascribe to him? Fondly do we hope—fervently do we pray—that this mighty scourge of war may speedily pass away. Yet, if God wills that it continue until all the wealth piled by the bondsman's two hundred and fifty years of unrequited toil shall be sunk, and until every drop of blood drawn with the lash shall be paid by another drawn with the sword, as was said three thousand years ago, so still it must be said, "The judgments of the Lord are true and righteous altogether."

With malice toward none; with charity for all; with firmness in the right, as God gives us to see the right, let us strive on to finish the work we are in; to bind up the nation's wounds; to care for him who shall have borne the battle, and for his widow, and his orphan—to do all which may achieve and cherish a just and lasting peace among ourselves, and with all nations.

ABRAHAM LINCOLN.

O CAPTAIN! MY CAPTAIN!

This not very characteristic production of the most individual of American poets was directly inspired by the assassination of Lincoln. Whitman had returned from his hospital service in Washington to his home in Brooklyn to complete the arrangements for printing "Drum-Taps," his Civil War poems, at his own expense. He was with his mother on the morning of April 15, 1865, when the news came that the President had been shot the night before. In a letter he says: "Mother prepared breakfast—and other meals afterward—as usual; but not a mouthful was eaten all day by either of us. We each drank half a cup of coffee; that was all. Little was said. We got every newspaper morning and evening, and the frequent extras of that period, and passed them silently to each other." Though his "Drum-Taps" was already printing, he began at once his Lincoln dirge, "When Lilacs Last in the Door-Yard Bloom'd," and the shorter lyric here reprinted.

O Captain! my Captain! our fearful trip is done,
The ship has weathered every rack, the prize we sought is won,
The port is near, the bells I hear, the people all exulting,
While follow eyes the steady keel, the vessel grim and daring;

WHILE LINCOLN

SPOKE AT

GETTYSBURG,

NOVEMBER

19, 1863

DURING THE

FAMOUS ADDRESS

IN DEDICATION

OF THE

CEMETERY

The most important American address is brief: "Fourscore and seven years ago our fathers brought forth on this continent a new nation, conceived in liberty, and dedicated to the proposition that all men are created equal. Now we are engaged in a great civil war, testing whether that nation, or any nation so conceived and so dedicated, can long endure. We are met on a great battlefield of that war. We have come to dedicate a portion of that field as a final resting-place for those who here gave their lives that that nation might live. It is altogether fitting and proper that we should do this. But in a larger sense, we cannot dedicate, we cannot consecrate, we cannot hallow this ground. The brave men, living and dead, who struggled here, have consecrated it far above our poor power to add or detract. The world will little note, nor long remember, what we say here, but it can never forget what they did here. It is for us, the living, rather, to be dedicated here to the unfinished work which they who fought here have thus far so nobly advanced. It is rather for us to be here dedicated to the great task remaining before us;—that from these honored dead, we take increased devotion to that cause for which they gave the last full measure of devotion;—that we here highly resolve that these dead shall not have died in vain, that this nation, under God, shall have a new birth of freedom, and that government of the people, by the people, for the people, shall not perish from the earth."

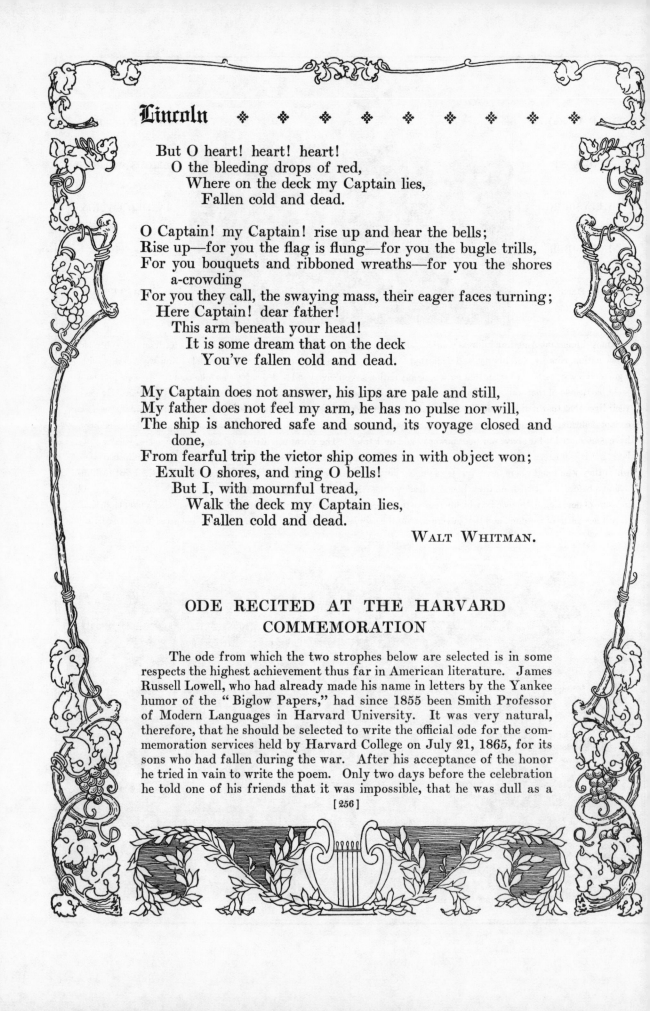

But O heart! heart! heart!
　O the bleeding drops of red,
　　Where on the deck my Captain lies,
　　　Fallen cold and dead.

O Captain! my Captain! rise up and hear the bells;
Rise up—for you the flag is flung—for you the bugle trills,
For you bouquets and ribboned wreaths—for you the shores
　a-crowding
For you they call, the swaying mass, their eager faces turning;
　Here Captain! dear father!
　　This arm beneath your head!
　　　It is some dream that on the deck
　　　　You've fallen cold and dead.

My Captain does not answer, his lips are pale and still,
My father does not feel my arm, he has no pulse nor will,
The ship is anchored safe and sound, its voyage closed and
　done,
From fearful trip the victor ship comes in with object won;
　Exult O shores, and ring O bells!
　　But I, with mournful tread,
　　　Walk the deck my Captain lies,
　　　　Fallen cold and dead.

WALT WHITMAN.

ODE RECITED AT THE HARVARD
COMMEMORATION

　　The ode from which the two strophes below are selected is in some respects the highest achievement thus far in American literature. James Russell Lowell, who had already made his name in letters by the Yankee humor of the "Biglow Papers," had since 1855 been Smith Professor of Modern Languages in Harvard University. It was very natural, therefore, that he should be selected to write the official ode for the commemoration services held by Harvard College on July 21, 1865, for its sons who had fallen during the war. After his acceptance of the honor he tried in vain to write the poem. Only two days before the celebration he told one of his friends that it was impossible, that he was dull as a

LINCOLN

THE LAST SITTING—ON THE DAY OF LEE'S SURRENDER

On April 9, 1865, the very day of the surrender of Lee at Appomattox, Lincoln, for the last time, went to the photographer's gallery. As he sits in simple fashion sharpening his pencil, the man of sorrows cannot forget the sense of weariness and pain that for four years has been unbroken. No elation of triumph lights the features. One task is ended—the Nation is saved. But another, scarcely less exacting, confronts him. The States which lay "out of their proper practical relation to the Union," in his own phrase, must be brought back into a proper practical relation. But this task was not for him. Only five days later the sad eyes reflected upon this page closed forever upon scenes of earthly turmoil. Bereft of Lincoln's heart and head, leaders attacked problems of reconstruction in ways that proved unwise. As the mists of passion and prejudice cleared away, both North and South came to feel that this patient, wise, and sympathetic ruler was one of the few really great men in history, and that he would live forever in the hearts of men made better by his presence during those four years of storm.

A NATION IN MOURNING—THE WASHINGTON PROCESSION AT LINCOLN'S FUNERAL

After his faithful service, Abraham Lincoln, the leader from whose wisdom and sympathy both North and South had most to hope, was not to survive the completion of his task. An assassin stole into his box at Ford's Theater on the evening of April 14th, shot him in the back of the head, and leaping upon the stage escaped by a rear door. The next morning at seven o'clock the President was dead. The remains were taken to his home in Springfield, Illinois, along the route by which he had traveled in 1861, on his way to take the oath as President. This picture shows the solemn procession that moved toward the railway station in Washington.

ALL PRESENT BUT THE COMMANDER-IN-CHIEF

The Grand Review of the Army, May 23–24, 1865.   As two hundred thousand troops marched in the bright May sunshine of 1865 down the main thoroughfare of the National capital, to the strains of martial music, waving their battle-rent flags amid the flashing of sabers and bayonets, one face was missing at the reviewing-stand.   Lincoln, the commander-in-chief, who through four years of struggle had kept faith with his army, was absent—dead by an assassin's bullet.   Thus one of the mightiest armies ever gathered passed in final review ere it melted into the walks of civil life.   No great victorious force ever turned so quickly and completely to the arts of peace.

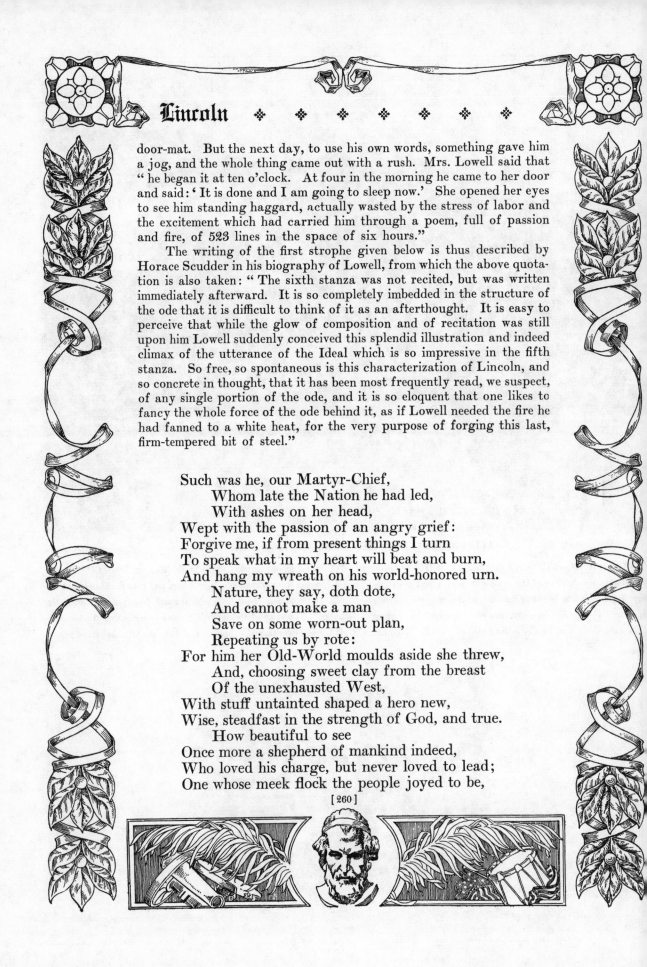

door-mat. But the next day, to use his own words, something gave him a jog, and the whole thing came out with a rush. Mrs. Lowell said that " he began it at ten o'clock. At four in the morning he came to her door and said: ' It is done and I am going to sleep now.' She opened her eyes to see him standing haggard, actually wasted by the stress of labor and the excitement which had carried him through a poem, full of passion and fire, of 523 lines in the space of six hours."

The writing of the first strophe given below is thus described by Horace Scudder in his biography of Lowell, from which the above quotation is also taken: " The sixth stanza was not recited, but was written immediately afterward. It is so completely imbedded in the structure of the ode that it is difficult to think of it as an afterthought. It is easy to perceive that while the glow of composition and of recitation was still upon him Lowell suddenly conceived this splendid illustration and indeed climax of the utterance of the Ideal which is so impressive in the fifth stanza. So free, so spontaneous is this characterization of Lincoln, and so concrete in thought, that it has been most frequently read, we suspect, of any single portion of the ode, and it is so eloquent that one likes to fancy the whole force of the ode behind it, as if Lowell needed the fire he had fanned to a white heat, for the very purpose of forging this last, firm-tempered bit of steel."

Such was he, our Martyr-Chief,
    Whom late the Nation he had led,
    With ashes on her head,
Wept with the passion of an angry grief:
Forgive me, if from present things I turn
To speak what in my heart will beat and burn,
And hang my wreath on his world-honored urn.
    Nature, they say, doth dote,
    And cannot make a man
    Save on some worn-out plan,
    Repeating us by rote:
For him her Old-World moulds aside she threw,
    And, choosing sweet clay from the breast
    Of the unexhausted West,
With stuff untainted shaped a hero new,
Wise, steadfast in the strength of God, and true.
    How beautiful to see
Once more a shepherd of mankind indeed,
Who loved his charge, but never loved to lead;
One whose meek flock the people joyed to be,

[260]

COPYRIGHT, 1911, REVIEW OF REVIEWS CO.

"SENDS ALL HER HANDMAID ARMIES BACK TO SPIN"

THE RETURN HOME OF THE SIXTEENTH MASSACHUSETTS INFANTRY, JULY 27, 1864

This scene of 1864, at the corner of Cambridge and Fourth Streets, East Cambridge, is in mournful contrast to the rejoicing which filled the nation the next year while Lowell was reading his ode in Harvard University. As these riders passed through Cambridge the Wilderness campaign had been fought, with little, apparently, accomplished to compensate for the fearful loss of life. Sherman was still struggling in the vicinity of Atlanta, far from his base of supplies, with no certainty of escaping an overwhelming defeat. Early had recently dashed into the outskirts of Washington. In fact an influential political party was about to declare the war a failure. So these Massachusetts troops returned with heavy hearts to be mustered out. Many of them reenlisted, to fight with the armies that captured Petersburg, and to be present at the surrender at Appomattox. Then they could return with those of whom Lowell sang: America "sends all her handmaid armies back to spin."

Lincoln ✦ ✦ ✦ ✦ ✦

Not lured by any cheat of birth,
But by his clear-grained human worth,
And brave old wisdom of sincerity!
They knew that outward grace is dust;
They could not choose but trust
In that sure-footed mind's unfaltering skill,
And supple-tempered will
That bent like perfect steel to spring again and thrust.
His was no lonely mountain-peak of mind,
Thrusting to thin air o'er our cloudy bars,
A sea-mark now, now lost in vapors blind;
Broad prairie rather, genial, level-lined,
Fruitful and friendly for all human kind,
Yet also nigh to heaven and loved of loftiest stars.
Nothing of Europe here,
Or, then, of Europe fronting mornward still,
Ere any names of Serf and Peer
Could Nature's equal scheme deface
And thwart her genial will;
Here was a type of the true elder race,
And one of Plutarch's men talked with us face to face.
I praise him not; it were too late;
And some innative weakness there must be
In him who condescends to victory
Such as the Present gives, and cannot wait,
Safe in himself as in a fate.
So always firmly he:
He knew to bide his time,
And can his fame abide,
Still patient in his simple faith sublime,
Till the wise years decide.
Great captains, with their guns and drums,
Disturb our judgment for the hour,
But at last silence comes;
These are all gone, and standing like a tower,
Our children shall behold his fame,
The kindly-earnest, brave, foreseeing man,
Sagacious, patient, dreading praise, not blame,
New birth of our new soil, the first American.

.   .   .   .   .

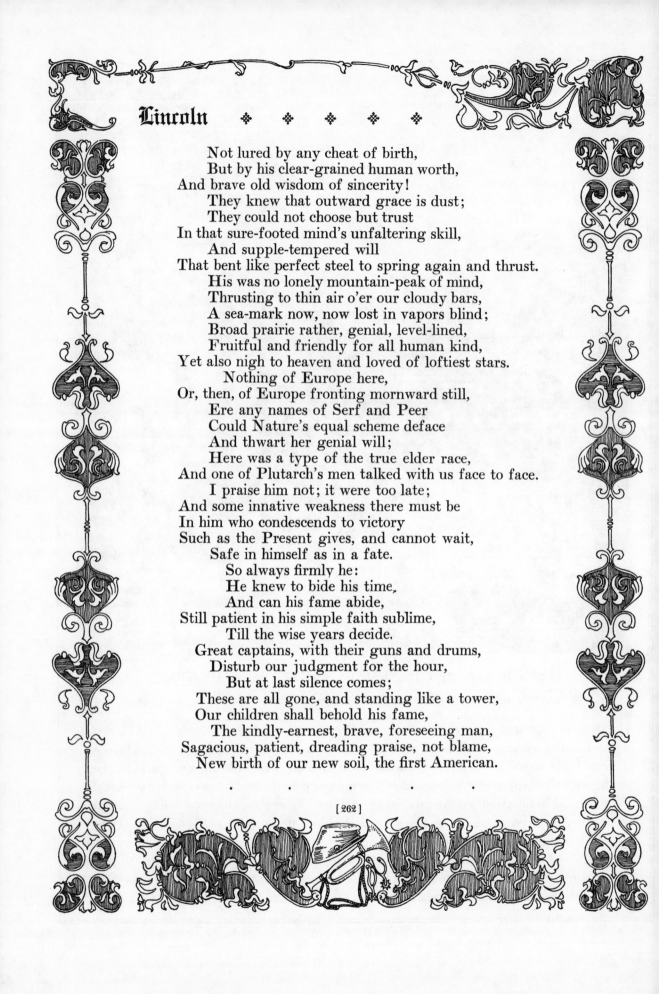

"NOT WITHOUT A PROUDER TREAD"—"LIFT THE HEART AND LIFT THE HEAD"

SOLDIERS AT THE DEDICATION OF THE BULL RUN MONUMENT, JUNE 10, 1865

As if to give pictorial expression to Lowell's sonorous lines, these scenes of 1865 have been preserved.   At the top is the Fifth Pennsylvania Heavy Artillery.   A thousand men stepping forward as a single man to the strains of music to which they had marched over the Virginia hills, reveal the practised movements of the veteran.   Below, some of the gaunt and hardened survivors of those four years look out at us.   Tanned by long exposure, toughened by numberless days and nights in sunshine and storm, these are the men who returned home in '65, adding their strength of character to the progress of their country,   Each had earned the right to feel the lofty mood Lowell expressed in his "Ode."   Each could feel the "tumult of elation" and the pride in motherland awaiting the morn of nobler day.

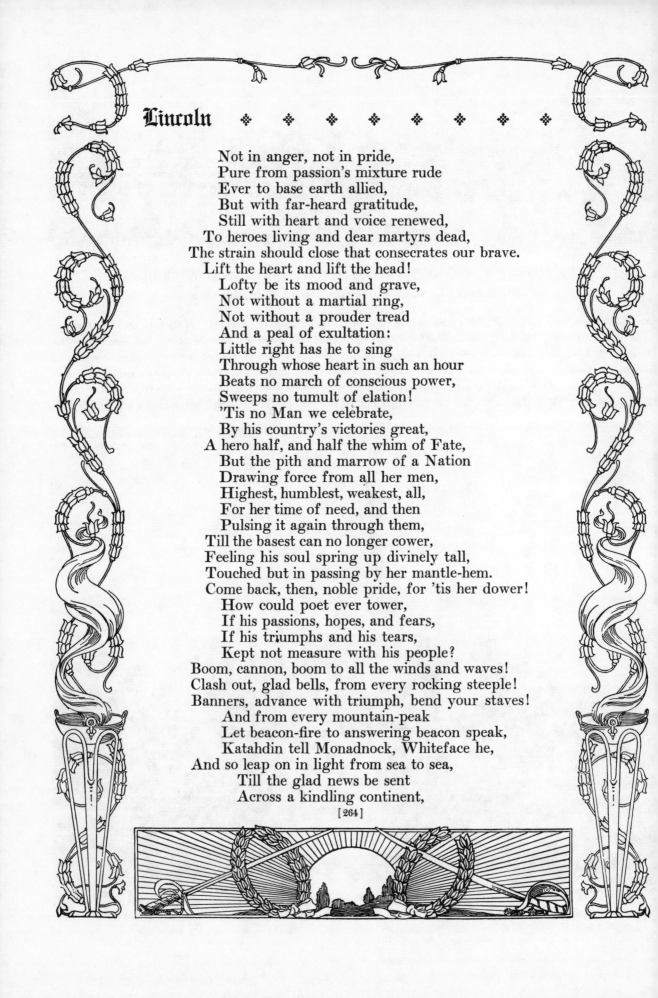

Lincoln ❖ ❖ ❖ ❖ ❖ ❖ ❖ ❖

Not in anger, not in pride,
Pure from passion's mixture rude
Ever to base earth allied,
But with far-heard gratitude,
Still with heart and voice renewed,
To heroes living and dear martyrs dead,
The strain should close that consecrates our brave.
Lift the heart and lift the head!
Lofty be its mood and grave,
Not without a martial ring,
Not without a prouder tread
And a peal of exultation:
Little right has he to sing
Through whose heart in such an hour
Beats no march of conscious power,
Sweeps no tumult of elation!
'Tis no Man we celebrate,
By his country's victories great,
A hero half, and half the whim of Fate,
But the pith and marrow of a Nation
Drawing force from all her men,
Highest, humblest, weakest, all,
For her time of need, and then
Pulsing it again through them,
Till the basest can no longer cower,
Feeling his soul spring up divinely tall,
Touched but in passing by her mantle-hem.
Come back, then, noble pride, for 'tis her dower!
How could poet ever tower,
If his passions, hopes, and fears,
If his triumphs and his tears,
Kept not measure with his people?
Boom, cannon, boom to all the winds and waves!
Clash out, glad bells, from every rocking steeple!
Banners, advance with triumph, bend your staves!
And from every mountain-peak
Let beacon-fire to answering beacon speak,
Katahdin tell Monadnock, Whiteface he,
And so leap on in light from sea to sea,
Till the glad news be sent
Across a kindling continent,

"WHERE FELL THE BRAVE"

DEDICATING THE MONUMENT AT BULL RUN, ON JUNE 10, 1865

This shaft was erected by the officers and men of General William Gamble's Separate Cavalry Brigade, stationed at Fairfax Court House during the preceding winter and spring. It is twenty-seven feet high, made of chocolate-colored sandstone, and bears on its top a 100-pound shell. The shells on the pedestals at each corner are of similar size. The inscription reads—"To the memory of the patriots who fell at Bull Run, July 21, 1861." The dedicatory exercises were conducted by the Rev. Dr. McCurdy, who read an appropriate service. After the singing of a special hymn for the occasion, the Fifth Pennsylvania Heavy Artillery executed a military parade and the Sixteenth Massachusetts Battery fired a salute. Judge Olin, who appears in white trousers and high hat, next delivered an eloquent address, and was followed by several generals. A little later in the day a second monument was dedicated on the field of Second Bull Run.

"NOT IN ANGER, NOT IN PRIDE"

Dedication of First Bull Run Monument, June 10, 1865.—A little more than a month before Lowell read his lofty ode for the sons of Harvard who had fallen in the Civil War, the group here preserved by the camera assembled to do honor to the "dear martyrs" who fell in the first great battle of the conflict. The site was on the hillside in front of the stone house, at the spot where on the afternoon of July 21, 1861, Ricketts and Griffin lost their batteries. In that battle the Federal forces had been entirely successful until early in the afternoon. Then the Confederates rallied on the brow of this hill, and the ground on which these men and women are gathered was the scene of a fierce struggle. The batteries were alternately captured by the Confederates and retaken by the Union forces, until the arrival of fresh troops in gray threw the Federal army into confusion and precipitated the panic of retreat. At the time

"TO HEROES LIVING AND DEAR MARTYRS DEAD"

of this picture, four years later, both soldier and citizen are standing calmly in the sunshine of the peaceful June day. "Not in anger, not in pride" do they look into our faces. At the left Judge Olin, with the cane, is standing behind a boy in a white shirt and quaint trousers who almost wistfully is gazing into the distance, as if the call of these mighty events had awakened in him a yearning for fame. To his left are Generals Thomas, Wilcox, Heintzelman, Dyer, and other veterans of many a hard-fought field who can feel the "march of conscious power" of which Lowell speaks. And the women with the flaring crinoline skirts and old-fashioned sleeves certainly may join in the "far-heard gratitude" this celebration was to express. After fifty years their emotions are brought home to the reader with the vividness of personal experience by the art of the photographer.

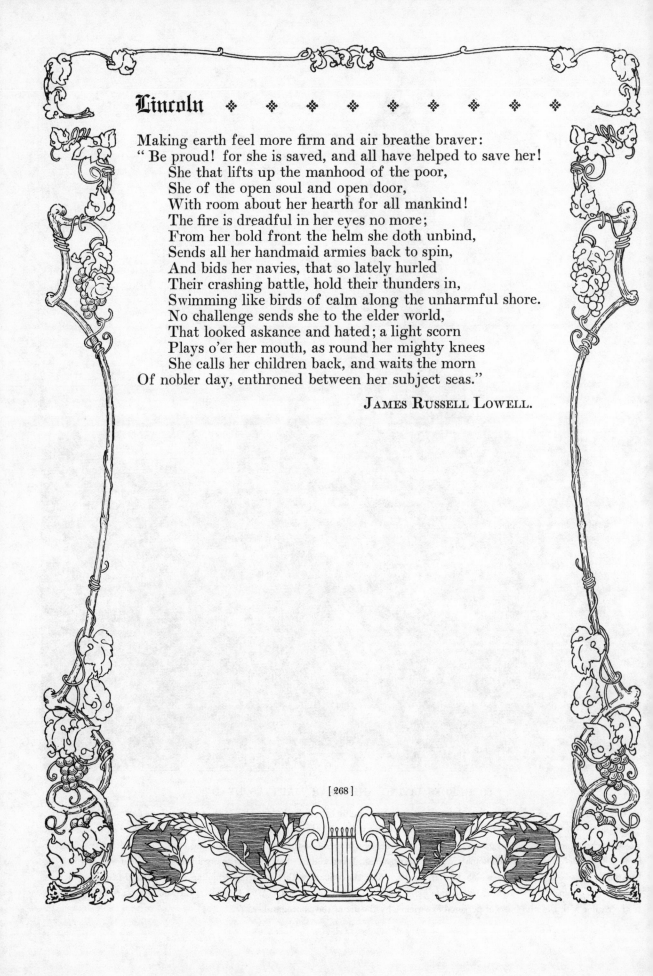

Lincoln ✦ ✦ ✦ ✦ ✦ ✦ ✦ ✦

Making earth feel more firm and air breathe braver:
" Be proud! for she is saved, and all have helped to save her!
   She that lifts up the manhood of the poor,
   She of the open soul and open door,
   With room about her hearth for all mankind!
   The fire is dreadful in her eyes no more;
   From her bold front the helm she doth unbind,
   Sends all her handmaid armies back to spin,
   And bids her navies, that so lately hurled
   Their crashing battle, hold their thunders in,
   Swimming like birds of calm along the unharmful shore.
   No challenge sends she to the elder world,
   That looked askance and hated; a light scorn
   Plays o'er her mouth, as round her mighty knees
   She calls her children back, and waits the morn
Of nobler day, enthroned between her subject seas."

JAMES RUSSELL LOWELL.

XII

———

THE
HERITAGE

———

THE HERITAGE

THE BLUE AND THE GRAY *

This national classic was suggested by an item in the New York *Tribune* in 1867. " The women of Columbus, Mississippi, animated by nobler sentiments than many of their sisters, have shown themselves impartial in their offerings made to the memory of the dead. They strewed flowers alike on the graves of the Confederate and of the National soldiers." The poem, prefaced by this item, was first published in the *Atlantic Monthly* for September, 1867, and at once attracted wide attention. The author was long on the New York Court of Appeals, and from 1892 was dean of the Law School of Cornell University.

By the flow of the inland river,
　Whence the fleets of iron have fled,
Where the blades of the grave-grass quiver,
　Asleep are the ranks of the dead:
　　Under the sod and the dew,
　　　Waiting the judgment-day;
　　Under the one, the Blue,
　　　Under the other, the Gray.

These in the robings of glory,
　Those in the gloom of defeat,
All with the battle-blood gory,
　In the dusk of eternity meet:
　　Under the sod and the dew,
　　　Waiting the judgment-day;
　　Under the laurel, the Blue,
　　　Under the willow, the Gray.

From the silence of sorrowful hours
　The desolate mourners go,
Lovingly laden with flowers
　Alike for the friend and the foe:

* Reprinted from " The Blue and the Gray and Other Poems" by arrangement with the publishers, Henry Holt and Company, New York.

THE BLUE AND THE GRAY

"BY THE FLOW OF THE INLAND RIVER—WHENCE THE FLEETS OF IRON HAVE FLED"

Finch's noble lines were evoked by a happening in a Mississippi town, as the opposite page sets forth. The war-time photographs show Union gunboats before they had left the river to peace. The four vessels on this page, *Baron DeKalb*, *Cincinnati*, and *Mound City* at the top, and the *Louisville* at the bottom, were among the most powerful of the Mississippi flotilla. They were all of the same class, 175 feet long and 51½ feet beam. Each carried three bow guns, four broadside guns on each side, and two stern guns. They were in addition plated with 2½-inch iron, yet they drew only six feet of water, and made nine miles an hour. They were constructed in the first year of the war by Captain James B. Eads, and some of them took part in every important action on the western rivers from the evacuation of Fort Henry to the capture of Mobile, 1864.

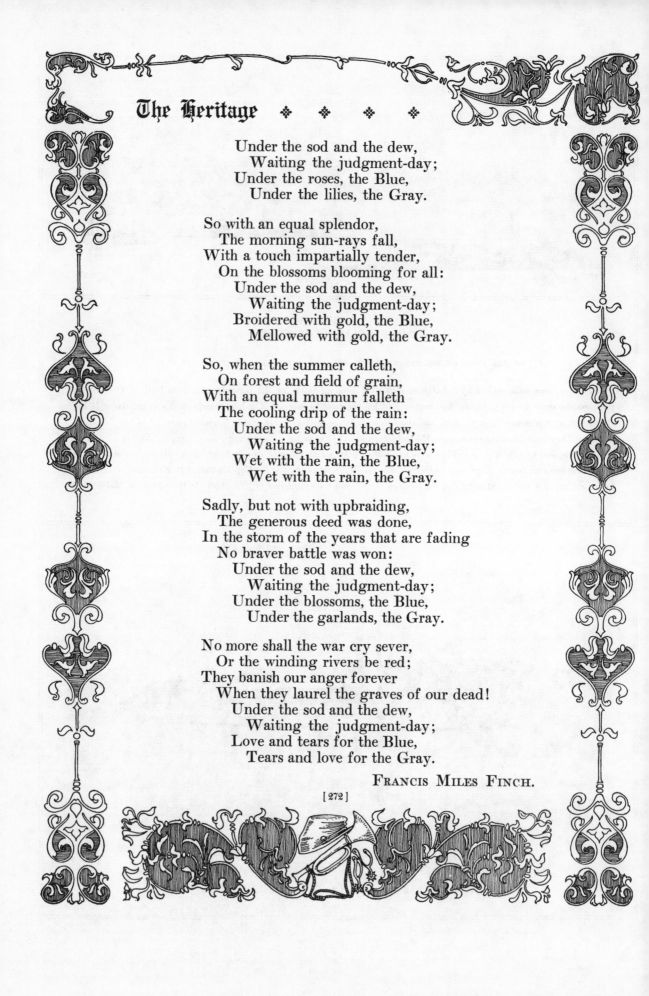

The Heritage ✦ ✦ ✦ ✦

Under the sod and the dew,
    Waiting the judgment-day;
Under the roses, the Blue,
    Under the lilies, the Gray.

So with an equal splendor,
    The morning sun-rays fall,
With a touch impartially tender,
    On the blossoms blooming for all:
        Under the sod and the dew,
            Waiting the judgment-day;
        Broidered with gold, the Blue,
            Mellowed with gold, the Gray.

So, when the summer calleth,
    On forest and field of grain,
With an equal murmur falleth
    The cooling drip of the rain:
        Under the sod and the dew,
            Waiting the judgment-day;
        Wet with the rain, the Blue,
            Wet with the rain, the Gray.

Sadly, but not with upbraiding,
    The generous deed was done,
In the storm of the years that are fading
    No braver battle was won:
        Under the sod and the dew,
            Waiting the judgment-day;
        Under the blossoms, the Blue,
            Under the garlands, the Gray.

No more shall the war cry sever,
    Or the winding rivers be red;
They banish our anger forever
    When they laurel the graves of our dead!
        Under the sod and the dew,
            Waiting the judgment-day;
        Love and tears for the Blue,
            Tears and love for the Gray.

FRANCIS MILES FINCH.

"THE BLOSSOMS BLOOMING FOR ALL"

These words of "The Blue and the Gray" might have been written for the tranquil scene here preserved by the war-time camera. All the foreground is bright with daisies, and the three graves under the trees by the cottage shine in the peaceful sunlight of a spring day. Nature asks not to which side belonged those now lying in their lowly beds—nor do we of any who fell in battle or perished in prison. The sentiment of "The Blue and the Gray" is at length the sentiment of the whole American people. The view is typical of the desolation that followed in the wake of the armies. On the right are the ruins of a line of houses; nothing remains but the crumbling foundations and the massive chimneys where hospitable fires once blazed in the wide fireplaces before throngs of merry young people. To the left are the remains of the humbler cottage. In the background are the woods where many a picnic made the days pass happily. The life of ease and quiet among these Arcadian surroundings was rudely ended by grim war. The hamlet lay in the path of a conquering army and was soon a waste place. But the gentle hand of Nature soon covered the unsightly wreckage.

A SOLDIER'S GRAVE

Break not his sweet repose—
Thou whom chance brings to this sequestered ground,
The sacred yard his ashes close,
But go thy way in silence; here no sound
Is ever heard but from the murmuring pines,
    Answering the sea's near murmur;
      Nor ever here comes rumor
Of anxious world or war's foregathering signs.
    The bleaching flag, the faded wreath,
    Mark the dead soldier's dust beneath,
    And show the death he chose;
Forgotten save by her who weeps alone,
And wrote his fameless name on this low stone:
    Break not his sweet repose.

JOHN ALBEE.

ODE AT MAGNOLIA CEMETERY *

Sung on the occasion of decorating the graves of the Confederate
dead, at Magnolia Cemetery, Charleston, on Memorial Day, April, 1867.

Sleep sweetly in your humble graves,
    Sleep, martyrs of a fallen cause;
Though yet no marble column craves
    The pilgrim here to pause.

In seeds of laurel in the earth
    The blossom of your fame is blown,
And somewhere, waiting for its birth,
    The shaft is in the stone!

Meanwhile, behalf the tardy years
    Which keep in trust your storied tombs,
Behold! your sisters bring their tears,
    And these memorial blooms.

* Used by permission of the B. F. Johnson Publishing Company, Richmond, Virginia, publishers of the Memorial Edition of the "Poems of
Henry Timrod."

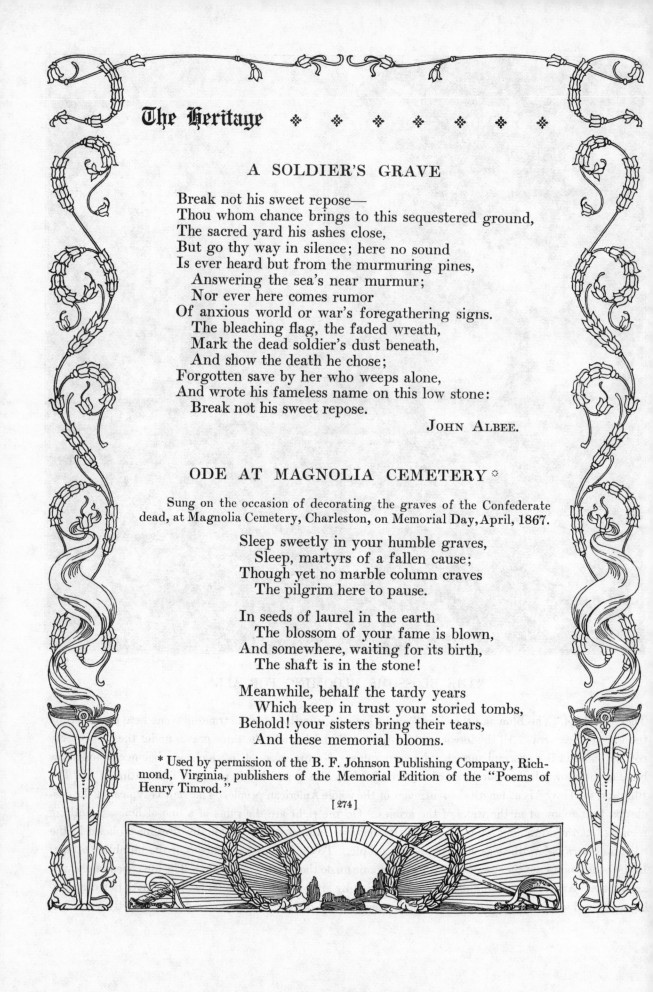

"BREAK NOT HIS SWEET REPOSE"

THE BURIAL-GROUND OF SAILORS WHO FELL AT HILTON HEAD IN 1861

This sequestered spot, the burial-place of the sailors who lost their lives in the capture of Hilton Head by the Federal fleet on November 7, 1861, might have been designed to fit the poem by John Albee. The live-oaks droop tenderly above it and cast a gloom around. Through it comes faintly "the sea's near murmur." But though the names of men like these may be unknown to fame, they are not forgotten in their quiet rest-ing-places. Each Memorial Day brings the gratitude of a nation that was saved because they dared to die.

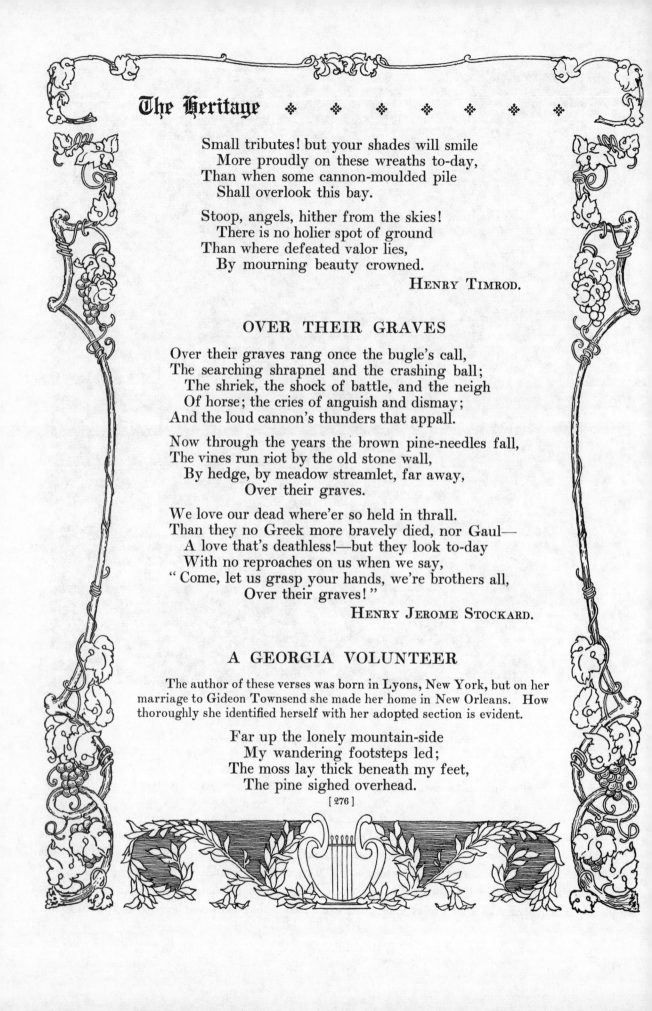

Small tributes! but your shades will smile
    More proudly on these wreaths to-day,
Than when some cannon-moulded pile
    Shall overlook this bay.

Stoop, angels, hither from the skies!
    There is no holier spot of ground
Than where defeated valor lies,
    By mourning beauty crowned.

HENRY TIMROD.

OVER THEIR GRAVES

Over their graves rang once the bugle's call,
The searching shrapnel and the crashing ball;
    The shriek, the shock of battle, and the neigh
    Of horse; the cries of anguish and dismay;
And the loud cannon's thunders that appall.

Now through the years the brown pine-needles fall,
The vines run riot by the old stone wall,
    By hedge, by meadow streamlet, far away,
        Over their graves.

We love our dead where'er so held in thrall.
Than they no Greek more bravely died, nor Gaul—
    A love that's deathless!—but they look to-day
    With no reproaches on us when we say,
"Come, let us grasp your hands, we're brothers all,
        Over their graves!"

HENRY JEROME STOCKARD.

A GEORGIA VOLUNTEER

The author of these verses was born in Lyons, New York, but on her marriage to Gideon Townsend she made her home in New Orleans. How thoroughly she identified herself with her adopted section is evident.

Far up the lonely mountain-side
    My wandering footsteps led;
The moss lay thick beneath my feet,
    The pine sighed overhead.

"WHERE DEFEATED VALOR LIES"

MAGNOLIA CEMETERY AT CHARLESTON—HERE TIMROD READ HIS "ODE"

This photograph preserves the resting-place of the Confederate soldiers over whom in 1867 Timrod read his last and finest production—the "Ode" presented opposite. This spreading tree is a fitting place for the utterance of one of the supreme poems in American literature. Timrod had spent his life in singing of his State and the South. He was fired by no ordinary devotion. But in no other effort did he light upon so lofty a subject, and express his emotions with so much of artistic restraint. The view above shows how appropriate to the scene were his lines. The gloom of these towering trees, the glint of marble slabs and columns, evokes at once the tender mood to which the genius of the Southern poet has given classic expression.

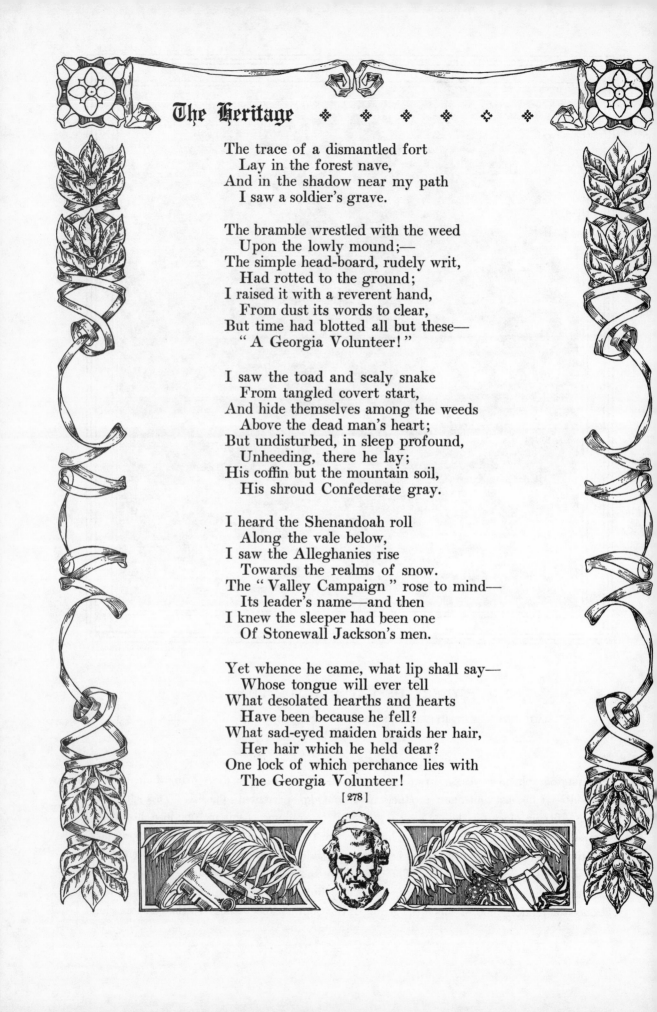

The Heritage

The trace of a dismantled fort
  Lay in the forest nave,
And in the shadow near my path
  I saw a soldier's grave.

The bramble wrestled with the weed
  Upon the lowly mound;—
The simple head-board, rudely writ,
  Had rotted to the ground;
I raised it with a reverent hand,
  From dust its words to clear,
But time had blotted all but these—
  " A Georgia Volunteer! "

I saw the toad and scaly snake
  From tangled covert start,
And hide themselves among the weeds
  Above the dead man's heart;
But undisturbed, in sleep profound,
  Unheeding, there he lay;
His coffin but the mountain soil,
  His shroud Confederate gray.

I heard the Shenandoah roll
  Along the vale below,
I saw the Alleghanies rise
  Towards the realms of snow.
The " Valley Campaign " rose to mind—
  Its leader's name—and then
I knew the sleeper had been one
  Of Stonewall Jackson's men.

Yet whence he came, what lip shall say—
  Whose tongue will ever tell
What desolated hearths and hearts
  Have been because he fell?
What sad-eyed maiden braids her hair,
  Her hair which he held dear?
One lock of which perchance lies with
  The Georgia Volunteer!

[278]

"OVER THEIR GRAVES RANG ONCE THE BUGLE'S CALL"

These resting places of soldiers upon the field of Bull Run, the first severe battle, remind Americans how widely the horror of war visited their land in 1861.   Not only by old stone walls such as Stockard speaks of, but also where rude head-boards were erected on the battle-fields, the crash of battle had roared.   Since 1862, when these pictures were taken, a grateful nation has converted these wild places into beautiful parks, better fit for preserving the names of those who met death where fell "The searching shrapnel and the crashing ball."

The Heritage ✦ ✦ ✦ ✦

What mother, with long watching eyes,
　　And white lips cold and dumb,
Waits with appalling patience for
　　Her darling boy to come?
Her boy! whose mountain grave swells up
　　But one of many a scar,
Cut on the face of our fair land,
　　By gory-handed war.

What fights he fought, what wounds he wore,
　　Are all unknown to fame;
Remember, on his lonely grave
　　There is not e'en a name!
That he fought well and bravely too,
　　And held his country dear,
We know, else he had never been
　　A Georgia Volunteer.

He sleeps—what need to question now
　　If he were wrong or right?
He knows, ere this, whose cause was just
　　In God the Father's sight.
He wields no warlike weapons now,
　　Returns no foeman's thrust—
Who but a coward would revile
　　An honest soldier's dust?

Roll, Shenandoah, proudly roll,
　　Adown thy rocky glen,
Above thee lies the grave of one
　　Of Stonewall Jackson's men.
Beneath the cedar and the pine,
　　In solitude austere,
Unknown, unnamed, forgotten, lies
　　A Georgia Volunteer.

MARY ASHLEY TOWNSEND.

WHERE SOME OF THE HEROIC DEAD LIE IN NATIONAL CEMETERIES

These wildernesses of headstones bring vividly to mind the resting-places of our heroic dead. There were in 1910 eighty-four national cemeteries situated in twenty-eight different states. In them are buried 207,075 known dead and 153,678 unknown, a total of 360,753. Of these the cem-

etery at Soldiers' Home in Washington contains 5,398 known dead, 288 unknown—a total of 5,686; the cemetery at City Point 3,719 known dead, 1,439 unknown—a total of 5,158; the one at Alexandria 3,401 known dead, 123 unknown—a total of 3,524. But these lack much of being the largest. At Vicksburg, 16,615 lie buried; at Nashville, 16,533; at Arlington, Virginia, 16,254; and Fredericksburg, Virginia, 15,273, of whom 12,785 are unknown.

CEMETERY AT SOLDIERS' HOME, WASHINGTON

SOLDIERS' GRAVES AT CITY POINT, VIRGINIA

GRAVES OF FEDERAL SOLDIERS, CHARLESTON, S. C.

IN THE SOLDIERS' CEMETERY AT ALEXANDRIA

A SWEEPING VIEW OF THE ALEXANDRIA "HEROIC DEAD"

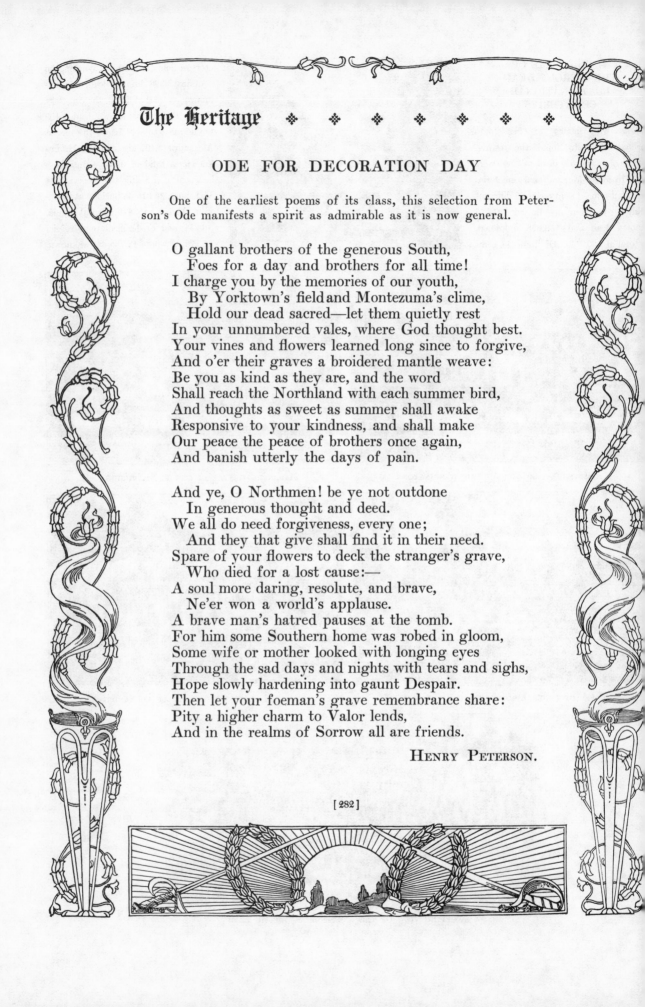

ODE FOR DECORATION DAY

One of the earliest poems of its class, this selection from Peterson's Ode manifests a spirit as admirable as it is now general.

O gallant brothers of the generous South,
    Foes for a day and brothers for all time!
I charge you by the memories of our youth,
    By Yorktown's field and Montezuma's clime,
    Hold our dead sacred—let them quietly rest
In your unnumbered vales, where God thought best.
Your vines and flowers learned long since to forgive,
And o'er their graves a broidered mantle weave:
Be you as kind as they are, and the word
Shall reach the Northland with each summer bird,
And thoughts as sweet as summer shall awake
Responsive to your kindness, and shall make
Our peace the peace of brothers once again,
And banish utterly the days of pain.

And ye, O Northmen! be ye not outdone
    In generous thought and deed.
We all do need forgiveness, every one;
    And they that give shall find it in their need.
Spare of your flowers to deck the stranger's grave,
    Who died for a lost cause:—
A soul more daring, resolute, and brave,
    Ne'er won a world's applause.
A brave man's hatred pauses at the tomb.
For him some Southern home was robed in gloom,
Some wife or mother looked with longing eyes
Through the sad days and nights with tears and sighs,
Hope slowly hardening into gaunt Despair.
Then let your foeman's grave remembrance share:
Pity a higher charm to Valor lends,
And in the realms of Sorrow all are friends.

HENRY PETERSON.

HOLLYWOOD CEMETERY IN RICHMOND, VIRGINIA
1,800 CONFEDERATE SOLDIERS LIE BURIED HERE

CONFEDERATE GRAVES IN THE WILDERNESS
REMINDERS OF THE BATTLE OF MAY 5-6, 1864

GRAVES OF FEDERAL SOLDIERS
NEAR BURNSIDE'S BRIDGE ON THE BATTLEFIELD OF ANTIETAM

A CORNER OF HOLLYWOOD CEMETERY
RICHMOND, VIRGINIA, IN 1865

The cemetery at Antietam, not far from the scene of the photograph above, taken soon after the battle on September 16–17, 1862, contains the graves of 4,684 soldiers, of which 1,829 are marked "unknown." Even a frail memorial like the one at the grave of the "Georgia Volunteer" usually fails to record the native heath of him who lies below, or to give any clue to the campaigns in which he fought. These soldiers, like their companions under the hemlocks in the Wilderness, must await the call of the judgment day. The Hollywood cemetery at Richmond contains a larger host. Eighteen thousand Confederate veterans there sleep in everlasting peace amid beautiful surroundings. Around them lie many of Virginia's famous sons, generation after generation of loved and honored names.

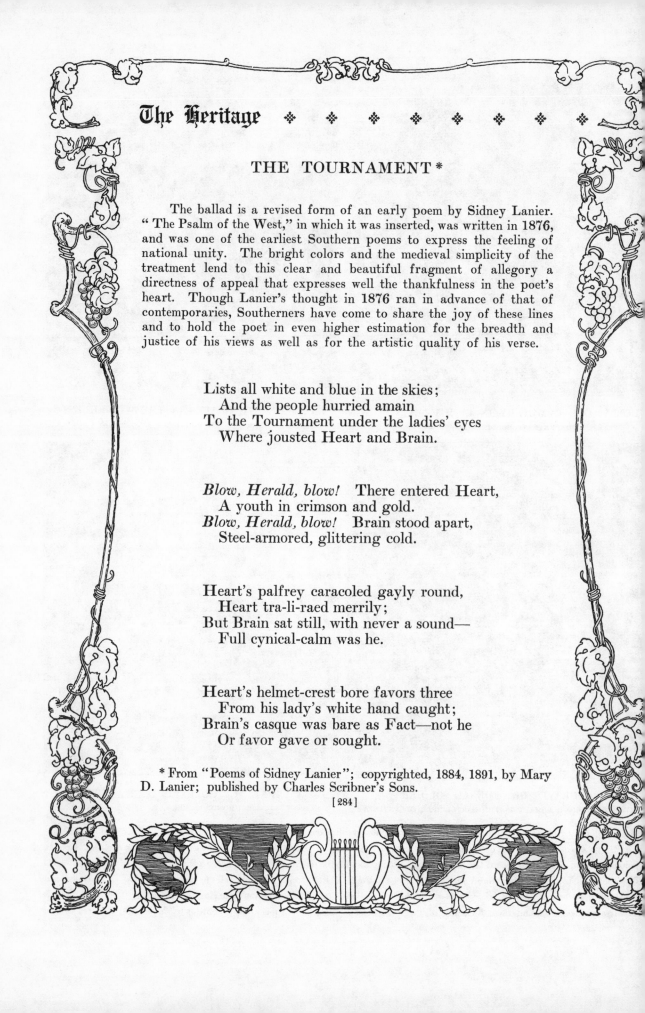

THE TOURNAMENT*

The ballad is a revised form of an early poem by Sidney Lanier. "The Psalm of the West," in which it was inserted, was written in 1876, and was one of the earliest Southern poems to express the feeling of national unity. The bright colors and the medieval simplicity of the treatment lend to this clear and beautiful fragment of allegory a directness of appeal that expresses well the thankfulness in the poet's heart. Though Lanier's thought in 1876 ran in advance of that of contemporaries, Southerners have come to share the joy of these lines and to hold the poet in even higher estimation for the breadth and justice of his views as well as for the artistic quality of his verse.

Lists all white and blue in the skies;
    And the people hurried amain
To the Tournament under the ladies' eyes
    Where jousted Heart and Brain.

Blow, Herald, blow! There entered Heart,
    A youth in crimson and gold.
Blow, Herald, blow! Brain stood apart,
    Steel-armored, glittering cold.

Heart's palfrey caracoled gayly round,
    Heart tra-li-raed merrily;
But Brain sat still, with never a sound—
    Full cynical-calm was he.

Heart's helmet-crest bore favors three
    From his lady's white hand caught;
Brain's casque was bare as Fact—not he
    Or favor gave or sought.

YORKTOWN—THE HOUSE WHERE CORNWALLIS SURRENDERED, 1781

MONUMENT TO HENRY CLAY AT RICHMOND

TOMB OF PRESIDENT POLK AT NASHVILLE

Peterson's poem preceding celebrates the heritage of glorious history common to North and South alike. The wartime views on this page are all Southern; yet every American can share the pride of beholding these spots — the house where Washington received Cornwallis's surrender; the tomb of Polk, leader of the nation when Scott and his soldiers fought in "Montezuma's clime"; the monument to the statesman Henry Clay; and the barracks at Baton Rouge, a stormy point under five flags—French in 1719,

HISTORIC GROUND AT BATON ROUGE, LOUISIANA

British in 1763, Spanish in 1779, American in 1810, and Confederate in 1861. Here nearly every prominent officer in the United States army since the Revolution did duty —Wilkinson and the first Wade Hampton, afterward Gaines and Jesup and Taylor, heroes of 1812. Here Winfield Scott saw his first service. Here Lafayette was received, and Andrew Jackson later. Here was the home of Zachary Taylor, and of his brilliant son "Dick," the Confederate general, who surrendered the largest Southern army.

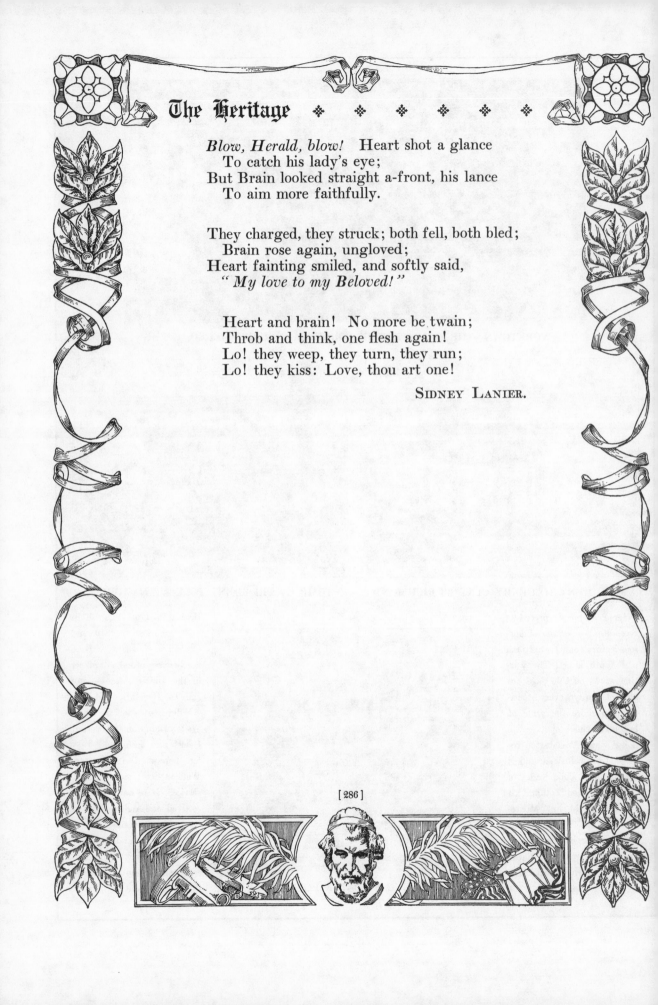

The Heritage ❖ ❖ ❖ ❖ ❖ ❖

Blow, Herald, blow! Heart shot a glance
  To catch his lady's eye;
But Brain looked straight a-front, his lance
  To aim more faithfully.

They charged, they struck; both fell, both bled;
  Brain rose again, ungloved;
Heart fainting smiled, and softly said,
" My love to my Beloved!"

Heart and brain! No more be twain;
Throb and think, one flesh again!
Lo! they weep, they turn, they run;
Lo! they kiss: Love, thou art one!

                    SIDNEY LANIER.

XIII

BROTHERHOOD

" HE REACHES THE HOME
HE LEFT SO PROSPEROUS
AND BEAUTIFUL"—*Grady*

RUINS OF THE
BERNARD HOUSE,
BATTLEFIELD OF
FREDERICKSBURG

THE FUTURE PRESIDENT OF THE CONFEDERACY, WITH HIS WIFE

THE FIRST OF SEVEN SCENES FROM THE LIFE OF JEFFERSON DAVIS

This picture, made from an old daguerreotype, forms as true a document of Jefferson Davis' human side as his letter concerning Grant on page 290.   Davis was born in Kentucky the year before Lincoln. His college education began in that State.   In 1842 he entered West Point.   Army service proved his ability to command.   In the Mexican War he won distinction as colonel of the First Mississippi Volunteers by the famous "reëntering angle" at Buena Vista.   As Senator from Mississippi and Secretary of War under President Pierce, he became the accepted leader of the Southern party in their insistence on the doctrine of States' rights.   His unanimous election as President of the Confederacy on February 8, 1861, by the Congress at Montgomery, Alabama, was unsought.   When the permanent government was established in 1862, he entered without opposition upon the six years' term.   When the stress of war turned his administration into a virtual dictatorship, he wielded enormous powers with the utmost fidelity.   His military training and experience had instilled him with such confidence in his military capacity that he maintained to the end a close control over all his generals.   His wife, who possessed all the charm of Southern womanhood, has left an account of her husband that forms one of the most intimate and winning biographies written by an American author.

"THE ROYAL FAMILY"—JEFFERSON DAVIS'S CHILDREN

The second scene in the series from Davis's career brings to mind the private sorrows that fell to his lot. On June 13, 1862, while a hundred thousand Union soldiers pressed at the very gates of Richmond, his infant son, William Howell, lay at the point of death. The harassed statesman and devoted father wrote Mrs. Davis: ". . . My heart sunk within me at the news of the suffering of my angel baby. Your telegram of the 12th gives assurance of the subsidence of disease. But the look of pain and exhaustion, the gentle complaint, 'I am tired,' which has for so many years oppressed me, seems to have been revived; and unless God spares me another such trial, what is to become of me, I don't know. Dr. Garnett will, I hope, reach you this morning. He carried with him what he regarded as a specific remedy. . . . My ease, my health, my property, my life, I can give to the cause of my country. The heroism which could lay my wife and children on any sacrificial altar is not mine. Spare us, good Lord." Yet he was subjected to peculiar trials. During the war a four-year-old son fell from a balcony and was instantly killed. Only two of his children survived him—Margaret, who married J. A. Hayes of Denver, Colorado, in 1877, and Varina Anne Davis, favorably known as a writer, honored at many a veterans' reunion, and beloved throughout the South as "Winnie, the Daughter of the Confederacy."

BROTHERHOOD

"LET US HAVE PEACE"

THE following significant sentences form part of the conclusion to General Grant's "Personal Memoirs":

"The war has made us a nation of great power and intelligence. We have but little to do to preserve peace, happiness and prosperity at home, and the respect of other nations. Our experience ought to teach us the necessity of the first; our power secures the latter.

"I feel that we are on the eve of a new era, when there is to be great harmony between the Federal and Confederate. I cannot stay to be a living witness to the correctness of this prophecy; but I feel it within me that it is to be so. The universally kind feeling expressed for me at a time when it was supposed that each day would prove my last, seemed to me the beginning of the answer to 'Let us have peace.'

"ULYSSES SIMPSON GRANT."

THE VOICE OF THE SOUTH

WHEN General Grant was dying at Mount McGregor the Boston *Globe* instructed its New Orleans correspondent to interview Jefferson Davis. Mr. Davis was not seen personally, but a few days later he penned the following letter:

"Dear Sir—Your request in behalf of a Boston journalist for me to prepare a criticism of General Grant's military career cannot be complied with for the following reasons:

"1. Gen. Grant is dying.

"2. Though he invaded our country, it was with an open hand, and, as far as I know, he abetted neither arson nor pillage, and has since the war, I believe, showed no malignity to Confederates either of the military or civil service.

"Therefore, instead of seeking to disturb the quiet of his closing hours, I would, if it were in my power, contribute to the peace of his mind and the comfort of his body.

[Signed] "JEFFERSON DAVIS."

THE INAUGURATION

THIRD OF SEVEN SCENES FROM THE LIFE OF JEFFERSON DAVIS

It is the eighteenth of February, 1861. The clock on the State House of Alabama points to the hour of one. Jefferson Davis is being inaugurated as President of the Confederate States of America. The only photograph of the memorable scene was made by A. C. McIntyre, the principal artist of Montgomery. Davis had been elected on February 9, 1861, by the provisional congress that had met there to form a Confederate Government. Although preferring high rank in the army to political position, Davis accepted. On February 18th he delivered a carefully prepared address to the throng here assembled. At the foot of the slope is the carriage of Judge Benajah Bibb, containing his daughter, who later became president of the Ladies' Memorial Association. On July 20, 1860, the seat of the new Confederate Government was transferred to Richmond, Virginia.

THE EULOGY OF SUMNER

This speech was delivered in the House of Representatives on April 28, 1874. Senator Charles Sumner of Massachusetts had died March 11, 1874, and the House followed the Senate in paying respect to his memory by suspending business. Lucius Q. C. Lamar, Congressman from Mississippi, was invited by the Massachusetts delegation to second the resolution. Only a perfunctory performance was expected, but as Lamar proceeded the stillness of the House and galleries became almost oppressive. Speaker Blaine sat motionless with tears running down his cheeks. Opponents in many a hot debate, Democrats and Republicans alike, were melted to tears. When he closed, all seemed to hold their breath, as if to prolong the spell; then a burst of hearty and sympathetic applause broke from all over the House and the galleries, such as had not been heard since the war. Of all the speeches delivered in both houses Lamar's alone was sent to all parts of the country by telegraph. The text here followed was from a copy in Lamar's own handwriting.

MR. SPEAKER: In rising to second the resolutions just offered, I desire to add a few remarks which have occurred to me as appropriate to the occasion. I believe that they express a sentiment which pervades the hearts of all the people whose representatives are here assembled. Strange as, in looking back upon the past, the assertion may seem, impossible as it would have been ten years ago to make it, it is not the less true that to-day Mississippi regrets the death of Charles Sumner, and sincerely unites in paying honors to his memory. Not because of the splendor of his intellect, though in him was extinguished one of the brightest of the lights which have illustrated the councils of the government for nearly a quarter of a century; not because of the high culture, the elegant scholarship, and the varied learning which revealed themselves so clearly in all his public efforts as to justify the application to him of Johnson's felicitous expression, " He touched nothing which he did not adorn; " not this, though these are qualities by no means, it is to be feared, so common in public places as to make their disappearance, in even a single instance, a matter of indifference; but because of those peculiar and strongly marked moral traits of his character which gave the coloring to the whole tenor of his singularly dramatic public career; traits which made him for a long period to a large portion of his

[292]

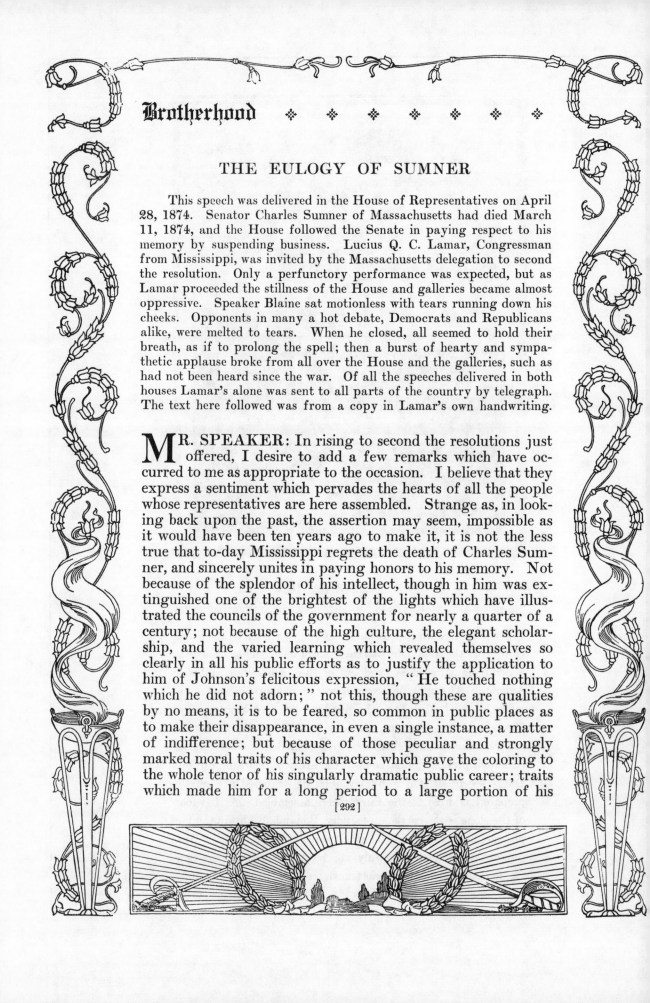

THE PRESIDENT OF THE CONFEDERACY

THE FOURTH OF SEVEN SCENES FROM THE LIFE OF JEFFERSON DAVIS—HIS WIDOW PRONOUNCED THIS THE ONLY WAR-TIME
PHOTOGRAPH

The trials of the Presidency were particularly severe to one of Davis's delicately balanced temperament. According to Mrs. Davis, "he was abnormally sensitive to disapprobation; even a child's disapproval discomposed him." She relates that one day, during the second year of the war, "he came home, about seven o'clock, from his office, staggered up to a sofa in his little private office and lay down. He declined dinner, and I remained by his side, anxious and afraid to ask what was the trouble which so oppressed him. In an hour or two he told me that the weight of responsibility oppressed him so that he felt he would give all his limbs to have some one with whom he could share it." But she adds in a later chapter, "As hope died out in the breasts of the rank and file of the Confederate army, the President's courage rose, and he was fertile in expedients to supply deficiencies, and calm in the contemplation of the destruction of his dearest hopes, and the violent death he expected to be his." In all his trials his wife was an unfailingly sympathetic companion.

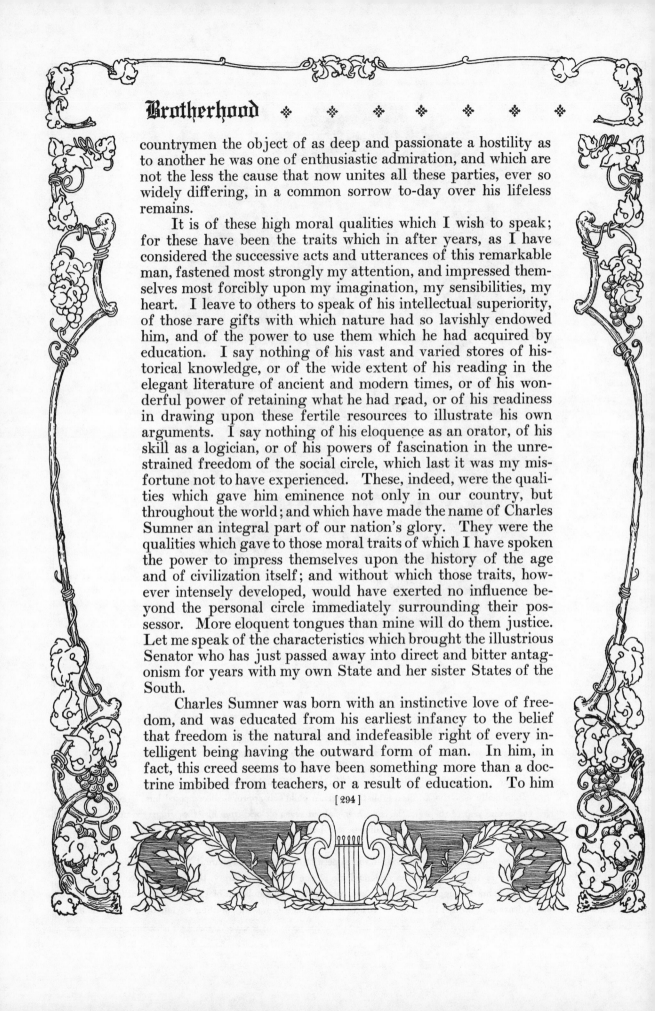

Brotherhood ❖ ❖ ❖ ❖ ❖ ❖ ❖

countrymen the object of as deep and passionate a hostility as
to another he was one of enthusiastic admiration, and which are
not the less the cause that now unites all these parties, ever so
widely differing, in a common sorrow to-day over his lifeless
remains.

It is of these high moral qualities which I wish to speak;
for these have been the traits which in after years, as I have
considered the successive acts and utterances of this remarkable
man, fastened most strongly my attention, and impressed themselves most forcibly upon my imagination, my sensibilities, my
heart. I leave to others to speak of his intellectual superiority,
of those rare gifts with which nature had so lavishly endowed
him, and of the power to use them which he had acquired by
education. I say nothing of his vast and varied stores of historical knowledge, or of the wide extent of his reading in the
elegant literature of ancient and modern times, or of his won-
derful power of retaining what he had read, or of his readiness
in drawing upon these fertile resources to illustrate his own
arguments. I say nothing of his eloquence as an orator, of his
skill as a logician, or of his powers of fascination in the unre-
strained freedom of the social circle, which last it was my misfortune not to have experienced. These, indeed, were the qualities which gave him eminence not only in our country, but
throughout the world; and which have made the name of Charles
Sumner an integral part of our nation's glory. They were the
qualities which gave to those moral traits of which I have spoken
the power to impress themselves upon the history of the age
and of civilization itself; and without which those traits, however intensely developed, would have exerted no influence beyond the personal circle immediately surrounding their pos-
sessor. More eloquent tongues than mine will do them justice.
Let me speak of the characteristics which brought the illustrious
Senator who has just passed away into direct and bitter antagonism for years with my own State and her sister States of the
South.

Charles Sumner was born with an instinctive love of freedom, and was educated from his earliest infancy to the belief
that freedom is the natural and indefeasible right of every intelligent being having the outward form of man. In him, in
fact, this creed seems to have been something more than a doctrine imbibed from teachers, or a result of education. To him

[294]

JEFFERSON DAVIS A PRISONER

PASSING THROUGH MACON, GEORGIA, IN AN AMBULANCE

Thus the motley crowd from street, doorway, and window gazed after the unfortunate President of the Confederate States on May 10, 1865. Davis had left Richmond on the night of April 2d, upon Lee's warning. In Danville, Virginia, he remained for a few days until word was brought of Lee's surrender. At Greensboro, North Carolina, he held a council of war with Generals Johnston and Beauregard, in which he reluctantly made provision for negotiations between Johnston and Sherman. He continued the trip south on April 14th, the day of Lincoln's assassination. At Charlotte, North Carolina, he was called forth by a group of Confederate cavalrymen, when he "expressed his own determination not to despair of the Confederacy but to remain with the last organized band upholding the flag." When he learned of the rejection at Washington of the terms agreed upon by Johnston and Sherman, he ordered Johnston to retreat with his cavalry. On April 26th, Davis continued his own journey. Only ten members of his cavalry escort were retained. In the early light of May 10th Lieut.-Col. B. D. Pritchard and troopers of the Fourth Michigan Cavalry came upon the encampment by the roadside in dense pine woods near Irwinville, Georgia, and captured the whole party.

JEFFERSON DAVIS

IN THE RIDING DRESS
HE WORE WHEN CAPTURED

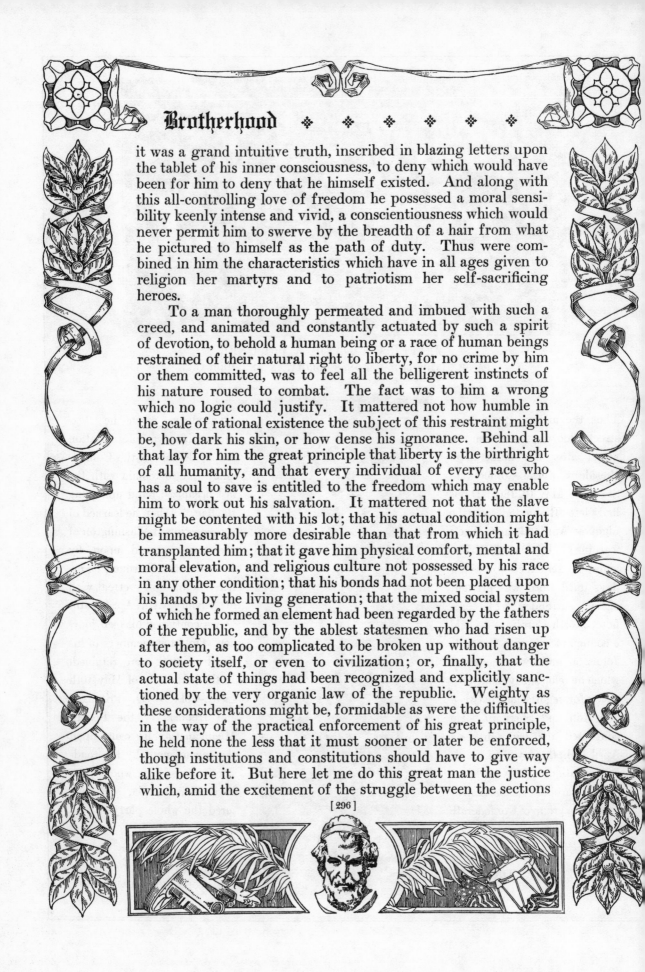

it was a grand intuitive truth, inscribed in blazing letters upon the tablet of his inner consciousness, to deny which would have been for him to deny that he himself existed. And along with this all-controlling love of freedom he possessed a moral sensibility keenly intense and vivid, a conscientiousness which would never permit him to swerve by the breadth of a hair from what he pictured to himself as the path of duty. Thus were combined in him the characteristics which have in all ages given to religion her martyrs and to patriotism her self-sacrificing heroes.

To a man thoroughly permeated and imbued with such a creed, and animated and constantly actuated by such a spirit of devotion, to behold a human being or a race of human beings restrained of their natural right to liberty, for no crime by him or them committed, was to feel all the belligerent instincts of his nature roused to combat. The fact was to him a wrong which no logic could justify. It mattered not how humble in the scale of rational existence the subject of this restraint might be, how dark his skin, or how dense his ignorance. Behind all that lay for him the great principle that liberty is the birthright of all humanity, and that every individual of every race who has a soul to save is entitled to the freedom which may enable him to work out his salvation. It mattered not that the slave might be contented with his lot; that his actual condition might be immeasurably more desirable than that from which it had transplanted him; that it gave him physical comfort, mental and moral elevation, and religious culture not possessed by his race in any other condition; that his bonds had not been placed upon his hands by the living generation; that the mixed social system of which he formed an element had been regarded by the fathers of the republic, and by the ablest statesmen who had risen up after them, as too complicated to be broken up without danger to society itself, or even to civilization; or, finally, that the actual state of things had been recognized and explicitly sanctioned by the very organic law of the republic. Weighty as these considerations might be, formidable as were the difficulties in the way of the practical enforcement of his great principle, he held none the less that it must sooner or later be enforced, though institutions and constitutions should have to give way alike before it. But here let me do this great man the justice which, amid the excitement of the struggle between the sections

At the top of the page appears the facsimile of the bail-bond signatures, including those of Jefferson Davis, Horace Greeley, and others.

SIGNATURES TO THE JEFFERSON DAVIS BAIL-BOND—HORACE GREELEY'S COMES THIRD

Jefferson Davis was captured near Irwinville, Georgia, on May 10, 1865, by a detachment of the Fourth Michigan Cavalry. On the way to Macon the party learned that a reward of $100,000 had been offered for the apprehension of Davis as one of the alleged accomplices of the assassination of Abraham Lincoln. It was later found that the testimony on which the charge was made was untrustworthy, some of the witnesses later retracting their statements. After a two-years' imprisonment in Fort Monroe he was indicted in Richmond for treason and liberated on bail. Of the many names attached to the document, the most conspicuous is that of Horace Greeley, editor of the *New York Tribune*, who had been prominent throughout the war as a molder of Northern sentiment. The passions born of the conflict were still raging, some of them in an intensified form. Greeley displayed unusual courage in subscribing his name to the bond. It appears just above that of Cornelius Vanderbilt, below Gerrit Smith's.

GREELEY READING THE "TRIBUNE"

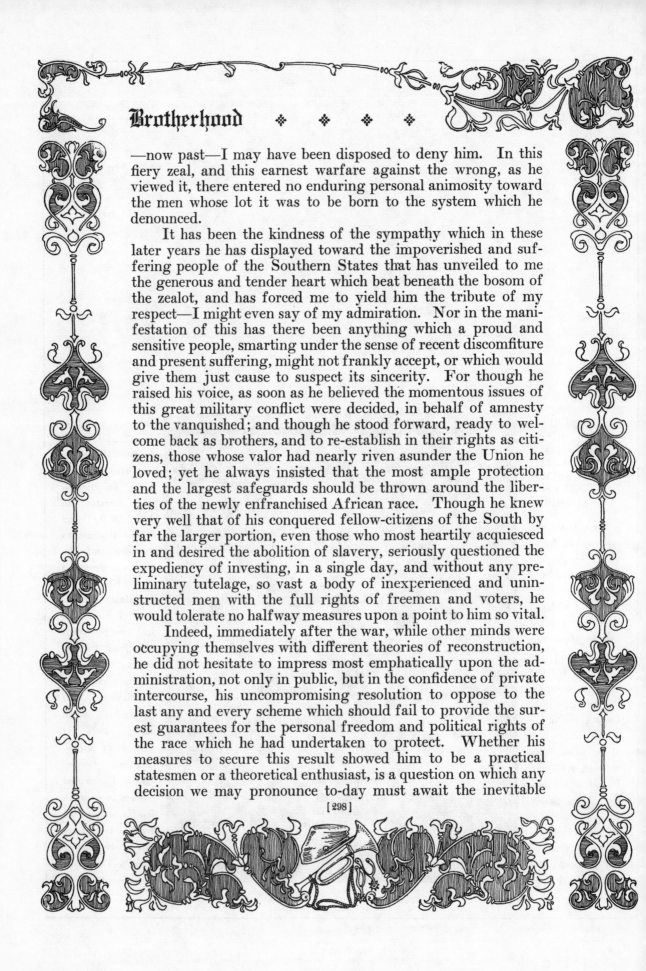

—now past—I may have been disposed to deny him. In this fiery zeal, and this earnest warfare against the wrong, as he viewed it, there entered no enduring personal animosity toward the men whose lot it was to be born to the system which he denounced.

It has been the kindness of the sympathy which in these later years he has displayed toward the impoverished and suffering people of the Southern States that has unveiled to me the generous and tender heart which beat beneath the bosom of the zealot, and has forced me to yield him the tribute of my respect—I might even say of my admiration. Nor in the manifestation of this has there been anything which a proud and sensitive people, smarting under the sense of recent discomfiture and present suffering, might not frankly accept, or which would give them just cause to suspect its sincerity. For though he raised his voice, as soon as he believed the momentous issues of this great military conflict were decided, in behalf of amnesty to the vanquished; and though he stood forward, ready to welcome back as brothers, and to re-establish in their rights as citizens, those whose valor had nearly riven asunder the Union he loved; yet he always insisted that the most ample protection and the largest safeguards should be thrown around the liberties of the newly enfranchised African race. Though he knew very well that of his conquered fellow-citizens of the South by far the larger portion, even those who most heartily acquiesced in and desired the abolition of slavery, seriously questioned the expediency of investing, in a single day, and without any preliminary tutelage, so vast a body of inexperienced and uninstructed men with the full rights of freemen and voters, he would tolerate no halfway measures upon a point to him so vital.

Indeed, immediately after the war, while other minds were occupying themselves with different theories of reconstruction, he did not hesitate to impress most emphatically upon the administration, not only in public, but in the confidence of private intercourse, his uncompromising resolution to oppose to the last any and every scheme which should fail to provide the surest guarantees for the personal freedom and political rights of the race which he had undertaken to protect. Whether his measures to secure this result showed him to be a practical statesmen or a theoretical enthusiast, is a question on which any decision we may pronounce to-day must await the inevitable

DAVIS AFTER HIS RELEASE FROM PRISON

THE LAST OF SEVEN SCENES FROM THE LIFE OF JEFFERSON DAVIS

On his return from Canada in 1868 Jefferson Davis paid a visit to Baltimore, and stood for this picture.   It reveals the lines of pain drawn by the sufferings of three years.   Twelve days after his capture he had been imprisoned in Fortress Monroe in a low cell.   There he was kept more than four months.   Then more comfortable quarters were assigned.   His attending physician, though a strong Republican, was completely won by the charm of the Southern gentleman and published an account of his prison life that aroused public sympathy for the most distinguished prisoner ever held in the United States.   On May 13, 1867, Davis was indicted for treason in the United States Circuit Court for the district of Virginia, whereupon he was admitted to bail for $100,000, signed by Horace Greeley and fourteen others.   When Davis was released he was greeted with deafening cheers, huzzas, and waving of hats.   He was included in the general amnesty of Christmas Day, 1868, and was released in February, 1869.   The twenty remaining years of his life were spent chiefly in Mississippi.

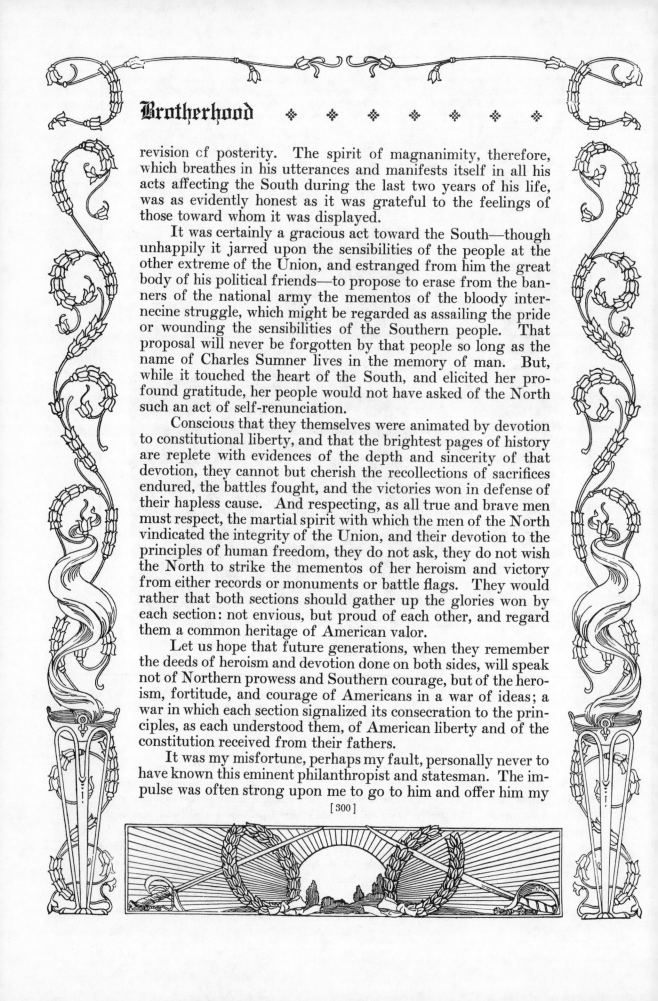

revision of posterity. The spirit of magnanimity, therefore, which breathes in his utterances and manifests itself in all his acts affecting the South during the last two years of his life, was as evidently honest as it was grateful to the feelings of those toward whom it was displayed.

It was certainly a gracious act toward the South—though unhappily it jarred upon the sensibilities of the people at the other extreme of the Union, and estranged from him the great body of his political friends—to propose to erase from the banners of the national army the mementos of the bloody internecine struggle, which might be regarded as assailing the pride or wounding the sensibilities of the Southern people. That proposal will never be forgotten by that people so long as the name of Charles Sumner lives in the memory of man. But, while it touched the heart of the South, and elicited her profound gratitude, her people would not have asked of the North such an act of self-renunciation.

Conscious that they themselves were animated by devotion to constitutional liberty, and that the brightest pages of history are replete with evidences of the depth and sincerity of that devotion, they cannot but cherish the recollections of sacrifices endured, the battles fought, and the victories won in defense of their hapless cause. And respecting, as all true and brave men must respect, the martial spirit with which the men of the North vindicated the integrity of the Union, and their devotion to the principles of human freedom, they do not ask, they do not wish the North to strike the mementos of her heroism and victory from either records or monuments or battle flags. They would rather that both sections should gather up the glories won by each section: not envious, but proud of each other, and regard them a common heritage of American valor.

Let us hope that future generations, when they remember the deeds of heroism and devotion done on both sides, will speak not of Northern prowess and Southern courage, but of the heroism, fortitude, and courage of Americans in a war of ideas; a war in which each section signalized its consecration to the principles, as each understood them, of American liberty and of the constitution received from their fathers.

It was my misfortune, perhaps my fault, personally never to have known this eminent philanthropist and statesman. The impulse was often strong upon me to go to him and offer him my

A PICTURE FULL OF MEANING TO READERS OF LAMAR'S "EULOGY"

NEGROES AT THE RUINS OF THE RICHMOND AND PETERSBURG BRIDGE AT RICHMOND IN APRIL, 1865

Everyone knows that the care-free black people sitting before the unruffled pool are in some way connected with the wreck of war that looms behind. A viewpoint of this relation, as warmly human as it is broad and national, is taken by Lamar in his "Eulogy of Sumner." Charles Sumner at the time of his death had for a generation been prominent in anti-slavery agitation. His oration in 1845 on "The True Grandeur of Nations" attracted attention even in England. With his election to the United States Senate, in 1851, at the age of forty, he stepped forward to a position of national leadership. Before and after the war few national figures aroused more opposition in the South than Charles Sumner. He created a storm in 1856 by his speech in the Senate on "The Crime Against Kansas," in which he reflected on South Carolina and on Senator Butler from that State. Preston Brooks, a South Carolina Representative and a relative of Butler, found Sumner alone at his desk in the Senate Chamber, and beat him over the head with a cane until Sumner fell senseless to the floor, receiving spinal injuries from which he never entirely recovered. Sumner, when able some years later to return to his seat, continued his opposition to slavery, and was prominent in securing to the freedmen citizenship and the ballot. No later than 1874, true patriotism had succeeded passion so notably that Lamar's "Eulogy" was greeted with warm applause by representatives of all sections.

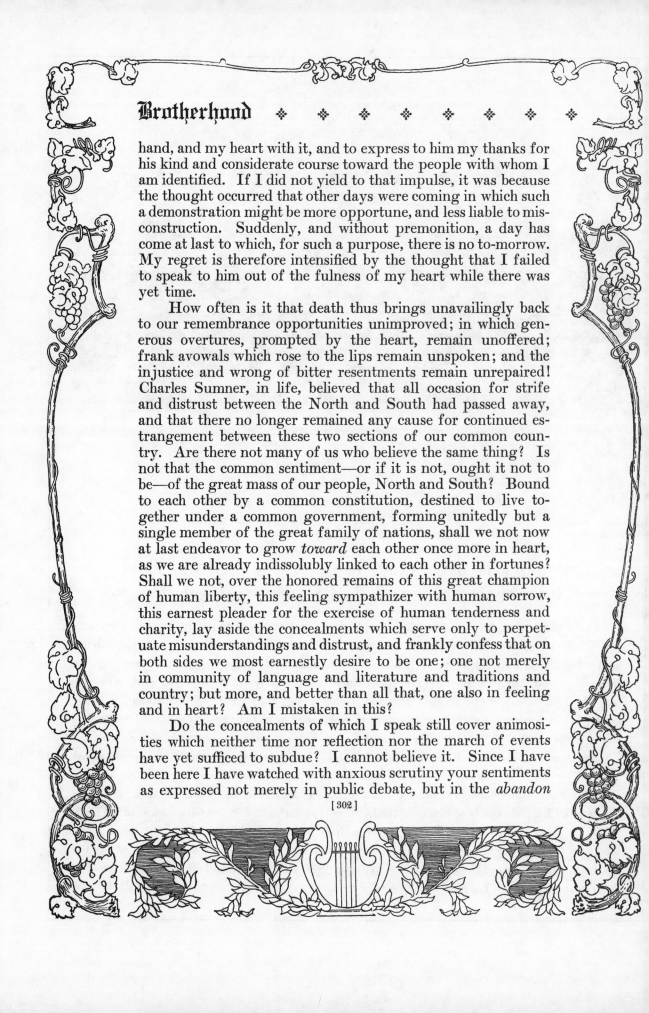

hand, and my heart with it, and to express to him my thanks for his kind and considerate course toward the people with whom I am identified. If I did not yield to that impulse, it was because the thought occurred that other days were coming in which such a demonstration might be more opportune, and less liable to misconstruction. Suddenly, and without premonition, a day has come at last to which, for such a purpose, there is no to-morrow. My regret is therefore intensified by the thought that I failed to speak to him out of the fulness of my heart while there was yet time.

How often is it that death thus brings unavailingly back to our remembrance opportunities unimproved; in which generous overtures, prompted by the heart, remain unoffered; frank avowals which rose to the lips remain unspoken; and the injustice and wrong of bitter resentments remain unrepaired! Charles Sumner, in life, believed that all occasion for strife and distrust between the North and South had passed away, and that there no longer remained any cause for continued estrangement between these two sections of our common country. Are there not many of us who believe the same thing? Is not that the common sentiment—or if it is not, ought it not to be—of the great mass of our people, North and South? Bound to each other by a common constitution, destined to live together under a common government, forming unitedly but a single member of the great family of nations, shall we not now at last endeavor to grow *toward* each other once more in heart, as we are already indissolubly linked to each other in fortunes? Shall we not, over the honored remains of this great champion of human liberty, this feeling sympathizer with human sorrow, this earnest pleader for the exercise of human tenderness and charity, lay aside the concealments which serve only to perpetuate misunderstandings and distrust, and frankly confess that on both sides we most earnestly desire to be one; one not merely in community of language and literature and traditions and country; but more, and better than all that, one also in feeling and in heart? Am I mistaken in this?

Do the concealments of which I speak still cover animosities which neither time nor reflection nor the march of events have yet sufficed to subdue? I cannot believe it. Since I have been here I have watched with anxious scrutiny your sentiments as expressed not merely in public debate, but in the *abandon*

CHARLES SUMNER—THE PORTRAIT BY BRADY

The single-mindedness, the moral grandeur stamped upon Sumner's features are revealed in this lifelike portrait. Even those whose political convictions were different, though equally intense, could agree with the estimate of his biographer, Moorfield Storey: "Charles Sumner was a great man in his absolute fidelity to principle—his un-flinching devotion to duty, his indifference to selfish considerations, his high scorn of anything petty or mean." He had convinced himself that suffrage was a right and not a privilege, and all the force of his intellect and char-acter was devoted to accomplishing what he thought was right. The eulogy by Lamar pays him fitting tribute.

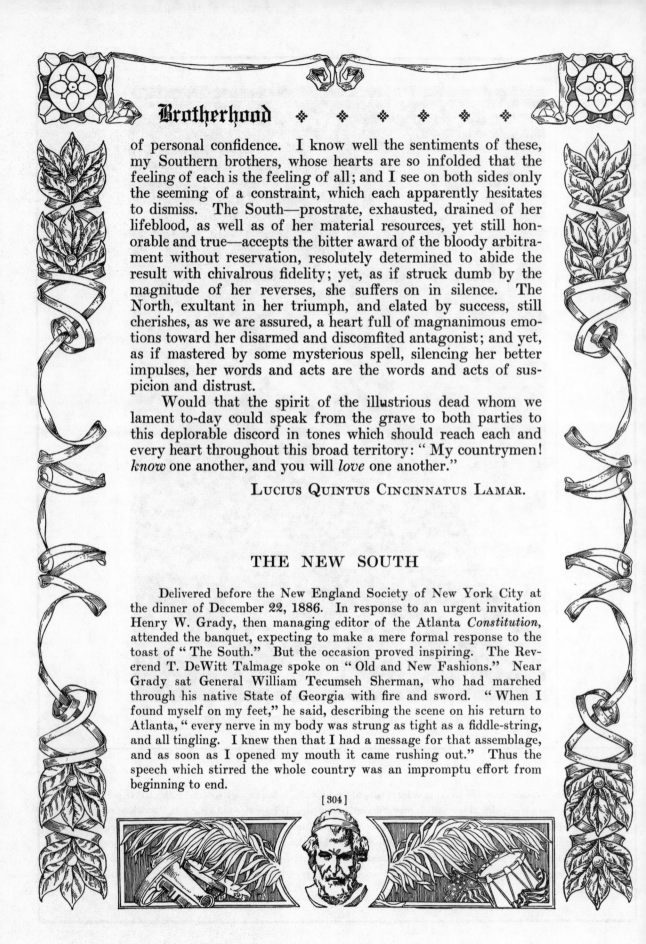

of personal confidence. I know well the sentiments of these, my Southern brothers, whose hearts are so infolded that the feeling of each is the feeling of all; and I see on both sides only the seeming of a constraint, which each apparently hesitates to dismiss. The South—prostrate, exhausted, drained of her lifeblood, as well as of her material resources, yet still honorable and true—accepts the bitter award of the bloody arbitrament without reservation, resolutely determined to abide the result with chivalrous fidelity; yet, as if struck dumb by the magnitude of her reverses, she suffers on in silence. The North, exultant in her triumph, and elated by success, still cherishes, as we are assured, a heart full of magnanimous emotions toward her disarmed and discomfited antagonist; and yet, as if mastered by some mysterious spell, silencing her better impulses, her words and acts are the words and acts of suspicion and distrust.

Would that the spirit of the illustrious dead whom we lament to-day could speak from the grave to both parties to this deplorable discord in tones which should reach each and every heart throughout this broad territory: " My countrymen! *know* one another, and you will *love* one another."

LUCIUS QUINTUS CINCINNATUS LAMAR.

THE NEW SOUTH

Delivered before the New England Society of New York City at the dinner of December 22, 1886. In response to an urgent invitation Henry W. Grady, then managing editor of the Atlanta *Constitution*, attended the banquet, expecting to make a mere formal response to the toast of " The South." But the occasion proved inspiring. The Reverend T. DeWitt Talmage spoke on " Old and New Fashions." Near Grady sat General William Tecumseh Sherman, who had marched through his native State of Georgia with fire and sword. " When I found myself on my feet," he said, describing the scene on his return to Atlanta, " every nerve in my body was strung as tight as a fiddle-string, and all tingling. I knew then that I had a message for that assemblage, and as soon as I opened my mouth it came rushing out." Thus the speech which stirred the whole country was an impromptu effort from beginning to end.

"WHILE OTHER MINDS WERE OCCUPYING THEMSELVES WITH DIFFERENT THEORIES OF RECONSTRUCTION."

A SCENE CONTEMPORARY WITH SUMNER'S "UNCOMPROMISING RESOLUTION" REFERRED TO BY LAMAR

The lively scene in Baton Rouge, Louisiana, just after the war, is typical of early reconstruction in the South. The wagon is filled with a military band, the flags are regimental colors, and the vehicle itself is a military wagon. The music has attracted not only a crowd of boys and men, but a woman with a child in her arms is standing in the door of the bakery where cakes and pies are advertised for sale, and in the second-story window above her another woman is gazing timidly from behind the shutter. Evidently the candidate for the State Senate is making some progress. Reconstruction in the South was not so long a period as some may suppose. The first attempts to reorganize the state governments, like the one here pictured, were under the protection of Federal military forces. The measures taken were sometimes harsh, but the execution of martial law was honest. Most of the governments were left in the hands of civil author- ities in 1868. "Carpet-baggers" and "scalawags" then held sway until the better class of citizens could come into control. But in 1874 their power was overthrown, except in Louisiana and South Carolina.

SOUTHERN EXPRESS OFFICE, RICHMOND

MILL ON JAMES RIVER AND KANAWHA CANAL

GALLEGO FLOUR MILLS, JAMES RIVER

GALLEGO FLOUR MILLS FROM THE CANAL

THE RICHMOND AND PETERSBURG RAILROAD STATION

REMAINS OF CARS NEAR THE STATION

"HIS TRADE DESTROYED"—ILLUSTRATIONS FOR GRADY'S WORDS

These few glimpses of ruined industries in the single Southern city of Richmond prove how discouraging a reality confronted the Confederate soldier on his return home. Even the words of the orator Grady are faint in comparison with the almost hopeless future that lay before his people in 1865. All their movable capital was exhausted. The banks had failed. The State and Confederate bonds were worthless. The railroads were ruined; the cities disconsolate; the labor system revolutionized. But, as Henry Watterson says, the South "was poor and in bondage; she was set free, and she had to go to work; she went to work, and she is richer than ever before.

FIRE-SWEPT HOMES

NOTHING BUT BARE WALLS

THE PATH OF DESTRUCTION

WORK OF THE FLAMES

A VISTA OF HAVOC

A ONCE BEAUTIFUL MANSION

"HE FINDS HIS HOUSE IN RUINS"—ILLUSTRATIONS FOR GRADY'S WORDS

On this page appear homes and public buildings wrecked by the conflagration during the evacuation of Richmond on the night of April 2, 1865. The flames swept up from the river, threatening to devour the whole town. The Union troops, arriving about eight o'clock on the morning of April 3d, found the city a scene of wild confusion. They were ordered to press into service every able-bodied man. Only with great difficulty were the flames extinguished by two o'clock. A beautiful residence-district lay utterly devastated.

COPYRIGHT. 1911, REVIEW OF REVIEWS CO.

A DESOLATE GARDEN

In the spring of 1865, this charming Southern garden in Petersburg did not bloom as had been its wont. The thundering cannon of Grant's besieging army had laid in ruins many a noble old mansion. Even where the non-combatants could dwell in comparative safety, they suffered for want of the necessaries of life. In the whole of Virginia there was not enough of either meat or bread to sustain the Confederate troops that had suffered far more severely than the citizens during the unusually hard winter just past. But after the war, the leaders, whose homes were in ruins, did not sit down in despair. The cities of the Southland arose in new beauty, and the manifold problems of a new era were studied with a courage Grady does well to praise. From the exhaustion of merciless war, from wreckage such as this, the South rose renewed like the fabled phenix.

A few steps across the garden, toward the same roofless home of the page facing, opens sadder destruction of the exquisite Georgian architecture. Toward the close of the siege, many scenes like this awaited the army photographer. Homes that had once reposed peacefully in the light of luxury and sparkled with gaiety now stood in ruins, grim tokens that Sherman's terse definition of war is true. And yet the South fought on. Never has the world seen greater devotion to a cause. Grander than this devotion was the resolute meeting of the problems left by the war. An entirely new social order, in which Southern leaders profoundly disbelieved, might well have appalled the stoutest heart. But the present prosperity of the whole section proves that hearts were not appalled. The dauntless energy of the Anglo-Saxon has gained again a victory more precious than any won in war.

The New South ❖ ❖ ❖ ❖

MY friends, Dr. Talmage has told you that the typical American is yet to come. Let me tell you that he has already come. Great types, like valuable plants, are slow to flower and fruit. But from the union of these colonists, Puritans and Cavaliers, from the straightening of their purposes and the crossing of their blood, slow perfecting through a century, came he who stands as the first typical American, the first who comprehended within himself all the strength and gentleness, all the majesty and grace of this republic—Abraham Lincoln. He was the sum of Puritan and Cavalier, for in his ardent nature were fused the virtues of both, and in the depths of his great soul the faults of both were lost. He was greater than Puritan, greater than Cavalier, in that he was American, and that in his honest form were first gathered the vast and thrilling forces of his ideal government—charging it with such tremendous meaning and elevating it so much above human suffering that martyrdom, though infamously aimed, came as a fitting crown to a life consecrated from the cradle to human liberty. Let us, each cherishing his traditions and honoring his fathers, build with reverent hands to the type of this simple but sublime life, in which all types are honored, and in our common glory as Americans there will be plenty and to spare for your forefathers and for mine.

Dr. Talmage has drawn for you, with a master's hand, the picture of your returning armies. He has told you how, in the pomp and circumstance of war, they came back to you, marching with proud and victorious tread, reading their glory in a nation's eyes! Will you bear with me while I tell you of another army that sought its home at the close of the late war— an army that marched home in defeat and not in victory—in pathos and not in splendor, but in glory that equaled yours, and to hearts as loving as ever welcomed heroes home! Let me picture to you the footsore Confederate soldier, as buttoning up in his faded gray jacket the parole which was to bear testimony to his children of his fidelity and faith, he turned his face southward from Appomattox in April, 1865. Think of him as ragged, half-starved, heavy-hearted, enfeebled by want and wounds; having fought to exhaustion, he surrenders his gun, wrings the hand of his comrades in silence, and lifting his tear-stained and pallid face for the last time to the graves that dot the old Virginia hills, pulls his gray cap over his brow and

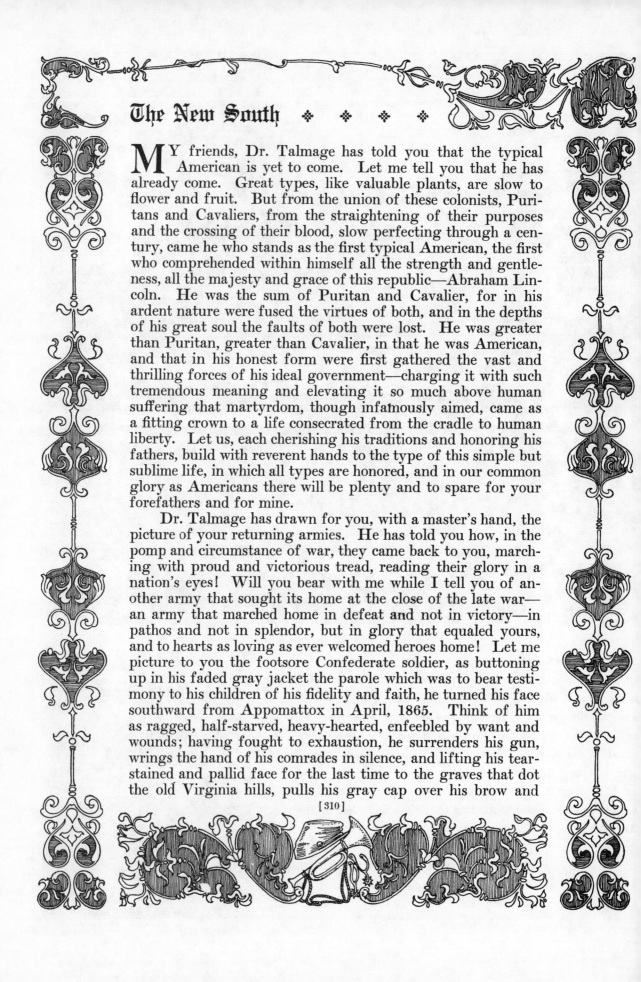

COPYRIGHT 1911, REVIEW OF REVIEWS CO.

"THIS HERO IN GRAY WITH THE HEART OF GOLD"

This portrait of a young Confederate volunteer caught the eye of the New York sculptor Ruckstuhl, while he was designing the magnificent monument to be erected in Baltimore by the Maryland Society of the Daughters of the Confederacy. The photograph was taken in April, 1861, when the boy soldier, Henry Howe Cook, had been promoted at the age of seventeen from the ranks of Company D, First Tennessee Regiment, to a lieutenancy in Company F of the Forty-fourth Tennessee, in B. R. Johnson's brigade. At the outbreak of the war proper arms were scarcer in the Confederacy than uniforms. Private Cook's trig costume contrasts sharply with the big hunting-knife and the old-fashioned pistol with its ramrod and percussion trigger. His glance is direct and fearless; yet he is almost too young to look blood-thirsty, even with the lethal weapon thrust in his belt. Working in the spirit which Grady so eloquently describes, he continued to rise after the war was over. As a lawyer he was eminently successful and in after years was honored by the people of Tennessee with the chancellorship in its court system.

begins the slow and painful journey. What does he find—let me ask you who went to your homes eager to find, in the welcome you had justly earned, full payment for four years' sacrifice—what does he find when, having followed the battle-stained cross against overwhelming odds, dreading death not half so much as surrender, he reaches the home he left so prosperous and beautiful? He finds his house in ruins, his farm devastated, his slaves free, his stock killed, his barn empty, his trade destroyed, his money worthless; his social system, feudal in its magnificence, swept away; his people without law or legal status; his comrades slain, and the burdens of others heavy on his shoulders. Crushed by defeat, his very traditions gone; without money, credit, employment, material, or training; and besides all this, confronted with the gravest problem that ever met human intelligence—the establishing of a status for the vast body of his liberated slaves.

What does he do—this hero in gray with a heart of gold? Does he sit down in sullenness and despair? Not for a day. Surely God, who had stripped him of his prosperity, inspired him in his adversity. As ruin was never before so overwhelming, never was restoration swifter. The soldier stepped from the trenches into the furrow; horses that had charged Federal guns marched before the plow, and fields that ran red with human blood in April were green with the harvest in June; women reared in luxury cut up their dresses and made breeches for their husbands, and, with a patience and a heroism that fit women always as a garment, gave their hands to work. There was little bitterness in all this. Cheerfulness and frankness prevailed. "Bill Arp" struck the key-note when he said: "Well, I killed as many of them as they did of me, and now I'm going to work." Or the soldier returning home after defeat and roasting some corn on the roadside, who made the remark to his comrades: "You may leave the South if you want to, but I am going to Sandersville, kiss my wife and raise a crop, and if the Yankees fool with me any more, I'll whip 'em again." I want to say to General Sherman—who is considered an able man in our parts, though some people think he is kind of careless about fire—that from the ashes he left us in 1864 we have raised a brave and beautiful city; that somehow or other we have caught the sunshine in the bricks and mortar of our homes, and have builded therein not one ignoble prejudice or memory.

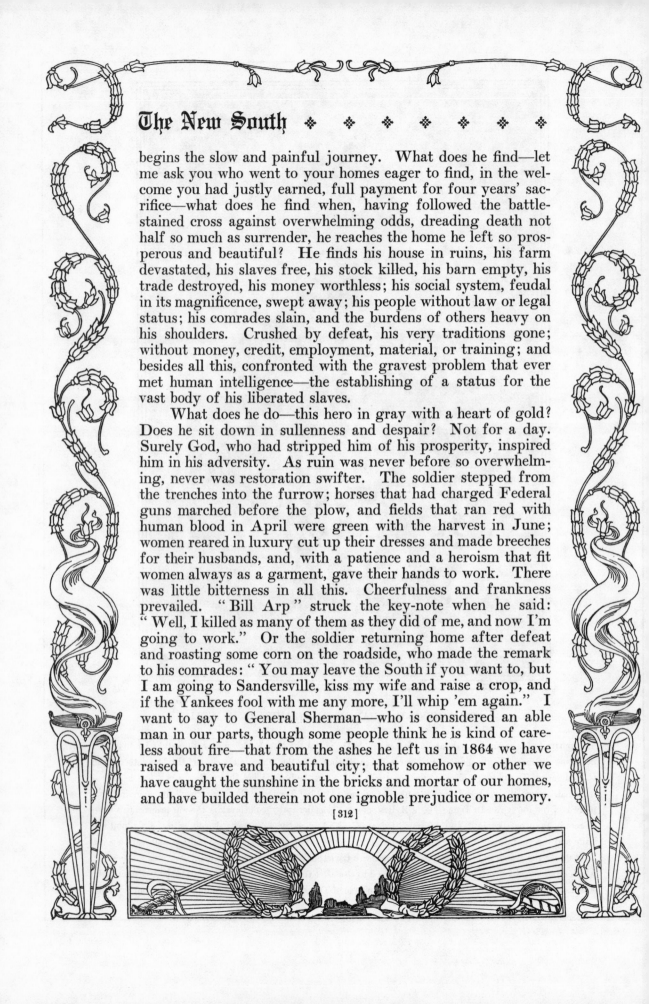

"HIS SOCIAL SYSTEM, FEUDAL IN ITS MAGNIFICENCE, SWEPT AWAY"

WADE HAMPTON'S GARDEN IN COLUMBIA, SOUTH CAROLINA

The plantation of the Hamptons, one of the finest in the whole South, fittingly illustrates Grady's allusion. The Wade Hampton here spoken of was not a states-right's man, but when secession was decided on he entered energetically into the preparations for war. "Hampton's Legion," raised and equipped from his private wealth, was prominent throughout the conflict. Hampton himself fought with them at Bull Run and up to the time he was wounded at Fair Oaks, in the Peninsula campaign. He was in the Gettysburg campaign as a leader of cavalry, being wounded three times in the battle. In 1864 he became especially distinguished for his fights against Sheridan in the Shenandoah. The ability displayed there was rewarded by Lee, who made him commander of all the cavalry in the Army of Northern Virginia. Hampton fought to the end, commanding the cavalry in Johnston's army at the time of his surrender. Even more creditable was his record after the war. Returning to the beautiful home where he had been reared in the "feudal magnificence" the ante-bellum system, he devoted his energies to rebuilding the South and securing full acceptance of the issues of the war. In 1876 he became Governor of South Carolina, and from 1878 to 1891 served as United States Senator. His career bears out Grady's speech.

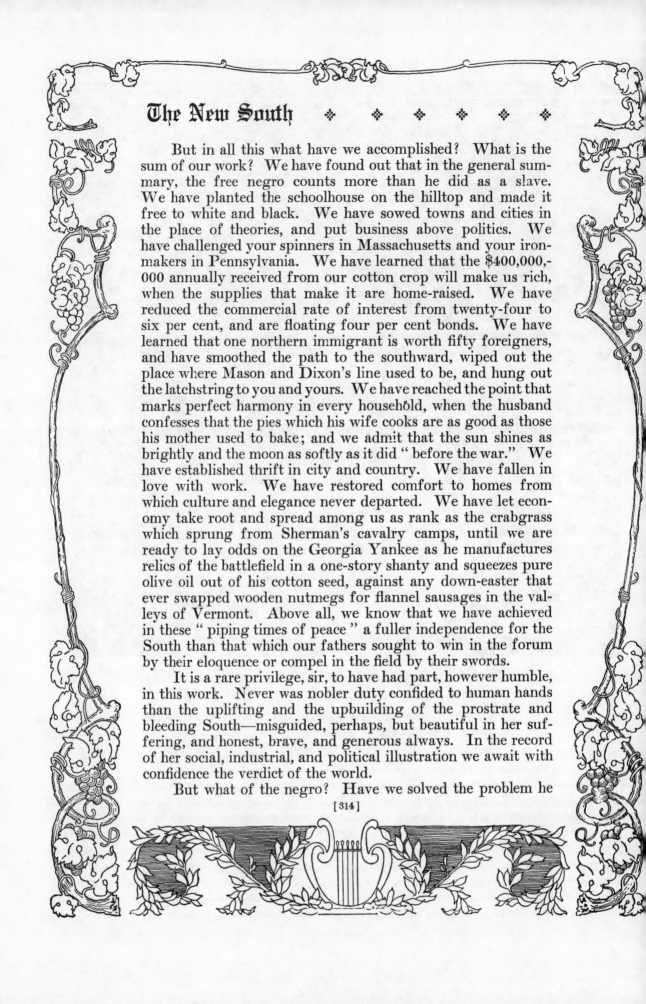

The New South ❖ ❖ ❖ ❖ ❖ ❖

But in all this what have we accomplished? What is the sum of our work? We have found out that in the general summary, the free negro counts more than he did as a slave. We have planted the schoolhouse on the hilltop and made it free to white and black. We have sowed towns and cities in the place of theories, and put business above politics. We have challenged your spinners in Massachusetts and your ironmakers in Pennsylvania. We have learned that the $400,000,-000 annually received from our cotton crop will make us rich, when the supplies that make it are home-raised. We have reduced the commercial rate of interest from twenty-four to six per cent, and are floating four per cent bonds. We have learned that one northern immigrant is worth fifty foreigners, and have smoothed the path to the southward, wiped out the place where Mason and Dixon's line used to be, and hung out the latchstring to you and yours. We have reached the point that marks perfect harmony in every household, when the husband confesses that the pies which his wife cooks are as good as those his mother used to bake; and we admit that the sun shines as brightly and the moon as softly as it did " before the war." We have established thrift in city and country. We have fallen in love with work. We have restored comfort to homes from which culture and elegance never departed. We have let economy take root and spread among us as rank as the crabgrass which sprung from Sherman's cavalry camps, until we are ready to lay odds on the Georgia Yankee as he manufactures relics of the battlefield in a one-story shanty and squeezes pure olive oil out of his cotton seed, against any down-easter that ever swapped wooden nutmegs for flannel sausages in the valleys of Vermont. Above all, we know that we have achieved in these " piping times of peace " a fuller independence for the South than that which our fathers sought to win in the forum by their eloquence or compel in the field by their swords.

It is a rare privilege, sir, to have had part, however humble, in this work. Never was nobler duty confided to human hands than the uplifting and the upbuilding of the prostrate and bleeding South—misguided, perhaps, but beautiful in her suffering, and honest, brave, and generous always. In the record of her social, industrial, and political illustration we await with confidence the verdict of the world.

But what of the negro? Have we solved the problem he

SHOT–RIDDLED HOMES IN FREDERICKSBURG, VIRGINIA

How widespread was the condition of affairs described by Grady as confronting the Confederate soldier on his return home, appears in such pictures. The havoc was the result of Burnside's bombardment of December 11, 1862. When the Confederate sharpshooters from the roofs and windows of the houses in Fredericksburg opened fire on the pontoniers, the Federal artillery at once returned the fire, at 7 A.M., and continued it incessantly until one o'clock in the afternoon. Despite a bombardment which laid the town in ruins, volunteers from the Seventh Michigan and Nineteenth Massachusetts finally had to be sent over to drive off the stubborn sharpshooters.

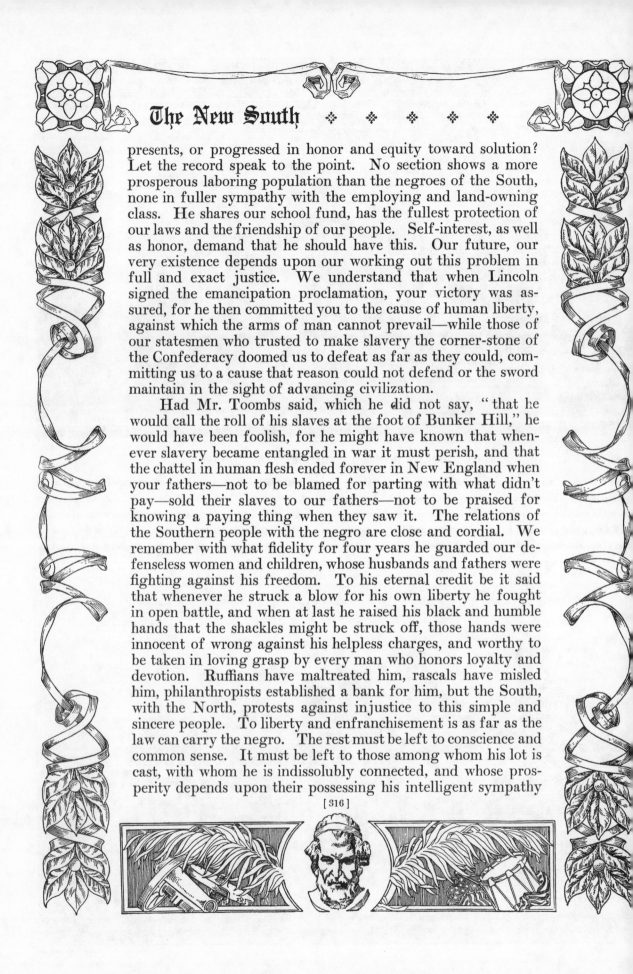

presents, or progressed in honor and equity toward solution? Let the record speak to the point. No section shows a more prosperous laboring population than the negroes of the South, none in fuller sympathy with the employing and land-owning class. He shares our school fund, has the fullest protection of our laws and the friendship of our people. Self-interest, as well as honor, demand that he should have this. Our future, our very existence depends upon our working out this problem in full and exact justice. We understand that when Lincoln signed the emancipation proclamation, your victory was assured, for he then committed you to the cause of human liberty, against which the arms of man cannot prevail—while those of our statesmen who trusted to make slavery the corner-stone of the Confederacy doomed us to defeat as far as they could, committing us to a cause that reason could not defend or the sword maintain in the sight of advancing civilization.

Had Mr. Toombs said, which he did not say, "that he would call the roll of his slaves at the foot of Bunker Hill," he would have been foolish, for he might have known that whenever slavery became entangled in war it must perish, and that the chattel in human flesh ended forever in New England when your fathers—not to be blamed for parting with what didn't pay—sold their slaves to our fathers—not to be praised for knowing a paying thing when they saw it. The relations of the Southern people with the negro are close and cordial. We remember with what fidelity for four years he guarded our defenseless women and children, whose husbands and fathers were fighting against his freedom. To his eternal credit be it said that whenever he struck a blow for his own liberty he fought in open battle, and when at last he raised his black and humble hands that the shackles might be struck off, those hands were innocent of wrong against his helpless charges, and worthy to be taken in loving grasp by every man who honors loyalty and devotion. Ruffians have maltreated him, rascals have misled him, philanthropists established a bank for him, but the South, with the North, protests against injustice to this simple and sincere people. To liberty and enfranchisement is as far as the law can carry the negro. The rest must be left to conscience and common sense. It must be left to those among whom his lot is cast, with whom he is indissolubly connected, and whose prosperity depends upon their possessing his intelligent sympathy

WHAT THE CONFEDERATE SOLDIER FOUND—A MISSISSIPPI VALLEY MILL

This gloomy scene is a reminder of the fate that befell the Mississippi valley and many another fertile region of the South. Western raids throughout the war destroyed hundreds of miles of railroad, burned the cars, and blew up the locomotives, fell upon tanneries and shoe-factories, wrecked arsenals, captured commissary stores, put the torch to cotton-factories, and in every possible way crippled the resources of the South for continuing the struggle. General Grant tells of an incident at his capture of Jackson, Mississippi, on May 14, 1863. Sherman was instructed to destroy "the railroads, bridges, factories, workshops, arsenals, and everything valuable for the support of the enemy." The two generals went into a very valuable cotton-factory, where the machinery was running at full speed and all the hands were at work, as if the city had not fallen into the hands of the enemy. While the military leaders stood there, hundreds of yards of canvas rolled out from the looms with the stamp of the Confederate Quartermaster's Department upon it. It was to be used in tents. After looking on the busy scene for a few minutes, the order was given for the place to be vacated, and within an hour the building and its warehouses were in flames. The next day the work of destruction was so thoroughly accomplished that "Jackson as a railroad center or Government depot of stores and military factories," it was reported, could be of little use for at least six months.

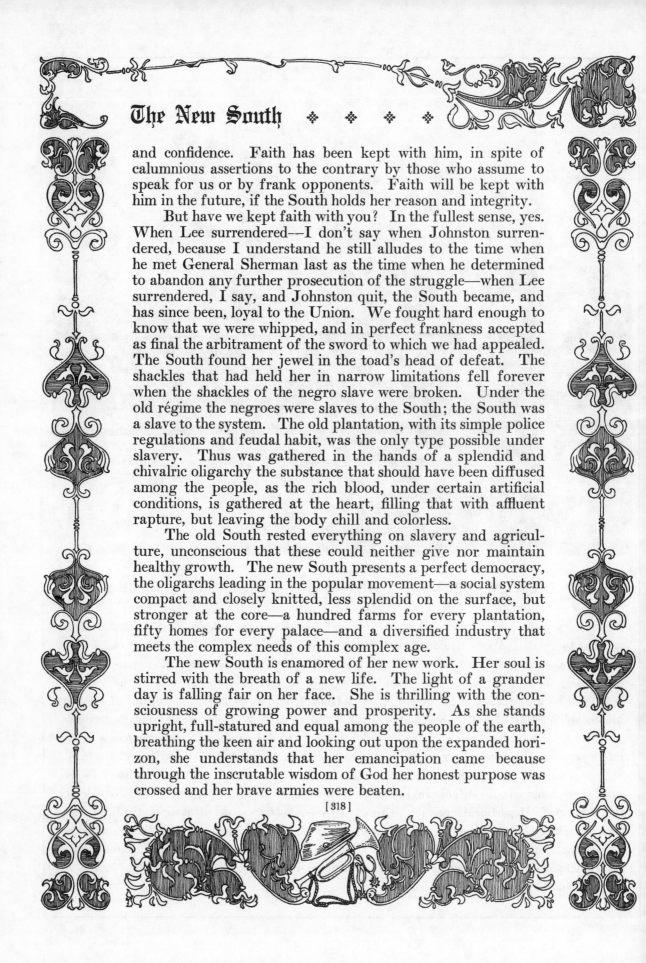

and confidence. Faith has been kept with him, in spite of calumnious assertions to the contrary by those who assume to speak for us or by frank opponents. Faith will be kept with him in the future, if the South holds her reason and integrity.

But have we kept faith with you? In the fullest sense, yes. When Lee surrendered—I don't say when Johnston surrendered, because I understand he still alludes to the time when he met General Sherman last as the time when he determined to abandon any further prosecution of the struggle—when Lee surrendered, I say, and Johnston quit, the South became, and has since been, loyal to the Union. We fought hard enough to know that we were whipped, and in perfect frankness accepted as final the arbitrament of the sword to which we had appealed. The South found her jewel in the toad's head of defeat. The shackles that had held her in narrow limitations fell forever when the shackles of the negro slave were broken. Under the old régime the negroes were slaves to the South; the South was a slave to the system. The old plantation, with its simple police regulations and feudal habit, was the only type possible under slavery. Thus was gathered in the hands of a splendid and chivalric oligarchy the substance that should have been diffused among the people, as the rich blood, under certain artificial conditions, is gathered at the heart, filling that with affluent rapture, but leaving the body chill and colorless.

The old South rested everything on slavery and agriculture, unconscious that these could neither give nor maintain healthy growth. The new South presents a perfect democracy, the oligarchs leading in the popular movement—a social system compact and closely knitted, less splendid on the surface, but stronger at the core—a hundred farms for every plantation, fifty homes for every palace—and a diversified industry that meets the complex needs of this complex age.

The new South is enamored of her new work. Her soul is stirred with the breath of a new life. The light of a grander day is falling fair on her face. She is thrilling with the consciousness of growing power and prosperity. As she stands upright, full-statured and equal among the people of the earth, breathing the keen air and looking out upon the expanded horizon, she understands that her emancipation came because through the inscrutable wisdom of God her honest purpose was crossed and her brave armies were beaten.

A COLONIAL MANSION IN RUINS—1865

Grady's returning Confederate soldier was a private in the ranks. But Southern officers, as well, rich and poor alike, found desolation at home in 1865. Compare with the preceding scenes the ruins of this handsome residence of the Pinckneys, one of the most distinguished Charleston families. It stood in the middle of a whole square, commanding a fine view of Charleston Harbor. When James Glenn arrived in 1743 as royal governor, he selected this mansion as his official residence. It was occupied in succession by Governors Glenn, Lyttleton, Boone, and Lord Charles Montague, while Charles Pinckney was in Europe and his son was attaining majority. During those years there were many stately dinners here. These ruins were the scene of Charleston's gayest colonial life.

The New South ❖ ❖ ❖ ❖ ❖ ❖

This is said in no spirit of time-serving or apology. The South has nothing for which to apologize. She believes that the late struggle between the States was war and not rebellion, revolution and not conspiracy, and that her convictions were as honest as yours. I should be unjust to the dauntless spirit of the South and to my own convictions if I did not make this plain in this presence. The South has nothing to take back. In my native town of Athens is a monument that crowns its central hill—a plain, white shaft. Deep cut into its shining side is a name dear to me above the names of men, that of a brave and simple man who died in a brave and simple faith. Not for all the glories of New England, from Plymouth Rock all the way, would I exchange the heritage he left me in his soldier's death. To the foot of that shaft I shall send my children's children to reverence him who ennobled their name with his heroic blood. But, sir, speaking from the shadow of that memory which I honor as I do nothing else on earth, I say that the cause in which he suffered and for which he gave his life was adjudged by higher and fuller wisdom than his or mine, and I am glad that the omniscient God held the balance of battle in His Almighty hand and that human slavery was swept forever from American soil—the American Union was saved from the wreck of war.

This message, Mr. President, comes to you from consecrated ground. Every foot of soil about the city in which I live is sacred as a battle-ground of the republic. Every hill that invests it is hallowed to you by the blood of your brothers who died for your victory, and doubly hallowed to us by the blood of those who died hopeless, but undaunted, in defeat— sacred soil to all of us, rich with memories that make us purer and stronger and better, silent but stanch witnesses in its red desolation of the matchless valor of American hearts and the deathless glory of American arms,—speaking an eloquent witness, in its white peace and prosperity, to the indissoluble union of American States and the imperishable brotherhood of the American people.

Now, what answer has New England to this message? Will she permit the prejudice of war to remain in the hearts of the conquerors, when it has died in the hearts of the conquered? Will she transmit this prejudice to the next generation, that in their hearts, which never felt the generous ardor of conflict, it

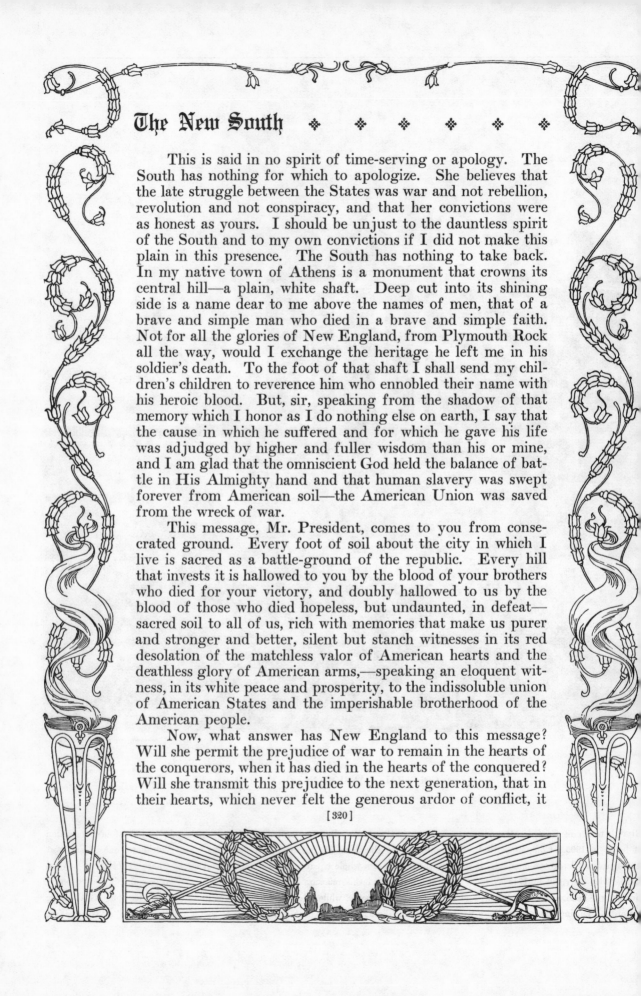

THE PINCKNEY HOUSE IN CHARLESTON, SOUTH CAROLINA

Here lived from 1769 the noted Charles Cotesworth Pinckney, after his return from school at Westminster and Oxford.   When the Revolution began he discontinued his practice of law and led a provincial regiment.   For two years he was one of Washingon's aides-decamp.   In 1780 his wife was evicted from the mansion by British troops when Sir Henry Clinton and Lord Cornwallis occupied the town. The history of his dwelling-place terminated in December, 1861.   A fire began on a wharf by the Cooper River, where some Negroes were cooking their supper.   It was blown into a hay store near by; it then spread swiftly before the gale to the banks of the Ashley, leaving behind nothing but a smoking wilderness of ruins.   The Pinckney mansion stood in its path.   The able-bodied men of the town were in service or drilling in the camps at the race-course, and little could be done to check its course till it reached the Ashley River.

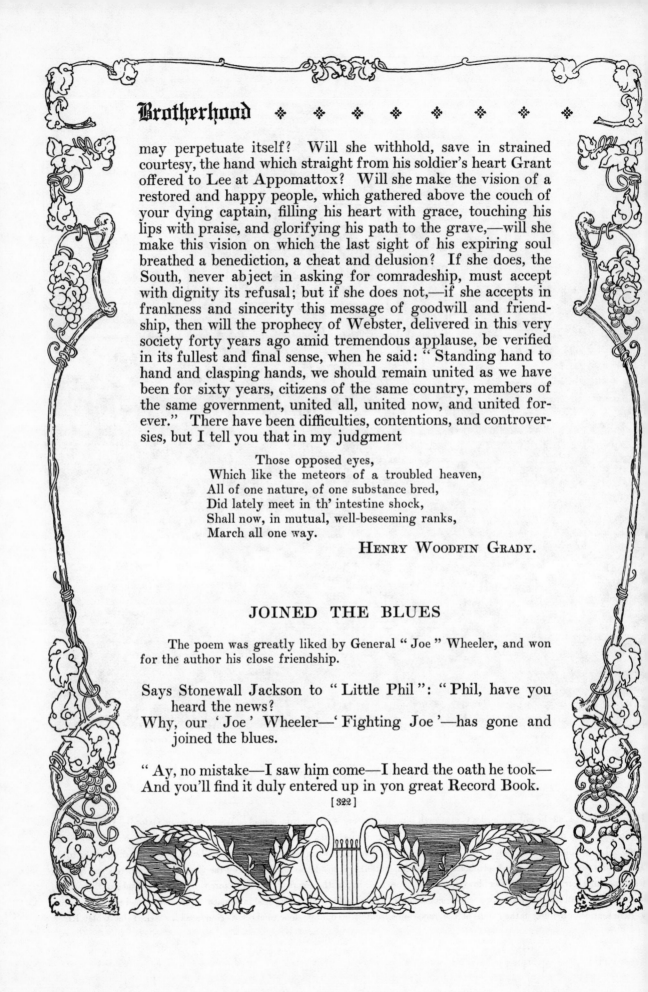

may perpetuate itself? Will she withhold, save in strained courtesy, the hand which straight from his soldier's heart Grant offered to Lee at Appomattox? Will she make the vision of a restored and happy people, which gathered above the couch of your dying captain, filling his heart with grace, touching his lips with praise, and glorifying his path to the grave,—will she make this vision on which the last sight of his expiring soul breathed a benediction, a cheat and delusion? If she does, the South, never abject in asking for comradeship, must accept with dignity its refusal; but if she does not,—if she accepts in frankness and sincerity this message of goodwill and friendship, then will the prophecy of Webster, delivered in this very society forty years ago amid tremendous applause, be verified in its fullest and final sense, when he said: "Standing hand to hand and clasping hands, we should remain united as we have been for sixty years, citizens of the same country, members of the same government, united all, united now, and united forever." There have been difficulties, contentions, and controversies, but I tell you that in my judgment

> Those opposed eyes,
> Which like the meteors of a troubled heaven,
> All of one nature, of one substance bred,
> Did lately meet in th' intestine shock,
> Shall now, in mutual, well-beseeming ranks,
> March all one way.

HENRY WOODFIN GRADY.

JOINED THE BLUES

The poem was greatly liked by General " Joe " Wheeler, and won for the author his close friendship.

Says Stonewall Jackson to " Little Phil ": " Phil, have you heard the news?
Why, our ' Joe ' Wheeler—' Fighting Joe '—has gone and joined the blues.

" Ay, no mistake—I saw him come—I heard the oath he took—
And you'll find it duly entered up in yon great Record Book.

"FROM THE ASHES LEFT US IN 1864"

The ruins of Atlanta here are the very scenes to which Grady was referring. The destruction of its industries Sherman declared to be a military necessity. Atlanta contained the largest foundries and machine-shops south of Richmond. It formed a railroad center for the central South, where provisions might be gathered and forwarded to the armies at the front. To destroy the Atlanta shops and railroads would therefore cripple the resources of the Confederacy. Railroads had been torn up to the south of the city even before its capture on September 2, 1864. But it was not until November 15th, when Sherman had completed all his arrangements for the march to the sea, that on every road leading into Atlanta the ties were burned, the rails torn up and then twisted so as to render them permanently useless. The buildings were first burned and the walls afterward razed to the ground. In the fire thus started the exploding of ammunition could be heard all night in the midst of the ruins. The flames soon spread to a block of stores and soon the heart of the city was burned out completely.

ON THE PAGE FACING,

THE SAME SPOT

FORTY-SIX YEARS

LATER

RUINS IN RICHMOND

AS THE WAR WAS

DRAWING

TO A CLOSE

THE USELESS SIGNALS

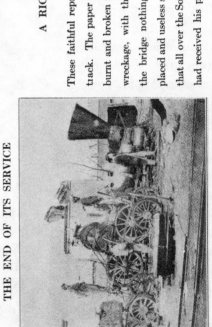

THE END OF ITS SERVICE

A RICHMOND PAPER MILL IN 1865

These faithful reproductions show the desolation war leaves in its track. The paper mill is a mass of ruins, with no power to turn the burnt and broken rollers. The railroad track is a heap of twisted wreckage, with the blasted engine hopelessly beyond repair. Of the bridge nothing remains but a row of granite pillars and the misplaced and useless signals. These views exhibit the stupendous task that all over the South awaited the returning Confederate soldier who had received his parole at the final surrenders and begun life again.

Below, Grady's declaration finds a vivid example. On the exact spot shown in the central picture of the opposite page has risen a modern mill to replace the blackened ruins. In place of the twisted rails are three well graded tracks. A reënforced concrete bridge replaces the broken causeway. In the distance the tall stacks of a busy city rise against the sky. The South is once more prosperous. Its sons have attacked the problems of the new era and have placed their section upon a basis for permanent advancement. The currents of national life are flowing through every part of its spacious territory, and it feels itself an integral and inseparable part of the mighty American republic. The hundreds of scenes in this and the preceding volumes have been from photographs taken in war time. Now that the volume is ended and the records of the campaigns are closed, an exception is made to show what the South has accomplished in less than half a century. Proud as all are of the devotion and courage of the South during the four years of war, prouder still should every American be of the splendid record of her peaceful victories in the forty years succeeding. For she has wrung victory from defeat and has provided for the whole world the spectacle of an enduring triumph—a progress without parallel.

"IT IS A RARE PRIVILEGE, SIR,

TO HAVE HAD ANY PART,

HOWEVER HUMBLE,

IN THIS WORK"

FORTY-SIX YEARS AFTER—THE RICHMOND PAPER MILL AND RAILROAD REBUILT

Brotherhood ❖ ❖ ❖ ❖ ❖ ❖ ❖

"Yes, 'Phil,' it is a change since then (we give the Lord due
    thanks)
When 'Joe' came swooping like a hawk upon your Sherman's
    flanks!

"Why, 'Phil,' you knew the trick yourself—but 'Joe' had all
    the points—
And we've yet to hear his horses died of stiff or rusty joints!

"But what of that?—the deed I saw to-day in yonder town
Leads all we did and all 'Joe' did in troopings up and down;

"For, 'Phil,' that oath shall be the heal of many a bleeding
    wound,
And many a Southland song shall yet to that same oath be
    tuned!

"The oath 'Joe' swore has done the work of thrice a score of
    years—
Ay, more than oath—he swore away mistrust and hate and
    tears!"

"Yes, yes," says "Phil," "he was, indeed, a right good worthy
    foe,
And well he knew, in those fierce days, to give us blow for blow.

"When 'Joe' came round to pay a call—the commissaries
    said—
Full many a swearing, grumbling 'Yank' went supperless to
    bed:

"He seemed to have a pesky knack—so Sherman used to say—
Of calling, when he should by rights be ninety miles away!

"Come, Stonewall, put your hand in mine,—'Joe's sworn old
    Samuel's oath—
We're never North or South again—he kissed the Book for
    both!"

JOHN JEROME ROONEY.

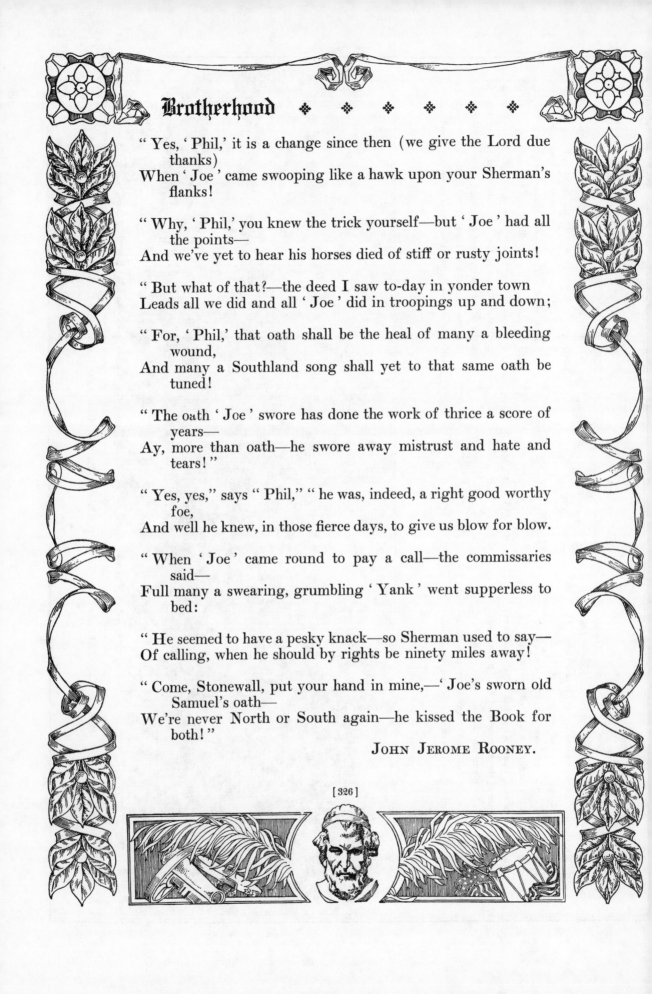

"JOE'S SWORN OLD SAMUEL'S OATH"

A post-bellum portrait of General Joseph Wheeler has been chosen to appear here as well as of "that loyal old Reb, Fitzhugh Lee"—in order to illustrate closely the poem. General Joseph Wheeler, a native of Georgia, was a brilliant Confederate cavalry leader in the Civil War. He graduated from West Point in 1859, entered the Confederate service in April, 1861, and fought at the head of a brigade at Shiloh. In the same year he was transferred to the cavalry. In 1863, as major-general, he commanded the cavalry at the battles of Chickamauga and Chattanooga, and protected Bragg's retreat southward. In 1864 he obstructed Sherman in his advance on Atlanta, as alluded to in the poem, and in the march to the sea. In 1865, as lieutenant-general, he commanded the cavalry in Johnston's army up to the surrender.

Brotherhood ❖ ❖ ❖ ❖

WHEELER'S BRIGADE AT SANTIAGO

'Neath the lances of the tropic sun
    The column is standing ready,
Awaiting the fateful command of one
      Whose word will ring out
      To an answering shout
    To prove it alert and steady.
And a stirring chorus all of them sung
    With singleness of endeavor,
Though some to " The Bonny Blue Flag " had swung
    And some to " The Union For Ever."

The order came sharp through the desperate air
    And the long ranks rose to follow,
Till their dancing banners shone more fair
      Than the brightest ray
      Of the Cuban day
    On the hill and jungled hollow;
And to " Maryland " some in the days gone by
    Had fought through the combat's rumble,
And some for " Freedom's Battle-Cry "
    Had seen the broad earth crumble.

Full many a widow weeps in the night
    Who had been a man's wife in the morning;
For the banners we loved we bore to the height
      Where the enemy stood
      As a hero should,
    His valor his country adorning;
But drops of pride with your tears of grief,
    Ye American women, mix ye!
For the North and South, with a Southern chief,
    Kept time to the tune of " Dixie."

WALLACE RICE.

"FOR THE NORTH AND THE SOUTH, WITH A SOUTHRON CHIEF,

KEPT TIME TO THE TUNE OF 'DIXIE'"

These two figures of '61 and '65 have a peculiar appropriateness for Wallace Rice's "Wheeler's Brigade at Santiago." They recall in detail the fullness of the warlike preparations in those distant days. The Union soldier is equipped with new uniform and shining musket, ready to repel any invader of the Nation's capital. More than once before the close of hostilities such services had been needed in the circle of forts that surrounded the city. The officer stands erect with the intensity and eagerness that characterized Southern troops in battle. A generation later, the Spanish war of 1898 became a magnificent occasion for proof that the hostile relations and feelings of the '60's had melted away. Those who had once stood in opposing ranks, and their sons with them, in '98 marched and fought shoulder to shoulder, inspired by love of the same country and devoted to the same high principles of human freedom.

UNION SOLDIER

ON GUARD OVER A PRISONER

IN WASHINGTON

1865

CONFEDERATE OFFICER

OF THE WASHINGTON ARTILLERY

OF NEW ORLEANS

1861

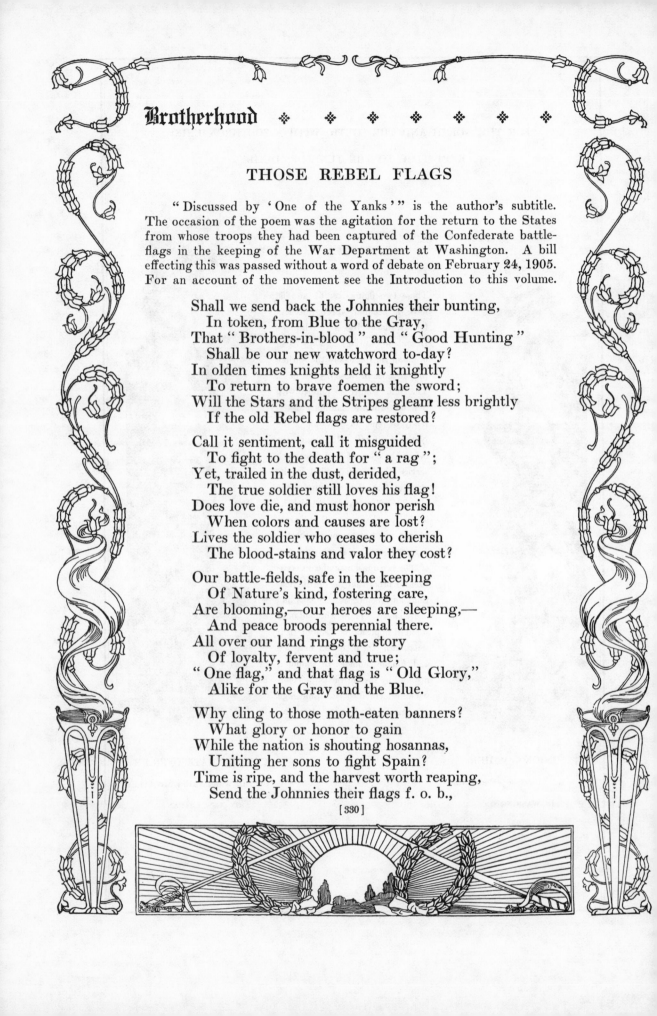

THOSE REBEL FLAGS

"Discussed by 'One of the Yanks'" is the author's subtitle. The occasion of the poem was the agitation for the return to the States from whose troops they had been captured of the Confederate battle-flags in the keeping of the War Department at Washington. A bill effecting this was passed without a word of debate on February 24, 1905. For an account of the movement see the Introduction to this volume.

Shall we send back the Johnnies their bunting,
    In token, from Blue to the Gray,
That "Brothers-in-blood" and "Good Hunting"
    Shall be our new watchword to-day?
In olden times knights held it knightly
    To return to brave foemen the sword;
Will the Stars and the Stripes gleam less brightly
    If the old Rebel flags are restored?

Call it sentiment, call it misguided
    To fight to the death for "a rag";
Yet, trailed in the dust, derided,
    The true soldier still loves his flag!
Does love die, and must honor perish
    When colors and causes are lost?
Lives the soldier who ceases to cherish
    The blood-stains and valor they cost?

Our battle-fields, safe in the keeping
    Of Nature's kind, fostering care,
Are blooming,—our heroes are sleeping,—
    And peace broods perennial there.
All over our land rings the story
    Of loyalty, fervent and true;
"One flag," and that flag is "Old Glory,"
    Alike for the Gray and the Blue.

Why cling to those moth-eaten banners?
    What glory or honor to gain
While the nation is shouting hosannas,
    Uniting her sons to fight Spain?
Time is ripe, and the harvest worth reaping,
    Send the Johnnies their flags f. o. b.,

"THAT LOYAL 'OLD REB' FITZHUGH LEE"

Since Jewett's lines apply to the Spanish War period, a portrait of "Fitz" Lee has been selected, taken many years after his days in the saddle as a Confederate cavalry leader. The nephew of Robert E. Lee was likewise a graduate of West Point, and was instructor in cavalry there from May, 1860, to the outbreak of the war. In nearly all the movements of the Army of Northern Virginia, he was a dashing cavalry leader. From March, 1865, to his surrender to General Meade at Farmville, April 7th, he was commander of all the cavalry of the army. That he was "loyal" appeared as early as 1874, when he delivered a patriotic address at Bunker Hill. His attitude on the return of Confederate battle-flags during his term as Governor of Virginia (1886–1890) is touched on in the Introduction to this volume. He served his country as consul-general at Havana from 1896, whence he was recalled in April, 1898, to be appointed major-general of volunteers and given command of the Seventh Army Corps. He too had "joined the Blues." Moreover, after the war he was made military governor of Havana and subsequently placed in command of the Department of Missouri. His death in 1905 was mourned nationally.

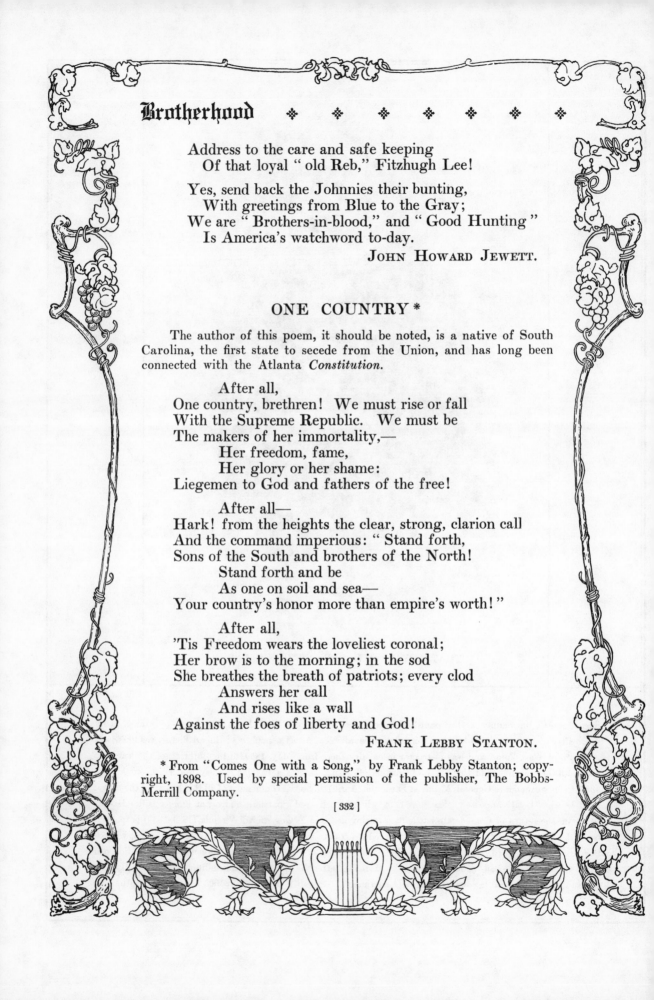

Address to the care and safe keeping
  Of that loyal " old Reb," Fitzhugh Lee!

Yes, send back the Johnnies their bunting,
  With greetings from Blue to the Gray;
We are " Brothers-in-blood," and " Good Hunting "
  Is America's watchword to-day.
JOHN HOWARD JEWETT.

ONE COUNTRY *

    The author of this poem, it should be noted, is a native of South
Carolina, the first state to secede from the Union, and has long been
connected with the Atlanta *Constitution.*

    After all,
One country, brethren! We must rise or fall
With the Supreme Republic. We must be
The makers of her immortality,—
    Her freedom, fame,
    Her glory or her shame:
Liegemen to God and fathers of the free!

    After all—
Hark! from the heights the clear, strong, clarion call
And the command imperious: " Stand forth,
Sons of the South and brothers of the North!
    Stand forth and be
    As one on soil and sea—
Your country's honor more than empire's worth! "

    After all,
'Tis Freedom wears the loveliest coronal;
Her brow is to the morning; in the sod
She breathes the breath of patriots; every clod
    Answers her call
    And rises like a wall
Against the foes of liberty and God!
FRANK LEBBY STANTON.

"AFTER ALL—ONE COUNTRY"

Here in Charleston, under the sunlight of a cloudless April day, rest the Parrott guns that from Morris Island pulverized the walls of Sumter, that hurled shot and shell across the bay—now silent, "after all." Flecks of shade from the live-oak leaves fall upon the polished barrels that for eighteen months had roared upon the distant foe. Now the silence is broken only by the rustle of the foliage above. Below, the daisies are beginning to hide the newly springing grass. The Stars and Stripes draped above the nearest gun-carriage is once more the flag of the whole American people. Peace has indeed come, and all over the land thanksgiving is ascending like an incense from hearts that have known the anguish of endless separation and the bitterness of unavailing sorrow—thanksgiving, too, for the issue of the conflict, which determined that America should forever wear the coronal of freedom and lead in the vanguard of human liberty.

Although taken long before the days of moving-picture films, this series of photographs preserves the progression of the celebration on April 14, 1865—the fourth anniversary of the evacuation of Sumter. The evening before, the news of Lee's surrender had reached Charleston and made the occasion one of national thanksgiving. The city was gay with flags; patriotic bands filled the air with music, and Dahlgren's fleet opened the day with the full national salute of twenty-one guns from every ship in the harbor. In Fort Sumter the Reverend Matthias Harris, who had helped to raise the flag over the fort, four years before, opened the services with prayer. Dr. Richard S. Storrs read that ever-beautiful passage beginning: "When the Lord turned again the captivity of Zion, we were like them that dream."

RAISING THE NATIONAL FLAG IN SUMTER, JUST FOUR YEARS AFTER ITS EVACUATION

Precisely at noon, General Anderson raised with his own hands the flag which had been lowered in 1861. Long-continued shouting and the boom of guns from every fort about the harbor was the salute to the banner that was held to be a symbol of the restored Union. In the address of Henry Ward Beecher the feeling of brotherhood to the South was prominent. These were his closing words, "We offer to the President of these United States our solemn congratulations that God has sustained his life and health under the unparalleled burdens and sufferings of four bloody years, and permitted him to behold this auspicious consummation of that national unity for which he has waited with so much patience and fortitude, and for which he has labored with such disinterested wisdom."

HENRY WARD BEECHER'S SPEECH OF BROTHERHOOD ON APRIL 14, 1865

WHEN PEACE DWELT AGAIN UPON FORT SUMTER

A spectator before that irregular pile of débris might never imagine that in 1861 Fort Sumter was a formidable work. Its walls then rose to a height of forty feet above high-water. Constructed of the best Carolina gray brick, laid in a mortar of pounded oyster-shells and cement, their thickness of five to ten feet made the stronghold seem impregnable. Despite the appearance in the picture, it proved so. The attack that began the war did very little damage, beyond the burning of the barracks. Two years later, Rear-Admiral Samuel F. Du Pont led a naval attack that was expected to capture the fort with little delay; yet the heavy bombardment made almost no impression. The ironclad that was nearest Sumter, the *Keokuk*, struck ninety times, was so badly injured that it sank the next morning. The *Weehawken* was hit fifty-three times; the *Passaic* thirty-five times, the *Montauk* fourteen times, the *Patapsco*, the fourth vessel in line, forty-seven times; and so on through the entire fleet. The fort, on the other hand, was hardly injured. At one point, where an 11-inch and a 15-inch shell struck at the same point at the same time, the wall was completely breached; on the outside

THE CRUMBLED WALLS FROM THE SAND BAR—1865

appeared a crater six feet high and eight feet wide. But the destruction shown in the picture was wrought by the bombardment from the land-batteries four months later. General Gillmore's guns opened on August 17th. Major John Johnson in "Battles and Leaders" makes this report of the effect of Gillmore's operations and of the work of the defenders: "When demolished by land-batteries of unprecedented range, the fort endured for more than eighteen months their almost constant fire, and for a hundred days and nights their utmost power until it could with truth be said that it at last tired out, and in this way silenced, the great guns that once had silenced it. From having been a desolate ruin, a shapeless pile of shattered walls and casemates, showing here and there the guns disabled and half-buried in splintered wrecks of carriages, its mounds of rubbish fairly reeking with the smoke and smell of powder, Fort Sumter under fire was transformed within a year into a powerful earthwork, impregnable to assault, and even supporting the other works at the entrance of Charleston harbor with six guns of the heaviest caliber." Above, it is a monument to the wastefulness of warfare.

WITHIN THE DESERTED FORT—1865

Here is the desolation inside the shattered walls of Sumter. The celebration of raising the flag on April 14, 1865, is now in the past. The
benches that had been crowded with listeners eager to catch every word
of the address by Henry Ward Beecher are now empty. The pavilion
in which he spoke is no longer gay with flags. The staff from which
"Old Glory" had floated to the applause of thousands stands bare.
Beyond are the shapeless ruins made by Gillmore's guns. Out in the
bay no ships dressed in flags are to be seen. For the whole nation is in
mourning. On the very evening of the flag-raising the bullet of Booth
had laid low the man through whose patience and statesmanship the
Sumter celebration had become possible. Trials more searching than
those of war awaited his sorrowing people.

APPENDIX

———

SONGS
OF THE
WAR DAYS

———

EDITED BY
JEANNE ROBERT FOSTER

"WHEN JOHNNY COMES MARCHING HOME"

THE MOST POPULAR WAR-TIME SONG OF THE MUSTERED-OUT MEN—THUS THEY
LOOKED AS THEY MARCHED HOME FROM TRENCHES AND FORTS, FROM BLOODY BAT-
TLEFIELDS, FROM HOSPITAL AND PRISON—BACK TO CITY, TOWN, AND COUNTRYSIDE

"SUCCESS TO THE ALABAMA"

THE ENGLISH MANOR HOUSE TO WHICH ADMIRAL SEMMES RE-PAIRED AFTER THE FAMOUS BATTLE—HIS CHIEF OFFICER, CAPTAIN KELL, IS STANDING AT THE EXTREME RIGHT.

In this charming photograph of Milbrook Manor House near Southampton, England, appears a scene of 1864 at the quiet country-place to which Admiral Semmes of the Confederate warship, *Alabama*, and his chief executive officer, Captain Kell, retired for rest and recuperation after the loss of their vessel in the battle with the U. S. S. *Kearsarge* off the coast of France. On the right of the picture is Captain Kell, convalescing from his wound in this green, shaded retreat. Exquisitely rendered by the camera are the hoopskirts, the flowing scarfs, and the old-fashioned blouses of the women in the picture. Under a glass the detail comes out with startling reality, and for a moment the atmosphere of the place and the time is restored. The beautiful, vine-clad manor house, with the quaint group of women, bring back to remembrance the history of the cruiser and of the *Kearsarge*, and the bravery of the men who fought during the most dramatic naval battle.

Songs of the War Days

Edited by Jeanne Robert Foster

"If a man were permitted to make all the ballads he need not care who should make the laws of a nation."

Andrew Fletcher

There is a strange, magical power in songs that spring from the hearts of men passing through great and passionate experience—the power to gather together again in after years a mirage of the emotions that begot them—a remembrance of the enthusiasm that incited men to perilous and heroic deeds. The question of actual literary merit has no place in the consideration of these war-songs; they were chronicles of events; they achieved universality, and on the field of battle they became the sublime pæans of a national crisis. Their words and melodies deserve a place in our records. The songs of the soldier boys, the spirited marching tunes, the sentimental ballads, the outbursts of fiery patriotism, must remain with us a legacy of unfailing inspiration and delight.

WHEN JOHNNY COMES MARCHING HOME

Patrick Sarsfield Gilmore

This rousing war-song was the one most sung by the soldiers returning from service.

When Johnny comes marching home again,
  Hurrah! Hurrah!
We'll give him a hearty welcome then,
  Hurrah! Hurrah!
The men will cheer, the boys will shout,
The ladies they will all turn out.

Chorus—
  And we'll all feel gay,
When Johnny comes marching home.

The old church-bell will peal with joy,
  Hurrah! Hurrah!
To welcome home our darling boy,
  Hurrah! Hurrah!
The village lads and lasses say
With roses they will strew the way.

THE BATTLECRY OF FREEDOM

George Frederick Root

One of the best of the many flag songs written during the war.

Yes, we'll rally round the flag, boys, we'll rally
    once again,
  Shouting the battlecry of freedom,
We will rally from the hillside, we'll gather
    from the plain,
  Shouting the battlecry of freedom.

Chorus—
  The Union forever, hurrah! boys, hurrah!
  Down with the traitor, up with the star,

While we rally round the flag, boys,
  Rally once again,
  Shouting the battle cry of Freedom.

We are springing to the call of our
    brothers gone before,
  Shouting the battlecry of freedom.
And we'll fill the vacant ranks with a
    million freemen more,
  Shouting the battlecry of freedom.

MARCHING THROUGH GEORGIA

Henry Clay Work

Written in honor of Sherman's famous march from Atlanta to the sea.

Bring the good old bugle, boys, we'll sing another
    song—
Sing it with a spirit that will start the world
    along—
Sing it as we used to sing it, fifty thousand strong,
While we were marching through Georgia.

Chorus—
  "Hurrah! Hurrah! we bring the jubilee,
    Hurrah! Hurrah! the flag that makes you
      free!"
  So we sang the chorus from Atlanta to the sea,
  While we were marching through Georgia.

How the darkeys shouted when they heard the
    joyful sound!
How the turkeys gobbled which our commissary
    found!
How the sweet potatoes even started from the
    ground,
While we were marching through Georgia.

THE SOUTHERN MARSEILLAISE

A. E. BLACKMAR, 1861

This was the rallying song of the Confederacy. It was sung throughout the South as early as 1861 while the soldiers were hurried to Virginia.

Sons of the South, awake to glory,
  A thousand voices bid you rise,
Your children, wives and grandsires hoary,
  Gaze on you now with trusting eyes,
  Gaze on you now with trusting eyes;
Your country every strong arm calling,
  To meet the hireling Northern band
  That comes to desolate the land
With fire and blood and scenes appalling,
  To arms, to arms, ye brave;
  Th' avenging sword unsheath!
March on! March on! All hearts resolved on
  victory or death.
March on! March on! All hearts resolved on
  victory or death.

Now, now, the dangerous storm is rolling,
  Which treacherous brothers madly raise,
The dogs of war let loose, are howling,
  And soon our peaceful towns may blaze,
  And soon our peaceful towns may blaze.
Shall fiends who basely plot our ruin,
  Unchecked, advance with guilty stride
  To spread destruction far and wide,
With Southron's blood their hands embruing?
  To arms, to arms, ye brave!
  Th' avenging sword unsheath!
March on! March on! All hearts resolved on
  victory or death,
March on! March on! All hearts resolved on
  victory or death.

BLUE COATS ARE OVER THE BORDER

Inscribed to Captain Mitchell.

Air—Blue Bonnets are over the Border.

The old song suggested this; a few lines are borrowed from it.

Kentucky's banner spreads
Its folds above our heads;
We are already famous in story.
Mount and make ready then,
Brave Duke and all his men;
Fight for our homes and Kentucky's old glory.

Chorus—

March! March! Brave Duke and all his men!
Haste, brave boys, now quickly march forward in
  order!

March! March! ye men of old Kentuck!
The horrid blue coats are over the border.

Morgan's men have great fame,
There is much in a name;
Ours must shine today as it ever has shone!

"THE SOUTHERN MARSEILLAISE"

These jolly fellows belong to the Fifth Company of the celebrated Washington Artillery. This was a crack regiment of New Orleans, where the Southern Marseillaise was popular, especially at the opening of the war, when this picture was taken. The young Confederates here are relaxing from discipline over their noonday meal. The frying-pan in the hand of the soldier to the right, also the negligent attitudes, reflect a care-free frame of mind. Their uniforms and accouterments still are spick-span and new. But a few weeks later they distinguished themselves at Shiloh.

As it shines o'er our dead,
Who for freedom have bled:
The foe for their deaths have now got to atone.

THE BONNIE BLUE FLAG

HARRY MACARTHY

South Carolina, the first state to secede from the Union, adopted a blue flag bearing a single white star in the center. Almost simultaneously with this change of flag there appeared the spirited song—"The Bonnie Blue Flag."

SONGS OF THE WAR DAYS

We are a band of brothers, and native to the soil,
Fighting for the property we gained by honest
toil;
And when our rights were threatened, the cry rose
near and far,
Hurrah for the Bonnie Blue Flag that bears a
single star!

Chorus—

Hurrah! Hurrah! for Southern Rights, hurrah!
Hurrah! for the Bonnie Blue Flag that bears a
single star!

As long as the Union was faithful to her trust,
Like friends and like brothers we were kind, we
were just;
But now when Northern treachery attempts our
rights to mar,
We hoist on high the Bonnie Blue Flag that bears
a single star.

VOLUNTEER SONG
Written for the Ladies' Military Fair held at New Orleans, 1861.
Published in *New Orleans Picayune*, April 28th, 1861, and sung
by the regiments departing for Virginia.

1

" Go soldiers, arm you for the fight,
God shield the cause of Justice, Right;
May all return with victory crowned,
May every heart with joy abound,
May each deserve the laurel crown,
Nor one to meet his lady's frown.

2

" Your cause is good, 'tis honor bright,
'Tis virtue, country, home and right;
Then should you die for love of these,
We'll waft your names upon the breeze:
The waves will sing your lullaby,
Your country mourn your latest sigh."

WE'LL BE FREE IN MARYLAND
ROBERT E. HOLTZ, January 30, 1862

During the years of the war nearly every musician was intent
on composing a new national song. Of the many compositions
offered the public, curiously enough, practically none of the more
ambitious attempts survive, while catchy doggerel such as "We'll
Be Free In Maryland" is still sung far and wide.

The boys down south in Dixie's land,
The boys down south in Dixie's land,
The boys down south in Dixie's land,
Will come and rescue Maryland.

Chorus—

If you will join the Dixie band,
Here's my heart and here's my hand,
If you will join the Dixie band;
We're fighting for a home.

We'll rally to Jeff Davis true,
Beauregard and Johnston, too,
Magruder, Price, and General Bragg,
And give three cheers for the Southern flag.

SLEEPING FOR THE FLAG
HENRY CLAY WORK

Henry C. Work's songs shared popularity during the war with
the melodies of Stephen Foster. "Sleeping For The Flag," "King-
dom Coming," "Brave Boys Are They," and "Marching Through
Georgia" were sung to glory in the '60's.

When the boys come home in triumph, brother,
With the laurels they shall gain;
When we go to give them welcome, brother,
We shall look for you in vain.
We shall wait for your returning, brother,
You were set forever free;
For your comrades left you sleeping, brother,
Underneath a Southern tree.

Chorus—
Sleeping to waken in this weary world no more;
Sleeping for your true lov'd country, brother,
Sleeping for the flag you bore.

You who were the first on duty, brother,
When " to arms " your leader cried,—
You have left the ranks forever,
You have laid your arms aside,
From the awful scenes of battle, brother,
You were set forever free;
When your comrades left you sleeping, brother,
Underneath the Southern tree.

WE ARE COMING, FATHER ABRAHAM
JAMES SLOAN GIBBONS

This song was written in 1862 just after Lincoln had issued his
call for 300,000 volunteers to fill the ranks of the army. It
was first printed in the *Evening Post*, July 16, 1862 and was
afterwards sung by the famous Hutchinson family. Lincoln
listened with bowed head to the song at the White House one
summer morning in 1864.

We are coming, Father Abraham, three hundred
thousand more,
From Mississippi's winding stream and from New
England's shore;

We leave our ploughs and workshops, our wives
  and children dear,
With hearts too full for utterance, with but a
  single tear;
We dare not look behind us, but steadfastly
  before:
We are coming, Father Abraham, three hundred
  thousand more!

Chorus—
We are coming, we are coming, our Union to
  restore:

division on the battlefield of Chickamauga. It is said to have
been sung by Captain Terry's regiment on the battlefield just
previous to the actual engagement.

The morning star is paling; the camp fires flicker
  low;
Our steeds are madly neighing; for the bugle bids
  us go:
So put the foot in stirrup and shake the bridle
  free,
For today the Texas Rangers must cross the
  Tennessee.

"FATHER ABRAHAM"

This photograph shows some of the members of the Twenty-second New York Infantry, who fought at the Second Battle of
Bull Run, Antietam, and Chancellorsville. It lost during service eleven officers and sixty-two men killed and mortally wounded
and one officer and twenty-eight enlisted men by disease. Notwithstanding, many of these men were among the first to enlist
again when Lincoln issued his call for 300,000 volunteers to fill the ranks of the army, a call that gave rise to the famous song of
that year, "We're Coming Father Abraham, Three Hundred Thousand Strong." Here they are at Harper's Ferry in '62 en-
joying the luxury of a visit from a lady whose light gown is attractively spread out over her ample hoop-skirt at the right of the picture.
It is interesting to study the formal manner in which the men are holding their rifles, and also the grouping around the drum.

We are coming, Father Abraham, three hundred
  thousand more,
We are coming, Father Abraham, three hundred
  thousand more.

You have called us, and we're coming, by Richmond's bloody tide
To lay us down, for Freedom's sake, our brothers'
  bones beside;
Or from foul treason's savage grasp to wrench the
  murderous blade,
And in the face of foreign foes its fragments to
  parade.
Six hundred thousand loyal men and true have
  gone before:
We are coming, Father Abraham, three hundred
  thousand more!

SONG OF THE TEXAS RANGERS
Mrs. J. D. Young
Air: *The Yellow Rose of Texas.*
This song was dedicated to Captain Dave Terry, a Texas
Ranger, who was conspicuous for bravery in General Wharton's

With Wharton for our leader, we'll chase the das-
  tard foe,
Till our horses bathe their fetlocks in the deep,
  blue Ohio.
'Tis joy to be a Ranger! to fight for dear Southland!
'Tis joy to follow Wharton, with his gallant,
  trusty band!
'Tis joy to see our Harrison plunge, like a meteor
  bright,
Into the thickest of the fray, and deal his deadly
  might.
O! who'd not be a Ranger and follow Wharton's
  cry!
And battle for his country, and, if needs be, die?

THE ALABAMA
Words by E. King   Music by F. W. Rasier
  While the greater number of naval war songs belongs to the
North, crystallizing around the names of Farragut and Winslow,
the heroism displayed by the small, scantily equipped Confederate
Navy, brought forth several lyrical tributes. This roystering

345

SONGS OF THE WAR DAYS

sea-song was dedicated to "Gallant Admiral Semmes of the *Alabama* and to the officers and seamen of the C. S. Navy."

> The wind blows off yon rocky shore,
> Boys, set your sails all free:
> And soon the booming cannon's roar
> Shall ring out merrily.
> Run up your bunting, caught a-peak,
> And swear, lads, to defend her:
> 'Gainst every foe, where'er we go,
> Our motto—" No surrender."

Chorus—

> Then sling the bowl, drink every soul
> A toast to the *Alabama*,
> Whate'er our lot, through storm or shot,
> Here's success to the *Alabama*.

THE SOUTHERN SOLDIER BOY

AIR: *The Boy with the Auburn Hair.*

As sung by Miss Sallie Partington, in the "Virginia Cavalier," Richmond, Va., 1863. Composed by Captain G. W. Alexander.

The sentiments of this song pleased the Confederate Soldiers, and for more than a year, the New Richmond Theater was nightly filled by "Blockade Rebels," who greeted with wild hurrahs, "Miss Sallie" the prima donna of the Confederacy.

> Bob Roebuck is my sweetheart's name,
> He's off to the wars and gone,
> He's fighting for his Nannie dear,
> His sword is buckled on;
> He's fighting for his own true love,
> His foes he does defy;
> He is the darling of my heart,
> My Southern soldier boy.

Chorus—

> Yo! ho! yo! ho! yo! ho! ho! ho! ho! ho! ho!
> He is my only joy,
> He is the darling of my heart,
> My Southern soldier boy.

"THE ZOUAVES"

J. HOWARD WAINWRIGHT

Published in New York *Evening Post*, 1861.

"The Zouaves" was one of the many spirited songs sung in memory of Col. Ephraim E. Ellsworth, of the New York Fire Zouaves. The Brooklyn Zouaves attained a place in history at the first day's battle at Gettysburg, by their efficiency under fire and the bravery of their Colonel.

> Onward, Zouaves,—Ellsworth's spirit leads us;
> Onward, Zouaves, for our country needs us;
> Onward, Zouaves, for our banner floats o'er us;
> Onward Zouaves, for the foe is before us.

Chorus—

> Onward Zouaves!
> Do nothing by halves:
> Home to the hilt, with the bay'net, Zouaves.

THE SONGS OF STEPHEN C. FOSTER

Stephen C. Foster, an American song-writer of Irish descent, was the most famous American folk-song writer of his day. While many of the songs antedate the actual years of the war, they were sung far and wide throughout the struggle and have continued to be popular down to the present day. Half a million copies were sold of "Swanee Rubber," and as many more of "My Old Kentucky Home" and "Massa's in the Cold, Cold Ground."

MY OLD KENTUCKY HOME, GOOD NIGHT

> The sun shines bright in the old Kentucky home;
>   'Tis summer, the darkeys are gay,
> The corn-top's ripe and the meadow's in the
>   bloom,
>   While the birds make music all the day.
> The young folks roll on the little cabin floor,
>   All merry, all happy and bright;
> By-'n-by hard times comes a-knocking at the
>   door:—
> Then my old Kentucky home, good-night!

Chorus—

> Weep no more, my lady,
> Oh! weep no more today!
> We will sing one song for the old Kentucky home,
> For the old Kentucky home, far away.

OLD FOLKS AT HOME

> Way down upon de Swanee Ribber,
>   Far, far away,
> Dere's wha my heart is turning ebber,
>   Dere's wha de old folks stay.
> All up and down de whole creation
>   Sadly I roam,
> Still longing for de old plantation,
>   And for de old folks at home!

Chorus—

> All de world am sad and dreary,
>   Ebery where I roam;
> Oh, darkeys, how my heart grows weary,
>   Far from de old folks at home!

CHEER, BOYS, CHEER

"Cheer, Boys, Cheer" was sung by every man who fought in a Southern Kentucky or Tennessee Regiment. General Basil Duke in his account of the battle of Shiloh, says—"Just as Breckinridge's Division was going into action, we came upon the left of it where the Kentucky troops were formed. The bullets commenced to fly thick and fast around us and simultaneously the regiment nearest us struck up the favorite song of the Kentuckians—'Cheer, Boys, Cheer.' The effect was inspiring beyond words."

Several versions of adapted words were sung to the melody of this song. One of the versions was dedicated to Horace Greeley and circulated throughout the north. The original "Cheer, Boys, Cheer," has, however, always remained closely identified with Southern sentiment.

Cheer, boys, cheer! no more of idle sorrow;
Courage! true hearts shall bear us on our way;
Hope points before and shows a bright tomorrow,
Let us forget the darkness of today:
Then farewell, England, much as we may love
      thee,
We'll dry the tears that we have shed before;
We'll not weep to sail in search of fortune;
Then farewell, England, farewell forevermore.

Chorus—
Then cheer, boys, cheer! for England, Mother
      England.
Cheer boys, cheer for the willing strong right
      hand;
Cheer, boys, cheer! there's wealth in honest labor;
Cheer, boys, cheer for the new and happy land.

TO CANAAN

This is an example of the many spontaneous lyrics sung to old tunes,—lyrics that were composed on the spur of occasions and soon afterwards consigned to oblivion.

Where are you going, soldiers,
With banner, gun and sword?
We're marching south to Canaan
To battle for the Lord.
What Captain leads your armies
Along the rebel coasts?
The mighty One of Israel,
His name is Lord of Hosts.

Chorus—
To Canaan, to Canaan,
The Lord has led us forth,
To blow before the heathen walls
The trumpets of the North.

DIXIE

The Original Version

Dixie was first written as a "walk-a-round" by an Ohioan, Dan Emmet, and was first sung in Dan Bryant's minstrel show on Broadway, New York, shortly before the war. It came into martial usage by accident and its stirring strains inspired the regiments on many a battlefield. Curiously enough it was adapted to patriotic words on both sides and remained popular with North and South alike after the struggle was over. Abraham Lincoln

loved the tune and considered the fact that it was truly representative of the "land of cotton" far more important than its lack of adherence to the strict laws of technical harmony. Twenty-two versions of the Confederate stanzas set to this famous melody have been collected by the Daughters of the Confederacy.

TO CANAAN
"WHERE ARE YOU GOING, SOLDIERS, WITH BANNER, GUN, AND SWORD?"

These soldiers so brilliant in brass buttons and gold braid, with gun and sword, were "Green Mountain Boys," members of the Sixth Vermont, stationed at Camp Griffin in 1861. The boy in the picture who stands so sturdily between the men has been enthused by the call of patriotism and hurried away from the mountains to join the army, inspired by the leaping rhythm of war songs like "Canaan." Many youngsters like him never returned to their homes after "the trumpets" had blown their final call.

I wish I was in de land ob cotton,
Old times dar am not forgotten;
Look away, look away, look away,
      Dixie Land.
In Dixie Land whar I was born in,
Early on one frosty mornin,'
Look away, look away, look away, Dixie Land.

Chorus—
Den I wish I was in Dixie,
      Hooray! Hooray!

In Dixie Land, I'll took my stand,
To lib and die in Dixie:
Away, away, away, down South in Dixie
Away, away, away, down South in Dixie.

DIXIE

Union adaptation by John Savage—one of the many versions of Dixie sung in the Northern states during the war.

Oh, the Starry Flag is the flag for me;
'Tis the flag of life, 'tis the flag of the free,
Then hurrah, hurrah, for the flag of the Union.
Oh, the Starry Flag is the flag for me.
'Tis the flag of life, 'tis the flag of the free.
We'll raise that starry banner, boys,
Where no power or wrath can face it;

    O'er town and field—
    The people's shield;
No treason can erase it;
    O'er all the land,
    That flag must stand,
Where the people's might shall place it.

I GOES TO FIGHT MIT SIGEL

"I goes to fight mit Sigel," is the great war-song of our German Civil War patriots, who fought with exceptional bravery for their beloved General and their adopted "Fatherland."

I've come shust now to tells you how,
I goes mit regimentals,
To schlauch dem voes of Liberty,
Like dem old Continentals,
Vot fights mit England long ago,
To save der Yankee Eagle;
Und now I gets my soldier clothes;
I'm going to fight mit Sigel.

When I comes from der Deutsche Countree,
I vorks sometimes at baking;
Den I keeps a lager beer saloon,
Und den I goes shoe making;
But now I was a sojer been
To save der Yankee Eagle;
To schlauch dem tam secession volks,
I'm going to fight mit Sigel.

TENTING ON THE OLD CAMP GROUND

Walter Kittridge

No song has been so widely sung since the war as "Tenting on the Old Camp Ground." For Memorial Day music, it shares honors with "Soldiers' Farewell."

We're tenting tonight on the old camp ground,
  Give us a song to cheer

Our weary hearts, a song of home,
  And friends we love so dear.

Chorus—
Many are the hearts that are weary tonight,
  Wishing for the war to cease;
Many are the hearts that are looking for the right,
  To see the dawn of peace.
Tenting tonight, tenting tonight,
  Tenting on the old camp ground.

We've been tenting tonight on the old camp ground,
  Thinking of days gone by,
Of the loved ones at home that gave us the hand,
  And the tear that said " Good-bye!"

We are tired of war on the old camp ground,
  Many are dead and gone,
Of the brave and true who've left their homes;
  Others been wounded long.

We've been fighting today on the old camp ground,
  Many are lying near;
Some are dead and some are dying,
  Many are in tears.

WE HAVE DRUNK FROM THE SAME CANTEEN

Charles Graham Halpine

There are bonds of all sorts in this world of ours,
Fetters of friendship and ties of flowers,
  And true lovers' knots, I ween;
The boy and the girl are bound by a kiss,
But there's never a bond, old friend, like this:
  We have drunk from the same canteen.

Chorus—
  The same canteen, my soldier friend,
  The same canteen,
  There's never a bond, old friend, like this!
  We have drunk from the same canteen.

It was sometimes water, and sometimes milk,
Sometimes applejack, fine as silk,
  But whatever the tipple has been,
We shared it together, in bane or bliss,
And I warm to you, friend, when I think of this:
  We have drunk from the same canteen.

GAY AND HAPPY

Private Henry Putnam, a descendant of Israel Putnam of historic fame, and a member of a New York regiment, wrote home from Cold Harbor the day before the battle, "We are quite gay in camp despite the prospect for battle to-morrow. To-night we have been singing and telling stories around the camp fire. I send you a paragraph of "Gay and Happy Still," which we sang tonight." The soldier was killed in the trenches the following day by the bullet of a Tennessee rifleman.

1

We're the boys that's gay and happy,
  Wheresoever we may be;
And we'll do our best to please you,
  If you will attentive be.

Chorus—

  So let the wide world wag as it will,
  We'll be gay and happy still,
  Gay and happy, gay and happy,
  We'll be gay and happy still.

2

We envy neither great nor wealthy,
  Poverty we ne'er despise;
Let us be contented, healthy,
  And the boon we dearly prize.

3

The rich have cares we little know of,
  All that glitters is not gold,
Merit's seldom made a show of,
  And true worth is rarely told.

THE GIRL I LEFT BEHIND ME
SAMUEL LOVER

The hour was sad I left the maid, a lingering
  farewell taking,
Her sighs and tears my steps delay'd, I thought
  her heart was breaking;
In hurried words her name I bless'd, I breathed
  the vows that bind me,
And to my heart in anguish press'd the girl I
  left behind me.

Then to the East we bore away, to win a name
  in story,
And there where dawns the sun of day, there
  dawns our sun of glory;
Both blazed in noon on Alma's height, where in
  the post assign'd me,
I shar'd the glory of that fight, Sweet Girl I Left
  Behind Me.

ONE I LEFT THERE

A Southern song of sentiment that equaled "Lorena" in popularity during the war.

1

Soft blows the breath of morning
  In my own valley fair,
For it's there the opening roses
  With fragrance scent the air,
With fragrance scent the air.
And with perfume fill the air,
But the breath of one I left there
  Is sweeter far to me.

2

Soft fall the dews of evening
  Around our valley bowers;
And they glisten on the grass plots
  And tremble on the flowers,
  And tremble on the flowers
Like jewels rich to see,
But the tears of one I left there
  Are richer gems to me.

"THE GIRL I LEFT"

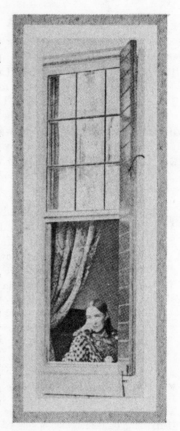

It is a strange chance of photography that preserved the wistful face of this wartime Yankee Girl at Fort Monroe, gazing from her window, to appear here. For "The Girl I Left Behind Me" was originally inscribed "To a Yankee Girl at Fort Monroe"! The demure lassie here, with the simple parting of the hair, the little bows and knots of ribbon on her dress, the plaid shawl drawn about her arm, the brocaded curtain above her head—all bring back the days that are gone. The jaunty words of the "Girl I Left Behind Me" bore an undercurrent of sadness, a fear that the waiting sweetheart might by the fortunes of war be condemned to spend a lifetime in unavailing sorrow. The tenderness and pathos of this song have made it live unto a later age. It strikes a note of universal tenderness.

THE FADED COAT OF BLUE
J. H. McNAUGHTON

"The Faded Coat of Blue" was sung extensively throughout the North during the war, in memory of the lads who were gathered with the bivouac of the dead.

My brave lad he sleeps in his faded coat of blue;
In a lonely grave unknown lies the heart that
  beat so true;
He sank faint and hungry among the famished
  brave,
And they laid him sad and lonely within his nameless grave.

Chorus—
No more the bugle calls the weary one,
Rest noble spirit, in thy grave unknown!
I'll find you and know you, among the good and
    true,
When a robe of white is giv'n for the faded coat
    of blue.

He cried, " Give me water and just a little crumb,
And my mother she will bless you through all the
        years to come;
Oh! tell my sweet sister, so gentle, good and true,
That I'll meet her up in heaven, in my faded coat
    of blue."

LORENA

This was the great sentimental song of the South during the
war period.

The years creep slowly by, Lorena;
    The snow is on the grass again;
The sun's low down the sky, Lorena;
    The frost gleams where the flowers have been.
But the heart throbs on as warmly now
    As when the summer days were nigh;
Oh! the sun can never dip so low
    Adown affection's cloudless sky.

A hundred months have passed, Lorena,
    Since last I held that hand in mine,
And felt the pulse beat fast, Lorena,
    Though mine beat faster far than thine.
A hundred months—'twas flowery May,
    When up the hilly slope we climbed,
To watch the dying of the day
    And hear the distant church bells chime.

MOTHER KISSED ME IN MY DREAM

Set to a plaintive melody—the words of this exquisite lyric
gave comfort to many a lonely soldier. It is recorded that a
wounded private of Colonel Benj. L. Higgins' 86th New York
Infantry sang this song to cheer his comrades while they were
halted in a piece of woods beyond the memorable wheat-field at
Gettysburg, on the morning of July 3d, 1863.

Lying on my dying bed
    Thro' the dark and silent night,
Praying for the coming day,
    Came a vision to my sight.
Near me stood the forms I loved,
    In the sunlight's mellow gleam:
Folding me unto her breast,
    Mother kissed me in my dream.

Comrades, tell her, when you write,
    That I did my duty well;
Say that when the battle raged,
    Fighting, in the van I fell;

Tell her, too, when on my bed
    Slowly ebbed my being's stream,
How I knew no peace until
    Mother kissed me in my dream.

O WRAP THE FLAG AROUND ME, BOYS

R. STEWART TAYLOR

O, wrap the flag around me, boys,
To die were far more sweet,
With Freedom's starry banner, boys,
To be my winding sheet.
In life I lov'd to see it wave,
And follow where it led,
And now my eyes grow dim, my hands
Would clasp its last bright shred.

Chorus—
Then ⎫
Yet ⎬ wrap the flag around me, boys,
So ⎭
To die were far more sweet,
With Freedom's starry emblem, boys,
To be my winding sheet.

COVER THEM OVER WITH BEAUTIFUL FLOWERS
Decoration Hymn.

E. F. STEWART

Cover them over with beautiful flow'rs,
Deck them with garlands, those brothers of ours,
Lying so silently night and day,
Sleeping the years of their manhood away,
Give them the meed they have won in the past,
Give them the honors their future forecast,
Give them the chaplets they won in the strife,
Give them the laurels they lost with their life.

Chorus—
Cover them over, yes, cover them over,
Parent, and husband, brother and lover;
Crown in your hearts those dead heroes of ours,
Cover them over with beautiful flow'rs.

JUST BEFORE THE BATTLE, MOTHER

GEORGE FREDERICK ROOT

Next in popularity to "When This Cruel War Is Over," was
the sentimental song "Just Before The Battle, Mother." Its
pathos and simplicity touched every heart.

Just before the battle, mother,
    I am thinking most of you,
While, upon the field, we're watching,
    With the enemy in view.

Comrades brave are round me lying,
  Filled with thoughts of home and God;
For well they know that, on the morrow,
  Some will sleep beneath the sod.

Chorus—

  Farewell, mother, you may never,
  You may never, mother,
  Press me to your breast again;
  But O, you'll not forget me,
  Mother, you will not forget me
  If I'm number'd with the slain.

LOW IN THE GROUND THEY'RE RESTING

COLLIN COE

Northern sentiment found vent in many beautiful Memorial Day Odes. Several of these possessed genuine poetic excellence.

  Low in the ground they're resting,
  Proudly the flag waves o'er them;
  Never more 'mid wars contesting
  To save the land that bore them!

Chorus—

Sleep, brave ones, rest, in hallow'd graves!
Our flag now proudly o'er you waves!
Vict'ry and fame, vict'ry and fame,
Loudly forever shall your brave deeds proclaim,
Loudly forever shall your brave deeds proclaim.

WEEPING, SAD AND LONELY

WHEN THIS CRUEL WAR IS OVER

CHARLES CARROLL SAWYER

Most popular of all in North and South alike was the song known as "When This Cruel War Is Over." It was heard in every camp, the Southern soldiers inserting "gray" for "blue" in the sixth line of the first stanza. It is doubtful if any other American song was ever upon so many tongues. One million copies were sold during the war.

  Dearest love, do you remember,
  When we last did meet,
  How you told me that you loved me,
  Kneeling at my feet?
  Oh, how proud you stood before me,
  In your suit of blue,
  When you vowed to me and country
  Ever to be true.

Chorus—

  Weeping, sad and lonely,
  Hopes and fears how vain!
  Yet praying, when this cruel war is over,
  Praying that we meet again!

POOR OLD SLAVE

This song, while not directly connected with the events of the war, was widely popular during the struggle.

  'Tis just one year ago today,
    That I remember well,
  I sat down by poor Nelly's side
    And a story she did tell.
  'Twas 'bout a poor unhappy slave,
    That lived for many a year;
  But now he's dead, and in his grave,
    No master does he fear.

"WHEN THIS CRUEL WAR IS OVER"

With the quaint style of hair-dressing that ruled in 1864, in flowered skirt and "Garibaldi blouse," this beautiful woman, the wife of a Federal army officer, was photographed in front of the winter quarters of Captain John R. Coxe, in February, at the headquarters of the Army of the Potomac, Brandy Station. She was even then looking at her soldier husband, who sat near her in his "suit of blue," or perhaps thinking of the three years of terrific fighting that had passed. Shiloh, Chickamauga, Chattanooga, Fredericksburg, Chancellorsville, Gettysburg—all of these had been fought and the toll of the "cruel war" was not yet complete.

Chorus—

  The poor old slave has gone to rest,
    We know that he is free;
  Disturb him not but let him rest,
    Way down in Tennessee.

NEGRO "SPIRITUALS"

Some of the negro chants or "spirituals" are particularly interesting because of their direct connection with the incidents of the Civil War. Their sources were generally obscure; their origin seeming to be either by gradual accretion or by an almost unconscious process of composition.

Colonel T. W. Higginson told the story of the beginning of one of these slave songs as related to him by a sturdy young oarsman of Ladies Island.

"Once we boys" he said "went to tote some rice and de nigger driver he keep a-callin' on us; and I say, 'O, de ole nigger-driver.' Den anudder said, 'Fust ting my mammy tole me was —notin' so bad as nigger drivers.' Den I make a 'sing,' just puttin' a word an' den anudder word." Thus, said Colonel Higginson, almost unconsciously a new song was created, which was repeated the second time with perfect recollection of the original melody and intonations.

The wild, sad strains of these primitive melodies, born of their desire for musical expression amid the dull, daily routine of cotton field and rice swamp, express above and beyond their plaintive lament, a simple trust in the future—in the happy land—the Canaan, toward which their yearning eyes were forever turned.

THE ENLISTED SOLDIERS

Sung by the Ninth Regiment U. S. Colored Troops at Benedict, Maryland, winter of 1863-4. General Armstrong calls this the Negro Battle Hymn. At Petersburg, July 29, 1864, a trooper of General Henry G. Thomas's brigade sat before the camp fire singing this "Negro Battle Hymn," "They look like Men of War." General Thomas describes the scene—the dark men with their white eyes and teeth, crouching over a smouldering camp fire, in dusky shadow, lit only by the feeble rays of the lanterns of the first sergeants dimly showing through the tents. After the terrible "Battle of the Crater" they sang these words no more.

> Hark! listen to the trumpeters,
> They call for volunteers,
> On Zion's bright and flowery mount—
> Behold the officers!

Chorus—

> They look like men,
> They look like men,
> They look like men of war.

MY FATHER, HOW LONG?

This primitive chant is thought by Mr. G. H. Allan, who wrote down the stanzas, to have originated from the Florida plantations. At the outbreak of the Civil War several negroes were thrown into jail at Georgetown, South Carolina, for singing the verses. Although the "spiritual" was an old one, the words were considered as being symbolical of new events. A little colored boy explained the matter tersely to Mr. Allan. "Dey tink de Lord mean fo' to say de Yankees call us."

> We'll fight for liberty,
> We'll fight for liberty,
> We'll fight for liberty,
> When de Lord will call us home.
> And it won't be long,
> And it won't be long,
> And it won't be long,
> When de Lord will call us home.

MANY THOUSAND GO

This "spiritual," to which the Civil War actually gave rise, was composed by nobody knows whom, although it is perhaps the most recent of the slave "spirituals" of which we have record. Lieut. Col. Trowbridge learned that it was first sung on the occasion when General Beauregard gathered the slaves from the Port Royal Islands to build fortifications at Hilton Head and Bay Point.

> No more peck o' corn for me,
> No more, no more;
> No more peck o' corn for me,
> Many tousand go.
>
> No more driver's lash for me,
> No more, no more;
> No more driver's lash for me,
> Many tousand go.

PRAY ON

This curious "spiritual" is one of those arising directly from the events of the war. When the news of approaching freedom reached the sea island rice plantations of the Port Royal Islands this chant was sung with great fervor by the negroes. The verses were annotated by Charles Pickard Ware.

> Pray on—pray on;
> Pray on, den light us over;
> Pray on—pray on,
> De Union break of day.
> My sister, you come to see baptize
> In de Union break of day,
> In de Union break of day.

MEET, O LORD

> Meet, O Lord, on de milk-white horse
> An' de nineteen vial in his han'.
> Drop on—drop on de crown on my head,
> And rolly in my Jesus arm;
> In dat mornin' all day,
> In dat mornin' all day,
> In dat mornin' all day,
> When Jesus de Christ been born.

COPYRIGHT, 1911, REVIEW OF REVIEWS CO.

"MEET, O LORD"

HILTON HEAD IN 1861—THE TIME AND PLACE OF THIS NEGRO SONG'S CREATION

This photograph appears here by a curious coincidence. With the presentation of the "spiritual" that commemorates an event of the war connected with the Confederate General Drayton, there has come to light a photograph of his home on Hilton Head in 1861. Through these gates, watched by loving eyes, he rode on the "milk-white horse," the morning of the engagement at Bay Point. Mr. W. F. Allen, who collected many slave-songs, was told that, "When de gun shoot at Bay Pint," General Drayton left a Negro boy holding his white war horse. He never returned to claim his steed and in some way the incident was commemorated in this "spiritual," which is still sung on the plantations of Hilton Head Island. Observe the Negro "mammies" on the porch and at the gate, also the luxuriance of foliage framing the Southern house in a bower of greenery. Members of the Third New Hampshire regiment face the reader; for the house is now a rendezvous of Federal troops.